In the Spirit of Joseph

Mary Cresp RSJ

© Mary Cresp 2005

All rights reserved. Except as provided by the Copyright Act 1968, no part of this publication may be reproduced, stored in a retrieval system or transmitted in any form or by any means without the prior written permission of the publisher.

Published by
Sisters of St Joseph of the Sacred Heart
PO Box 1508 North Sydney NSW 2059
Australia.

Cresp, Mary.
In the Spirit of Joseph.

Includes index.
ISBN 0 9579976 4 7.

1. Joseph, Saint. 2. Sisters of Saint Joseph. 3. Spiritual life.
I. Sisters of St. Joseph of the Sacred Heart.
II. Title.

255.976

<u>Cover</u>: Painting, "St Joseph". Ann Steenbergen RSJ (Goulburn).
Used with permission.

<u>Photos</u>: Mary Cresp RSJ

Wholly disc converted and photoset, printed and bound by Gillingham Printers Pty Ltd of Adelaide South Australia

Dedicated to

Nancy O'Connor CSJ
(died Aug 1, 2004)

Friend,

   mentor,

      outstanding Sister of St Joseph

Contents

Introduction   xiii

Ch. 1   **The Spirit of Joseph Tells God's Story**   1

    Part 1.1
- We are a word of God   1
- Joseph's word of faith   3
- Joseph's vocation   5
- Charism is a word of God   7
- The Charism of Joseph   9

    Part 1.2
- Tapping into the charism   12
- Sisters of St Joseph, Le Puy, France   12
- Father Médaille and the founding Sisters   14
- Refounding and Expansion   17
- Father Woods, co-founder of the Sisters of St Joseph, Australia   20
- Meeting with Mary MacKillop   22
- Sisters of St Joseph, Australia   23
- Re-Sourcing the Charism   25
  - *God's love*   26
  - *God's will*   28
  - *The Eucharist*   29

    Part 1.3
- Changed Context for Sisters St Joseph   29
- Beyond Sisterhoods   31
- Charism fostered   33
- Associates   35
- Volunteers   36
- A spirit of partnership   38

Ch. 2   **The Spirit of Joseph Breaks Boundaries**   41

    Part 2.1
- Breaking through fear   41

Joseph the new patriarch	43
The new demands change	44
The new involves pain	46

Part 2.2

Beginning a new thing	48
Life out of death	51
Frontier women	53
Going farther	54
Australian response	56
Sisters of the Outback	60
Foolishness and Prudence	63
Taking the spirit forward	65

Part 2.3

The New Enlivens	69
Renewal – Re-new-ing	74
The spirit of Joseph lived in partnership	75
Overcoming fear	78
Reaching into the new	79
The "more"	83

Ch. 3 The Spirit of Joseph Finds God in the Ordinary   87

Part 3.1

The Incarnation	87
Joseph and the Ordinary	89
Joseph the Family Man	92
Joseph the Worker	94
Joseph's Religious Practice	96

Part 3.2

A spirituality in the world	99
Double Union	101
Sisters of St Joseph and the Ordinary	102
Enculturating the Ordinary	104
The "Ordinary" in Australia	107
Living the "Ordinary"	109
Identification with people	*110*
Practicality	*111*
Part of Local Community	*113*
Hard Work	*115*
Egalitarianism	*117*
God's Presence	*118*

Part 3.3
  Dualism   122
  Integrating spirituality and religion
    with daily life   123
  Partnership with lay groups   127

Portrait of a Sister of St Joseph   **129**

Ch. 4   The Spirit of Joseph Acts Justly   131

Part 4.1
  Justice and religion   131
  Justice and Scripture   132
  What is justice?   135
  Joseph and justice   137
  Joseph and the justice of compassion   138

Part 4.2
  Promoting justice in a world
    of systematised injustice   140
  Unity and Reconciliation   143
  To be prophetic   144
    Poverty   *145*
    Chastity   *148*
    Obedience   *151*

Part 4.3
  Globalisation   158
  Furthering the spirit   161
    Sponsored Ministries   *162*
    Inservice Training   *162*
    Outreach   *163*
  Changing cultures that promote injustice   165
  "If you want peace, work for justice"   168

Ch. 5   The Spirit of Joseph Brings Together   171

Part 5.1
  Communion   171
  God as communion   172
  The communion of the Body of Christ   174
  Christian Community   175

Joseph and community	178
Self-gift	*179*
Bonding	*180*
Hospitality	*181*

Part 5.2

Sisters of St Joseph as community	183
Inclusivity	186
Hospitality	189
Restoring unity	190
Inter-religious relations	*192*
Being with	194
Presence	*196*
Kindness	199
Relating	201
Compassion	*202*
Mutuality	*203*

Part 5.3

"Being With" today	205
Building Community in a changing world	207
Establishing relationships of mutuality	*210*
Being communities for mission	*212*

Spirituality from Père Médaille   **215**

Ch. 6   The Spirit of Joseph Walks Humbly   **217**

Part 6.1

We come from the earth	217
Humus	218
Human	220
Humility	222
Humour	225
Joseph walked humbly	226
Joseph's greatness	*227*
Joseph and the earth	*228*
Joseph and Divine Providence	*229*

Part 6.2
    Sisters of St Joseph and humility   230
- *Truth* — *238*
- *Humanness* — *242*
- *Trust in Divine Providence* — *246*
- *Earthiness* — *249*
- *Humour* — *251*

Part 6.3
- Walking in Humility — 254
- Trusting in Divine Providence — 256
- Being earthy — 257

Ch. 7   The Spirit of Joseph Engages Pain   261

Part 7.1
- The place of pain — 261
- Joseph engaged pain — 266

Part 7.2
- Self-emptying — 269
- Under the Southern Cross — 272
- The cross – an ongoing foundational image — 278
- Experience of the Cross — 280
  - *Suffering for the sake of mission* — *280*
  - *Persecution* — *284*
  - *Betrayal* — *286*
  - *Identification with those who suffer* — *288*
  - *Misuse of power* — *291*
  - *Laying down one's life* — *294*

Part 7.3
- Giving of self — 299

Woods' Epistle of the Institute of St Joseph   **303**

Ch. 8	**The Spirit of Joseph Localises Church**		**305**
	Part 8.1		
	The Church is Catholic		305
	The Church is Communion		308
	The Church is Local		310
	The Communion of Saints		312
	Joseph as Patron of the Church		313
	Joseph and Collegiality		315
	Part 8.2		
	Bringing into Communion		317
	Re-establishing the local Church		319
	Power Structures		322
	Bishops	*322*	
	Priests	*327*	
	Convent Life	*333*	
	Part 8.3		
	Mission to *communio*		335
	Expressing *communio* in relationships		336
	Associates	*336*	
	Other lay groups	*337*	
	Sisters of St Joseph	*339*	
	Ordained Ministers	*341*	
	The St Joseph Movement		343

Epilogue	**347**
List of Primitive Documents Used	**352**
List of Newsletters, Congregational Periodicals	**353**
Index of Scripture References	**354**
Index of Names, Places and Subjects	**355**

Introduction

Dear Reader,

Spirit lives. It develops in people's lives and is passed on from one generation to the next. So when attempting to trace the spirit of Joseph, I needed to meet real people. From them I learnt of Joseph's spirit. Let me introduce you to these people now; their stories will form the shape of this book.

The first is Joseph, the husband of Mary. We know little about him. Many legends and not many facts have been handed down to us. All we know for certain is that he was a Jew, born in the time of the occupation of Judea by the Romans; he eventually married Mary, the mother of Jesus; he came from a royal Jewish line and he worked with his hands.

The second person is a Jesuit priest, born in 1610 in Carcassonne, France, and sent during the 1640's to give missions to the spiritually-starved people of the Auvergne region in that country. He is Jean-Pierre Médaille. With him is a group of six women who come from various towns and villages of the region. Françoise Eyraud, Claude Chastel, Marguerite Burdier and three Annas – Anna Chalayer, Anna Vey and Anna Brun – made up the first documented community of the Sisters of St Joseph formed by Father Médaille. The Church dignitary who, in 1650, approved this radical new group, is Henri de Maupas, Bishop of Le Puy and Count of Velay.

Mother St John Fontbonne is next in line. Born Jeanne Fontbonne on March 31, 1759, in the small hill town of Bas-en-Basset overlooking the Le Loire valley, she went to school with the Sisters of St Joseph first in her home town and then at Le Puy. She was to join the Sisters, be appointed Superior of the Convent in Monistrol and endure the ravages and dislocation of the Revolution before, in 1807, being summoned by Cardinal Fesch to re-establish the Sisters of St Joseph in his diocese of Lyon.

Go forward some fifty-four years to the far-off land of Australia. Here, in the south-east of the State of South Australia, the tiny village of Penola has harboured the dreams of an English priest, Father Julian Tenison Woods, born in Southwark, London, in 1832. With him is a young, Melbourne-born woman, Mary MacKillop. She is the first child of Scottish migrants who met and married in Australia, giving birth to this, their first child, on January 15th, 1842. Over the next few years, the dreams of Woods and MacKillop were to combine and give rise to a new group of Sisters of St Joseph, suited to the unique conditions and times of a pioneer land.

Members of these two forms of Sisters of St Joseph comprise the next group. We will call on their stories as we consider the "Spirit of Joseph". I thank the 800 and more Sisters whom I've interviewed around Australia, New Zealand, USA, Canada, England/Wales, Ireland, France, Italy, Peru and India, who have opened up to me their living of Joseph's spirit.

Finally, there is a whole host of people who, largely unacknowledged, have ensured that the way of Joseph continues to be a gift to the Church. These are families, lay groups, benefactors, Associates and co-workers with the Sisters, young people re-interpreting the spirit of Joseph, individuals – little bands of people who have identified with what might be called the "Josephite way" of carrying out the mission given to us in Baptism. Thank you to all these whose insights have contributed to this book.

All of these people share what might be recognised as bearing a "family resemblance" in charism. This is not to say that the characteristics they bear belong only to them. Sisters of St Joseph and those who identify with the charism of St Joseph, for example, are not the only ones who find God in the ordinary circumstances of daily life. Jesuit spirituality is based on this premise. And Josephites are not the only ones who might be described as "down to earth" or "earthy". Franciscans might object were we to claim this.

But just as the elements of facial features are common to everyone and yet their particular arrangement enables us to identify a family resemblance, so, too, the characteristics of charism shared by those who identify with the tradition of Joseph tend to establish bonds between them. This book attempts to describe these features and the resulting bonds.

Three terms used continuously in the book need to be defined. The first is "Charism". As this is the subject of Chapter One, I leave its definition for your reading. The second is "spirit". We use the term in many ways, but in the main, its sense in this book is impetus producing particular qualities of character displayed by persons and through which the action of the Holy Spirit is revealed. Spirit is passed on in living people rather than being contained in documents. Therefore, the content of this book comes from stories of the lived spirit of Joseph.

The third definition is of a term that occupies a lot of space in the literature and commercial activities of today – "spirituality". I find the explanation of David Ranson helpful for an understanding of the complexities of the term. He says,
> (The) reason why there is a great deal which is ambiguous when we speak about `spirituality' is because of the different ways in which the two formative cultures in the West deal with the subject. Possibly, our approach to `spirituality' arises from whether our preference is for Hebrew or Greek. If our orientation is towards Greek,

> then we conceive of the `spiritual' as immaterial, beyond matter, supersensory, ethereal – connection with a `spiritual' world. Alternatively, from the Hebraic context, `spirituality' is concerned with force and energy, a vitality in life, a `coming awake', and increased awareness about life and a deepened sensitivity to its murmurs and rhythms.[1]

With David, I prefer the second emphasis of spirituality as "attentiveness to life" that "awakens within us the awareness of a deepened relationship with ourselves and with others, with the world and with some greater sense of meaning"[2] – which is encapsulated for me in relationship with the Other (God) and the meaning that that relationship gives to my life.

In reading this book, too, note that the format followed in each chapter has three parts. Part One deals with background information and highlights characteristics of the spirit traditionally associated with Joseph. Part Two describes how Sisters of St Joseph in history have responded to urgings of the Holy Spirit in such a way that the characteristics of spirit they show are associated with that of Joseph. Part Three outlines present trends indicating that the Holy Spirit continues to call people to mission in these same characteristic ways.

Acknowledgement of sources is found in the footnotes. Any unreferenced material comes from oral interviews I conducted with Sisters, Associates and others who identify with the spirit of Joseph around the world. Again, I thank them for their contribution to this work; in them the spirit of Joseph continues to live and to be passed on.

---

[1] Ranson, David. *Across the Great Divide: Bridging Spirituality and Religion Today.* Sydney Australia: St Pauls Publications 2002. pp. 16, 17
[2] Ibid. p. 17.

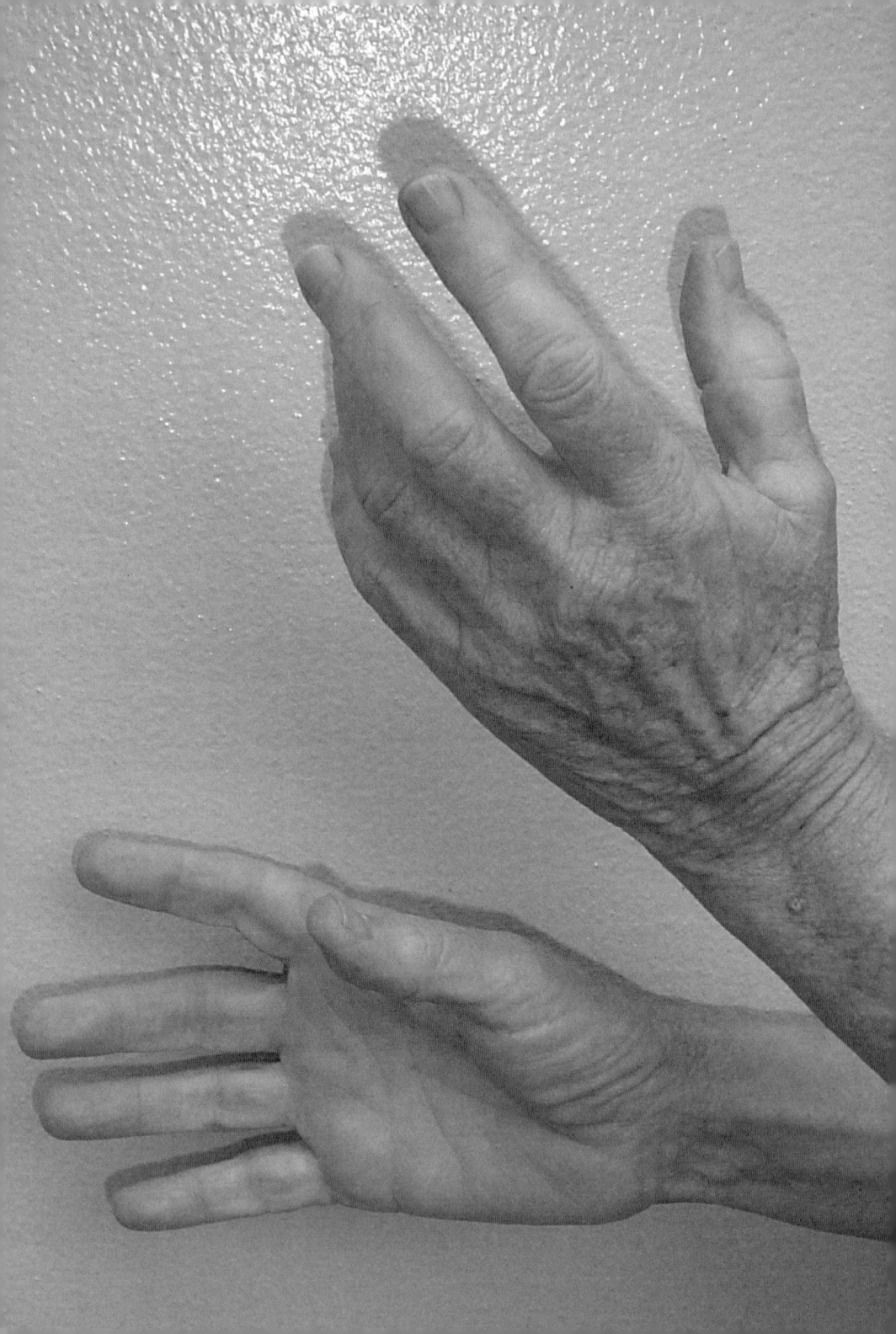

CHAPTER ONE

The spirit of Joseph ......

tells God's story.

"Joseph, son of David, have no fear about taking Mary as your wife. It is by the Holy Spirit that she has conceived this child!" (Mt 1:20)

1.1 PART ONE: The spirit is revealed

We are a word of God:
A story is told of a disciple and his Master. The diligent disciple would go to the great teacher day after day, month after month and would sit at his feet basking in the Master's instruction. The Master would always teach his disciple through stories. One day the disciple asked, "Master, why do you labor to teach me through stories; would it not be faster to teach me directly?" The teacher answered, "Bring me some water." Now the disciple knew his teacher to be a very formal and disciplined man. He had never asked for water at this time of the day. Nevertheless, he went immediately to fetch it. Taking a clean brass waterpot from the ashram kitchen, the disciple went to the well, filled the pot with water and returned. He offered it to his teacher who then spoke: "Why have you brought me a pot when I asked only for water?"[1]

God tells wonderful stories! And through these stories we are given the life-water who is God. We are the "pot" wherein the story of God is brought to our world. We are, as it were, a word

---

[1] Waiver granted http://www.callofstory.org/en/storytelling/whytell.asp

of God. Words are spoken in all sorts of ways. Words can be symbols, or drawings, or objects. God communicates in happenings, in images, in persons and, yes, in words.

The Word of God made flesh is Jesus. In his life and being the fullness of God is revealed. But each of us, too, is a word or communication of God, as is the whole of creation. We learn about God, Hopkins says, through seeing the world, and so it becomes a word: "The world is charged with the grandeur of God."[2] And St Francis of Assisi told his brothers to "preach by their deeds",[3] since they, in themselves and their actions, were a word of God.

If each of us is called to be a word of God, the way that word is uttered is through the Spirit. St Basil describes the Spirit as "the Breath of God who always accompanies the Word".[4] God created humanity, we are told in Genesis, by "breathing" life into the form made of clay.[5] So life is a gift or "grace" of God. The gift tells us something about the giver. In itself, then, being born tells us something about God – our answering the call to life points to life's source. No wonder joy and awe accompany birth. God is there!

All the more is this so when, as Christians, we are born anew by Baptism and enter into a graced family relationship with God. St Paul says that we become a "letter from Christ" written "not with ink but with the Spirit of the living God."[6] Through the Spirit we share in God's own life. In so far as we remain in tune with that grace, we will continue, as we develop and grow, to image God in our personalities and our way of being. We will tell God's story.

---

[2] Gerard Manley Hopkins, "God's Grandeur".
[3] Regis J Armstrong & Ignatius C Brady. *Francis and Clare, The Complete Works*. New York: Paulist Press, 1982. p. 122
[4] Cited by Denis Edwards in *Breath of Life*. New York: Orbis Books, 2004. p. 26.
[5] Gen. 2: 7.
[6] 2 Cor. 3: 3.

Joseph's word of faith

What story of God was told in Joseph? Because we have no biographical details of his life, we have to deduce them from the faith-writings of the Gospels. What we can say is that Joseph was open to God's action in him and so he was able to be in intimate relationship, as close as father is to son, with the Word enfleshed. Their relationship mirrored for us the kind of God Jesus described in his stories, such as that of the Prodigal Father, or the mother giving birth.[7]

Being open to God's action in our lives is traditionally referred to as having faith in God. It is only when we have a relationship of faith with another that we allow them to influence and guide us. Our baptismal gift from God was the grace to enter into such a faith relationship. Pope John Paul II names Joseph's faith as one of the essential characteristics of his response to God. "To believe", he says, "means to live in history open to God's initiative, to the creative force of his Word, who became flesh in Christ, uniting himself forever to our humanity."[8] In faith, Joseph allowed God to act in his life. And in so "doing God's will", Joseph became an instrument through whom God was revealed enfleshed among us in Jesus.

Like Joseph, all the baptised are called to reveal God in our world through being open to "doing God's will". We trust God enough to know that full life is what God wants for us. This aspect of faith, doing God's will, is called the virtue of obedience. The root meaning of "obedience" is "on account of hearing." Artists frequently depict Joseph as cupping his ear, to indicate Joseph's obedience. Committed to doing the will of God, all the baptised must listen "with a servant's ear" to God's voice. We can't delude ourselves that we have a direct line to God, and so we listen for the word of God in the dialogue

---

[7] Lk. 15:11-32; Jn 16:21-23.
[8] Angelus Address on Fourth Sunday of Advent, Vatican City, Dec. 23, 2001 (Zenit.org).

between our own hearts and the community of scripture, Church, religious community and wider society (or the 'signs of the times').

Openness to God's will was one of the first aspects noted by the early Church as characterizing Joseph. They expressed this in different ways, including what is of pertinence to us, in their conversations about Joseph being a virgin. Actually, the point of their arguments was not Joseph – rather they were concerned about protecting belief in the divine origin of Jesus.[9] But behind their statements is also a cultural understanding, even in pagan society, that saw virginity as a sign of absolute focus on God's will. So when some of the Church Fathers, such as Augustine, insisted that Joseph was a virgin, they tapped into the popular mind which readily agreed with what St Paul says:

> The unmarried man is busy with the Lord's affairs, concerned with pleasing the Lord; but the married man is busy with this world's demands and occupied with pleasing his wife. This means he is divided. The virgin … is concerned with things of the Lord, in pursuit of holiness in body and spirit.[10]

Western culture today does not see in virginity a symbol of an undivided heart. But what Paul is referring to, being totally committed towards carrying out God's purpose in our lives, is demanded of every Christian, whether married or not. A focus on God's will and inner listening, enables the story of God's love to be told in the lives of those who identify with the spirit of Joseph.

---

[9] Church fathers such as Jerome and Augustine insisted that Joseph, like Mary, was a virgin. Others concluded that he must have been an old man no longer sexually active, so that Mary's virginity could be protected. What both arguments were trying to affirm was faith in the divinity of Christ. Reading back into the Gospels details about Joseph's personal life is not the point of the Gospels anyway, and on the basis of historical evidence, cannot be verified or refuted.

[10] 1Cor. 7: 32-34

Joseph's vocation

When we obey the will of God for our lives at the deepest level, we find our "call" or "vocation". The root meaning of the word 'vocation', from the Latin 'vocare', is, of course, 'call'. Joseph's first and primary call came at birth when he respond to life and thus became a word of God in his person. This word continued to be "spoken" throughout his life, as, at each stage of his development, he became more deeply who he was made to be. Through the words of scripture and its interpretation by community elders,[11] he would have remained in tune with the word of God, allowing it to influence life decisions and to give shape to the truth of God within him.

Matthew's gospel tells us that another important way in which Joseph heard what he was being called to was through the language of the inner self, the unconscious, where, St Paul says, God speaks.[12] This language is that of the symbol, often experienced in dreams or touched at a conscious level for us in things like theatre, poetry, music or art. For the ancient peoples, the dream was a messenger of God. "Let the prophet who has a dream recount his dream: let him who has my word speak my word truthfully," charged Jeremiah.[13]

It was through listening to God in his dreams that Joseph learnt his vocation.[14] "If ever Joseph had wondered, 'Who am I?' or 'Why am I here?'", says Louise Perrotta, "this was God's mind-boggling answer."[15] Through attending to the dream, Joseph learnt that he, along with Mary, was to play an active part in the

---

[11] John Paul II says, "It is ... by the light and with the strength of the word of God that my own vocation can be discovered and understood, loved, and followed and my own mission carried out." *Pastores dabo vobis* (On the Formation of Priests in the Circumstances of the Present Day), 1992, par. 47.
[12] Ref., for example, Rom. 5:5, Rom 10:8, Phil 2:13, 1 Thess 2:13, Eph 2:22, Eph 3:17, where God is described as being at the centre of our being.
[13] Jer. 23:28.
[14] Mt 1: 20-23
[15] Louise Bourassa Perrotta. *Saint Joseph, His Life and His Role in the Church Today*. Huntington: Our Sunday Visitor, 2000. p 35.

coming of the Messiah. In bringing the gift of himself and allowing the Holy Spirit to work through him, Joseph enabled God's story to take shape.

Christian belief is that God's dream takes perfect shape in Jesus. The early Church saw that this dream continued to be lived out in their being the Body of Christ.[16] Through them, Christ acted by way of the ordinary talents they brought to the service of the community. The creative breath of the Spirit enabled these gifts (*charisma* in Greek) to be sign and instrument of God's presence among them. Not every gift said the same thing, since all were different according to the role of the person, their character and abilities. But together they contributed to the whole.[17]

When groups of Christians gather around leaders with whom they find their particular gift to be compatible, it is said that they share the same "charism". They find their vocation in that way of carrying out mission. Sicari says that the unique vocation of each person is "a response to the charismatic call of the Spirit".[18] The response of Joseph and of the early Christians to their vocation enabled the Spirit to work through them, so that God's story of love in Jesus continued to be told. This, too, is our call.

---

[16] For example, "I live now, not I, but Christ lives within me." Gal. 2:20. Seventeenth-century French mysticism was particularly aware of this call. A noted spiritual director of the time, J J Olier, writes in his "Mémoires": "All apostolic persons and the apostles are Christ-bearers: they take Our Lord with them wherever they go; they are, as it were, sacraments bearing Christ in order that under their appearance and through them he may proclaim the glory of his Father. Jean-Jacques Olier, 1608-1657. From "Jesus Living in Mary: Handbook of the Spirituality of St Louis de Monfort". http://www.ewtn.com/library/Montfort/Handbook/Frenchs.htm

[17] W. Harrington. ("Charism", in J. A Komonchak, M. Collins and D. A. Lane eds, *The New Dictionary of Theology,* Wilmington, DE: Michael Glazier Inc., 1987, p. 180), states that the word "charism" owes its use in religious language to St. Paul. "It is a supernatural gift bestowed by the Holy Spirit for building up the body of Christ. A charism is a gift which has its source in the *charis* - grace or favor - of God and which is destined 'for the common good,' (1 Cor 12: 7)." Paul goes on to describe some of the gifts of the Spirit to the Church.

[18] Antonio Maria Sicari. "Ecclesial Movements: A New Framework for Ancient Charisms", *Communio,* Vol XXIX, No. 2, Summer 2002. p 296.

Charism is a word of God

Through the characteristics of the charism (or gift) that we identify with in carrying out Christ's mission and in which we recognise our vocation, God's story is told in a particular way. Charism becomes the "pot" in which the story is carried. What the charism looks like will depend to a large extent on how the founders of the group we join established it. And an important factor in how they established it is the understanding of God that attracted them and impelled them to portray it in the way they carried out their mission. For instance, those whose impression of God is primarily as the secret lover would have a very different focus and method in ministry from those expressing God's strong wish for social justice. Thus, each group gathered around a charism will present in their story a different 'face' of God. Like a multi-faceted diamond, the variety of charisms or gifts enable the Church to respond to its vocation to be sacrament of Christ and light to the nations.

The word "charism" dropped out of current usage for centuries, but the essential understanding that the Spirit provides for the needs of the mission did not. When in 1873 Mary MacKillop[19] wrote her pamphlet explaining the necessity for a different kind of Religious Congregation in Australia, her friend in London, Lady Georgina Fullerton, introduced the text with this comment: "Each race, each clime, each society have different requirements and the Holy Ghost breathes into the hearts which He inspires to work for others the peculiar spirit destined to provide for those wants."[20] However, the consciousness that it is the whole Church and not just Religious and clerics who share in these gifts of the Spirit for mission was not one that most Catholics had at the time.

---

[19] See Introduction.
[20] Mrs Augustus Craven. *Life of Lady G. C. Fullerton*. London 1888. Translated from the French by H J Coleridge, ed. Notes taken from copy in Mitchell Library, Sydney by Evelyn Pickering RSJ, 1983.

"Vatican II," says Sicari, "rediscovered the charismatic dimension of the Church."[21] As a result of this rediscovery there has been a phenomenal burgeoning of lay movements that have sprung up around the world to involve ordinary people in extending Christ's ministry among us. For their part, Religious Congregations were given the specific task by Vatican II of reclaiming their charism, basing the process on "both a constant return to the sources of the whole of the Christian life (the Gospel) - and to the primitive inspiration of the institutes and their adaptation to the changed conditions of our time".[22] In doing this, Religious have not only relocated their ambit of ministry among the poor, but they have discovered that their charisms are broader than their particular expression of it. Lay people share the same gifts as they do and interpret them for their way of life.

The charisms of groups within the Church complement and sustain one another, enabling the mission of Jesus to be ever new, to meet new worlds and changing needs across a wide spectrum of society. A definition of "charism" in this context might be as follows: Charism is
- a gift of the Spirit
- given to persons
- taken up by a group
- to carry out the mission of Jesus
- characterised by particular ways of being and serving and
- reflective of a particular experience of God's presence in our world.

I think of charisms as rivers flowing around the world with tributaries or channels carrying the charism into different places and times. Each river has its own characteristics, and through its

---

[21] Sicari, "Ecclesial Movements", 298.
[22] *Perfectae Caritatis* 1965, par. 1.

many channels (Religious and lay people who share the same spirit) it waters our world, making visible and active the particular aspects of God's love that each group is gifted to portray. Another image of charism is offered by the Sisters of St Joseph in France. They see the charism as the soil, in which roots from different groups in the Church – Religious, Associates, lay groups – are planted. From this soil the roots produce a trunk, the charism, which in turn puts forth the particular expressions of the charism, branches, as it were, of the same tree.[23]

The Charism of Joseph

During the Middle Ages, the figure of Joseph as patron became popular especially among ordinary folk struggling to survive in times of war, plague and famine. Their society was one where a system of patronage meant that lower classes were utterly dependent on the good graces of patrons for education, work, housing, welfare and Christian burial.[24] In return, obedience, loyalty and honour were expected. The pyramidal structure of such a society was well entrenched; for them it "mirrored" the heavenly realm where God, angels and saints were arranged in descending order of importance. The notion of saints being "patrons" before God's throne fitted easily into popular imagination, especially when feelings of powerlessness and helplessness against the vagaries of life were constant companions.

So at a time when plagues like the Black Death wiped out a third of the population and when knowledge of medicine was primitive, the picture of Joseph possibly dying in the loving arms of Jesus and Mary touched the anxieties of most people. Joseph became the "patron of a happy death". He could intercede on behalf of the petitioner for God's mercy at this

---

[23] Soeurs de Saint Joseph, *Par-delà Toutes Frontières*. Rome: Editions du Signe, 1998. p 35.
[24] Bodies being left to rot in fields or to be eaten by wild animals was not unknown.

most vulnerable of moments. Confraternities whose ministry was to care for the body after death and give it dignified burial named themselves after Joseph.

Similarly, in a society which had begun to organise craftsmen into guilds, the forerunners of unions, identification with Joseph the artisan[25] was a natural step. Joseph was the patron of workers. He was offered, too, as a model of fathers. While a patriarchal structure was supposedly upheld by the heavenly order, the absence from their families of many men due to wars and trade meant that the skills of fathering were not valued. Especially during the late Middle Ages, real efforts were made by preachers to exhort men to restore this imbalance and, like Joseph, to properly care for and treasure their families.

On the popular front, then, the figure of Joseph was familiar to many, since his role in the ordinary facets of life allowed them to align themselves with one whose power before God was great and who could then provide heavenly patronage and hope. But is there a deeper gifting of Joseph that might be recognised as a Spirit-gift – "charism" – still operating in our world today?

The critical questions here are: "What role did Joseph play in God's plan of salvation? How did Joseph's gift contribute to mission? What were the characteristics of his being and serving? How did these tell of God's presence in his world?" The answers to these questions make up the fabric of this book.

In one way, Joseph's is a unique gift. Given the family structure of his day, only he could correspond with the invitation of God to "legitimise" the birth of Jesus and to provide the context in which the Word could be enfleshed. But God's story of presence

---

[25] Anne Hennessy. *In Search of a Patron: Re-discovering St. Joseph through a Social Context Approach to Gospel Studies,* Unpublished Monograph, Sisters of St Joseph of Orange, California, 2002. p 42. As will be noted in a later chapter, the Greek word used in Scripture to describe Joseph's work is *tekton,* denoting "a person who works with hard substances."

with us still takes shape through the ongoing mission of the Body of Christ. Are there people whose particular gifts for mission are similar to those of Joseph?

We are well aware of, say, the Franciscan movement emanating from the figure of Francis of Assisi. The experience of God's nearness and personal love at a time when rural societies were falling apart and urban life tended to swallow people up into anonymity was vital for Christ's mission in the twelfth and thirteenth centuries. It still speaks to us today.

Is there a Josephite way of ministry? And if so, do others besides Religious Congregations named after Joseph share in this way? Our experience tells us that they do. We Sisters have become very conscious of this fact especially in recent years when we have handed over to lay leadership the management of institutions formerly administered by ourselves.

The enthusiasm with which lay people identify themselves with the charism bears out the realisation that they breathe the same characteristics of Spirit as we do. Associates and other lay groups express that charism in ministry. Indeed where was this spirit first caught if not in our families living their faith?[26] Psychologists tell us that we are attracted by what we have the potential for ourselves. Do those who have tapped into the river we might name the Movement of St Joseph continue to tell of God in the same way as Joseph did?

---

[26] A typical story is one where a Sister was regretting being assigned to Western Australia, far from her father in Victoria (as far as San Francisco is from New York). "My dear girl", her father said, "If you are sent to the West that means that God has something special for you to do there, which no-one else could do, and it would be very wrong for me to stop you going. As I told you before, you are not to think of me, only to do God's will."

1.2 PART TWO: The spirit unfolds.

<u>Tapping into the charism</u>
We do know that Julian Tenison Woods tapped into the river of the St Joseph charism when, as a young seminarian, he met with the Sisters of St Joseph in France during a holiday there in 1853. What struck him was their simplicity; the picture of God that he caught from them was that God's presence is with ordinary people in lowly walks of life. It was the spirit of these Sisters, he said, that inspired him years later in the founding of the Australian Sisters of St Joseph.

When he came to Australia, Julian found in Mary MacKillop the same spirit. And when he told her of the Sisters of St Joseph in France, Mary recognised what was in her. At first she and Father Woods considered the possibility of getting Sisters from France or of her going to France to join them. She wrote to her mother at the time:
> "I have such an earnest longing for the Order of St Joseph and know well how hard it will be to get it established here, but everything God blesses will prosper, and surely His blessing attends this holy Order; none other is so fitted for the wants of this Colony ... but unless Sisters come from France, it will be long before there are enough of us for the work that is to be done".[27]

Since there was no money for either option, what resulted was the creation of the Australian Sisters of St Joseph. It's as though Julian and Mary dipped into the stream of the charism shared by the Sisters of St Joseph in France and gave its waters a channel which enabled it to flow into this country.

<u>Sisters of St Joseph, Le Puy, France.</u>
What is the story of these French Sisters of St Joseph who inspired the Australian founding? It is generally accepted that

---

[27] Archives of Sisters of St Joseph, Sydney. Cited in Sheila McCreanor, ed. *Mary MacKillop & Flora*. Sydney: Sisters St Joseph, 2004. p. 15.

the official recognition by Bishop of Le Puy in the year 1650, marks the foundation of the Sisters of St Joseph.[28] In a time of great trauma, the area around Le Puy was still recovering from the effects of the Protestant Reformation and the Wars of Religion, and a series of failed crops throughout the land was accompanied by widespread destitution. It was a time also of intense spiritual renewal among the nobility. Sodalities where people met to pray and discuss religion were set up, and confraternities of mercy, giving help to the poor, were numerous.

Under the influence particularly of Cardinal Pierre de Bérulle (1575-1629), the Carmelite Sisters reformed by Teresa of Avila had been introduced into France from Spain earlier that century. Here they quickly spread and had profound affect on the spirituality of the period. As devotion to St Joseph had featured prominently in the life of St Teresa, it was natural that he was associated with the spiritual renewal of 17th century France. This was promoted further by a number of Jesuit spiritual writers who were part of the Bérullian movement. Anne Hennessy notes:

> Preachers, including the Jesuit home missionaries in France, presented Joseph as the model for married men: a faithful provider, a respectful spouse, a nurturing and protecting provider for his family. For people of higher social standing and education, ... Joseph was the person closest to the Incarnation and the Redemption. His own contemplation of the Mystery of Jesus and Mary was example and content for the mystical circles that influenced French Catholic spirituality of the Ancien Régime.[29]

At the time, Religious Life for women was, by the order of Rome, monastic. A large dowry was required, and only the

---

[28] Marie-Louise Gondal in *Les Origines des Soeurs de Saint-Joseph au XVII Siècle* (Paris: Cerf, 2000), argues that 1650 is merely the institutional approval of a movement begun in a neighbouring diocese at least nine years before.
[29] Hennessy, *In Search of a Patron*, p. 2.

higher classes could hope to enter this way of life. Apostolic work, such as the teaching of girls, the care of orphans, etc., was done within the monastery. For a nun to be seen outside the walls was a scandal and brought disrepute to the whole group. It was presumed she was escaping the convent. Strict rules governed enclosure.

While most Bishops carried out the Roman edict in the strictest terms, there was a way they could get around the ruling. Bishops had civic powers as well as Church powers. On behalf of the State they could recognise groups of women who lived like nuns as "residential confraternities", if they were needed for the good of the diocese and if they didn't look like nuns.[30]

Father Médaille and the founding Sisters

In the 1640's a young Jesuit, Jean Pierre Médaille, was assigned to the giving of Missions in the region around Le Puy, and in the course of doing this, he met groups of village women who wished to become nuns but were not eligible to do so. So when Médaille realised that this scattered group of women he was working with had a vocation to Religious Life, he gathered them at Le Puy whose bishop, Henri de Maupas, was glad to have such a group of Sisters. Besides, he needed them to run his House of Charity for orphans. October 15th, 1650, marks the official recognition of their foundation in Le Puy.

Médaille set about giving the six women, Françoise Eyraud, Claudia Chastel, Anna Chaleyer, Anna Vey, Anna Brun and Marguerite Burdier,[31] a rule which enabled them to live as

---

[30] Ref. M. Dortel-Claudot. *The Evolution of the Canonical Status of Religious Institutes With Simple Vows from the 16th Century Until the New Code.* Trans. M. R. MacGinley, Institute of Religious Studies, Sydney, 1989.

[31] Françoise Eyraud, 39 years of age, came from Le Puy and was the first superior of the group. Claudia Chastel was from Mende, a widow of a soldier killed in war, and the only one of the group who could, at the founding, read and write. Anna Chaleyer was 46 years of age and from Lyon. Anna Vey was about 15 years of age, from St Jeures de Bonne. Anna Brun was from Le Puy, an orphan, 15 years old. Marguerite Burdier was 24 years old, had a strong personality and seems to have had great influence on the growth of the Congregation.

religious without cloister. Their whole reason for being was to come into union with the uncreated Trinity through living in union with the created trinity of Jesus, Mary and Joseph **in** service of the "dear neighbour".

The Holy Family, according to this popular devotion of the time, was an earthly image of the divine Trinity – in other words, it told God's story.[32] So in honour of the Father, the Sisters were to strive to be perfectly open to God's will like Mary, obedient to grace; in honour of the Son they were to be totally empty of self as was the Son incarnate, Jesus, who gave himself totally in zeal "for souls"; in honour of the Spirit, the union of Father and Son in love, they were to practice perfect love like Joseph, model of those who serve Jesus and Mary, "one in the service of each other and one in the service of the neighbour without distinction".[33] He refers to union with God and neighbour as the "double union". In summary, they were, he instructed them, to live in such a way that their Congregation might bear the name of "The Congregation of God's Great Love".

The structure of the group conformed to social customs of the time. They wore the dress of widows, since widows were the only group of women who could legally arrange their own affairs. They lived in small, unnoticeable groups and accompanied each other wherever they visited or worked – scandal prevented any woman from going out alone. A saying of the era was "Either a husband or a wall"! Thus a number of rules given by Médaille are there simply to guard against what would have given scandal to that society, since scandal would have destroyed the whole experiment and put paid to the "little design" going forward.

---

[32] The "Two Trinities" was a devotion promoted by the 17th century French School of Spirituality.
[33] Primitive Constitution of the Sisters of St Joseph, Le Puy.

There were two different ways of belonging to the Sisters. One was for those who formed the main body, making simple vows of poverty, chastity and obedience; the other was for "Agregées" (the word means "joined" or "associated"), generally poor country women who pledged themselves to maintain attachment to the Congregation and shared in the life in so far as they could. Both groups were full members of the Congregation.[34] In both country and city the Sisters trained Confraternities of Mercy consisting of married or single laywomen who worked with them in ministry. The formation of these women was the same as for novices.

The Sisters' work was to do whatever was needed, whatever was in the power of women to do – although they were warned not to do work that was being covered in the local area by the cloistered Congregations, such as teaching girls from the higher and middle classes. They taught trades, especially lace and ribbon-making, so that women could earn money for the family; they took care of orphans, the sick, the abandoned; catechetical instruction was always included. Especially in the small villages they did much to restore the dignity of Church buildings and to encourage priests, often poorly educated and lonely.

It seems that the pressure to be "real nuns" was constant. There is a theory that one community wanted to become monastic "Adorers of the Eucharist," and that one of the founding Sisters wrote in alarm to Father Médaille. Whatever lay behind his reply, his pamphlet on the Eucharist as a model of *apostolic* Religious Life was the result. It was written as a letter to the recipient, most likely Marguerite Burdier. Through the literary form of metaphor, Médaille urges the Sisters to cling to their

---

[34] Records show the agregées soon did take the three devotional vows. In the 19th century, this arrangement was to give way to the monastic structure of "Lay" and "Choir" Sisters. See Patricia Byrne. "Vows in the History of Sisters of St Joseph"; Unpublished paper presented October 10, 1998, Annette Walters Memorial: Symposium on Vowed Life, St Paul, MN.

apostolic character, empty of self, so that through the humble bread of their little group, God can feed and nourish the world.

> Here in describing what she (Marguerite) knows and believes about the Eucharist, Médaille tells her – and us! This is your life! The mystery of our immersion in the mission of unioning love that is total and double is that "love of loves" which awakens in us the whole extent of holy loves. It is the meaning and purpose of her life. In fact, her life, our life, seized by God's enduring love, is to be that same enduring love – constant, unconditional, and life giving. It is to be the most "pure and perfect love" (par. 20) and will be that limitless love that is described in Ephesians as having the length, breadth, height and depth of Christ's love. (Eph. 3:18)[35]

By 1654 Father Médaille was required by his superiors to withdraw from directing the Sisters. Bishop de Maupas was also given another diocese, but since his replacement fully approved of the Sisters, they were able to flourish. The Sisterhood spread widely and was greatly loved throughout France. As times changed, their ministries gradually focussed on education and health care. But details of how the Congregation developed in the first 150 years have been lost owing to the trauma of the revolution – during which at least five Sisters were guillotined.

Refounding and Expansion

After the Revolution, the Sisters gradually came together again in small groups and attempted to continue their apostolate and recover properties. In Lyon, 1807, Cardinal Fesch (the uncle of Napoleon and a Constitution priest), called on Mother St John Fontbonne, to re-form the Congregation in his diocese. Napoleon had demanded of Rome that Religious should have a common structure of a central house with over-all superior under the bishop in each diocese, so Mother St John adopted this

---

[35] Bette Moslander. Unpublished paper, July 2003.

new arrangement.[36] Napoleon did not approve of monastic orders either – apostolic groups were favoured now. And since the fashion of a widow's bonnet and shawl of a century before had also changed, the Sisters thought it advisable to adopt a more monastic form of dress.

From Lyon the Sisters spread quickly into neighbouring areas of France and Italy. In 1836, the influential Countess de la Rochejacquelein financed the journey of six Sisters to go to St Louis, United States of America. Bishop Rosati was looking for Sisters to work with the indigenous people and to teach the deaf. The Sisters of St Joseph, the countess affirmed, were ideally suited to conditions in a pioneering country. Their rule allowed them to meet whatever needs presented themselves. For instance, they could teach boys, which other women's groups often could not. So it was that the little missionary band settled in Carondelet, a small village near St Louis and now a suburb of the city.

From this small beginning, the Sisters in the United States pushed out west, north and east. Early efforts in the 1860s to centralise into one Congregation were resisted by different foundations under Bishops who did not want a system where the "superior" would be from another diocese. Those who were in dioceses led by friends of the then Archbishop of St Louis did agree to centralise, and so they applied for and gained papal (or pontifical) approval. This gave the major superior elected by the Sisters more independence, although they still needed the authorisation of the local Bishop to minister in a diocese. For those who remained diocesan, the local Bishop, as their highest

---

[36] Edward Udovic ("Jean-Baptiste Etienne and the Vincentian Revival" in *Vincentian Studies Institute Monographs No.2)* says: "Napoleon had an obsession for order, uniformity, and centralization. He also was abysmally ignorant of religious issues. In 1807, he formulated a plan to bring the governmentally approved communities of sisters into one group organized under the common title of 'sisters of charity.' In each diocese, these sisters were to come under the authority of the bishop."

"superior", had the final say in Sisters' lives. The two systems grew up together in United States and Canada.[37] At the time of writing, there are 23 diocesan groups of Sisters of St Joseph in USA, and the Sisters of St Joseph of Carondelet (pontifical) are divided into four provinces and three vice-provinces. In 1966 all groups came together to form the Federation of Sisters of St Joseph in USA. The same process took place in Canada, with the five English-speaking diocesan groups forming a Federation there.[38]

Meanwhile, in Europe, the Sisters of St Joseph scattered in dioceses in France and Italy, established foundations in other countries – northern and southern Europe, India, South and Central America, Africa. This expansion continued throughout the 19th and 20th centuries.[39]

Sometimes the movement involved withdrawals and amalgamations. For instance, the thriving communities in Russia[40] were forced to withdraw with the onset of atheistic communism in the 1920s. Especially since Vatican II some smaller diocesan groups in France have come together to form a new Congregation. The "Institute of St Joseph" centred at Le Puy is made up of six such groups. Federations of Sisters of St Joseph have been formed in France and Italy. The Argentinian

---

[37] Sister Michael Bourne SSJ describes the same process undergone by the Sisters of St Joseph of Annecy in the 1890s and explains: "Papal approbation is a decree of official recognition of a Congregation, not just locally by the Bishops, but by the Holy See. It might be described as conferring universal or 'catholic' status rather than diocesan status. It gives the Congregation a stability in the Church which ensures its preservation even if a specific government should refuse recognition or expel its members, confiscate its property and commit other acts of injustice and attempted destruction." *His Mercy is From Age to Age,* Llantarnam Abbey, Wales: Sisters of St Joseph of Annecy, 1982. p. 146.
[38] One French-speaking foundation has joined the Federation in France.
[39] Many North American Congregations have established missions and foundations in South America. For example, the Sisters of St Joseph of Carondelet went to Peru in 1962 and now have a vice-province there. See Mary McGlone CSJ,, *Comunidad para el Mundo,,* Lima, Peru : Centro de Estudios y Publicaciones CEP, 2004.
[40] The Sisters of St Joseph of Chambéry went to Russia in 1863. There were more than 100 Sisters there when, under communism, some were imprisoned, the others expelled in the early 1920s.

Sisters of St Joseph have formed an association with others in South America who belong to either a European or North American Province.[41] Similarly the different foundations in India and Africa are looking at ways they can collaborate in acknowledgement of their common roots in Le Puy. The story of the Sisters of St Joseph begun in France in 1650 and now spread to every continent is not just one founding story, but an ongoing series of foundings and adaptations, changing in structure and form in order to portray the constancy of God's great love to an ever-changing society.

Father Woods, co-founder of the Sisters of St Joseph, Australia

When Julian Tenison Woods came to Australia in 1854 at the age of 22, he brought with him a wealth of experience and learning in the arts, science and in religion. He had had a chequered upbringing in England where the practice of Catholicism was patchy, newly re-establishing itself more strongly in the wake of the English Reformation.

Of delicate health, Julian had received a spiritual awakening when 16 years old and had subsequently lived as a third-order Franciscan; later he had joined the Passionists where he was professed but left because of illness, as was also the case when he entered the Marist Fathers' Novitiate in France. During those years he came under the influence of priests noted for their spiritual leadership – Tracterian convert from Anglicanism Frederick Oakeley, Passionist Ignatius Spencer, Wilfred Faber,[42] Marist Fathers Faure and Julian Eymard[43] and, briefly, the Curé of Ars.

---

[41] For instance, the Sisters of St Joseph, Brazil, are a Province of the Sisters of St Joseph of Chambéry, France (with its Generalate in Rome).
[42] Wilfrid Faber (1814-1863) was the founder, under Newman, of the London Oratory and was a composer of many sentimental, if popular, hymns of the time.
[43] St Julian Eymard was to become founder of a new Religious Order of Priests, the Blessed Sacrament Fathers.

During his time in France he had met with the Sisters of St Joseph. Later he wrote of this meeting:

> It was while I was in the Auvergne that I formed the idea of the Sisters of St Joseph. I found that in many parts of France a convent system prevailed that was of great assistance to the church in every way. The daughters of farmers and humble people were the sources from which the convents were recruited. They were not highly educated nor, probably, very refined; but they lived a life of great edification, and supplied most of the wants that could be supplied by religious communities. ... They lived in great poverty and simplicity and there was no fine-ladyism about them; but they were of the people and were loved by them.[44]

Julian's broad, almost "panoramic" experience in spirituality and religious life was to be further enriched by a short tutelage under the Jesuit Fathers in South Australia when, in 1856, Julian resumed his studies for the priesthood and was finally ordained for the Adelaide diocese the next year. South Australia was at that time a struggling colony of a few thousand people. Unlike other areas in Australia, it had been colonised by free settlers, not convicts. Many of these people were non-Conformists (or Dissenters) and the principles of religious equality and freedom had been established as part of the colony's founding vision in 1836. But with three quarters of its area being non-arable desert and lacking gold and other precious minerals, its development depended almost entirely upon the largess of the influential, mainly English Protestant families whose imported wealth secured what fertile land there was and offered employment to its citizens.

Of the small and scattered population only about one tenth were Catholic. Because religion did not receive public monies and most Catholics were farm labourers and servants with no social

---

[44] Julian Tenison Woods. *Memoirs*. Dictated to and transcribed by Miss Anne Bulger at Elizabeth St, Sydney, between 1887 and 1889. Unfinished Manuscript, Archives, Sisters of St Joseph, Sydney.

status, support of the Church was meagre. When its second Bishop arrived in Adelaide in 1859, not only did he find few material resources but what he called a 'deplorable lack of priests' and an almost non-existent Catholic school system.[45]

Bishop Geoghegan was to remain in Adelaide for barely two years. However, he did make impassioned efforts to address the situation whereby, as Mary MacKillop was later to describe it, families were in danger of losing their faith "because of too infrequent contact with their pastors and too few opportunities to attend to their spiritual duties".[46] Consequently there was heightened awareness among the Catholic population that they must make attempts to educate children and to form a faith identity.

Meeting with Mary MacKillop

In particular, the question was addressed by Father Woods as he visited as best he could the parish to which he was assigned, spanning 57,000 square kilometres (22,000 square miles) located in the south-eastern region of the colony. There, in the small, isolated township of Penola, he met in 1861 the young governess, Mary MacKillop with whom he kept in contact and of whose desire for Religious Life he was well aware. However, it seemed as though this desire could not be fulfilled. She longed to live a way of life wholly dependent on God's Providence and serving the most needy. In Melbourne she had had a passing encounter with the Sisters of Mercy but was not drawn to them; and it seemed that only in far-off Europe would there be the kind of group whose call corresponded with hers.

Moreover, since the age of 15, Mary had been the financial mainstay of her large family – her parents and seven surviving

---

[45] Marie Foale. *The Josephite Story: The Sisters of St Joseph, Their Foundation and Early History 1866 – 1893*. Sydney: Sisters of St Joseph, 1989. p. 6.
[46] MacKillop Mary. *Necessity for the Institute*. Pamphlet written in 1873, London. Archives, Sisters of St Joseph.

brothers and sisters. Scottish migrants, Alexander and Flora MacKillop had fallen on hard times early in their marriage and had been obliged to accept the charity of relatives and frequent disruptions to family life in the search for work and lodging. There is pathos in Mary's description of these years – "My life as a child was one of sorrow, my home, when I had it, a most unhappy one."

Yet it was from her parents that Mary had received the foundations for a faith that would sustain her throughout life. "My Father," she wrote, "had been educated for the Church and had studied very deeply. From him I learnt so much of the teachings of our holy Faith. He had studied for seven years in Rome alone and under the Jesuit Fathers; thus all I heard from him made me love the ways of our holy Faith ... and made me have a great affection for the Society of Jesus."[47] Her mother's trust in Divine Providence inspired Mary at last to take the plunge and to entrust the financial cares of her family to God's care even though debts, incurred in large part through the impetuousness of her father, were still pending. On March 19th, 1866, Mary put aside the fashionable clothes of the time to don a simple black dress and bonnet to indicate her intention and from that time, under the direction of Father Woods, lived a rule of life and signed herself "Mary – Sister of St Joseph."

Sisters of St Joseph, Australia

In one way, then, it was a transplanted seed that took root in Penola in the little stable transformed into a schoolhouse where Mary MacKillop began what she saw as God's work. What grew up in Australia from this transplanted seed was, however, a thoroughly Australian tree.

Like their French counterparts, the members of this group were simple women, many not highly educated and coming

---

[47] Letter to Msgr Kirby, May 27, 1873. Archives, Sisters of St Joseph, North Sydney.

necessarily from the non-privileged classes - since that is where most Catholics stood on the social scale. In the 1650s, the Sisters of St Joseph went against the accepted model of Religious Life of the time to live a life among the people without cloister and in small groups. In the 1860s in Australia, the Sisters of St Joseph caused some scandal to those who associated women religious "with the upper classes of society and believed they should lead secluded lives in large buildings surrounded by extensive grounds".[48] These Josephites, it was asserted, were not "real nuns" – they walked the streets and lived in twos and threes in rented houses identical to those of the families they served.

The Australian Sisters of St Joseph shared with the Sisters of Le Puy a strong Jesuit influence in their formative years. Mary had conducted the Penola school for little over a year when Father Woods called her and a companion to the more populated Adelaide to begin the enterprise there. His efforts to establish a Catholic system of education had been boosted by his appointment as diocesan Director of Schools, and he saw the Sisters as the means by which this aim could be reached. The Austrian Jesuits had worked over a large area of South Australia for many years, and their influence rivalled that of the Irish clergy in that State. As confessors and advisers to Mary and the Sisters, they were involved with the fledgling Sisterhood from the beginning.

When circumstances led to the excommunication of Mary MacKillop[49] and eventually forced Father Woods out of the diocese, it was the Jesuits who extended practical help to the Sisters of St Joseph and took over their direction. When Mary MacKillop went to Rome to have the Rule approved, it was again a Jesuit, Father Anderledy, who instructed her in law

---

[48] Foale, *The Josephite Story,* p.23.
[49] This part of the story will be developed in a later chapter.

pertaining to Religious Life and gave her a solid understanding of Church authority. As a result, her clarity about these matters was to be a hallmark for the rest of her life.

Rapid expansion featured these Sisters of St Joseph too, and soon they were in all parts of Australia and New Zealand. Like their French counterparts, they served above all in country parishes and lived in small groups of two or three, not demanding more than what the people could afford to provide. Early on in their development, differing understandings of the relationship of Bishops to the group led to the formation of diocesan-based Josephites as opposed to those of pontifical rite with central governance. The two forms of Josephite life burgeoned side by side, and eventually, in the 1960s, the diocesan congregations formed a Federation and some are now pontifical.

Meanwhile overseas foundations in Peru and Ireland have been established and outreach to Papua New Guinea, East Timor and other South American, Asian and African countries extends the story of God's compassionate love on a wider front. Recent years have seen both groups of Sisters of St Joseph founded in Australia joyfully acknowledging their common roots and exploring closer links.

Re-Sourcing the Charism
The original rule written by Julian for the Sisters of St Joseph in Australia lacks Médaille's theological depth. Nevertheless there are strong parallels evident in the spirituality alluded to or presumed. The history of the Irish Church, where most priests in Australia came from, had been tied up with the French seminary system and therefore of the French School of Spirituality. What these priests taught, then, was strongly influenced by this spirituality. Its devotions were theirs, and they brought these to Australia. Julian had had direct contact with it in France as a Marist novice; Mary MacKillop's early

instruction in the faith had been shaped by it. The rule, then, reflected many of the same features of spirituality as that given by Médaille in 1650.

God's love: The primary experience of God for both the Sisters of St Joseph founded in Le Puy and those founded in Australia over two hundred years later is that God is love. Especially since the visions of St Margaret Mary Alacoque,[50] God's great love incarnated in Jesus had been promoted in devotion to the Sacred Heart. In 1856, at the urgent entreaties of the French bishops, Pope Pius IX extended the feast of the Sacred Heart to the universal Church and for the greater part of the 19th, and, indeed, the 20th century, this devotion was a prime symbol of Catholicism.

After the Revolution most surviving manuscripts of Father Médaille's teachings had been lost.[51] However, in their absence, as evidence from the archives of various branches of Sisters of St Joseph shows, the Sisters readily adopted devotion to the Sacred Heart as expressing their group nature.

A lively example is provided by Mother Bernard Gosselin, founder of the Sisters of St Joseph of Orange in California, whose book of prayers in honour of the Sacred Heart is thumb-marked to fragmentation.[52] Her establishment of this new branch of the Congregation was the result of a dream:

> She was in the convent chapel, kneeling at the back of the room after Mass. She stared at the crucifix above the altar, and it was suddenly replaced with a statue of the Sacred Heart. It seemed to grow until it was life-size, and then it began to walk down the aisle as if seeking someone. She

---

[50] A Visitation nun, Paray-le-Monial, France, whose visions began in 1673. The popularity of the devotion was aided by the simplicity of its practices and its visual appeal (the Jesuits, for instance, used the image on title pages of publications and in their churches).

[51] For instance, copies of the manuscripts of *The Eucharistic Letter* were only rediscovered in Lyons in the 1960's when Jesuit Fr Nepper was doing research on Médaille.

[52] Prayer Book in Archives, Sisters of St Joseph of Orange. Mother Bernard founded the Sisters in California from La Grange in 1912.

could see it quite distinctly, and the thought came vividly to her mind, "Even his feet are beautiful." When He got near enough to her, He pointed to her, looking directly into her face. "It's you I want", He said. "I want you to do something for me; and you will accomplish it through devotion to my Sacred Heart."[53]

Her dedication of the beautiful (recently renovated) Motherhouse chapel to the Sacred Heart of Jesus is a constant reminder of the response. So, too, in 1960 the Mother General of the Sisters of St Joseph of Rochester could reflect,

That the Sisters of Saint Joseph should practice and promote a special devotion to the Sacred Heart of Jesus is not surprising. ... Our maxims,[54] the spiritual legacy of our founder, are full of exhortations to the "most perfect love possible." Father Médaille's "Means to Transformation in Christ" (Spiritual Legacy) is a beautiful summary of this devotion, which is "wholly directed to the love of God himself."[55]

In Australia, the Church in the time of Mary MacKillop and Julian Tenison Woods promoted with vigour this same devotion. The teaching of St John Eudes that the Sacred Heart is a "Furnace of Divine Love" is one that was familiar to them. Mary's Retreat Notes of 1871, later put into a circular to her Sisters, describe in the highly-embellished language of the Victorian era the source of her *charism*, and therefore of her characteristic approach to mission:

'Say, wilt thou be my lover? Wilt thou seek for happiness in Me? Wilt thou suffer me to teach thee? Wilt thou become simple and gentle as all my true lovers are?' ... My little

---

[53] Brad Geagley. *A Compassionate Presence: the Story of the Sisters of St Joseph of Orange.* Orange: Sisters of St Joseph of Orange, 1996.
[54] Fr Médaille produced a book of Maxims which the Sisters founded under his direction have always used as a source of inspiration.
[55] Mother M. Helene, Circular letter to the Sisters, January 6, 1960. The final quote of the excerpt is taken from the Encyclical of Pius XII, "*Haurietus Aquas.*" On the other side of the Atlantic, the Sisters of St Joseph of Annecy, from 1873 on, renewed each year the consecration of the Congregation to the Sacred Heart. (Bourne, *His Mercy is From Age to Age* p. 113).

> one,.... I have asked you to come to me that I might tell you how I loved you, and ask you, for My love, to call My other children back to me.'[56]

The orientation of the charism was to be perpetuated for the Australian Sisters of St Joseph by the addition to their name of a sub-title, "of the Sacred Heart".

God's will: Openness to God's will is an essential ingredient in the way Sisters of St Joseph tell God's story. Jesus had declared that his real familyare those who hear the will of God and do it (Mt. 12:48). For Mary MacKillop, God's will was like "a very dear book which I am never tired of reading, which has always some new charm for me".[57] Julian had written in the first rule of the Sisters of St Joseph:

> Their whole desire must be to love God and to love nothing else, neither friends, riches, comforts, worldly news, nor even worldly knowledge; and, finally, they must cease to love their own wills, and learn to be subject to all, for the love of God.[58]

In the Holy Family, Médaille saw full openness to God's will. For him, as later for Mary and Julian, this attitude is based on a relationship of overflowing confidence in God's love. In his book containing a hundred maxims for the Sisters of St Joseph[59], Médaille offers a wealth of advice on developing such a relationship: for example,

> Accept without hesitation the loss of all good and the suffering of all evil, rather than the failure, however slight, to fulfill the holy will of God. (Maxim 13)

> Be always ready to obey peacefully, indifferent to all that is not against God's will: to live or to die, to be healthy or ill, happy or unhappy, loved or persecuted, finding always your complete contentment solely in fulfilling God's will. (Maxim 72)

---

[56] Circular, 21 May 1907.
[57] Letter to Monsignor Kirby, May 22nd, 1873.
[58] Rule approved by Bishop L. B. Sheil, Bishop of Adelaide, December 17, 1868.
[59] Publications of the *Maxims of the Little Institute* are multiple. A particularly fine commentary is produced by Marcia Allen, *Love's Design: An Invitation to Reflect on the Maxims of the Little Institute.* Kansas: Sisters of St Joseph of Concordia, 1998.

> Live out your life with one desire only: to be always what God wants you to be, in nature, grace and glory, for time and for eternity. (Maxim 73)

The Eucharist: For both Médaille and the Australian founders, the sacrament of the Eucharist was seen to be the prime narrator of God's story, what Vatican II would call the "source and summit" of Christian life.[60] Signifying and enabling union with God and each other, the Eucharist provided a model for Religious. Like Jesus expressing God's nature in the total giving of self for the life of others, Sisters were urged to live in complete self-giving. The Eucharist, says Médaille, "constitutes all our holy and pure loves on earth".[61] Julian similarly exhorts his Sisters:

> Let us then, dear Sisters, see in Jesus the Superior of our community, Who dwells amongst us, and Who goes before us in all things in the self-denying example He gives.[62]

On the pilgrimage of faith lived out as a Sister of St Joseph, the story of God's love has continued to be told through the years by those who have shared the charism of St Joseph, open to God's dream and, by the power of the Spirit, enabling the Word to become incarnate in and through their obedience to that Word.

1.3 PART THREE: The spirit lives into the now

<u>Changed Context for Sisters of St Joseph</u>
> In the history of the Church we encounter one constant that is revealed with greater force especially in moments of cultural and ecclesial crisis or in times of epoch-making change: the

---

[60] Documents of Vatican II, *Decree on the Ministry and Life of Priests,* par. 5.
[61] *The Eucharistic Letter,* Translation InterCongregational Research Team, Federation of the Sisters of St Joseph, USA, 1973. par. 1.
[62] Written by Fr Woods and printed under the two different titles by Mary MacKillop (*Book of Instructions*) and the Diocesan Sisters of St Joseph (*Explanation of the Rule and Constitution of the Sisters of St Joseph*). Archives, Sisters of St Joseph, Sydney.

> great gifts of sanctity that .. (Christ) presents to .. (the Church).[63]

In the past, the charism given visibility in the Church through Sisters of St Joseph has been gift. Does the shape of this gift still speak to our age? A feature of post-modern culture is the fundamentally-changed attitude towards sex and the former sign-value of virginity and thus of celibacy. As already noted, in the popular mind it now rarely symbolises absolute focus on God. In pagan times, figures such as the Roman Vestal Virgins who gave their lives to keeping the gift of fire alight, had symbolised total commitment to public service.[64] Ancient philosophies which informed Christian thought had also maintained that virginity signified the perfect human being.[65] These cultural understandings influenced peoples' attitudes to the significance of virginity.

So it was that the order of Virgins in the early Church was valued since, being a life "above the course of nature", it signified a "heavenly" life of union with God, symbolised in the image of "Spouse of Christ". St Ambrose could declare,

> Virginity has brought from heaven that which it may imitate on earth. And not unfittingly has she (the virgin) sought her manner of life from heaven, who has found for herself a Spouse in heaven. She, passing beyond the clouds, air, angels, and stars, has found the Word of God in the very bosom of the Father, and has drawn Him into herself with her whole heart. [66]

---

[63] Fidel Gonzales Fernandez. "Charisms and Movements in the History of the Church", *The Ecclesial Movements in the Pastoral Concern of the Bishops,* Vatican City: Pontifical Council for the Laity, 2000. p. 71.

[64] The worship of Vesta was only abolished in 380 AD by the emperor Theodosius. So valued was the service the virgins provided that it took on religious significance, demanding total commitment, symbolised by their vow of chastity. Being buried alive was the punishment for breaking this vow.

[65] In folk etymology the word virgin comes from vir (Latin. 'man') and gyne (Greek. 'woman'), a man-woman or androgyne, a complete person. A virgin has the whole potential of the total original human being. http://www.phreak.co.uk/head/articles/manwoman.html

[66] Ambrose, *Concerning Virgins,* To Marcellina, his sister. Book 1. Chapter 1. http://www.newadvent.org/fathers/34071.htm

But in the cultural context of postmodern society, the symbolic language of virginity has changed. Does that mean that religious consecration as a Sister of St Joseph no longer has value? Sandra Schneiders asserts that the opposite is the case. This new era, rather than being hostile to consecrated celibacy, offers it an opportunity for its "greatest witness value":

> Freely chosen, religiously motivated, publicly lived, chaste nonmarriage cannot fail to raise questions in our sex-saturated and pleasure-obsessed culture. ... The choice to willingly forego both marriage and sex is a genuine conundrum within a rampantly narcissistic and hedonistic culture.[67]

While this may be the case, however, a big challenge for Religious is to tell the story of God they are gifted with in a language that can be understood by our culture. It must, too, tell the truth. In the past, its symbols often set Religious apart from the rest of the Church. As Sisters of St Joseph interpret their identity and meaning for today, they have necessarily tapped into the urging of the Spirit that raises awareness that it is the whole Church and not just clergy and Religious who are involved in its mission. That mission is to be sign and instrument of union with God and of unity with all peoples.[68] Religious must nurture this awareness.

Beyond Sisterhoods

Leading up to Vatican II, the Church had already been on a journey of reclaiming the notion of total Church involvement in mission. The Catholic Action movement in the time of Pius XI had called forth the gifts of lay people for mission, even though, in the main, laity were tightly controlled in this action by the clergy. The Young Christian Workers movement had enabled people to bring the light of the Gospel to their work situations.

---

[67] Sandra M. Schneiders. *Selling All,* New York: Paulist Press, 2001. p. 131.
[68] Vatican II, *Dogmatic Constitution on the Church,* par.1.

The encyclical of Pius XII on the Mystical Body of Christ had provided the theological basis for a changing image of Church.

The background to this growing awareness was historical. Structures in the primitive Church had reflected the basic Christian experience of God as relational – Trinitarian. For the Christian (as for the Jew), God's revealing action took place in the formation of a people. Church leadership preserved this experience in consulting one another as a collegial group and in service of the community.

However, a later pyramidal structure of Church organisation had, for much of subsequent history, contributed to stereotyping of the Church as clergy first, then Religious and finally lay people, in order of "importance". In the popular imagination, those in the higher ranks were closer to God than those in the lower. The laity were the ones to be ministered to. They were recipients of the ministration of clergy and Religious rather than missioners in their own right.

Vatican II challenged us to invert the pyramid. We begin with the laity. The Holy Spirit endows different charisms or gifts to the whole people of God, all called to holiness and mission. From what Sicari calls "a *charismatically formed* laity"[69] will emerge priesthood, religious life and dedicated lay life. Together, the whole Church – lay, religious and cleric – will live out their mission in a variety of ways but will gather around the particular charisms given them.

David Ranson sees that Religious play a particular role in inverting the pyramidal image of Church and thus promoting the Church's reclaimed self-understanding:
> It is important to remind ourselves that a Religious Order does not exhaust the expression of a charism; the charism, around which a Religious Order has developed and lives, exists

---

[69] Sicari, "Ecclesial Movements", p. 296.

> unacknowledged perhaps in the hearts and lives of many people who are not members of a Religious Order. It will always be the task of Religious Orders to recognize this, in humility, and to foster their charism beyond their own structures in creative and constructive ways so that the ecclesial community is alive with the fullness of the Spirit.[70]

As inheritors of the charism given in the tradition of Joseph, Sisters of St Joseph are taking up the challenge. Through their encouragement of lay groups who have recognised in themselves the spirit of Joseph, Sisters are in turn recognising and fostering that charism in the laity. In this way they help promote a revitalised image of Church for mission and enable the breath of the Spirit to speak to our world.

Charism fostered
One way in which they are fostering the charism of St Joseph is by providing opportunities for spiritual growth among people who work with them. The first Sisters of St Joseph in Le Puy were born with an understanding of being in partnership. While the "Agregées" (associated Sisters) were full members of the Congregation, co-workers were always engaged with the Sisters in their works as Confraternities of Mercy. Today, **co-workers** make up the numerical bulk of those carrying out ministry according to the way of St Joseph.

Programs of formation for co-workers are an important feature of the ministrations of Sisters of St Joseph at the present time. While these programs may have been started with a certain amount of anxiety on the part of Sisters "to preserve their charism", it is now well recognised that the charism isn't *"theirs"*. The urging of the Spirit is already present in the lives of these co-workers, and the theological and spiritual formation offered by the programs simply taps into "the great gifts of sanctity" that Christ presents to the Church in this era[71].

---
[70] David Ranson. "What is the Gift of Religious to Tomorrow's Church?" *Compass: A Review of Topical Theology,* Chevalier Press, Sydney, Vol 29, Summer, 1995. p. 15.
[71] Fernandez, "Charisms and Movements", p. 71.

For instance, the Sisters of St Joseph of Orange, USA, run a 12-unit module as required training for the Health-Care workers. The units cover such topics as the spiritual heritage of the Sisters of St Joseph, the health-care ministry and its theological underpinnings, personal development and spirituality, justice, ethics and formation of community. All of these are integrated within the framework of method, values and mission that arise from the charism. In the business world, this integration can be revolutionary. The director of St Joseph's Healthcare, Hamilton (Canada) says:

> We see values-based care as the demonstrative way of living our mission. It engenders pride, leadership, excellence and compassion. ... At the end of the day, when you or a loved one enters a health care facility, what really matters is quality care, competence and compassion.[72]

Other programs such as the Australian "Colloquiums" for teachers and other co-workers similarly raise awareness of partnership in mission. One participant says that when she went to her first Colloquium experience, she had a sensation of "coming home".

> I was overwhelmed by the Sisters' hospitality. Over the weekend, that became a kind of symbol for everything else that happened. It touched into my spirituality and developed it. I could see Saint Joseph and Mary MacKillop as role models for how Jesus wants us to reach out to other people in love. I felt I belonged.

The Principal of St Bruno's School (formerly run by the Sisters) in Lyons, France, sums up this approach in a reflection on his experience:

> I understood that the Sisters of St Joseph of Lyon wanted to consider me, a layman, as a partner, a true collaborator, and not as a substitute for an assistant to the Superior. .. Throughout these years, the Federation of the Sisters of St Joseph offered me numerous opportunities of nourishing my mind, of finding more enlightenment in our procedures and

---

[72] Dr Kevin Smith, President and CEO, St Joseph's Healthcare, Hamilton.

projects, thanks to days of sharing and of analysis. I will never cease to praise those occasions when we would meet our colleagues, inciting us through our daily work to stress the essentials, to establish the priorities of values for which we are to work.[73]

Associates

The **Associate** movement is a widespread phenomenon of our times among the different groups of Sisters of St Joseph. This movement provides both a structure which recognises the charism present in those who are not Sisters and a forum for bonding in that spirit. Most Associate groups would identify with the statement of hope expressed in the "Handbook of Josephite Associates"–

> to enter into a spirit of communion between the Associates and Sisters by sharing love, simplicity, homeliness and generosity, with St Joseph as model in his caring for Jesus and Mary and the Universal Church in the modern world.[74]

The aim of the movement is primarily to raise awareness among Associates of the Spirit's gifting so that it is nurtured and strengthened. The charism is lived out in the lay situation – parishes, "workplace, families and friendships".[75] Therefore it is not expected that Associates should work in the specific ministries of the Sisters; instead, they interpret the spirit for their own lay lives[76]. Some groups of Sisters of St Joseph do offer a volunteer program for Associates and opportunities to live for short periods in community with them. But the direction, if it is truly a lay movement, will not be from the Sisters to join them,

---

[73] "Testimony of Mr François Petinataud" in *Proceedings of the International Forum,* Le Puy-Lyon, August 7-10, 1993; An International Gathering of the Federations and Congregations of St Joseph: "Rooted to Bear Fruit". pp 51, 52
[74] *Handbook of Associates of the Sisters of St Joseph of the Sacred Heart.* p.7.
[75] Associates – Sisters of St Joseph of Carondelet.
[76] There are also Associates of Sisters of St Joseph who are diocesan priests – they must interpret the spirit for their clerical lives. It goes without saying that these priests do not belong to a Religious Order. The Society of St Joseph in USA and the Oblates of St Joseph in Rome are but two of a number of clerical orders who identify with the charism of St Joseph. Fr. Stramare Tarcisio OSJ has compiled a list of over 200 Religious Congregations named after St Joseph. The scope of this book deals only with those having some association with Le Puy.

even as "companions on the journey". Rather it will foster the understanding of the Spirit endowing charisms among the whole of God's people, some of whom will be called to express that charism in Religious Life, but most of whom respond to it in "friendship, prayer and service"[77] according to their own circumstances in life..

The sharing of spiritual resources by the Sisters continues to be important in this evolution. One Associate explains:
> Being an Associate has turned my life around – I am part of a movement that is growing in love. These people are my extended family and we have the support and love of the Sisters.

Another stressed the "ordinariness" she found among the Sisters. Invited to a cup of tea, she was taken to the kitchen "just as I would with my neighbours". From this small incident she and her husband were to respond to the spirit-gift within themselves as Associates to reach out to other families in trouble. Members of the strong Associate movement of the Sisters of St Joseph of the Sacred Heart in Peru say they feel "lucky" to share the Josephite charism.
> The Sisters have taught us a new way of living in solidarity with the most disadvantaged people in our country. We enjoy the sense of being part of a big family whose identity becomes stronger through love, courage and the challenge of these hard times.

Volunteers

Volunteer programs invite lay people to be involved with Sisters in ministry for short or longer periods. Appropriate formation accompanies these, and so the story of God's love continues to be told upon an ever-widening front.

In some countries, volunteers have taken on a more permanent and independent identity. In Sydney, Australia, a group called

---

[77] Mission Statement, *Handbook of Associates of the Sisters of St Joseph of the Sacred Heart*. p.3.

Josephite Community Aid (JCA) has established a way of life which aims, through friendship, to "empower poorer people to become self supporting in their own lives". A Sister of St Joseph who believed that fewer young people entering Religious Life did not mean less generosity among them, called on volunteers to live the charism of St Joseph in a way that spoke today. JCA is the result.

Since their beginnings in 1986, the special focus of JCA service has been refugees and mentally disabled street people. Now in three communities, they are considering possible expansion into other locations around Australia. The group has a thorough spiritual and community formation, and their motto, "Never see a need without doing something about it", is taken from the first rule of the Julian Tenison Woods, echoing that of Médaille some 200 years earlier:
> ... they will undertake all the spiritual and corporal works of mercy of which women are capable.

A feature of JCA is the way many recipients of their friendship in turn become members of the group themselves. One such is Margaret whose family were refugees and who became a full-time volunteer for JCA. In her work she was joined by twenty-one year old Moses:
> He was kidnapped from his home at just 11 years of age and forced to become a child soldier. After three years, he escaped and spent three and a half months walking to Kenya where he sought refuge in a refugee camp. He came to Australia in January this year and came into contact with JCA in June. ...
> Margaret says, "He's great because he comes with me and interprets. One day we thought we had managed to invite a family to the beach for a day in the school holidays. When we arrived to pick them up they were all still in pyjamas and wanted to give us food. We knew only a couple of Denka words but knew "Yallah" means "hurry". Still no progress. Finally one of the children understood. I asked them to wear shorts and swimmers but the little kid dressed up in a suit. He

wore that. It was hilarious because they hadn't seen the sea before. They couldn't believe the waves kept coming and going. They didn't care about appearances – they just went in to swim in their underwear." [78]

A spirit of partnership

To promote true partnership Sisters and lay groups need to keep each other in support and prayer. We live in a world where many people are in reaction to fear, where the powers of evil are too big for us, where there seems to be a widespread retreat into areas of safety, particularly with regard to religion. Yet it was over the chaos that the creative Spirit brooded. As Sisters of St Joseph have reflected,

> Out of the chaos of our time, a new kind of world, a new age, is coming into being. It is a world with immense potential for creating a global community and a world with equally immense capabilities for self-annihilation and destruction unparalleled in recorded human history. [79]

The Spirit has long been at work, setting up around our world groups of people whose understanding of God is such that they know that to be the Community of God's Great or Compassionate Love gives a power greater than any evil. Being swamped by a sense of insignificance and powerlessness does not acknowledge God's providential love for our world. Father Timothy Radcliffe, the General of the Dominican Order, says this:

> For most of my life, our Christian hope was propped up by its secularized child, a belief in progress. There were new inventions every year...But since the end of the Cold War that confidence in progress has gone. ... We Christians have no road map for humanity. We have no more idea than anyone else what will happen to humanity in the next hundred or thousand years. So, with the disappearance of confidence in progress, we have to recover a genuinely Christian hope. If

---

[78] See JCA website, http://www.jcaid.com
[79] USA Federation of Sisters of St Joseph, "Celebration of a Charism", 1986.

we may do so, then humanity will discover in us something for which it longs and which is ours to give.[80]

I believe our hope lies in the possibilities for God's kingdom that Jesus put before us – the communion of all peoples with God and each other. A characteristic of those who share the charism based in the tradition of St Joseph is that we make good white ants.[81] We act locally and we are persistent in the face of immense odds.

But in a global world, collaboration is needed. Being in communion with those who share our Josephite way of ministering in the Church, making connections and supporting one another, is an important way of fostering hope in our world. The charism given to us, with its focus of portraying in our lives and ministries the story of God's compassionate, freeing love, can strengthen the communion of lay and religious as promulgated by Vatican II ("That they may be one"). Pope John Paul II takes up the same theme in introducing the year of the Eucharist:

> The Eucharist is not merely an expression of communion in the Church's life; it is also a *project of solidarity* for all of humanity. In the celebration of the Eucharist the Church constantly renews its awareness of being a "sign and instrument" not only of intimate union with God but also of the unity of the whole human race.[82]

In living into the charism of St Joseph we tell God's story of communion and love.

---

[80] *The Tablet,* August 16th, 2003. p. 1.
[81] Sir Henry Parkes, politician, founder of Australia's public school system of education and violently anti-Catholic, once declared in a speech, "The Sisters of Saint Joseph are like white ants; when once they enter a locality, you cannot even starve them out!" In the *Tasmanian Mercury.* Oatlands, Tasmania, June 1896. (In Australia, if not other parts of the world, termites are referred to as "white ants").
[82] John Paul II, *Mane Nobiscum Domine,* October 2004. par 27

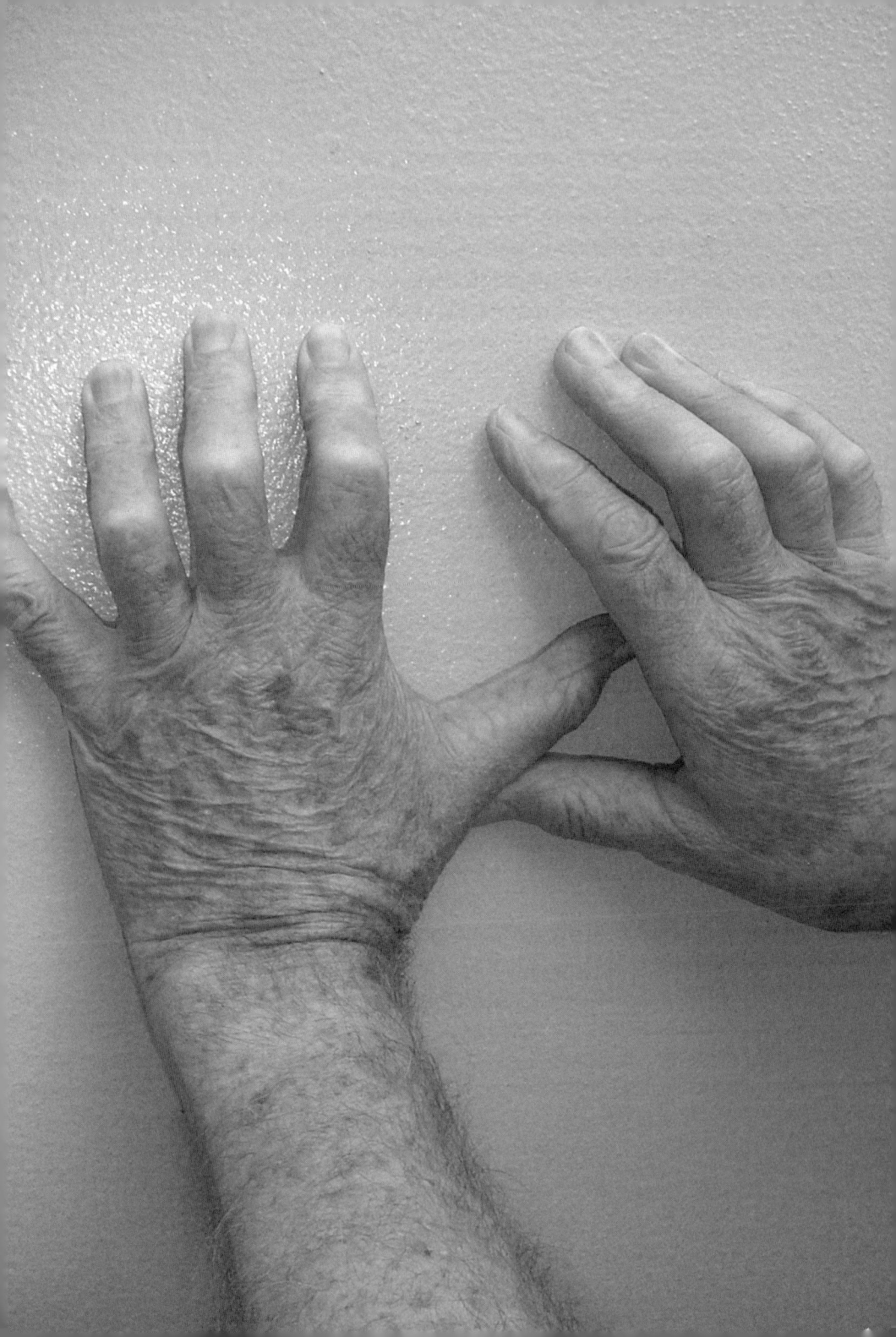

CHAPTER TWO

The spirit of Joseph ......

breaks boundaries.

"Get up, take the child and his mother, and flee to Egypt." (Mt 2:13)

2.1 PART ONE: The spirit is revealed

<u>Breaking through fear</u>
When Abraham Lincoln was accused of being too soft on former Confederate soldiers he said that the best way to overcome your enemies is to make them your friends[83]. In today's society, perhaps the most common enemy we have is fear. Fear is one of the strongest emotions we can experience in life. As enemy it can paralyse us or propel us into violent action, hate and destruction. What the power of the Spirit can do is help us make the enemy of fear into a friend.

We know from Scripture that a sign of the Spirit's work is creation. When the Spirit works creatively with fear, we find that, rather than destroying the source of the fear, the Spirit engenders new life from that very circumstance. Is it not especially important for us in this age of terrorism to learn how to invest positive power, rather than negative, irrational reaction, into the realm of fear? Our faith offers us such an opportunity.

For Christians, the most wonderful example of what the Spirit does with our fear is the resurrection of Jesus Christ. Out of

---

[83] The exact quote is "Am I not destroying my enemies when I make friends of them?"

death itself came new life. Nature demonstrates this too, in its own way. The evolutionary process is one that requires the death of one stage in order for the new to emerge. As Denis Edwards says:

> At every stage in this process, and at many points along the way, something that is genuinely new occurs. And while the new is completely dependent on its preexisting components, it is not reducible to its components."[84]

The figure of Joseph in the Gospels similarly demonstrates for us the action of the Spirit in our dealing with fear. We are not told in the Gospels about the emotional turmoil Joseph must have experienced when he found that Mary was pregnant not by him. But we are told he was faced with a dilemma. The law of Moses directed the procedure for formal or informal divorce in such a case. But his dream directed him not to fear but rather to take Mary as his wife. Internal fear can present itself as confusion, and often this can be harder to deal with than physical threat. Authors Paul Molinari and Anne Hennessy describe his resolution of the struggle:

> Although his moral security was rooted in fulfilling what his religion told him and in being loyal to a God of Law, Joseph, the simple pious Jew, knew the difference between fidelity to God and mere observance of the Law. Still, it must have been a shock for someone who knew God within the context of the Law to encounter the Spirit who `breaks the law'! However, like the holy people of his tradition, when the God-who-goes-beyond-the-Law called him Joseph responded, however many or probing were the questions of his steadfast heart.[85]

This action of breaking through the barriers of fear was to propel the "inbreaking of God" by which Joseph was to become a key player in God's plan of salvation.

> Joseph's legal paternity is what legitimates Jesus' title as "Messiah". In a very real sense we are able to speak, then, of

---

[84] Edwards, *Breath of Life*, p. 44-45.
[85] Molinari Paul & Hennessy Anne. *The Vocation and Mission of Joseph & Mary,* Dublin: Veritas Publications, 1992. p. 12

Joseph's "birthing of the Messiah", his essential role in the Incarnation, his enabling of the inbreaking of God's universal commonwealth of love in Jesus.[86]

From Joseph we learn that neither common sense nor religious regulation can confine God's action in our lives. Risk-taking is part of the Christian enterprise. "Fear not," Jesus says, when waters threaten to overwhelm us or when death is all around. "Perfect love drives out fear."[87] This is the kind of love that is shown in the actions of Joseph.

<u>Joseph the new patriarch</u>
In keeping with the presentation of Joseph as being intimately associated with the new era being ushered in by Jesus, Matthew uses the literary tradition of "haggadic midrash" – taking figures and happenings from the books of the Old Testament Pentateuch and applying them to current situations. Louise Perrotta makes the point:

> From his first appearance in Matthew's Gospel, Joseph walks the edge between tradition and newness. He is a key player in a divine plan that is a surprising departure from the ordinary. Yet like Jesus, he is firmly rooted in the tradition of Israel.[88]

So it is that Matthew draws Joseph into the Pentateuch tradition of the patriarchs.[89] The Pentateuch Joseph was protector and saviour of his father Israel (Jacob) and his family. From Egypt, Joseph's land of exile, Moses had saved his people from the persecutor Pharaoh and had led a covenanted people back home. The new patriarch, Joseph, saves Jesus from Herod and ushers in the new Moses who will bring salvation to all peoples,

---

[86] Margaret Shannon and Bill Russell. *The Just One*, Cobourg Ontario: Villa St Joseph, 1990. p. 19.
[87] 1 John 4:18. Refer also, Mt 8:26, Mk 5:36, Lk 5:10, Jn 14:27, Acts 27:24, etc.
[88] Perrotta, *Saint Joseph,* p. 29.
[89] Note that Médaille's rule stipulates loving service of each other and the neighbour "in honour of Saint Joseph their Patriarch". To consider Joseph as patriarch is not to imply approval of patriarchy as a system. As a theological tool it allows us to touch into tradition in reflecting on his role within salvation history.

making them one family in God. In one phrase, it seems, Matthew intends to remind us of God's saving work which would be brought to perfection in Jesus.

Likewise, he associates this Joseph with well-known characteristics of the patriarchs. Like Abraham of old, Joseph responds to God's command and, "taking the child and his mother", sets out into an unknown land. "Do not be afraid!" the angel has told him (Mt. 1:20).

> Such words of reassurance as "do not be afraid" are found in all the accounts of the calls of patriarchs and prophets. They are usually associated with the promise of God's 'being with' the person chosen for the mission. The task to be accomplished, being difficult and beyond human capacities, demanded that the Giver of the mission be at the side of the person called.[90]

To allow God to do the impossible through you demands courage. It also demands a certain amount of rashness. The old Abraham had been promised, despite the odds, that he would be father to a great nation. That his son was called Isaac, a name derived from the word "laughter", recalls the reaction of the aged Sarah to the foolish prediction of her son's birth. Similarly the patriarch Joseph, prisoner of the pharaoh, had believed enough in his dreams that they eventually saved his father and family. Now Matthew's Joseph is asked to step foolishly into nothingness, taking on the responsibilities of "a husband and father without being either 'in totum'"[91] and trusting that God's plan would produce a progeny that even he could not dream of.

<u>The new demands change</u>
To each of the patriarchs, the covenant made between God and the chosen people had needed to be renewed. Salvation history certainly didn't go in a straight line. Human structures were lost;

---
[90] Molinari & Hennessy, *The Vocation and Mission of Joseph & Mary*, p. 17.
[91] Molinari & Hennessy, *The Vocation and Mission of Joseph & Mary*, p. 20

peoples were dispersed; promises were forgotten. In the different stages of history, people were called to change their hearts and begin their relationship with God anew.

Newness was a feature, too, in the way they expressed their hope for a Messiah. "See the earlier things have come to pass," God says in Isaiah. "New ones I now foretell."[92] "Lo, I am about to create new heavens and a new earth."[93]

The process that allows the new to happen in life involves both an outer and inner movement. Change will happen to us for as long as this earth is living. It is an exterior thing – changes in one's life situation, work practices, global events, for example. But for human beings to successfully negotiate these changes, an inner transition has to take place. The emotions are involved, and therefore a psychological or spiritual reorientation has to take place before the change can be integrated into a person's life. James Zullo describes the process as a threefold movement from one state through a bridging period or transition into a new life-situation. He quotes change-agent William Bridges in explaining that "there can be any number of changes, but unless there are transitions, nothing will be different when the dust clears".[94]

In the spiritual life, the term "conversion" is usually applied to this process. While it can apply to a radical change in one's orientation in life, "conversion" is also the constant re-directing of the heart to God, allowing the Spirit to lead us to a new place in our relationship with that God. It was not enough for God to give Moses the terms of the covenant. The people of Israel had to accept them in their hearts – otherwise, they would return to the golden calf as easily as before.

---

[92] Is 42:9
[93] Is 65:17
[94] James R. Zullo. "Navigating Transitions", *The Works,* Winter 2001. p. 47.

Conversion also requires an ability to discern what is of the Spirit and what is not. In the 16th century, St Ignatius of Loyola reflected on how those truly directed by the Spirit have done this through the ages. He suggests that love of God must motivate us and that we should note the effects of decisions in the inner movements of our hearts. Decisions not of God will produce anxiety and dis-ease, while "true spiritual gladness and joy" will result from those that are in accord with God's will for us.[95] For the creative Spirit to do the new thing, we must have what Gerard Hughes calls "that fundamental disposition which says, 'Thy Kingdom come, not mine: Thy Will be done, not mine'".[96] This attitude will allow us to find God in places and situations we least expect.

That God is a "God of Surprises" is not a modern discovery. Biblical narrative is full of examples of those who are required to step out beyond the expected norm and to risk all in order to allow the new to be born. Israel itself, with most of its people exiled and seemingly barren, destroyed and without hope, is exhorted to
> Enlarge the space for your tent,
> Spread out your tent cloths unsparingly;
> Lengthen your ropes and make firm your stakes (Is. 54:2).

In the face of defeat, the people of Israel were to build and make way for the "new heaven" and "new earth" that God would bring about (Is. 66).

The new involves pain

Acute sensitivity to the things of God can lead us to scary places. We can be very vulnerable while on the journey of transition, a period Zullo calls "liminality".[97] Coming from the certainty of our past, we can be led by change through a wilderness as painful as any Exodus journey. Depending on the

---

[95] Spiritual Exercises of St Ignatius, "On the Discernment of Spirits", First Rule.
[96] Gerard Hughes. *The God of Surprises,* Lond.: Darton, Longman & Todd. 1986. p. 147.
[97] Zullo, "Navigating Transitions", p. 47.

severity of the change, the period of transition is one that often involves pain and loneliness. But go on this journey we must, if we are to grow and if we are to find meaning in our lives.

In our celebrations of the Eucharist, our resolve to go on this journey is joined with that of Christ. With him we declare that through the Spirit, God leads us to new life in and through what appears as death. As Pope John Paul II said when he declared 2005 as the Year of the Eucharist:

> In the Eucharist, Christ makes present to us anew *the sacrifice offered once for all on Golgotha*. Present in the Eucharist as the Risen Lord, he nonetheless bears the marks of his passion, of which every Mass is a "memorial", as the Liturgy reminds us in the acclamation following the consecration: "We announce your death, Lord, we proclaim your resurrection". At the same time, while the Eucharist makes present what occurred in the past, it also *impels us towards the future, when Christ will come again* at the end of history. This "eschatological" aspect makes the Sacrament of the Eucharist an event which draws us into itself and fills our Christian journey with hope.[98]

The Spirit-led journey of Joseph broke through the barriers of his situation into the pain that leads to new life. In his doing so, a "new family" would be established by Jesus. This new covenant would be based not on the bonds of patriarchy but on relationship with God and availability for mission.

> Neither Joseph nor Jesus conformed to the expectations of their society. ... Joseph had also formed a "new family of God". He accepted the pregnant Mary as his wife, and he accepted her child Jesus as his own although both actions threatened his reputation, his "honor". Joseph abandoned the familiar and secure webs of kinship and professional relationships to go into Egypt in order to protect his unusual "family".[99]

---

[98] Apostolic Letter, "Mane Nobiscum Domine", par 15.
[99] Hennessy, *In Search of a Patron,* p. 56.

For those living the charism gifted to Joseph, openness to the new witnesses to and confirms that gift. There is connection with what has gone before, but in going through the pain of breaking through barriers, a new thing is done according to the movement of the Spirit for new life. A poem of Sister Anna Marie Mack, Sister St Joseph in Philadelphia, USA, says it all:

To St Joseph – Patron of Risk-Takers.

*You took the risk unsure
of anything save love and faith;
made no demand, humbly
gave your word and life
to greater gamble: Mother, Son.
At what expense, such recompense!*[100]

2.2 PART TWO: The spirit unfolds.

Beginning a new thing

The founding stories of the Sisters of St Joseph, like the story of Joseph, demonstrate the characteristic of breaking through boundaries into a new way of being. "Every authentic charism," says the document *Mutuae Relationes*, "brings an element of real originality in the spiritual life of the Church along with fresh initiatives for action".[101]

The Sisters of St Joseph formed in Le Puy in the middle of the 17th century were not the first to embark on apostolic religious life for women in the face of Rome's prohibition. Francis de Sales and Jane Frances de Chantal had attempted to establish the Visitation Sisters in 1610 as an apostolic group combining

---

[100] Sr Marie De Montfort, ed. *Time and Eternity; Poems by Sisters of St Joseph.* Llantarnam: Sisters of St Joseph of Annecy, Llantarnam Abbey, 1999. p. 15.
[101] *Mutuae Relationes,* Rome, Sacred Congregation for Religious and for Secular Institutes, May 14, 1978. par. 12.

works of charity with contemplation. However, they had not been able to withstand the pressure to conform to the rule of enclosure. Where they failed, the 1638 foundation of the Daughters of Charity by St Vincent de Paul succeeded in enabling a women's group to break through the barriers of Church law to bring hope to the poor.

The Sisters of St Joseph were but one of many groups that sprang up in the 17th century to do apostolic work.[102] By the time of Jean Pierre Médaille's death in 1669, though, most of these had disappeared, while the Sisters of St Joseph were flourishing. However, the way they survived was not by employing the same methods of Vincent de Paul,[103] but by being unnoticeable. Theirs was what Médaille called a "Little Design" whereby they avoided public and Church attention, living in small groups in the way of ordinary people under the authority of the local bishop[104]. No large monasteries marked their presence. Nor did their membership come from the higher classes, aiming for grand things for the betterment of the poor. Theirs was a simple life and they did not threaten established powers as did a Mary Ward[105] or other women of note.

Another point in their favour was that the Sisters' lifestyle did not appear too different from that of the confraternities of devout women, already a familiar sight in southern France:
> (Father Medaille) proposed continued presence and action in their own milieu, but with a "new manner of life". They consecrated themselves by simple vows and their little communities could show forth that the life of the sisters is

---

[102] In France alone, in spite of the Council of Trent renewing mandatory enclosure, more than 90 uncloistered apostolic communities of women were founded in the 17th century..

[103] Vincent de Paul called his Daughters a "company". They renewed their vows each year, thus avoiding stipulations for Religious.

[104] The 1654 memoirs of the Town-Fathers in Le Puy indicate that it was five years before they found out that the women managing the local "hôpital" were Religious.

[105] Mary Ward founded The Institute of the Blessed Virgin Mary in 1609. The model for the order was the Society of Jesus, but the venture was suppressed and Mary excommunicated and imprisoned for a time. Her companions maintained her ideals and the Congregation was reinstated under a changed rule after Mary's death.

"totally consecrated to the pure and perfect love of God," all "union and charity among themselves and towards every sort of neighbor." Their types of service, their forms of action in the house or outside will be those which are practiced all around them, those which they have practiced with the Ladies of Mercy before becoming Sisters of Saint Joseph, service in the hospitals, visiting the poor and prisoners, orphanages, care for women of ill repute, spiritual direction of lay persons, preparation for marriage, "and even instruction of young girls in places where religious already established are not taking care of them".[106]

No doubt, too, it was the character of the women who made up the first communities of the Sisters of St Joseph that ensured their growth. While social and church systems required that official guidance and approbation came only through the men founders (Médaille and de Maupas), "clearly the religious energy of the women who offered to work for the service of God and neighbour was the creative force that made the community of the Sisters of St Joseph possible."[107] Through their living out of the "Little Design", the action of the Spirit leading towards acceptance of apostolic women Religious was able to take root and develop. It is noteworthy that by 1684 a local bishop could comment, "The Sisters' charitable works make them respected by everyone as true Religious in the Church of God."[108] It would take more than another two hundred years, however, before the Vatican would recognise apostolic women's groups as officially Religious.

---

[106] Thérèse (Marguerite) Vacher. *Des "régulières" dans le siècle: Les soeurs de Saint-Joseph du Père Médaille aux XVII et XVIII siècles.* (Concerning Religious Women in the Century: The Sisters of Saint Joseph of Father Médaille in the 17th and 18th Centuries) 1992. Trans. Mary R. Boyle and Roberta Archibald. SSJ Center for Spirituality, Philadelphia, Sept – Oct., 1999. The phrases in quotation marks are taken from Médaille's primitive *Constitutions for the Little Congregation of the Daughters of St Joseph.* Session Four. p. 161.
[107] Carol K. Coburn & Martha Smith. *Spirited Lives*. Chapel Hill (USA): University of North Caroline Press, 1999. p. 22 The authors also point our that "Acceptance came more readily because their members, unlike upper-class women, could work for a living without censure and were unlikely to be potential claimants to a family inheritance – the issue that had caused trouble for early Visitation and Ursuline nuns. p. 24.
[108] Notes of lecture by Pat Byrne SSJ, Concordia, Kansas, July 2003.

Life out of death
The ability to be creative in a hostile situation is a mark of the Spirit, and one that is typical of the spirit of Joseph. In Genesis we are told that creation happened in the chaos.[109] When a person is creative, energy is found despite the difficulties, and new life emerges. Mother St John Fontbonne is one who fitted into this category. One commentator remarks, "As a worthy heir of Father Médaille, with courage and wisdom, she had 'dared' when all seemed lost."[110]

Previous to her re-founding the Sisters of St Joseph after the French Revolution, Mother St John had, in her younger years, been constantly referred to as "the life of the party".[111] Shortly after profession as a Sister of St Joseph she was assigned to Monistrol, an area of great need. With the boldness born out of simplicity, she asked the Bishop for facilities to establish a workshop where the poor could produce goods for sale so that they could help themselves. The laying of the foundation stone for this workshop in a renovated building was probably what was locally remembered as the occasion when the young superior was invited by the bishop to bless the stone along with him![112]

In 1790, the parish priest of Monistrol took the oath by which he aligned himself with the separation of the Church in France from papal authority. In the following year, a complaint was made that the Sisters were not taking part in the constitutional "Mass" and religious ceremonies. In fact, when the apostate priest went to the hospital chapel to give Benediction, not one of them had been present. In September an attempt was made to

---
[109] Genesis 1: 2: "Now the earth was a formless void, there was darkness over the deep, with a divine wind sweeping over the waters."
[110] Anne Françoise Trapeaux. "Mother St John Fontbonne" in *Proceedings of the International Forum, Le Puy – Lyon,* Aug 7-10, 1993, p. 59.
[111] Ref. Desclée De Brouwer & Cie eds, *Mère Saint Jean Fontbonne,* Paris-Bruges: Cie, 1929. Chs. 1-4.
[112] De Brouwer & Cie, *Mère Saint Jean Fontbonne,* p. 42.

persuade the Sisters to support the constitutional church. However, the deputation was met at the door by a determined Mother St John who declared, "It's useless for you to meet the community; here the head speaks for the body!" "What a woman!" was the response. "We can't win against her!"[113]

When eventually Mother St John and her blood-sister, Sister Thérèse, were imprisoned, it is said that they and those who shared their fate transformed their cell into a virtual chapel. They had been condemned to death but were saved by the assassination of Robespierre in 1795 – to the said annoyance of Mother St John who took it that she was not worthy to become a martyr! Since they could not retrieve their property, she continued her apostolate from her parents' house in Bas-en-Basset, while the revolution continued to work itself out until the signing of the Concordat by Pius VII and Napoleon in 1801.[114]

In order to respond to the 1807 call of Cardinal Fesch to re-establish the Sisters of St Joseph, Mother St John set out on a new journey "without knowing where she was going".[115] One of her first duties was to revise the constitutions, governance structures and form of dress to make it possible for the Sisters to minister in changed civic conditions.[116] Once the Congregation was re-founded, numbers quickly grew as former members rejoined and new candidates presented themselves. In 1816 the Motherhouse was established in Lyon itself, in a former

---

[113] De Brouwer & Cie, *Mère Saint Jean Fontbonne*, p. 49.
[114] This agreement reconciled France with Rome, recognising the "Catholic religion as the religion of the great majority of French" (rather than "the State religion") and allowing Catholicity to be publicly practised in the country according to agreed conditions. The Concordat was promulgated in Paris in April 1802.
[115] Trapeaux, "Mother St John Fontbonne", p.60.
[116] Under Napoleon, Religious Congregations had to submit their constitutions for governmental approval. The conditions he set down for Religious were based on a hierarchical structure. "Napoleon," says Edward Udovic, "had an obsession for order, uniformity, and centralization." (Edward.Udovic, "Jean-Baptiste Etienne", p. 82).

Carthusian monastery, badly in need of repair. From there Sisters were soon missioned throughout the world.

Frontier women

The same spirit which had characterised Mother St John was to accompany these Sisters who broke into the new world. Mme de la Rochejaquelein[117] associated this spirit with the flexibility that featured their rule and occupations:

> They give themselves to all the works of mercy, they take charge of free schools or boarding schools, hospitals, asylums for foundlings or for the aged: they may look after prisoners; attend on the poor and the sick in their houses; take care of the infected – they are ready for anything.[118]

From small beginnings in Carondelet, Sisters of St Joseph soon joined those Religious recognised in USA and Canada as "frontier women". In their book *Spirited Lives*, Coburn and Smith note that

> American sisters were some of the first white women brought in to "civilize" newly forming towns and other areas of settlement. ... The scarcity of clergy meant that women religious often functioned as surrogate priests at baptisms, at religious services and ceremonies, and at the death bed. .. The sisters' ability to accommodate and adapt to rugged, and sometimes dangerous, frontier conditions enabled them to provide much needed educational and social services to men, women and children in a variety of Western settings, counteracting the often hostile, anti-Catholic attitudes prevalent in nineteenth-century America.[119]

Illustrative of this spirit is the story of a group of Sisters on their trek from Carondelet to Arizona in 1870. They had volunteered in response to a request by the priest at Tucson to teach there. The journey required them to travel across the country by rail to San Francisco, thence by ship to San Diego and over the

---

[117] The Countess paid for the passage of the Sisters to St Louis, USA.
[118] Archives of the Archdiocese of St Louis, cited by Patricia Byrne, "Sisters of St Joseph: The Americanization of a French Tradition", *U. S. Catholic Historian*. p. 249.
[119] Coburn and Smith, *Spirited Lives,* pp. 98, 99.

Rockies to Tucson. Their diary records delight at the natural beauty they encountered, dismay when those appointed to meet them at posts along the way did not appear, bravery as they found alternate means of resuming the journey and a good serve of humour that enabled them to cope with the extreme physical difficulties. In Lower California, for example, when they stopped for lunch, they fossicked for gold.

> Seeing quantities of it, we proposed getting a sack and filling it. Just think, a sack of gold! – but we soon learned by experience that 'all that glitters is not gold'.[120]

Next day they celebrated the feast of the Patronage of St Joseph by picking desert wild flowers and forming a procession in front of the travelling party, "picturing themselves in Egypt with their holy patron".[121]

Going farther

As they pushed out into new areas, the Sisters often found that, like Joseph, they had to go beyond the requirements of law to allow the Spirit to break through. In Mount Hope, Canada, in 1869, a migrant woman presented herself at the orphanage there, begging the Sisters to take her five children, since her husband was in jail in their own country and she had no means of supporting them. Realising there were few options for a woman by herself in this isolated area, the Sisters stretched the rules, inviting her to stay with the children and to pay her way by helping at the orphanage.[122] In days when "humanity" was not a feature of institutions, it is significant that this spirit broke through the barriers of what was deemed appropriate, to reveal this aspect of the charism that dares.

---

[120] Mary Lucida Savage. *The Congregation of Saint Joseph of Carondelet*. St Louis, Herder Book Co., 1927. p. 252. Coburn and Smith describe in graphic details the extreme physical difficulties of the trip, including an incident where the wagon in which they were travelling "teetered over 17 feet of water" before it could be stabilised. *Spirited Lives,* p. 109.

[121] Savage, *The Congregation of Saint Joseph of Carondelet,* p. 109.

[122] This story is illustrated in Veronica O'Reilly CSJ, *Frontier Women: Sisters of St Joseph,* Turin, Italy: Editions SADIFIA Media, 1986. p. 13.

Years before in Annecy, then part of the Savoy separate from France, a letter had come from a priest in India, begging for Sisters to come to that land to nurse and educate the children. For the time it was an innovation for women to branch out into the "foreign missions". Rather than allowing themselves to be paralysed by the war and political uncertainty of their own country, Abbé Neyret urged them, they should reach beyond:

> Providence is rich in expedients and it is easy for God to remove all obstacles. .. On account of the increasing troubles in our poor Europe, and the general distress which is resulting from them, I must no longer delay to give you instructions to direct you in the choice of the Sisters you send.[123]

So it was in the midst of turmoil that the Sisters decided in 1849 to send volunteers into this new area of need, into a new country holding unknown fears. Ideal conditions are rarely the scene of the kind of spirit shown by Joseph. It is in the chaos that the Spirit continues to create the new thing.

A feature of the creative spirit is adaptability. Being able to cope with all kinds of circumstances has always characterised the lives of the Sisters. An amusing vignette from the early days of the Indian mission illustrates this. With a ship needing to be met and all other Sisters ill, the remaining Sister, Mother St John (de Maurienne) had to embark on the long journey to carry out this task.

> So far there had only been one aspirant to the religious life – a young woman of Irish parentage. She had just begun her canonical year and her mistress of novices was Mother St John herself. So at her departure from Kamptee the 'novitiate' had to travel with her. Thus it came about that the first novitiate in India was in a bullock cart![124]

---

[123] Bourne, *His Mercy is From Age to Age*, p. 67.
[124] Bourne, *His Mercy is From Age to Age*, p. 86. The canonical year of Novitiate is one where the novice is provided with intensive training in spirituality that is meant to provide the foundation for the rest of her Religious Life. This is done under the tutelage of a novice director.

A similar kind of enterprise is shown in the stories of Sisters arriving at Kansas City in 1866 where their only provisions were a cow and a building with walls but no furniture;[125] or of the Colorado Sisters in the 1870s who, in order to find suitable lottery prizes to raise funds for a new mission, "dug for gems and crystals, hiked mountains, explored caves and panned river beds".[126]

Again, the ability to survive events that should have rung the death-knell to the Sisterhood is a mark of the spirit. When, in the name of Revolutionary principles, laicisation of social services in France, including education, was carried out in the 1880s, Sisters in the Savoy were thus made redundant. Their response was to start a new venture by setting up private Catholic schools[127] and providing catechism lessons outside school hours for those in community schools. During this same period, the features of this same spirit were being taken up by a new Sisterhood of St Joseph in Australia.

Australian response
Indeed, it was in response to an 1851 Act of Parliament restricting government funds to compulsory, secular education that prompted Bishop Geoghegan in Adelaide ten years later, to forbid Catholics to send their children to these schools and instead begin a separate system of education for themselves. Geoghegan regarded the government schools not only as godless but as positively hostile to Catholicism, favouring Protestant philosophy and religious indifference. It was all well and good for the Bishop to insist that alternate schools be set up, but the poverty of the Catholic population made this an impossibility. The Bishop having died barely two years after writing his Pastoral Letter, and his successor not appointed until three years later, the state of Catholic education was a still-unsolved

---

[125] Coburn & Smith, *Spirited Lives,* p. 102.
[126] Coburn & Smith, *Spirited Lives,* p. 121.
[127] These schools were free to those who could not afford fees.

problem when Father Woods put to Mary MacKillop his dream of Sisters of St Joseph serving with the same spirit as those he had seen in France.

The dream was totally impractical. The Sisters were to
> live among and like the poor whom they were serving. They were to own neither houses, land nor money in their own right and were to subsist solely on such school fees as they might receive and the gratuitous offerings of the local people.[128]

With the instruction to "do all the good they (could)",[129] the Sisters soon found themselves also involved in visiting jails and hospitals, caring for reformed prostitutes and managing charitable institutions for orphans, the destitute and the socially disadvantaged.
> Although conscious of their limitations, particularly their financial insecurity, they were prepared to take initiatives and use ingenious methods to achieve their aims. Moreover, they took risks and stepped outside the general norms for nineteenth century sisters' behaviour. In particular, they went out into the city streets in pairs and asked the more affluent for donations of money or goods to be used for the benefit of the people in their institutions. ... When South Australians observed the good work they were doing, people of all faiths, or of none, responded generously to their appeals for help.[130]

In their Spirit-response to the apparent foolishness of a life totally dependent on God's providence, the Sisters of St Joseph were to become a corner-stone of the Catholic history of Australia.

Fintan Sheehan says that while founders are people of their own time and environment, there is always an element of real

---

[128] Foale, *The Josephite Story*, p. 18. Rome was to change the clause about not owning property when Mary MacKillop presented the rule for approval. But dependence on the charity of the local parish for their sustenance was, until the granting of stipends in 1968, a feature of the life of the Sisters of St Joseph.

[129] Sisters of St Joseph, *Book of Instructions,* Archives, Sydney.

[130] Marie Foale. *Think of the Ravens: The Sisters of St Joseph in Social Welfare,* Adelaide: Sisters of St Joseph, 2001. pp. 4, 5.

originality about the enterprise. Founders, future-oriented, are "agents of social transformation".[131] This was certainly the case with Mary MacKillop and Julian Tenison Woods. The Irish-born clergy of the time were not used to Religious Sisters living in areas where Mass might be celebrated once in six months. They were disturbed by the thought that "convents" might be hessian tents or "humpies", set among those of the people they served. Like their French counterparts, Sisters were sent in twos and threes where they became part of the town community.[132] This was a scandal to those used to the large, enclosed communities of "real nuns".

In her paper published in London, *The Necessity for the Institute*, Mary MacKillop explained why it was imperative that Sisters not require grand convents nor impose hardships on the people. The people were poor, their poverty often exacerbated by drunkenness, and they lived in small communities widely scattered across the vast country of Australia. Catholics were few in number and many were in situations where practice of the faith was difficult because their spouse was Protestant or of no faith. By sharing their lives, Sisters were able to reach them in ways that would break down hostilities. Thus, said Mary, "what would seem out of place in Europe (was) still the very reverse in most parts of Australia".

---

[131] Fintan D. Sheehan. "Charism as Empowerment to Discern, to Decide, to Act, to Assess", *Review for Religious,* March-April 1988.p. 164

[132] Vacher points out that in re-founding, Mother St John "reproduced the kind of structure she had known before the Revolution" which resulted in the "creation or recreation of a great number of small houses composed of two or three sisters." *Des "régulières",* p. 370, 371.

A feature of originality is the suspicion with which it is received, especially in the realm of religion. As the Vatican document, *Mutuae Relationes* says, the venture "may appear unseasonable to many".[133] For example, there may well be, as Ann Gilroy suspects, a connection between two happenings during Mary MacKillop's visit to southern New Zealand in the 1890s. The Sisters of another Congregation who lived in a large convent next to the cathedral were "unable" to accommodate her and asked a nearby family to do so. At the same time, the bishop of the diocese received a letter from his friend, Bishop Reynolds in South Australia, warning him,
> to beware of Mary as she was a troublemaker in the Australian church. He suggested that it would be inadvisable to allow her too close contact with women religious in (New Zealand) in case she infected them with her ideas.[134]

The same Spirit that urged Joseph to go beyond the boundaries of suspicion and fear to "gamble" upon God's protection was present with Mary MacKillop. In 1871 she heard that Bishop Sheil was about to make drastic changes to the rule previously approved by him and according to which the Sisters had made their vows. The new rule would introduce Lay Sisters and each convent would be autonomous, under the direct authority of the parish priest. Thus the unity of the Sisterhood and egalitarianism, a vital characteristic of the Australian society in which they were immersed, would be lost. Mary could respect the Bishop's right to do what he thought best for the diocese, but she felt she had to make known the fact that she could not align herself with these conditions and remain true to her call. She wrote, then, to the Bishop:
> I know you can withdraw your approbation from (the rule) and if our good God so wills it, I am resigned. But oh, pardon me, my Lord, if I say that I cannot in conscience see the Rule altered and remain as a Sister. I am your child, my Lord, your

---

[133] *Mutuae Relationes, par 12.*
[134] Anne Gilroy RSJ. "Mary MacKillop and the Challenge to Her Daughters". *The Australasian Catholic Record,* Vol 72, Jan. 1995. p. 62.

> humble helpless child. I want to please you, but above all to please God and do His holy will. If then in any way it may please Him that you should alter the Rule, then, my Lord, I feel I must take the alternative you offered and leave the Institute until it may please God to give me in some other place what my soul desires.[135]

The excommunication of Mary shortly afterwards for "disobedience and insubordination" did not lessen her belief that God would break through the obstacles to show the way. She knew that new life is not born without pain, and so she was ready to risk all out of the conviction that God's will would be done in her.[136]

Sisters of the Outback

In Australia, the symbolism of the outback is similar to that of the "frontier" for United States and Canada. With two thirds of the population clinging to the fertile coastal cities, the desert interior of the country presented for the first European inhabitants a formidable wasteland.

> It is the 'outback' that reinforced the already established sense of isolation born of Australia's geographical remoteness from the home countries. The outback fostered its own sense of isolation. Only the brave – the spiritually content – could meet the challenge of the outback. Australia, though a strangely beautiful country, rich in mineral wealth, is a country of uncertain seasons, or relentless droughts and devastating floods that test the spirit of those who dare to conquer it. Out of its very vastness and openness is born that sense of isolation which engenders a strong individualism and a consciousness that the country must learn to stand alone –

---

[135] Mary MacKillop to Bishop Sheil, September 10, 1871. Archives, Sisters of St Joseph, Sydney.
[136] When writing of the emotional effect of the excommunication, Mary describes how she couldn't sleep: "I thought of the awful nature of the sentence, and all that I had ever felt when hearing of such things before came back to my mind. I thought of the state in which I was supposing I should die before morning, but with this thought came a calm resigning of myself into the arms of my good God ... In the end I went to sleep very happily with more loving confidence in my good God than I had felt for a long time. Letter of Mary MacKillop to Father J. T. Woods, Nov. 15th, 1871. Archives, Sisters of St Joseph, Sydney, Australia.

even while it desires contact with other countries and cultures – and rely on its own resources if it is to survive.[137]

It was to the far-flung families of the "bush" that Mary MacKillop and Julian Tenison Woods dedicated their primary concern. The Sisters of St Joseph quickly became known as "Sisters of the Outback". Here they shared the lot of the people they served. So it was that early Sisters found themselves travelling for days on end by bullock wagon to remote mining towns where their "convent" was a white-washed tent, the same as those of the workers, or to little communities of railroad constructors or farmers opening up marginal land.[138]

Most of South Australia has poor rainfall[139] and uncertain mineral deposits, and so Sisters' stays in these locations were often temporary, as people moved from one area to another to gain more stable livelihoods. But the Sisters suffered the consequences of their zeal. As Marie Foale says,

> The Sisters of St Joseph were poor and resembled the poor among whom they lived and worked, in that their mortality rate was high. During the years 1873 – 1881, when very few of them had celebrated their fortieth birthdays, eighteen young sisters died.[140] ... Illness often struck where the sisters had insufficient good food and warm clothing for their needs, were inadequately housed or had to work in draughty, unlined buildings.[141]

---

[137] Daniel Lyne. *Mary MacKillop: Spirituality and Charisms*. Sydney: Sisters of St Joseph, 1983. p. 43.
[138] Even in the fertile country of New Zealand, this motif was to stand. In 1897 when visiting the Sisters, Mary MacKillop met the parish priest of a sizeable town, Queenstown, who "thought it foolish to expect two or three Sisters to live in such an out-of-the-way place as Arrowtown "(where Sisters are described as "labouring away in the lonely mountains for the sake of a few children, even though deprived of the help and consolation of daily Mass"): Anne Marie Power RSJ. *Sisters of St Joseph of the Sacred Heart: New Zealand Story*, Auckland: Sisters of St Joseph, 1983. p. 89.
[139] South Australia is the driest State of the driest continent of the world!
[140] Most were in their twenties. Tuberculosis was a common killer.
[141] Foale, *The Josephite Story*. p. 142.

Local tradition in at least one isolated area has it that the Sisters were starving because the Catholics were so poor they could not pay school fees and had little to share with them. It was the Lutheran community who saved them by giving them cabbages.[142]

In the Queensland outback the Sisters became known as "women of the west". Here they shared with their counterparts, the wives of stockmen, miners and sheep shearers, the hot and rough conditions that have produced a ruggedness to their characters that speaks of courage, endurance and resourcefulness. The first foundation in far-off Queensland had been made in January 1870. Mary and her companions had had to beg their fare from Adelaide, since the Bishop could provide no funds.

The story of the hardships they suffered makes for torrid reading. While the physical hardships were formidable, the insults and abuse of some clergy, for reasons unclear, were even more so. One incident tells of a priest preventing the Sisters from accessing the plentiful water supply he had at the presbytery and church, and them having to obtain it from a Jewish man, carrying it in buckets "at great inconvenience".[143] Verbal abuse from the pulpit was frequent.[144] Before her hurriedly leaving the Congregation from Copperfield, a harsh, remote mining town, one of the young Sisters had written to Mary MacKillop complaining of "unspeakable things" the parish priest had forcibly done to her. Mary MacKillop referred to her later with tenderness and compassion, although no records exist to show what happened to her.[145]

---

[142] And other food, no doubt. But the cabbages must have made an impression!
[143] Paul Gardiner. *An Extraordinary Australian: Mary MacKillop*, Sydney: E. J. Dwyer, David Ell Press, 1993. p. 216. The Sisters had 18 boarders at the time and taught over 200 pupils at the school.
[144] Gardiner, *Mary MacKillop*, p. 216.
[145] Her name was even removed from family records.

Such was the cost of going where no other Religious were free to go. Joseph had pushed out into Egypt to save the Christ-child; it was in order to make possible the revelation of Christ's love among them that the Sisters undertook such risks:

> In small or poorer towns, or in scattered villages, or in remote places in the bush, ... priests can seldom visit, there being so few of them for the heavy work of the missions. ... (It) is in these latter places that the faith of children is most endangered.[146]

The "pioneering spirit" that characterised Mary MacKillop was to be a feature of her whole life and this she passed on to her Sisters. Even later in life, she was known to venture into the "bush" around Sydney. Ignoring convention, she would borrow a horse and buggy from the Jesuit Fathers in North Sydney and drive herself and a novice to Greenwich Village to give religious instruction:

> This preparation of the children ... involved a visitation of one isolated house after another, trudging along unmade roads in rain and clammy heat, sitting in tin-roofed shacks for hours, persuading parents to allow their children to attend instructions, and many other incidental tasks such as discreetly arranging that the poorer children should be as well-dressed as their better-off companions on their First Communion day.[147]

Foolishness and Prudence

Sisters of St Joseph are not alone in taking risks for the sake of God's reign. All Religious communities have by nature what some authors call "a bias of foolishness". However, it is maintained, "it should be said that foolishness and rationality can be complementary."[148] Early Sisters of St Joseph were to learn this lesson.

---

[146] Mary MacKillop, *Necessity for the Institute*.
[147] Osmond Thorpe. *Mary MacKillop,* Sydney: Sisters of St Joseph, 1957. Revised and with End Notes 1994. p. 182. The "bush village" referred to is now a suburb of modern Sydney!
[148] Lawrence Cada, I. Raymond Fitz, Gertrude Foley, Thomas Giardino, Carol Lichtenberg. *Shaping the Coming Age of Religious Life,* N. Y: Crossroad, 1979. p. 117.

In the case of Mary MacKillop and her Sisters, it was Father Woods who would provide this lesson. Obviously heading for a breakdown, he displayed erratic behaviour during the time Mary was in Queensland. In this state, his fascination with psychic phenomena, mistaken for spirituality, increased dramatically. He regarded two Sisters claiming to have visions as saints; he himself wrote of visitations of the devil and made wild prophecies about future events and dates of deaths.

When Mary suggested that he should check what was happening to him with another priest, he reproached her for giving into "temptation" by judging as the "world" judges, saying he had Our Lady's guarantee that he would not err in directing the Sisters. At the same time, despite the failure of fund-raising efforts and Mary's urging that he be "more prudent and more simply distrustful in some things", he blithely maintained that "he had a heavenly assurance that he would never want for money, and prepared to go further into debt by building additions to the convent (in Adelaide)".[149]

As background to the eventual excommunication of Mary MacKillop and banishment of Father Woods to another diocese, these experiences were to prove a sober reminder to the Sisters that delusion and risk-taking were not the same thing. The difference lies in whether or not self-aggrandisement is at its heart. Cuskelly comments:
> With very little resources (Mary MacKillop) gambled; but gambling for the good of others, not for personal gain; gambling on God's Providence to support you in a worthy cause becomes the virtue of Christian trust."[150]

Even in the execution of this trust, prudence serves its purpose. During one meeting when Mary was struggling with the Bishop

---

[149] Gardiner, *Mary MacKillop*, p. 87.
[150] E. James Cuskelly. "Mother Mary MacKillop and Australian Spirituality". *The Australasian Catholic Record*, Vol 72, Jan. 1995. p. 5.

of Brisbane about the future of the Sisters in his diocese, she took with her the astute Sister Josephine who recalled:

> I was with Mother at the interview and the Bishop was very nice, but determined to have his own way. The promises on both sides were verbal. So when he went out, I said to Mother she ought to give her promise in writing and so should he – that was what business people did. She asked him for it in that way. He got very red and then he gave his written promise not to interfere with the Sisters, and she gave hers not to remove them until he was ready to supply our places.[151]

Theirs was the prudence of Joseph who, on returning from Egypt, went to Nazareth instead of Bethlehem, seeing that "Archelaus, the least competent and most brutal of the three sons among whom Herod's domain had been divided",[152] would be an even greater threat than his father had been.

Taking the spirit forward

Even with prudence, those gifted with the spirit of Joseph find that they are constantly being called to push out into the new. In the 1650s, Father Médaille had set out for his Sisters in Le Puy a rule of life whose practical application took on the nature of a motto as they pushed forward into new areas of need: "(Sisters) will undertake all the spiritual and corporal works of mercy of which women are capable and in keeping with their rank and activities, all done in the same lowly and self-emptying humility."[153] In his Maxims he spelled this out further – the Sisters were to "imitate the most zealous and embrace in desire the salvation and perfection of a whole world; everything they undertook was to be "for God's glory".[154]

Over two hundred years later a similar motto from the rule of Father Woods provided for the Australian Sisters of St Joseph an impetus to overcome all obstacles in their zeal for God's

---

[151] Gardiner, *Mary MacKillop*, p. 230. Note 4.
[152] Perrotta, *Saint Joseph*, p. 44.
[153] *Règelements of the Daughters of St Joseph* under heading, "The Goal of the Association".
[154] Maxims 7, 8 of Médaille's *Maxims of the Little Institute*. Translation as in Marcia Allen, *Love's Design.*, p. 7.

reign: "(The) Sisters must do all the good they can, and never see an evil without trying how they may remedy it, and this for the glory of God, the good of souls, and the prevention of sin in the world." [155]

The women who took up the challenge to reveal God's love as Sisters of St Joseph often had to travel through darkness and uncertainty in order to do so. Père Piron may have assured the Sisters gathered with Mother St John in 1808, "You are few in number, but like a swarm of bees you will spread everywhere",[156] but they had no surety that they would, indeed, be found eventually in every continent of the world. As a young woman Mary MacKillop may have been told by an old retired doctor that he saw her "at the head of a long train of virgins in brown" and that she would be excommunicated but "the Pope will set you all right again",[157] but being a woman of common sense and faith, she put no credence on such comments, instead trusting God alone.

So it is that without guarantees, thousands of Sisters have been lured by a spirit that breaks through boundaries for the sake of God's reign. Stories of this spirit come to us from all around the world. For instance, the Sisters in France who ministered to the alienated and unchurched of their own country in their founding years, showed the same missionary spirit that later found them on foreign soil. This spirit led the Sisters in Annecy to establish the Indian mission in 1849. Even there they did not settle. Fifteen years later they sent missionaries from India to protestant England, to work "like Jesus and the Apostles, that is, among the children and the poor".[158]

---

[155] *A Book of Instructions, Archives, Sisters of St Joseph, Sydney.*
[156] Sister M. Immaculata. *Like a Swarm of Bees: Sisters of St Joseph of Buffalo*, Derby N. Y.: Society of St Paul, 1957. p. 16.
[157] Memoirs of Annie and Donald MacKillop, siblings of Mary. Archives, Sisters of St Joseph, Sydney.
[158] Mother Louise Flavie, letter to Bishop Clifford, Archives, Sisters of St Joseph of Annecy, Llantharnum, Wales.

The Spirit's urge to go forward into new areas resulted in the sisterhood expanding throughout the nineteenth century. Sisters of St Joseph were found in Italy, Switzerland and other European countries by the mid-1800s. In 1856, "Sisters from Chambéry were the first Catholic religious in Scandinavia after the Reformation".[159]

Two years afterwards, another group was to set out for Brazil. Sisters were in Russia for 54 years before being expelled after the Revolution in 1917. They have been in Algeria since 1868. In 1882, the Maurienne Sisters founded the Congregation Argentina.[160] From 1891 to 1914 when they were expelled, the Sisters of St Joseph of Lyon were in Armenia. Wonderful accounts of their lives there are recorded in a monthly review published by the Congregation, *Le Règne de Dieu*. One story tells how the Sisters were having trouble extricating themselves from the mud on an unfamiliar track. A girl ran after them begging them to come to her house where her little brother was ill. The baby did die, but only after the Sisters, with the mother's tacit permission, baptised him, and "the angels added another little brother to their number".[161]

Adaptability has been a feature of the Sisters' presence wherever they have gone. For example, in their founding days, in St Louis and later in Philadelphia, the Sisters of St Joseph were asked to take charge of boys' asylums when other congregations, whose rules prohibited care of boys, had to abandon them. As Margaret Brennan explains:
> The rule had no specific prohibition against caring for boys, though there was never a clear precedent. This left them free to teach both sexes in parochial schools as well, and indeed to take up any work a bishop or pastor might ask of them.

---

[159] Benedicte De Vaublanc. "Sisters of Saint Joseph Today: Their Expansion and the Movement Toward Unity". Unpublished paper, 1994.
[160] De Vaublanc, "Sisters of Saint Joseph Today".
[161] *Le Règne de Dieu*, Sisters of St Joseph of Lyon, No 1, Janvier 1912. p. 20. Translation mine.

> This flexibility was a strong factor in the growth of the congregation in the United States.[162]

Similarly, since they did not have restrictions about nursing men, the Sisters were able to go beyond the disapproval of polite society that considered "nursing a nonrelative male (to be) obscene".[163] The fact that they cared indiscriminately for victims of epidemics and disasters and particularly of the Civil War helped overcome the anti-Catholic prejudices of 19th century America.

The Australian Sisters, said Mary MacKillop, were missionaries:
> It is in a truly missionary spirit of poverty that under the direction of their Superiors they hold themselves ready to go on the shortest notice and without a murmur wherever obedience and the cause of the dear little ones of the Church require it. But they know well that solicitude as to their own temporary wants, necessity of securing *beforehand* a house to live in, and such things, are the greatest possible drawbacks to a true missionary spirit.[164]

At a time when Australia was not one country but a collection of independent colonies, she saw that the call was for Sisters to go beyond their own familiar settings into the unknown. As she wrote to Monsignor Kirby in Rome, "the work has not been intended by our good God for Bathurst, or for Adelaide, or for Queensland alone, it is for the poor of all Australia.[165]

That vision was soon to be extended overseas, as in October 1883, a group of Sisters crossed the Tasman Sea to the South Island of New Zealand. Again, this new foundation was made at a time of great uncertainty, when an investigation was being conducted by the Bishop of Adelaide purportedly on orders from

---

[162] Margaret Brennan. *Persistence of Vision: Portrait of Mother Stanislaus Leary, a 19th Century Maverick.* Privately printed, Sisters of St. Joseph of Rochester, 2005. Page references from unpublished text.
[163] Coburn and Smith, *Spirited Lives,* p. 190.
[164] *Necessity for the Institute.*
[165] Letter to Monsignor Kirby, August 10, 1874.

Rome but in reality in a private effort to gain power over the Congregation. The result of it was the banishment of Mary from Adelaide to Sydney – a move which in the end was to see a new spurt of growth for the Congregation and the means of its mission spreading throughout Australia and beyond.

It is not only breaking through physical barriers that demand the missionary grace of the Spirit. Sometimes the personal barriers can be as formidable as any cultural or physical obstacle. Sister Raymond, one of the first Sisters to go to New Zealand, was left in charge when the first superior returned to Australia. Lack of confidence caused her to write to Mary MacKillop:

> I hope dear Mother, you will soon send us someone in (Sister Calasanctius') place as Provincial. I do not think I will ever be able to manage here. The Sisters will want someone that can look after their school and be a help to them that way. I am of very little use; besides I am afraid I will not be able to manage. It is not like Australia where we could get help or advice at any time.[166]

The fact that this same Sister was to effectively serve as Provincial twice, for a total of 23 years, does not negate the fact that she had to overcome grave fears about her ability to lead. The spirit that caused Joseph to go beyond requirements of law, that impelled him to brave the unfamiliarity of a new country and to enter into the unexpected ways of God, is the spirit that has continued to invite Sisters of St Joseph to venture farther throughout the histories of the various Congregations.

2.3 PART THREE: The spirit lives into the now

<u>The New Enlivens</u>
Walter Kasper writes, "Whenever something new arises, whenever life is awakened and reality reaches ecstatically beyond itself, in all seeking and striving, in every ferment and

---

[166] Letter from Sister Raymond Smyth to Mary MacKillop, 17 September 1884.

birth, and even more in the beauty of creation, something of the being and activity of God's Spirit is manifested." [167]

Even in times of consolidation and predictability, the spirit of creatively breaking through boundaries into the new is a constant feature in the stories of different groups of Sisters of St Joseph. This is despite that fact that, by the dawning of the twentieth century, most groups had entered into the maturity stage of growth, having been re-founded or established in the previous century, and therefore already past the creative introductory and growth stages of organisations.

A characteristic of the maturity stage is maintenance and expansion of what has already been achieved, a suring-up of membership and a system of uniformity that enables efficiency and direction.[168] This stage is marked by competition, and the Sisters of St Joseph have been no exception to this. Older Sisters from all over the world referred in interviews to the competitiveness of these years that saw women being urged to enter one branch of the Sisters of St Joseph as opposed to another because it was "better". There was a sense of betrayal if someone entered a Congregation other than the one that educated or nurtured them.

The features of this stage were made more intense by the completion of the codification of Canon Law and its promulgation in 1917-18. While the effects of World War I and the traumas of the Depression delayed its impact somewhat, two factors contributed to it rendering the specific identity of Religious Congregations comparatively bland and non-differentiated. The first was that constitutions had to be re-written to conform with the new code, with the result that

---

[167] Walter Kasper, *The God of Jesus Christ,* Lond.: SCM, 1983. p. 227.
[168] For instance, in the Minutes of each of the three General Chapters of the Sisters of St Joseph of the Sacred Heart (Sydney) between 1916 and 1925, "uniformity" is an expressed concern. Archives, Sisters of St Joseph, Sydney.

references to distinguishing characteristics of individual Congregations tended to be lost, at least in legal documentation. The second was that major superiors had to send to Rome at regular intervals a detailed account of how the code was being observed in the daily lives of communities. Thus conformity was imposed, during years when world events likewise favoured stability, constancy and certainty.

Despite this fact, there were multiple opportunities for Sisters of St Joseph and those who shared their gift to recognise themselves in a spirit that breaks through boundaries. Even before the Code was completed, one of the effects of the Vatican's giving apostolic Congregations canonical status in 1900[169] was that more stringent observation was already being given to their activities. Creative means of dealing with this were sometimes called for. For instance, an investigation was held in 1909 about the services of Sisters in hospitals in America.

> The Vatican prelate was particularly interested in whether men were patients, whether the sisters did bandaging or gave baths, massages, or "other personal services", and whether sisters assisted in operations, "especially on the bodies of men". A superior in the St Paul province[170] penned a very diplomatic letter in response. Telling the cleric that the sisters did have male patients, never gave massages, and performed only "slight bandaging now and then", she described the operating room: "At times Sisters may be found in the vicinity of the operating rooms, so as to see that whatever is needed is duly provided: but .. nothing is done or allowed that could conflict with the strictest rules of religious modesty." In reality, some sisters had received special training as operating room nurses, and archival photographs reveal that for some sisters, being in the "vicinity of the operating room" clearly meant standing over the operating table next to the surgeon.[171]

---

[169] This meant that women's apostolic Congregations were accepted as an official part of Church mission as Religious, just as Monastic Orders were Religious.
[170] Sisters of St Joseph of Carondelet.
[171] Coburn and Smith, *Spirited Lives,* p. 203.

A different example of how obstacles are overcome is provided by the Sisters of St Joseph of Tipton (USA) who had established the Good Samaritan Hospital in Kokomo under great difficulties in 1913. The Ku Klux Klan was particularly virulent in that part of Indiana in the 1920s. As a movement, it flourished "by its appeal to bigotry, ignorance and fear."[172] Their tactics included not only attacking the Sisters, but also erecting in 1924 the Howard County Hospital in direct competition. One night a dishevelled, poor-looking gentleman was brought to its doors in urgent need of treatment. Not realising that he was a prominent sympathiser, the staff evicted him without ceremony and so his friends took him on to the smaller, struggling Good Samaritan Hospital. There, without question, he was taken in and treated with dignity. When he died in 1935 it was found that this man had left his entire fortune to the Good Samaritan Hospital: "it was through his providential gift that the Sisters were enabled to purchase the former Howard County Hospital (which by now had closed), so that once again it might be used for community service."[173]

Mavericks are often the bearers of a spirit that reflects the risk-taking of Joseph. Geagley tells of the drive of Mother Francis Lirette of the Sisters of St Joseph of Orange, California. She was an astute business woman, who during the Great Depression years, used the opportunity
> to pick up some really fine properties at a fraction of their value. To be sure, it sometimes seemed that payrolls could not be met, or mortgages paid on time, but these were small considerations in the greater scheme of things. Mother Francis would not let anything like a Depression stop her.[174]

The fact that this same woman caused heartache to her Sisters when she seemingly turned her back on them to start a new branch of the Sisterhood in Australia, does not take from her

---

[172] M. Gerard Maher and Caroline Daele. *A Modest Violet Grew: Historical Sketch of the Sisters of St Joseph, Tipton, Indiana*. Tipton: Sisters of St Joseph, 1950. p. 48.
[173] Maher & Daele, *A Modest Violet Grew*, p. 49.
[174] Geagley, *A Compassionate Presence*, p. 152.

role in establishing the foundations for what is now a major health system, providing services throughout California and other USA States with outreach to the most disadvantaged.[175]

When she came to Australia, Mother Francis struck up a close friendship with another strong woman, Mother Leone Ryan, the then Superior General of Mary MacKillop's Sisters of St Joseph of the Sacred Heart. Francis and Leone were peas in a pod. A great educationalist, Mother Leone realised that the tent flaps needed to be widened if the Church was to continue its work of evangelisation in schools. In 1958 she arranged with the Archdiocese of Sydney to open the Catholic Training College run by the Sisters to lay teachers and secured places for them in the Catholic Education system.

Previously, in 1954, she had approved the establishment of "Motor Missions" where Sisters travelled from town to town, training catechists and taking catechism classes in State schools.[176] This was to become one of the major ministries of the Sisters. With the advent of television came televised catechism lessons, then (but no longer, of course) paid for by the State government. A large Catechism Correspondence School reached children in remote areas and gave them personal contact with the Sisters.

In the area of nursing, too, the Sisters of St Joseph in Australia showed the same spirit of initiative that marked other Sisters of St Joseph around the world. Ordered by the Archbishop of

---

[175] The branch of the Sisters of St Joseph founded in Australia by Mother Francis in now reunited with its motherhouse in Orange, California. The Health System of the Sisters of St Joseph of Orange (around 200 Sisters) is now spread throughout California, West Texas and Eastern New Mexico and provides medical services through 15 hospitals, 3 home health agencies, hospice care, outpatient and mobile services and other facilities.

[176] Most States in Australia and New Zealand at the time allowed for an hour's Religious Instruction to be given in the schools by qualified personnel of the different denominations. Even though Australian Bishops had decreed that all Catholic children were to attend Catholic schools, the post-war influx of migrants and geographical factors made this an impossibility. Consequently many thousands of children were lacking adequate Religious Instruction.

Sydney in 1936 to take over the maternity hospital left to them in a Will, Sisters trained in mothercraft nursing were sent to gain qualifications in obstetrics, being among the first women Religious given permission by Rome to do so. Under the leadership of the legendary Sister Anne Byrne, not only were buildings constructed and hosts of collaborators engaged to raise funds, but the programme of nursing training and services given was deemed to be first class, with care of the most disadvantaged extending across the city.[177]

Renewal – Re-new-ing

"Heaven is not for cowards", quoted Mother Bernard Gosselin in 1913.[178] The challenges posed by Vatican II were certainly not met with cowardice by Sisters of St Joseph, along with other Religious. As the various documents were issued from the Council, they were received with general enthusiasm. Renewal of Religious Congregations was to be based, the documents said, on both a constant return to the sources of the whole of the Christian life (the Gospel) - and to the primitive inspiration of the institutes and their adaptation to the changed conditions of our time.[179]

However, the confusion of the years following Vatican II presented a formidable barrier to a smooth transition from former ways of living Religious life to those urged by the Council. Many women came to see that for them, entering the Congregation had been a response to the urgent needs of the apostolate after World War II rather than to Religious Life. With the realisation that holiness and Church mission involves all the baptised and not just priests and Religious, they made the move to take up apostolic life as lay members of the Church.

---

[177] Unfortunately, with recent changes in health care, St Margaret's Hospital could not survive as a stand-alone hospital and was closed in 1997.
[178] Letter to Sr Patricia, January 6, 1913. Archives, Sisters of St Joseph of Orange.
[179] *Decree on the Appropriate Renewal of the Religious Life* par. 2.

While the gifts of former members continue to enrich Church mission, Sisters of St Joseph have had to work through their experience of diminishment. Believing that, as for all evolution, this death is leading to new life, they are searching for their meaning in a new era. What role and purpose do they have today? For so long, they have been seen as "teachers" or "nurses". However, ministry does not define a group. Questions about what has characterised our spirit in the past, about our corporate mission, how we would ideally like to be and how we stand in relationship with others in the Church and wider society, are all connected with our identity. In particular, in the context of a Church which now understands itself to be *communio* – signifying and bringing about union with God and each other – Religious need to see themselves as having a particular role to play in the total mission of the Church but in true partnership with the lay faithful.

The spirit of Joseph lived in partnership.

The complementarity of Religious and lay life as a way of portraying the face of God among us is one that has yet to break through commonly held stereotypes and traditional assumptions. Society and Church tend to set roles over against one another rather than emphasise their interdependence. It seems that the lesson taught by Paul that all need one another and that no one role is more important than the other[180] – indeed, as Jesus said, those held in highest esteem are to take the lowest rank of servant[181] – is one that Christianity is yet to be convinced of.

The trend to separate consecrated life over against lay life is a result of what happens in the collective unconscious of cultures. Anthropologists have shown that a community's encounter with Holy Mystery, or the "Other", is extended and renewed by the symbols and rituals they erect to recall it to memory. Often the

---

[180] 1 Cor. 12, especially "The eye cannot say to the hand, "I do not need you" any more than the head can say to the feet, "I do not need you."
[181] Mark 10: 44. "Whoever wants to rank first among you must serve the needs of all."

symbol will be certain persons set aside to reflect in their beings the union with the Godhead originally experienced. Priests, monks, shamans, gurus or, as has happened with Christian (and Buddhist) women, nuns, have traditionally held these roles.

Being associated with the sacred, these persons can become "sacralised", that is, they can be looked upon as being holy in themselves, rather than being reminders of God. (The story comes to mind of the man who grabbed a shovel when a Sister fell – she could not be touched because she was "holy"!)

The letter of Peter points out that the community of Jesus was to regard itself in total as a "holy nation" – "God's people" – who would "proclaim the glorious works" of God.[182] It is still a novel idea to some lay people that Baptism calls them to involvement as Church on mission to our world. They still regard themselves primarily as the ones "ministered to" by the "professionals", clergy and Religious.

Especially since Vatican II many Religious have put effort into "desacralising" their image, trying to raise awareness among laity of their call to holiness and mission and to find ways of expressing the complementarity of the role of consecrated persons *with* that of laity and clergy.[183] The discovery that their founders often exemplified this attitude and willingly shared their spiritual resources with lay groups in their time has been an impetus to reinterpret that attitude for our time. For instance, the fact that novices and members of the Confraternities of Mercy were offered the same training in Le Puy has encouraged Sisters of St Joseph to look at creative ways to share spiritual resources today.

---

[182] 1 Peter 2: 9–10.
[183] The efforts of pre-Vatican II Religious was, I consider, integrally directed to forming laity who would take up involvement in Jesus' mission.

Besides the programs of formation described in the last chapter, other ventures seek to foster partnership among those attracted by the spirit given to Joseph. To mark the tenth anniversary since the Beatification of Mary MacKillop,[184] the Sisters of St Joseph in Australia have launched a program of different modules which are available to volunteers, co-workers, Associates, students in general – and candidates who wish to become Sisters.[185]

The elements of this program are such that novices will have the company of members of the wider Church, including lay groups who share the charism of St Joseph, during their time of formation as Sisters. The Canonical Year, since it deals specifically with personal issues and Josephite community life, is for novices only, but still serves as one module among others.[186] This new initiative, it is hoped, will not only develop a consciousness of the context of Religious Life as partnership in mission but also lessen the effects of exclusivity which can surround the life of novices.[187] At the same time, it recognises the particularity and identity of Religious Life in this mission.

Eileen McNerney of the Sisters of St Joseph of Orange is convinced of the need for Sisters to foster the spirit of Joseph among lay people.
> "The power of Jesus – this light that we are asked and empowered to bring to the world, is very strong and very needed. ... This mission has been passed on to us (Sisters of St Joseph). Now it's our opportunity to pass it on to others – those who believe in our mission and want to take an active role in bettering our neighbourhoods," she continued. "This mission that we refer to as the mission of St Joseph is not just

---

[184] Mary MacKillop was beatified by Pope John Paul II in Sydney on January 19th, 1995.
[185] The program is offered as a distance education unit through the Broken Bay Institute of the School of Divinity, University of Sydney, and may be taken for credit or audited.
[186] Other modules deal with topics such as Mission, Theology of Church, Josephite Spirituality, etc.
[187] They join novices of other Congregations for various components of this year, for example, lectures and processes of a theology of vows, etc.

the mission of the Sisters. It's a significant piece of the mission of Jesus...Sisters and lay ministers working together to extend the mission of Jesus and be of assistance to the "dear neighbour".[188]

As yet, structures that give identity to lay groups who share the spirit of Joseph are not nearly as defined as those for Religious. How these can be strengthened, without creating thereby another "church" as it were, is a task that continues to challenge.

Overcoming fear

In the meantime, the characteristics of spirit that featured in the lives of Sisters since their founding years are as much in evidence as they ever were. A story is told of how the Sisters in India in 1978 had to break through fear to establish a Leprosy Clinic in Prathipadu. The fact that one of their own Sisters had been wrongly diagnosed with leprosy and could illustrate that, having lived with them for some years, she had not contacted it, was seen as an indicator of God's providence, giving them confidence to venture into the project.[189]

In late 1986, the Council of the Sisters of St Joseph of Orange asked each member of the community to re-examine her life and ask the questions, "How can each one of us renew our spiritual, communal and ministerial life? How can each of us help the Congregation continue to make options for the poor a concrete reality? How can we move beyond our comfort zone?"[190]

Sister Elena Jaramillo is typical of those who answered the challenge, she by volunteering to work with refugees in San Salvador. With fear and anxiety, she and a Sister of St Joseph of Carondelet accompanied the refugees to their destination, knowing their presence as "foreigners" meant that the militia was less likely to attack the group. Since then there has been no

---

[188] "What is Hope and Life?" *Focus*, Fall 1999. Sisters of St Joseph of Orange. p. 8.
[189] Bourne, *His Mercy is From Age to Age,* p. 190.
[190] *Focus,* Fall 1999. p. 4. Sister Elena goes on to say, "I am grateful for (the Sisters), their prayers, support and love. All their support makes the mission in Central America possible."

question of her not returning to San Salvador, even though re-entry each time is hard and frightening. One day while visiting a neighbouring community, Sister Elena took shelter with other women in a small adobe church as bombs were being dropped. "That morning, hearing and seeing the weeping and wailing of mothers and fathers as their children were massacred, was more than one could bear," she recalls.

Overcoming fear can have a domesticated face. One of the interviewees, a Sister of St Joseph in Australia, explains:
> I was on a Motor Mission at the time. I was driving home from a distant place by myself one night and the car broke down. It was an isolated spot and getting dark. I prayed like anything to St Joseph! A motor-bike went past. At that time there were lots of stories about bikie gangs and their violence; this rider looked ferocious, all tattooed, you know, so I was quite relieved when he went on. But then he turned around and came back! I was petrified. But I tried not to show it, and went forward to him smiling and explaining my predicament. He was wonderful to me! He fixed up the car, and soon we were both on our way.

Another Sister in USA said that when she was in a mission area she often had to take a deep breath and trust in God. She was once called out to help a woman who was in labour. "I wasn't trained as a nurse," she said, "but as always I did the best I could – there was no-one else. On the way out I grabbed a book about delivering babies, and we got on fine."

<u>Reaching into the new</u>
The missionary spirit that lured the founders into territories unfamiliar to them continues to be claimed by the Sisters. The Sisters of St Joseph of Philadelphia wrote in their Directional Paper for the 1989 Chapter:
> We recognize as part of our graced heritage taking risks and creatively using limited resources to accomplish more than seemed possible, responding to the new needs of each era,

steadily serving the poor, and educating ourselves for mission.

This has meant the continued expansion of Sisters into areas of need in Africa, South and Central America, Asia and Polynesia. The Sisters of St Joseph of Chambéry are now in Czechoslovakia where the Church has once again reorganized.[191] In Pakistan they minister to the 1% Christians and 98% Muslim population through education, offering the one group an opportunity to recognize their human dignity and the other "an open and welcoming Church."[192] The Indian Province made a foundation in Tanzania in 2002. From Brazil they went to Mozambique. Sisters of St Joseph of Lyon in Mexico have formed a vibrant province.

The Sisters of St Joseph of the Sacred Heart in Peru have come to know the many other missionaries from Congregations of St Joseph in Canada, United States and other areas with whom they feel a bond of spirit. Ireland, too, having for so long sent women overseas to join groups of Sisters of St Joseph as missionaries, has now received back the ministrations of Sisters in the "home-missions" of need.[193] Even in this move, constant openness to conversion is required. A new culture now operates in their homeland. What the Sisters of St Joseph of Carondelet found when they took their first novice in Peru, they can identify with: "Instead of being the North American (or Australian, or repatriating Irish!) Sisters who are here to change things, all of a sudden you realize that you are the one who has to be changed!"[194]

---

[191] *Message Aux Amis,* Soeurs de Saint Joseph de Chambéry, Province de France, Sept. 2003. p. 2
[192] *Message Aux Amis,* p. 4
[193] Sisters of St Joseph of Annecy, Chambéry and Lyon have had ministries in Ireland since the early 1900's. Sisters of St Joseph of the Sacred Heart approved in the 1995 Chapter the return of Sisters born in Ireland for ministry or retirement.
[194] McGlone, *Comunidad para el Mundo,* p. 320. Bracketed inserts mine.

In an ever-changing world, adaptations in methods of ministry are being constantly demanded. The "village missions" of India are an example of how Sisters have adapted methods to suit local needs.

> Certain Sisters go in twos to the villages at the request of the priests to whose parishes the villages are attached. The Sisters normally spend a month in the village catechising; they prepare people for the sacraments, for the blessing or rectification of marriages, ... The actual catechising is done at night after work in the fields is finished at sundown and the evening meal prepared and consumed. Consequently the Sisters' busiest time is from 10.00 p.m. till 2.00 a.m. or even later. Their lodging is usually a hut, or if anything resembling a church, they sleep on the sacristy floor.[195]

In Australia's tropical Kimberley region, Sisters arrived at the aboriginal settlement of Yaruman in the 1960s and, since there were no buildings there, lived in a caravan and taught under a tree. Having local elders involved in running the school and passing on their own language was, for its time, an innovation that has since been accepted across much of the country.

Sisters of St Joseph of Annecy in Tambacounda, Senegal, use a system of "minimal education" called "alphabetisation" where totally illiterate people are taught the basics for trade and housekeeping. Like most ventures, hardship has been part of the experience of these Sisters also. In 1965 when they were beginning a mission in Coudiry, an explosion caused by faulty electricity destroyed everything on the night of their arrival. "We had nothing left except the clothes we were wearing, our profession crucifixes and a medal of Our Lady. We certainly suffered but we were not discouraged."[196]

During the Indonesian occupation of Timor-Leste (East Timor), Sisters from Sydney began in 1994 a "visiting" ministry to that

---

[195] Bourne, *His Mercy is From Age to Age*, p. 195, 196.
[196] Bourne, *His Mercy is From Age to Age*, p 249.

country at the request of Bishop Belo. Rather than establish a foundation in East Timor (impossible at that time), he asked the Sisters to produce education materials in the Tetum language to help preserve the people's culture, then threatened by the imposition of Indonesian systems. Until self-determination in 1999, the Mary MacKillop Institute of East Timorese Studies was able to take into East Timor beautifully illustrated texts in catechetics, health and basic education, to be printed there and which they then instructed teachers to use. The destruction by retreating Indonesian soldiers of all schools, libraries, printing presses, public buildings and facilities (as well as homes) meant that the whole project had to be started again in the year 2000. This has been done and the Sisters continue to maintain a constant (roving) presence in Timor-Leste. To their joy they have learnt that Sisters of St Joseph of Chambéry from Brazil are now serving in a remote area of that poorest of countries.

In home countries, too, sensitivity to what provides more effective means of evangelisation and service has seen Sisters of St Joseph of Chambéry in France venture into neighbourhood pastoral care in areas of high migrant population. Living in communities of two or three in flats peopled mainly by refugees and psychiatric patients, they are "neighbours" to those who are alienated In Lyon, a House of Welcome for families needing accommodation during hospital visits and treatment is run by a community made up of Sisters from the various Congregations of the French Federation. An Associate directs the facility.

In United States and Canada, a variation of the practice of the 17th century Le Puy Sisters to "divide the city" into sections and minister to the needs of that area has meant the establishment of neighbourhood houses where, after surveying the needs as expressed by the local population, services are offered in accordance with these needs. A feature is the involvement of volunteers from the area, so that an awareness of their own gifts then raises a sense of dignity in the people themselves.

The lay community of Josephite Community Aid in Sydney names this spirit of adaptation as "flexibility":

> We have to be able to read where people are "at". Flexibility means being there for others as they need us and being sensitive to what those needs are. It means being able to respond to the situation; to go with the flow. The person is more important than the plan. It is about acceptance of young or old, rich or poor. We avoid anything that would prevent us from being open to God's call to serve.[197]

It was that spirit that drove Joseph into Egypt to ensure God's presence with us in Jesus.

The "more"

Joan Duffy, Congregational Leader of the Sisters of St Joseph of Boston at the time of writing, makes this reflection: "Each time we allow the paradoxes of life to expand our soul, holy mystery, cosmic, mystery, Paschal Mystery embraces us and calls us to 'the more'."[198]

This has been the experience of those especially who, with Joseph, find themselves urged by the Spirit to open themselves to an awareness of new 'signs of the times'. The newsletter of the Sisters of St Joseph of Boston, *Soundings,* draws a connection between the situation of the first Sisters in Le Puy and themselves who, with revelations of former abuse by Church personnel, find themselves in the new space of scandal and alienation:

> In seventeenth century France our first sisters expanded the boundaries of religious life... They looked beyond these established norms and envisioned a style of religious life that reaches out in healing presence to the dear neighbour. In our own day the erosion of trust in church, political, and corporate arenas continues to impel us to "challenge structures wherever they oppress or imprison people". (CSJ Constitution, "Spirit and Purpose", 9.) Fidelity to this vision is the healing

---

[197] "Our Spirit". *Josephite Community Aid* (booklet produced by the group for private circulation.)
[198] *Soundings*, Vol 24, Summer 2002. Sisters of St Joseph of Boston. p. 2

> presence we offer to all whose lives we touch... Much has changed yet our charism continues to call us to fashion new and creative ways of connecting neighbour with neighbour and neighbour with God.[199]

An outstanding example of one who lived her life as a Sister of St Joseph open to new possibilities and ready to go forward into new territory wherever changing circumstances required it, was Nancy O'Connor, to whom this book is dedicated. The tributes paid after her sudden death on August 1, 2004, attest to the difference her presence made in the lives of so many. On completing her term of leadership of the Congregation in 2002, she took on a project for children not covered by health insurance in her State of California, USA. The comment of a colleague, Rich Statuto, reflects the extent to which she led across boundaries of professionalism into those areas that speak of ministry for the sake of God's reign:

> "She was a friend and spiritual guide to the members of our executive team," he said, "and she continually reminded us that we are a healthcare ministry and not just an affiliation of hospitals. She showed us that our true job is to treat the whole person and to bring all people into union with God and with one another."
>
> "She was always a risk taker, and under her leadership we grew rapidly but strategically – she always reminded us to remain focussed upon responding to the needs of the people living within our communities."

Because of Nancy's response to life, all at her funeral could sing,

> *He put a new song into my mouth*
> *A hymn to our God* (Ps. 40:4).

At each Eucharist we recall and re-present the memory of one who crossed the barriers of death into new life and, through the

---

[199] *Soundings*, Vol 25, Summer 2003. Sisters of St Joseph of Boston. p. 3

Spirit, enables us to do the same. The example of Sisters who, like us, have entered with Christ into this covenant, continues to inspire us. In and through them God's reign has continued to be extended into new times and places. They have done this often at great peril to themselves. One of the hymns composed for the beatification of Mary MacKillop recalls these women:

> If I could tell the love of God
> I'd sing of women seen as fools
> Because, in Joseph's hidden way
> They crossed an empty land with trust.[200]

Joseph took Jesus and Mary across the empty land into a place of safety so that the new action of the Spirit might be fruitful. These women each had their empty lands to cross – deserts of fear, new horizons, initiatives not tried before, with no map to go by, spurred on by a love "that overcomes fear." "For God's foolishness is wiser than human wisdom, and God's weakness is stronger than human strength"(1 Cor 1:22-25).

---

[200] "If I could tell the love of God" Lyrics N. Rowe, Music C. Willcock. Sydney: Sisters St Joseph. 1995.

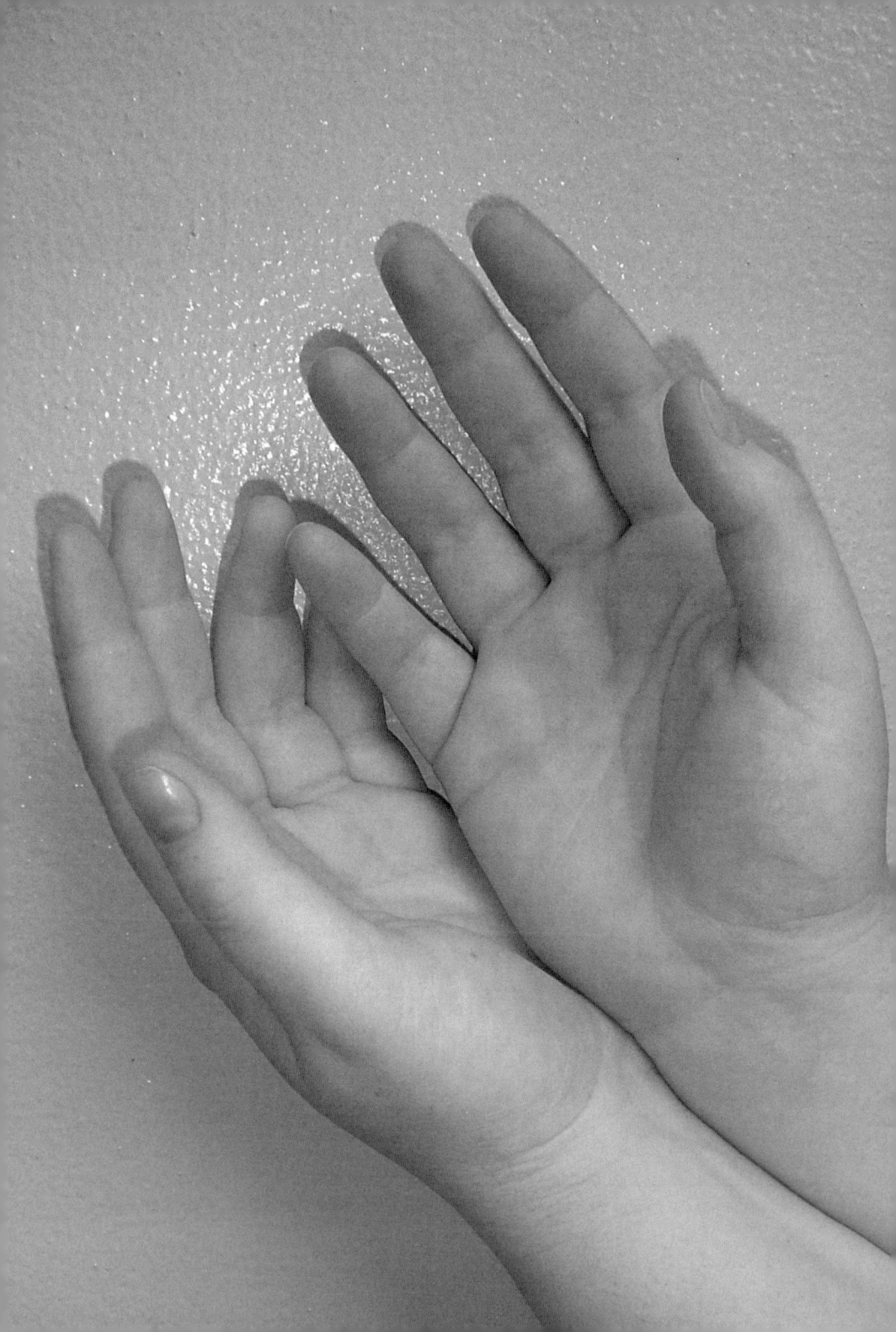

CHAPTER THREE

The Spirit of Joseph ......

finds God in the ordinary.

Is not this the carpenter's son? (Mt. 13:55)

3.1 PART ONE: The spirit is revealed

The Incarnation
To quote Abraham Lincoln again: "God must love plain, ordinary folk very much, seeing he has made so many of them."[1] That union with God is found in ordinary life is a truth that people in general seem to find hard to believe. God is the Holy One. Holiness is union with God.

But for the Christian, that belief is tied up with our understanding of the Incarnation – that in Jesus, God has been revealed enfleshed among us. In the earthly life and death of Jesus, we can know God. Jesus Christ is the Way to, the Truth about, and the Life in, union with God. So union with God is attained as, through the gracious outpouring of the Spirit, we grow into union with the risen Christ. And union with Christ means to be in union with the members of his Body, on this earth, who continue to carry out the mission of Jesus (to reveal God and bring all peoples into union with God) through loving service of the neighbour. Indeed, for the Christian, it is our love of neighbour which indicates and effects our love of God.[2]

---

[1] Cited by Richard Foley. *Saint Joseph, Patron of the Triumph*, Goleta CA: Queenship Publishing, 2002. p. 40.
[2] Jn 4:7 – *"Beloved, let us love one another; for love is of God and those who love are born of God and know God."*

In the Incarnation we understand the Word to have become truly human. So there was no suspension of the ordinary processes of how we develop emotionally, physically and intellectually for Jesus. Nor was there any "pre-knowledge" of events or non-interaction in the normal social structures of his time. God was revealed in one who shared our lot, so that humanity could share life with God, and all of creation could find its fulfilment in its creator.[3] St Paul sees this coming of Jesus as a threshold event in history. Adam ushered in the first period; Moses the second, where union with God in a people was marked by the giving of the law;[4] and now, the time of the Messiah, when all humanity can be a people in union with God by being 'justified by faith' (Gal 3:24), which 'works itself out through love' (Gal 5:6), the 'fulfilment of the law' (Rom 13:10)".[5]

The reflections of Vatican II highlighted the fact that, rather than disregarding the world and ordinary life, the Incarnation showed God's presence in these. The writings of St John set "the world" against "the spirit".[6] Unfortunately, this fact has been used at times in the history of the Church to deny the goodness of creation, giving the impression that holiness is only achieved by living apart from "the world".[7] Language lacks the capacity to differentiate between a world which is an end in itself and a world which, with all of creation, will only find its fulfilment in God. When the world is an end in itself, people follow their base inclinations so that vices, such as dishonesty, immorality, greed, disunity and violence, are simply ways of promoting one's short-term goals. This is the "world" that is to be rejected. When Christians reject such vices for a perspective of life that goes beyond this world, where values come out of love of God,

---

[3] Rom 8:21 – because creation itself will be set free from its bondage to decay and obtain the glorious liberty of the children of God.
[4] Gal. 3:19.
[5] Raymond Brown, Joseph Fitzmyer, Roland Murphy. *The New Jerome Biblical Commentary*. London: Chapman, 1990. p 1391.
[6] For example, 1John Ch. 4.
[7] The "world" in John can be compared with the "flesh" in Paul.

neighbour and creation, the self is not the be-all and end-all. In this, we are united with God who is totally self-giving, as we learn from Jesus, who revealed God to us in pouring himself out in death.

At the Second Vatican Council, the Bishops saw that the Christian belief in the Incarnation has implications for our attitude towards creation, society and the "normal" activities of human beings. They called not for a rejection of the created world but for a choosing of values which enable God's reign to take root in that world. They proposed an "integration" of daily life and faith and a "harmonisation" of faith and culture. Rather than set up opposition between faith and life, the Gospel is to throw light on how life can be "lived to the full" through knowing the "freedom of the children of God".[8]

> To those .. who believe in divine love, He (Christ) gives assurance that the way of love lies open to all and that the effort to establish a universal community (of brothers and sisters) is not a hopeless one. He cautions them at the same time that this love is not something to be reserved for important matters, but must be pursued chiefly in the ordinary circumstances of life.[9]

Joseph and the Ordinary

Mary and Joseph, critical players in the unfolding of the Incarnation, lived very ordinary lives. This fact provides Christianity with an important insight into where union with God is to be found. So often, the figures of Jesus, Mary and Joseph in their life in Nazareth are irrelevant to those trying to find spiritual meaning in their lives. How can we make a connection with them and our current situations? Anne Hennessy suggests that we need to stop putting them in holy pictures and place them in their historical setting. With regard to Joseph, it is time, she says, to move him "out of the rarefied

---

[8] See particularly the document, *"The Church Today"* (*Gaudiem et Spes*).
[9] *Gaudiem et Spes*, par. 38.

atmosphere of traditional Catholic iconography and place him in a more universal and realistic context, facing the dilemmas of ordinary daily life".[10]

So what was "ordinary life" for Joseph? The intention of the Gospels is not to give us a history of characters involved nor to give us a description of their social backgrounds. But we are fortunate today, through the discoveries of archaeologists, social scientists, anthropologists and scripture scholars, to be able to construct a picture of what life was like in the time of Joseph. The limitations of our ability to do this are acknowledged: no-one can with certitude "reproduce" a period in history. But we can appreciate what is known of the times and thus to picture more realistically the events described in the Gospels.

The context of life for Joseph was the isolated village of Nazareth in first-century Galilee. This was a peasant world, one where pockets of people lived in small hamlets among the rocky outcrops of southern Galilee. These hamlets "would consist of peasants who worked their own land, tenant farmers who worked land belonging to others, and craftspersons who served their needs".[11] As such, these village people occupied the "lower rung of the social and economic ladder"[12] of Jewish society.

Nazareth at the time would probably have been made up of about 300 to 400 people. It was situated at a short walking-distance[13] from the large city of Sepphoris which Herod was re-constructing over the period of years surrounding the birth of Jesus. But being away from the thoroughfares connecting this

---

[10] Hennessy, *In Search of a Patron*. p. 52.
[11] Elizabeth Johnson. *Truly Our Sister: A Theology of Mary in the Communion of Saints*. New York: Continuum International Publishing, 2003. p. 141.
[12] Johnson, *Truly Our Sister*, p. 143.
[13] Around 3.5 miles, or 5.6 kilometres.

city with others, Nazareth was inconspicuous and of no importance.

Houses in the village were dug into the hillsides with a frontage of two or three rooms of local stone and daub and clustered together around a courtyard to form a compound. Roofing was of reeds and packed mud.

> In the unroofed, common courtyard, inhabitants of the domestic units, most likely an extended family or close kinship group, shared an oven, a cistern that held water, and a millstone for grinding grain, indicating that this was the kitchen where food was prepared and cooked in the open air. Domestic animals also lived here. ...
> Living at a subsistence level, households by and large grew their own food, did their own building, and sewed their own clothes from cloth that they spun and wove, mostly woollen cloth from sheep.[14]

This was a patriarchal society, where the village was governed by the elders, and entrance in and out of its walls was supervised by its men.[15] Various levels of solidarity that ruled village behaviour served to shape the characters and interactions of the inhabitants.

But life was far from peaceful in this area. In 4 BCE,[16] Sepphoris had been flattened by the Romans when it revolted against the occupation. Many people had been sold into slavery and two thousand crucified on the hillsides around Nazareth.[17] Having come under Roman rule some sixty years before, the region had moved into a market economy and, most tellingly, had been subjected to internal and foreign (Roman) taxation. Thus the meagre supplies eked from primitive farming methods were taken up to sustain the cultured lifestyle of the ruling

---

[14] Johnson, *Truly Our Sister*, p. 143.
[15] Hennessy, *In Search of a Patron*, p 51.
[16] The terms BCE and CE are used for "Before the Common Era" and "Common Era" respectively.
[17] Perrotta, *Saint Joseph*, p. 94.

classes. "More often than not, there was no .. surplus, placing the rural population on a narrow margin between subsistence and famine."[18] Consequences of being unable to pay the taxes could be loss of one's land, going into tenancy under an absentee landlord, moving to the cities in search of patronage or being sold into slavery.

Other changes, too, made life difficult for the ordinary person. Small plots of land, divided and sub-divided according to traditional inheritance laws, could rarely sustain a family. This fact, together with the multiplicity of taxes and the seeping effects of previous Greek occupation and now Roman, had meant the break-up of families – as Perrotta explains, not so much of the nuclear family as the extended family. "In this area, where geographical mobility has been unknown and occupations are handed down from father to sons, this is a big change indeed."[19]

Joseph the Family Man

The details of Joseph's situation in Nazareth with regard to extended family are unknown. But whatever the case, he and Mary would have lived within a compound, sharing daily life with others to whom he was bound by "blood, occupation, religious practice, patronage and membership in a household".[20]

Joseph may or may not have been the head of his household, since this role was traditionally filled by whoever was the eldest male in the group. As part of a wider family, his concern would have been to conform to the standards of honour which governed the roles each person was to fulfil. To break these would bring shame on the group.

---

[18] Johnson, *Truly Our Sister*, p. 145.
[19] Perrotta, *Saint Joseph*, p. 95.
[20] Hennessy, *In Search of a Patron*, p. 47.

Life in all its aspects was shared: there was no such thing as "privacy". Goods and values were common resources. A household was not a place where you could get away from the world or from work. It was the centre in which all the members carried out the tasks required to sustain the group. Thus, as Anne Hennessy says, "Joseph's family responsibilities were played out in a public arena."[21]

Joseph's life with Mary would have begun with the "common human event"[22] of asking her to be his wife. Jewish practice of the time required the active consent of the woman, even if the marriage was an arranged one. The time of betrothal was more than an engagement: it was a legal commitment that was completed when the bride joined her husband's household about a year later. Thus, the code of honour that was broken when Mary was found to be pregnant "before they came together" was no light matter. "Both Joseph and his beloved, at the mercy of their fellow religionists in a closed village society, must have known the pain of being despised by 'good' people who had not been called beyond human and divine laws."[23]

"It was through the exercise of his fatherhood that Joseph was called to serve the person and mission of Jesus,"[24] said Pope John Paul II. As father Joseph had fulfilled the requirements of law in having Jesus circumcised and named, ensuring his lineage. He socialised him into manhood and passed on to him the skills of his trade. His was the duty to instruct Jesus in the Law and to oversee his religious and moral development.

What Joseph was like as a person we can only surmise. But it is a fact that,

---

[21] Hennessy, *In Search of a Patron*, p. 50.
[22] Perrotta, *Saint Joseph*, p. 30.
[23] Molinari & Hennessy, *The Vocation and Mission of Joseph & Mary*, p. 14.
[24] *Redemptoris Custos*, par. 8.

> for many years, whenever Jesus had used that familial word (Abba), he had meant 'Joseph'. From among all the images of God that Jesus had learned in his life as a pious Jew, he applied the familiar name of his foster-father to his God, his heavenly father.[25]

Joseph's family life, lived in a world of violence and fear, of hardship and social constraint, nevertheless provided the foundation for some of the most important understandings we have as Christians about our relationship with God.

Joseph the Worker

Joseph, we are told, was a *tekton* – a person who works with hard substances.[26] Archaeological evidence tells us that the bulk of these substances was most likely stone, since timber was not plentiful and there was ample use of the limestone and basalt deposits in the area.[27] Public works such as water systems in Sepphoris and domestic constructions such as grinding stones and storage areas used these materials excavated out of the hills. Ovens were made out of brick. Wood would have been used for ploughs, door frames and small items of furniture. A more accurate description of Joseph's trade, then, would be "builder", since there was no such thing as a specialised "carpenter".

It is known that builders worked in groups and that these men were often related.

> Because few villages in ancient Palestine were large enough to support a family of builders consistently, these craftsmen were known to travel around the region. So it is possible that Joseph was rooted in a kin or trade group in Nazareth, but

---

[25] Perrotta, *Saint Joseph*, pp. 53, 54.

[26] The Greek word in Mk 6:3 and Mt 13:55, traditionally been translated as "carpenter", has a far wider sense. Anne Hennessy says that even in the 16th century, the Carmelite scholar, Jerome Gracián, acknowledged that Joseph could have been a smith, but his "scholarship gave way to his piety and (he) rejected the idea on the grounds that an anvil would have been too heavy for Joseph to carry to Egypt and back, and that the dirt and noise of the forge would not have been appropriate for the home of the Holy Family."!! (*In Search of a Patron*, p. 42).

[27] Even if forestation was heavier than it is today, relics such as the first-century boat raised from the Sea of Galilee in 1986 and made of several types of wood, show that it was probably difficult to obtain a sustained supply of specialised timbers.

was accustomed to travelling with other builders throughout Palestine.[28]

Anne Hennessy raises the possibility that Joseph may have worked in nearby Sepphoris as a hired labourer. If so, the situation would have been stressful for Joseph. In re-building the city, Herod adopted the architectural styles of pagan Rome, constructed to impress. Therefore, local builders found themselves directed by overseers and engineers from Rome.

> They had to employ unfamiliar methods to make an architectural statement on behalf of their corrupt ruler and their pagan oppressors. They were not working for people like themselves, or on projects with which they were familiar. They were, instead, building massive structures which by their size alone would erase any sign of individual workmanship or talent. The workers in Sepphoris did heavy construction work without the benefit of machinery, but with the constant threat of physical injury or even death.[29]

Involved in these interactions would have been the system of "patron-client relationships"[30] that would have determined availability and conditions of work. This system, which applied also to social standing, depended on the beneficence of well-disposed males in positions of influence whose "patronage" brought them honour and status. Joseph and those he worked with would have had to cultivate these contacts, giving and receiving hospitality and gifts.

However, Joseph's work-life involved far more than building and its associated activities. He would also have been a small-time farmer. Johnson explains that,

> even families of craftsmen like Joseph the *tekton* cultivated a plot of land for basic foodstuffs, including grains (mostly wheat, but also some barley), olives for oil, and grapes for wine. A kitchen garden near the compound would supply

---

[28] Hennessy, *In Search of a Patron*, p. 48.
[29] Hennessy, *In Search of a Patron*, p. 45.
[30] Hennessy, *In Search of a Patron*, p. 50

legumes, vegetables, and leeks, while orchard trees producing figs, dates, and nuts supplemented the basic diet. Most families kept a number of small animals, mostly sheep and goats but perhaps also some cows. These provided dairy products, occasional meat, and skins and wool for making clothing.[31]

Scholars note that the parables of Jesus all use the imagery of fields, animals and harvesting, and of workers lining up for hire, rather than that of a tradesman working quietly in his "carpenter's shop". This is one more indication that the experience of Joseph and the growing Jesus would have been just this: the constant, hard work of caring for the home "plot", producing food and tending animals as well as labouring at the building trade.

In Joseph we see one who, in his work, grew into union with God. Gerard Manley Hopkins recognises this in his poem entitled "Work".

> It is not only prayer that gives glory to God but work.
> Smiting on an anvil, sawing a beam, whitewashing a wall,
> Driving horses, reaping, scouring – everything gives God
> Glory. To lift up hands in prayer gives God glory.
> But a man with a dung-fork in his hand,
> Or a woman with a slop-pail,
> They give God glory too.[32]

Joseph's Religious Practice

"Everyday piety," says Johnson, "was anchored by two institutions, the family household and the public assembly or synagogue."[33] The primary setting for religious observance was the home. Praying twice a day, morning and evening, was the common practice. Purity laws determined foods eaten, hygiene and sexual intercourse. The purpose of these laws was to honour God, the all-holy One, in whose presence no

---

[31] Johnson, *Truly Our Sister,* p. 200.
[32] Hopkins, Gerard Manly. *Collected Works.*
[33] Johnson, *Truly Our Sister,* p. 169.

contamination should be allowed. Children were instructed in the Law, and Sabbath rituals and rest were observed in this home-space – consisting, it must be remembered, of more than one nuclear family. Johnson quotes the *Schema* as encapsulating these "defining aspects of Jewish life":

> Hear O Israel, the Lord our God, the Lord is one. And you shall love the Lord your God with all your heart, and with all your soul, and with all your might. And these words which I command you this day shall be upon your heart. You shall teach them diligently to your children and shall speak of them when you sit in your house, and when you walk by the way, and when you lie down, and when you rise up (Deut. 6:4—5).[34]

Luke's Gospel describes Jesus in Nazareth as going to the synagogue, "as his custom was, on the sabbath day".[35] Despite this, archaeology has so far failed to unearth remains of a pre-70 CE synagogue in the village. However, as Johnson notes, the Greek word *synagogë* means "assembly".[36] Just as the Christian concept of "church" can refer to either the people or the building, so too, the "synagogue" can denote the people gathered, be it in a building or in an open space. In a village like Nazareth, the equivalent of a town square could have served this purpose.

At this assembly, people came together for public prayer and reading of scripture. Inspirational instruction was given and the Torah explained. At various times of the year they also gathered for religious festivals and to observe fast days. Celebrations of funerals, marriages and initiation ceremonies would have called for further gatherings as would some aspects of public business such as local law proceedings and decisions concerning village life.

---

[34] Johnson, *Truly Our Sister*, p. 169.
[35] Lk 4:16.
[36] Johnson, *Truly Our Sister*, p. 167. The author makes the point also that Luke, being from the city, would not have been familiar with the arrangements of country life.

These assemblies would probably have been led by male household heads who also took responsibility for the observance of moral behaviour, an integral part of social and religious life. Thus love of neighbour, provision for the poor and kindness to the stranger, were part of worship of God: "And you shall observe all my statutes and all my ordinances, and do them: I am the Lord."[37]

According to the Books of Exodus and Deuteronomy, every male Israelite was required to visit the Temple in Jerusalem three times a year. Given their poverty, the demands of distance (four days' journey) and the need to attend to flocks and harvest, religious pilgrimages to Jerusalem might not have been frequent events for the peasant peoples of Galilee. But we do read in Luke's Gospel that Mary and Joseph did so every year.[38]

For the Jew, the Temple ensured and concretised God's worship. Jerusalem was a symbol of God's presence among them as a people. Gathered to offer sacrifice, study, pray and celebrate, they could experience themselves as the assembly of God's people. The spiritual meaning of political events that marked their history as a people was recalled in this place. God had been with them in these events. They had been shaped as God's people through these events. "Going up to Jerusalem" on pilgrimage would have solidified their identity as a people covenanted to God in what others might regard as "accidents of history" but which, for them, contained the revelation of who God was for them and their relationship with that God. Little wonder then, that a series of invaders who tried to destroy Jewish self-understanding, chose to destroy the Temple.

In summary, the figure of Joseph "in the daily rounds of ordinary life in Galilee, in Sabbath rest and prayer, and,

---

[37] As spelled out in Leviticus Chapter 19.
[38] Again, Luke may have imposed an urban expectation on this peasant population in this statement.

occasionally, in festival pilgrimages to the temple in Jerusalem"[39] is one that demonstrates union with God in the ordinary. In his tercentenary address given to the Sisters of St Joseph of Carondelet, Jesuit Father Gaudefroy said of Joseph,
> Buried in the nameless masses and taken up with our petty human affairs, he was the personification of the saintliness of an active life in the world. The distinguishing note of his career is that he did all sheerly as a tool in the hand of God.[40]

3.2 PART TWO: The spirit unfolds.

<u>A spirituality in the world</u>
In 17th century France, Sisters of St Joseph, living "like Religious outside cloister",[41] were seen to be doing a revolutionary thing. The roots of this judgement lie partly in ideas of holiness that have come down to us through history. Herbert Alphonso explains that in the first centuries of the Christian era, the ideal of holiness was martyrdom. In yielding their lives, martyrs joined Jesus whose death made visible the total outpouring of God's love, given "for the life of the world".

When the classical era of persecution was ended, holiness came to be signified by the "living martyrdom" of monastic life,
> so that even lay Christians who aspired to holiness strove to mould their lives on a kind of "flight from the world". This lasted fairly well through the Middle Ages until St Thomas Aquinas, recapturing the insights of St Augustine, placed the essence of Christian holiness fairly and squarely in *charity* or *love* – love which both leads to, and is the fruit of, union. Unfortunately, however, ... the accent on the ascetical-monastic "flight-from-the-world" understanding of Christian holiness continued somehow to prevail in practice. With the

---

[39] Johnson, *Truly Our Sister*, p. 165.
[40] Gaudefroy, "*Return to the Fountainhead."* Tercentenary Address published by the Sisters of St Joseph of Carondelet (St Louis, Missouri), p. 95. Quoted in Dolorita Marie Dougherty et al, *The Sisters of St Joseph of Carondelet,* Herder Book Co., St Louis, 1966. p. 24.
[41] Marguerite Burdier's description of themselves, 1683. Vacher, *Des "régulières",* Session Five, p. 238.

> advent of the renaissance movements of a markedly apostolic spirituality – notably that of Ignatius Loyola ... and Francis de Sales, ... – the understanding of Christian holiness as focussed on union with God (the union of love), in whatever state or condition of life in the world, was once again highlighted in both theory and practice.[42]

The founding of the Sisters of St Joseph at a time when the influence of Ignatius Loyola and Francis de Sales were at their height determined the "worldly" character of the Congregation. The Jesuit Médaille portrayed in the documents he wrote for the Sisters the Ignatian understanding of God "as loving and active in human affairs; a personal God with a personal interest in individuals".[43] Likewise, the works of Francis de Sales were avidly absorbed by the Sisters. Canonised soon after his death[44], the Savoie Francis was a hero throughout the south of France. Because the Visitation Nuns whom he had founded had been forced to become monastic, many Sisters of St Joseph popularly regarded themselves as inheritors of his ideals of contemplation in action.[45]

The writings of Francis were addressed to ordinary people living in the "world". They were based on the premise that "it is an error, it is even a heresy",[46] to hold that piety is incompatible with any state of life. Likewise, the primitive constitutions of the Sisters of St Joseph maintained that the Sisters' concern was to be the neighbour's "sanctification" or "holiness"– not merely their salvation".[47] Sisters were to give

---

[42] Herbert Alphonso. "The Idea of Holiness in Christianity", *Pro Dialogo*, Bulletin 92, 1996/2. p. 243
[43] Anne Hennessy. *The Influence of Ignatian Spirituality on the Primitive Documents of the Sisters of Saint Joseph*. Berkley, California: Sisters of St Joseph of Orange, 1983. p 168.
[44] Francis de Sales died in Lyon in 1622, was beatified in 1661 and canonised in 1665.
[45] This belief was sustained even after the Revolution, particularly by the Sisters of St Joseph of Annecy whose Mother House occupies the former monastery of the Visitation Sisters.
[46] From his treatise, "An Introduction to the Devout Life".
[47] Throughout the *Constitutions*, Médaille urges Sisters to "contribute" through their service to the "salvation and perfection" of the neighbour. The term "perfection", as he used it, means "fullness of life", "wholeness", "holiness".

spiritual formation to women, particularly to members of the Confraternities of Mercy who helped them in their charitable works; records show that they also led retreats and gave inspirational instruction to parishioners.[48]

<u>Double Union</u>
The devotion of the "Two Trinities" was to provide for the Sisters the formula by which they were to understand their mission.[49] In the zeal of Jesus, the openness of Mary and the unifying love of Joseph, the gracious presence of the Father, the self-giving of the Son and the unifying love of the Spirit were made visible on earth. So, too, the Sisters were to signify and effect the "double union", making present in union of neighbour with neighbour the union of neighbour with God.

For Médaille, the Eucharist was a model of this double union. Jesus unites heaven and earth – he is in himself the "double union". When we celebrate the Eucharist, we are taken, by the power of the Spirit, into Jesus' self-gift or sacrifice made so that all might be united to God. So the Sisters of St Joseph are to be totally given to God, in giving self to the neighbour.

> In summary, as our dear Savior in the Holy Eucharist appears to us as being not at all given to self but totally given to God his Father and the souls redeemed by his Precious Blood, so, my dear Daughter, our Little Design and those who belong to it will not be given to self, will be totally lost and emptied of self in God and for God, and with that, will be completely given to the dear neighbor; (in short, they will be) entirely given to God and the dear neighbour, not at all given to self.[50]

The place in which the "double union" with God and neighbour was to be achieved was this world. "Sisters of St Joseph, living in the manner of religious, were necessarily in touch with the

---

[48] Vacher, *Des "régulières"*, Session Five. p. 261.
[49] Probably, because this formula was simple, it was a "memory device for those members of the Congregation who were illiterate." Hennessy, *The Influence of Ignatian Spirituality*. p. 99.
[50] *The Eucharistic Letter*. par. 42.

world, with people, in a way of life by design not separate from them."[51] "The place of service becomes the place of union with God and with every neighbour, while leading the world to God."[52]

Sisters of St Joseph and the Ordinary

The world which saw the birth of the Sisters of St Joseph in the 1650s was centred in the Auvergne, an area of France considered by the elite of society to be, as Bishop de Maupas said, "the most uncouth region" of the country.[53]

This was an agrarian society. Ravaged by the Wars of Religion from which it was slowly recovering, it had also suffered a series of failed crops causing further hardship and suffering. The majority of families eked out some sort of living,[54] tilling the lands of often-absentee lords to whom they payed taxes in a percentage of produce and animals. From a young age, all family members were required to work in the fields. The old and sick were left alone all day to fend for themselves and to mind infants. Travel was restricted and tolls were charged to go over a lord's property and to enter towns.

Fear was an ever-present reality. Fighting between rival gangs and noble challengers often razed the countryside. Nature was scary, because it controlled life. Wild animals roamed the countryside. Famine was a constant threat. People were nearly always hungry, and mothers in particular were malnourished. Disease was rampant. Indeed, in one month, July 1650, 27% of the population of 15,000 in Le Puy died from the plague.

---

[51] Patricia Byrne. "Vows in the History of Sisters of St Joseph".
[52] Vacher, *Des "régulières"*, Session Three, p. 118.
[53] Byrne, Patricia. "French Roots of a Women's Movement: The Sisters of St Joseph 1650 – 1836". PhD Dissertation, Boston College, Boston 1985. p. 32.
[54] Even as late as 1957, life in the Auvergne was described as being full of difficulty. An article by Walker Howell in the *National Geographic Magazine*, September 1957, comments: "Auvergne is not a rich land. The Auvergnat works hard for little reward. Farmers and laborers toil until dark, and women spend hours on their knees beside rivers and streams, submerging their hands in icy water to do the family washing." "Lafayette's Homeland, Auvergne" , p. 427.

Ten per cent of this population, however, could count on land, taxes and privilege to assure a secure lifestyle. The opening up of trade to far shores brought a variety of food to their tables: no monotonous fare of rye bread, beans and turnips for them. Well-ventilated housing on country estates contrasted with the stinking, dark hovels which the peasants shared with animals.

At this time, too, there was a rising middle class, the bourgeoisie. This class consisted of people like lawyers or bankers. They, with the tradespeople, formed a buffer between the aristocracy and the very poor. Life for them was not easy. For example, it took 10 years for a bourgeoisie woman to earn enough money for a dowry if she wanted to enter the monastery. Together, the two levels of this 90% of the population supported the lifestyle of the top 10% and were dependent on them.

Class position was seen in this world to be determined by God.[55] Morality demanded faithfulness to the duties of one's state of life wherever birth had determined. Consequently there was little movement from one class to the other.

However, concern for morality did encourage betterment of one's situation within social strata. Education was seen as a way to reform society through reforming the characters of its members. By the 17th century an awareness of the importance of mothers as family moral guides was growing. Therefore education for girls was being embraced; until then it had been the prerogative of boys. Girls' schooling, funded by the bourgeoisie of the town, was conducted by enclosed nuns in buildings physically attached to the monastery. Teaching itself was seen as a lowly profession and even for the Jesuits who

---

[55] This conviction was to be long-lasting. For example, the hymn "All things bright and beautiful" contains the verse, "The rich man in his castle, The poor man at his gate, He made them high or lowly, And ordered their estate." Words by Cecil F Alexander, <u>Hymns for Little Children,</u> 1848.

conducted 50% of the boys' schools in France at the time, it was considered a form of mortification!

Most towns cared for the sick and the improvident poor by establishing an "hôpital" (for vagabonds, orphans, handicapped, beggars and itinerants), an "Hotel-Dieu" (for the sick, injured – especially veterans – and dying) and a Maladerie (smaller houses for foundlings, incurables and others). In general, attitudes towards those served were paternalistic and sought to distinguish the "deserving" from the "undeserving".

Religion and politics at this time were intermingled to the point of fusion. Prelates had civic powers. Groups such as Religious Orders had to get "letters patent" from the civil authority for legal standing and the right to receive bequests and legacies. French kings viewed Rome's decrees on religious matters as laws from a foreign legislator. Power clashes over land and rule between lay nobility and bishops were frequent.

It was against this background that the Sisters of St Joseph began their mission of opening the "dear neighbour" to union with God and each other through their various ministries. "These little groups of women," says Vacher, "scattered in the country, lived the way of the people's ordinary life."[56] In this, they resembled Joseph. With a background not unlike theirs, he was gifted by the Spirit in his ordinary life – disturbed, even chaotic as it was – to signify and enable union with God's incarnate presence in our world.

Enculturating the Ordinary
By the time of their refounding after the Revolution, the Sisters of St Joseph were thoroughly identified in the popular mind with ordinary life. They were to carry this reputation with them when they set out for foreign shores. Although, as Patricia

---

[56] Vacher, *Des régulières,* Session Four, p. 161.

Byrne points out, the Sisters who left France for the United States in 1836 began their ministry among their compatriots, they soon became identified with the common population of their new country. She attributes this in part to the fact that from the beginning their teaching of the deaf and of other specialised groups of children required interaction with government authorities; this "provided incentive to learn English and provoked interaction with the American milieu".[57]

Other factors led to the "Americanisation" of the Sisters. From the beginning a steady stream of women having no French language entered the Congregation and this necessitated the translation of the constitutions into English. Unlike most other Religious whose rules precluded the care of boys, the Sisters of St Joseph were able to take on this charge. Thus, because "bishops were anxious to have sisters for male orphanages, and pastors often preferred a community who could teach boys in the parochial school, since a parish could ill afford separate institutions for boys and girls",[58] preference was given to these Sisters. Consequently, they had greater visibility and increased membership; having expanded rapidly, they found themselves independent of France in organisation and in allegiance to local bishops. This sense of separation from France was formalised in 1860 when a system of general government was adopted by the Sisters of Carondelet with provinces in St Louis, St Paul, Albany and Los Angeles. Many groups in other dioceses throughout United States and Canada chose diocesan government.

Migrants themselves, or children of migrant families, the American Sisters of St Joseph shared the poverty of their lay counterparts. Their identity was with the local Church which itself was multi-cultural, and they became deeply involved in

---

[57] Byrne, "The Americanization of a French Tradition", p. 253.
[58] Byrne, "The Americanization of a French Tradition", p. 254.

parish life. Because this was an age of bigotry, they found themselves suffering the same fate as the rest of a Catholic subculture. To avoid outright abuse, they wore the "garb of ordinary women"[59] for travel; they put up with insults and struggled against enormous odds to bring a sense of dignity to the Catholic poor. They worked hard to maintain themselves, supplementing their income with funds earned through needlework, lace-making and a variety of menial tasks such as washing clothes. They served as nurses and housekeepers in the Civil War and in the Spanish American War. In Canada the Sisters played a leading role in the battle against the cholera and typhoid epidemics of 1854. Trekking through snow in the north, wild deserts in the west, and steamy bogs in the south, American Sisters served their "own" people. "Slavish work," says Byrne, "was the price paid by many sisters to secure a niche in the society, both ecclesiastical and civil, of the United States of America."[60]

Within the lives of Sisters themselves, there were some inner tensions caused by the clash of French and American cultural practices, but these were soon overcome by the weight of local membership if nothing else. At her election as Superior General of the Philadelphia Congregation in 1884, we are told, Mother Mary John Kieran asked the Bishop if she could dispense with Sisters kissing her hand. When he gave permission she wrote in her diary, "That was a relief!"[61]

In India, Africa, South and Central America and other countries, the same ability to adopt and integrate the behaviour patterns of

---

[59] Evangeline Thomas *Footprints on the Frontier*. Maryland: Newman Press, 1948. p. 79. Margaret Brennan gives a vivid description of bigotry at work in her work, *Persistence of Vision*. "Religious did not wear habits when they travelled in those days. Anti-Catholic, anti-foreign, anti-Irish sentiments of the Know-Nothings were high; religious never knew whom they might meet on a long journey, or how insulting and even dangerous such a confrontation might be. Frightening incidents had erupted around the country: riots, street violence, Catholic churches bombed and convents burned. It seemed best to avoid trouble." p. 2.
[60] Byrne, "The Americanization of a French Tradition", p. 262.
[61] Byrne, "The Americanization of a French Tradition", p. 264.

the surrounding culture has enabled the Sisters of St Joseph to become part of the warp and woof of local, ordinary life. For example, when Sisters arrived in Yanam, India, in 1849, they were shocked by the different, un-European customs they encountered. It was not long, however, before they could write to a new group of Sisters coming as missionaries, "What a happiness it is for us to welcome you! Come quickly. We have put the rice on to cook!"[62] In truly "meeting the neighbour in every place,"[63] Sisters of St Joseph have found God in the ordinary.

The "Ordinary" in Australia

Mary MacKillop knew that ordinary life in Australia in the 1860s was very different from that of Europe. In her pamphlet, *The Necessity for the Institute*, she prefaced her description of conditions in this country with the words, "It is an Australian who writes this, one brought up in the midst of the many evils she tries to describe, and who has over and over again heard pious priests and zealous Bishops sadly deplore a state of things which they could not remedy."

What the bishops could not remedy was the toll made on pastors ministering in an untamed land, harsh and alien to Europeans, and unyielding in the demands on health and spirit. Catholics were poor, many from convict or servant backgrounds, and they had little influence in political affairs. Anti-Catholic bigotry was a feature of the country right from the beginning. Sometimes the response of Catholics, especially clergy, did not help the situation. Gathered from all parts of Europe, these priests were often rejects from Religious Orders there or from dioceses where they had caused trouble. The number of priests

---

[62] Bourne, *His Mercy is From Age to Age*, p. 77. Another lively example is that of Sisters who went from California and Australia to Papua New Guinea. They were soon joining in local customs and speaking pidgin with the best of them although, Geagley says, "they never mastered roasted cat"!

[63] *Comme un Grain de Séneve – Les Sœurs de Saint Joseph*, Epinay-sur-Seine (France): Editions Cif, 1982. p. 14.

and bishops was small, and there was a good deal of hostility between those who had come from Ireland (the majority) and those from England or other countries.

Pockets of people in the cities clustered around the coast and in tiny settlements scattered at vast distances from one another across properties as large as whole countries in Europe, separated from each other by thick bushland or formidable deserts – these were the objects of bishops' concern. Aboriginal populations, decimated through introduced disease and deliberate massacres and poisonings, were also a preoccupation of some bishops. But there was little they could do, since lack of church personnel and restrictive government policies frustrated early attempts to engage with the issue. There was open enmity and fear among white settlers as Aboriginal peoples tried to defend their land, as recorded in the Memoirs of Father Woods, for example:

> At the close of the first day's journey, they passed by a newly built hut where there was a woman with three children who implored them to stay as she was alone and was afraid of the blacks. They had just speared six of the horses and the husband had gone away to seek assistance. ... The woman was a Catholic and he (Father Woods) was anxious to say Mass for her the next day and give her the sacraments. Night came on and the settler did not return, so a watch had to be kept. In the middle of the night the dogs gave warning that the blacks were about. Father had only one charge in an old double barrelled gun, but fortunately the natives made no attack. In the morning Father said Mass in the hut, and this was the manner in those days in which he travelled and carried the sacraments amongst the settlers.[64]

The discovery of gold in Victoria and New South Wales had brought hordes of migrants to the east coast of Australia. This caused a problem to regions such as South Australia where marginal farming land and lack of minerals could support only a

---

[64] *Memoirs of J. E. Tenison Woods.*

relatively small population. While their husbands went off to the goldfields, women were left there to support the family in whatever ways they could. Schooling was virtually nil, especially away from the cities.

This was the ordinary world of Mary MacKillop. She had known at first hand the effects of dislocation and dysfunction in her family, as her father searched for work as far away as New Zealand and coped with the indignity of failure in wild schemes for fame and fortune. Poverty and hardship were her daily realities. To the enterprise of establishing the Sisters of St Joseph she could bring nothing but herself and, while knowing suffering would still be involved, a belief that "God can make us very happy even in this world".[65]

Living the "Ordinary"
A critical factor in the founding stories of the Sisters of St Joseph in France and in Australia is that these founders came from among the people they served. When Julian Tenison Woods reflected on his meeting with the Sisters of St Joseph in France he recalled:

> I had been accustomed to regard a nun as one on whom a great deal of money had to be spent, and who must be raised above the laboring classes, both in means and in education. I felt instinctively that a nun, to be one with the poor and a servant of the poor, should belong to the humbler classes, especially as the immense wants of the Church in that direction could only be effectively and abundantly recruited from that class. But when I saw how the want was supplied in France, I made up my mind that I would use all my efforts to extend these institutions to my own country.[66]

The six women who made up the first community in Le Puy, those who joined the Congregations in America and other countries, and the first members of the Sisters of St Joseph of

---
[65] Letter to her mother, Nov. 27, 1866. Archives, Sisters of St Joseph, Sydney.
[66] *Memoirs, J. E. T. Woods.*

the Sacred Heart in Australia, brought with them the traits that accompany an ability to find God in the ordinary life of the common people. These traits provide a number of distinguishing characteristics for the foundations of these Congregations.

Identification with the common people: "Home is where the heart is," they say. The type of housing chosen by Sisters of St Joseph can give an indication their hearts being among the people. In the early years of the Institute, the Sisters in France often lived in the same physical building, with their own quarters, as the people to whom they ministered – "the people could see the sisters living in their midst, and that their presence was often, in itself, constructive and apostolic".[67] Until the Revolution, this was the pattern: small country houses or accommodation shared with or in close proximity to the people. It is noteworthy that the Sisters in Vienne who, towards the end of the 1600s, accepted a number of noble ladies as members and obtained housing away from the hospital, were the one Congregation that became monastic. They did not survive the Revolution.

In 1853, the Sisters of St Joseph of Annecy were beginning a ministry at Chens. Sister Michael Bourne tells us that the sponsor, the Marquis de Costa de Beauregard, wanted them to live at his castle but they refused.

> "Poor religious do not live in castles!"
> "But everything will be provided gratis!"
> "Monsieur, we are very grateful for what you give us and we accept it as an alms, but in witness to our vow of poverty we must live in an ordinary house, earn our own living and do our own housework. If we depart from this God will not bless our apostolate."[68]

---

[67] Vacher, *Des régulières,* p 272.
[68] Bourne, *His Mercy is From Age to Age,* pp 76, 77.

The Sisters who went to St Louis in 1836 began their ministry in a log cabin where the boarders shared a dormitory (separated by a curtain) and so cold they had to shake the snow from the bedcovers and break the ice in their washing bowls each morning. When Mary MacKillop and her companions were moving from Penola to Adelaide in 1867, only people of means could afford the fabrics and furnishings shipped to South Australia from London. Mary warned Father Woods, then, that their home should be "particularly simple; it was to be neat and clean, but there were to be no carpets or nice curtains".[69]

It is a fact that large numbers of novices, health requirements and convenience has resulted over the years in large motherhouses being built and some convents being places "set apart", especially during the twentieth century. However, most people remember the simple house in suburbs or country towns, built next to the church or school perhaps, but no different in appearance from other people's houses. The heart of the Sisters was with the people they served.

Practicality: An ability to put your hand to anything, or at least to 'have a go', is another feature that has typified Sisters of St Joseph. From lace-making to teaching, to nursing, digging foundations for buildings, sewing clothes, running commercial businesses, farming, cooking and housekeeping – there isn't an occupation that Sisters of St Joseph haven't been involved in. To these projects they have often brought a hard-headedness that has won them the respect of their lay counterparts. Surviving documentation shows that in Le Puy, Sisters entered into market contracts for the lace they produced, reserving around 12% of the proceeds to live on, the rest supporting ministry and enabling women workers to supplement an otherwise meagre family income.[70] In 1766 for example, the inhabitants of Craponne

---

[69] Gardiner, *Mary MacKillop*, p. 64.
[70] Patricia Byrne. Lectures given at Concordia, June 2003. A particular instruction in the early Constitution written by Médaille was that Sisters should provide for poor single women

requested Royal *Lettres Patentes* from Louis XV in favour of the Sisters of St Joseph, arguing, "without the help of the lace making, what would become of this district?"[71]

The subject of cows comes up frequently in stories surrounding Sisters of St Joseph. In 1860, Mother Saint John Facemaz was General Superior of Carondelet. She had come from a little village in the mountains of Moutiers, France. When she arrived in Carondelet, she was asked what she could do. She said, "The only thing I know how to do is take care of cows and chickens." "And then," says De Vaublanc, "they made her Mistress of Novices and later Superior General!"[72]

Sister Xavier Cunningham, a pioneer of the Sisters of St Joseph of Concordia, received an award from the Holstein-Fresian Association of Kansas, "for notable accomplishments in building character in boys, in exemplifying improved practices in dairy farming and in breeding a superior herd of Holstein-Fresian cattle. .. Starting with two cows and no experience in dairying,…"[73]

A willingness to get involved in whatever might benefit the disadvantaged underlies many of the activities undertaken by the Sisters. In 1883, we are told, Sisters taught night school in New York "to accommodate children and adults who worked in the city's factories".[74] In South Australia in the 1890s, Sisters taught

---

who would otherwise in danger of "losing their honor; they (the Sisters) will work to lodge them somewhere and to give them the means to work at earning their living." Translation of *Constitutions for the Little Congregation of the Daughters of St Joseph* by Research Team, USA Federation of Sisters of St Joseph, 1979.

[71] Vacher, *Des régulières,* p. 262.
[72] De Vaublanc, "Sisters of Saint Joseph Today".
[73] Nephrology, Archives, Sisters of St Joseph of Concordia.
[74] Coburn & Smith, *Spirited Lives,* p. 135. The authors go on to note the cost to Sisters themselves, quoting the comments of a Sister: "Don't you remember the crowds of girls we had to teach at night after teaching all day? My eyes were nearly blind when we got through. Sisters Dominica and poor De Sales used to teach big young men with beards in the basement. It used to be ten o'clock before they got home. Then we had to do our washing and ironing on Saturday and take our turn to sit up with Mother Philomene every night until she died."

reading at night to illiterate adults at Burra, a copper-mining town where "ignorant Catholics" were a despised minority. In Africa, the pride of people at being able to write their name for the first time has given impetus to the Sisters whose belief in the dignity of each person urges them on.[75] Such scenarios have been repeated around the globe.

Particularly during periods of hardship, people have appreciated the practical hope of the Sisters. "When things were at their blackest during the Depression," said one Sister in Baden, USA, "our family could count on the Sisters. They would keep people's hope up. And I know they helped some people find work, including my father." Creativity and involvement in life is needed to be made in order to do things like that. During these same years, a Sister in Port Lincoln (South Australia) who did the cooking for the boarding school used her "spare time" in the afternoons to run sewing lessons for women so that they could make clothes for their families. The same response was made by a Sister-cook in Wanganui, New Zealand. "She had her head in heaven and her feet on the ground"[76] is a comment that has been made of many Sisters of St Joseph.

Part of Local Community: Separation of church and state did not exist in France prior to the Revolution, and so to be involved in church apostolate was to be involved in local community. Perhaps that is one reason why Sisters of St Joseph have understood themselves, in their foundational being, to be integrally concerned with issues broader than purely "religious". This is a trait found around the world.

Working to "improve social conditions" in the town has led Sisters, like those in Newport (Wales) in the 1870s, to organise small, manageable activities that helped people beyond Catholic

---

[75] Bourne, *His Mercy is From Age to Age,* p. 249.
[76] Said of Sister Jeanne Bird, Sisters of St Joseph of Orange. Geagley, *A Compassionate Presence,* p. 255.

circles see what they could do themselves. Bourne notes that at the time "it was no unusual thing to hear a girl say, 'Sister, we were bored when we had nothing to do. Now it's different'."[77] An 1880s account of Adelong, Australia, records:

> The Sisters not only taught religion and basic subjects but, through the children, introduced to the rugged, hardworking folk a gentle culture in the form of music and art. The harsh life of the women tended to be softened and refined by the influence of the Sisters and by the imitation of what was considered their 'orderly' methods of housekeeping.[78]

In our own time, Sisters like Sister Marie Charles in St Louis, USA, have become recognised "treasures" as their involvement in local affairs has brought a new sense of worth and dignity to otherwise depressed groups. In downtown Carondelet, Marie Charles noted that the run-down condition of a decaying slum area promoted a reputation for drug-dealing and general crime. With the involvement of Council and other "contacts", she began a scheme of buying old houses which they would then renovate and sell, which enabled them to buy others and do the same. The result is that the old part of the city has been rehabilitated and a new freshness and pride has spread to the whole neighbourhood. Practical, discreet help for the poor in the area further adds to a growing sense of community.

Remembering how the Sisters used to walk the streets after the evening meal, talking to those they met, one woman said, "The Sisters of St Joseph aren't 'holier than thou!' They act so normal! They're not plastic nuns!" Sisters playing in bands of the local town, taking part in fundraising activities for charities, helping with sports events, being available to baby-sit so that

---

[77] Bourne, *His Mercy is From Age to Age*, p. 131.
[78] Srs Michael Glass and Celsus O'Grady eds., *Their Story: 1882 – 1982*. Rhodes, Australia: Sisters of St Joseph of Goulburn, 1982. p. 9.

parents can take part in a parish retreat[79] or just have a night out – all of these things point out where God is.

Hard Work: Father Marius Nepper SJ in France describes Sisters of St Joseph as having their "sleeves rolled up for ministry".[80] With no knowledge of their Le Puy counterparts, an Australian songwriter writes of the Sisters of St Joseph here, and in particular, of Mary MacKillop,

> "She set out to make a difference
> in a roll-your-sleeves-up way."[81]

In every part of the world, it seems, there are Sisters of St Joseph who are known for their hard work. Bourne tells of Sister St John Paulie supervising construction work in India at the turn of the twentieth century:

> She was evidently a master-builder and would not accept any slovenly work from the men to whom she became "a terror". She not only supervised but she worked like a Trojan and expected everyone else to keep pace with her.[82]

Geagley comments on the "strong work ethic" of the Sisters of St Joseph of Orange.[83] Older Sisters there still recall the days when they taught all day and then came home to dig foundations for the new hospital building before the evening meal. "The girls have taken to the work like hot tamales," their foundress, Mother Bernard Gosselin, is reported to have said.[84]

Similarly, stories of Sisters getting up at 4.30 in the morning to do the community washing, to paint walls "before the neighbors were awake,"[85] to carry out repair work so that ministry could begin, or to complete university courses while doing full-time

---

[79] One interviewee told of a priest who asked if the Sisters in a city parish would babysit on a weekend gathering for families. They agreed to help out and he replied, "You can ask the St Joseph's to do anything. I've asked three other communities, and they wouldn't hear me out."
[80] Marius Nepper SJ. "Portrait of a Sister of St Joseph". See p. 130.
[81] James Long. "A Vision for Australia" in songbook, *If I Could Tell the Love of God*, p. 18.
[82] Bourne, *His Mercy is From Age to Age*, p. 197.
[83] Geagley, *A Compassionate Presence*, p. 83.
[84] Geagley, *A Compassionate Presence*, p. 114.
[85] Coburn and Smith, *Spirited Lives*, p. 214.

ministry – these are common in Josephite memory around the world. The following is a typical scenario:

> As a music teacher, you were teaching at night and all day Saturday, on the lunch hour and before school. .. I was going all day and Saturday from 9.00 in the morning to 4.00 in the afternoon. I also played the organ in church. I was doing some choir work in the classrooms at school. I was busy all the time.[86]

While the terms "workaholism" and "Sisters of St Joseph" have sometimes been synonymous, the reputation is one that has been gained largely out of the zeal Sisters have had for the apostolate, often in the face of extreme difficulties. Financial poverty was another factor – both on the part of the Sisters themselves, who had to make do with what was available, and on the part of the parishes and institutions in which they worked. They did not want "their" children to be deprived, so they worked harder. And when a sandstorm blows the wall down, for example,[87] and there are no builders in the isolated areas where Sisters often laboured, there is nothing else to do but to "roll up your sleeves" and start to remedy the situation.

However, a work ethic becomes a problem when work gets in the way of its purpose – growth into the heart of God, incarnate among us. The danger of Sisters gaining their sense of self from the amount of work they do is still one that some have to deal with, especially as they age. Father Médaille had warned the Sisters over three hundred years ago, "Let them also watch diligently to remove obstacles to the holiness of their vocation by too great a multiplicity of tasks."[88] Mary MacKillop had

---

[86] Elizabeth Smyth and Linda Wicks. *Wisdom Raises Her Voice,* Toronto: Sisters of St Joseph (Transcontinental Printing), 2001. p. 140. Permission for this author to use extracts from *Wisdom Raises Her Voice* and *Compassion Builds a House* (Bisson) as noted on p. 354.
[87] Glass and O'Grady, *Their Story,* p. 31. A sandstorm blew in one side of the school while classes were in progress in Wallendbeen, NSW (Australia).
[88] *Constitutions for the Little Congregation of the Daughters of St Joseph,* p. 9.

written in her time, "We must look before us, do what we do well and refuse undertaking too much."[89]

Egalitarianism: While the 17th century French class system was part of the ordinary world known by the Sisters in Le Puy, their lower class backgrounds introduced to the Sisterhood an element of comparative egalitarianism that would have been novel for those times. "Open to women of all classes, it did not limit its mission to any particular type of activity and did not require a large dowry, lengthy preparation for entrance, or education."[90]

In the "melting pot" of cultures in United States, this spirit was furthered by the steps taken in their American constitutions to safeguard against class (and ethnic) divisions in community by urging Sisters to lay aside "all worldly considerations of personal qualities, and of advantages, which they enjoyed in the world, all pretensions to privileges and favors …, (so that they may) labor with perfect union of will to procure the glory of God and the salvation of their neighbour".[91]

Unity was the concern of Mary MacKillop, too, in upholding the egalitarianism that was a mark of the Sisterhood she founded. Some Catholics of the time, especially priests, were shocked by the fact that no dowry was required to be a Sister of St Joseph and that their membership, drawn from all classes, admitted of no distinctions. Mary MacKillop suffered much because she refused to divide the Sisters into "choir" and "lay" Sisters.
When Bishop Sheil threatened to introduce this division in a revised rule, Mary explained that she could not be part of such a Congregation since such changes went against everything that

---

[89] Letter to Sister Raymond, Provincial, New Zealand, 15 August 1900. The context was concern about the overwork of Sisters. Archives, Sisters of St Joseph, Sydney.
[90] Coburn and Smith, *Spirited Lives,* p. 26.
[91] *Constitution,* Sisters of St Joseph, 1860. Quoted by Coburn & Smith, *Spirited Lives,* p. 87.

she believed about the spirit given by God to the Sisters of St Joseph.[92]

To be identified with the ordinary people, Sisters needed to be sensitive to what would alienate them. Mary was in touch with the Australian culture where class distinctions would belie a belief in the presence of God in each person. Sisters of St Joseph elsewhere in the world were soon to express the same belief by doing away with a system of "choir" and "lay" Sisters that had grown up in post-Revolutionary France.

Awareness of God's Presence: It is one thing to be identified with the common people, but to have the eyes and ears to know the ordinary as the place of God's self-revelation requires reflection on the deeper meaning of daily routines. Faith sees beneath appearances.

To ensure Sisters had opportunity to bring the light of faith to bear on their lives, Father Médaille arranged for structures to be built into the their timetable for such reflection:
> Both the Constitutions and Règlements ask the sisters constantly to review their experience in prayer, in the service of the neighbor, and in community life. This review was done by individuals daily in the examen; and as a community weekly in the Sunday conference, as well as at special times set apart monthly and yearly. Why? Not to keep a moral scorecard, but to search, individually and corporately, for the action of grace among them, to take cognizance of whether or not they were responding, in order that they might know and follow God's desire.[93]

These same structures were part of the rule for Sisters of St Joseph of the Sacred Heart in Australia. Daily meditation and practices such as ringing a "Presence of God" bell at intervals

---

[92] Mary MacKillop to Bishop Sheil, September 10th, 1871.
[93] Patricia Byrne. "Re-conceiving Identity in a Time of Crisis". Paper presented for the U.S. Federation of the Sisters of St. Joseph 'Sound the Trumpets' National Event, June 27, 2000. p. 13.

during recreation had the same goal of lifting the heart to God in the circumstances in which Sisters found themselves.[94]

Structures also allowed for periods of silence in order to give space for Sisters to listen to their interior "voice", God at the centre of our being. A problem arose, however, when this structure became an end in itself. Not all newly-professed had the advantage of having a superior like one Sister who recalled that to go shopping seemed to be the prime time for them to do "pastoral visitation". After her first experience, the then-young Sister hesitantly said to the superior, "I thought we weren't supposed to talk to people in the street". Her Irish-born superior answered, "Ah, to be sure, my dear, Jesus would expect us to!"

It might have helped other young Sisters to come to a similar judgement had they known that when Father Médaille wrote the rule about "keeping silence in crowded places" he was actually talking about public toilets![95] While many Sisters could see the point of observing silence at night in order to foster "recollection and union with God"[96] in one's heart, the dilemma caused by seemingly opposing spirits of engagement with God's people and yet conforming to what was a decorum issue did not make sense[97]. One Sister-nurse who attended on her death-bed an Australian ex-Mother General who had imposed this rule most strictly and had forbidden Sisters to speak to parishioners outside the church, heard the dying, now-mellowed Sister say, "Where are the Sisters? They're in their parishes, talking to the people!" "That rule didn't fit us!" said

---

[94] The Le Puy Sisters of St Joseph were instructed, "During the day, one of the Sisters, at least hourly, will be responsible for reminding the others of the presence of God". *The Règlements*, p. 11

[95] Byrne, Notes of lecture, June 2003.

[96] *Constitutions for the Little Congregation of the Daughters of St Joseph,* p. 34.

[97] In interviews with older Sisters right around the world, problems with the rule of silence as written in former rules came up in all interviews and had been a constant neuralgic point in their lives.

one interviewee. Yet in the modern world of constant noise, the challenge to nourish a consciousness of God's presence in the depths of our own being and in our encounters with others and creation is now greater than ever.

The structure of communal prayer provides the orientation for Sisters' service. After devotional prayers together, the Sisters in Le Puy were instructed by Médaille to also share "the experiences of their meditation in humility and candor with each other".[98] Because the contemplation of God was to be *in* the apostolate, "Divine Office has never been a part of the spiritual traditions handed down and lived in the communities of St Joseph in the course of the centuries".[99] Community Prayer Books attest to the fact that, until Vatican II, the common prayers of the Sisters were, like those of most Catholics, devotional – litanies, the Rosary, the Little Office of the Virgin Mary on specific days, and so on.[100]

While these exercises presume a common faith, they do not encourage the bonding that comes with exchange of spiritual convictions. Efforts have been made by Sisters of St Joseph in recent years to retrieve the primitive practice of "sharing of the heart" in community prayer and/or theological reflection groups.

Finding God in the ordinary ideally results in Sisters being led
> to penetrate more deeply
> into the mystery and mission of Christ
> in the one movement of prayer and service.[101]

However, especially with the rise of Jansenism, a spirit of dualism tended to separate prayer and action as well as the Sisters' life inside and outside the house, even while the presence of God was being sought in the apostolate. Vacher

---

[98] *Règlements*, p. 9.
[99] Vacher, *Des régulières,* Session Three, p. 122.
[100] Members of lay sodalities often recited the same prayers.
[101] *Constitutions of the Sisters of St Joseph of the Sacred Heart*, 1986, p. 6.

explains, "in spite of their good will and their desire to support the sisters in their spiritual life, the pastors and other ecclesiastical delegates were not always in a position to understand how an authentic consecrated life could be lived in the world".[102]

Thus, the language of "leaving the world" and being in opposition to "the world" adhered to the thought patterns of Catholics of the time regarding apostolic Religious life. Father Woods used fighting words in admonishing his Sisters at Lochinvar in 1887 to "strictly keep your rule in its letter and its spirit, and like the stones in the sling of David, you will be weapons with which the Sacred Heart will defeat the pride and the infidelity of the world".[103]

Customs such as Sisters eating apart from "seculars" accentuated the dichotomy between "normal" life and "sacred" life. According to records of Chapters[104] of Sisters of St Joseph of the Sacred Heart during the 1880s into the 1920s – a period when, in the normal life cycle of organisations, uniformity becomes an issue – legislation was made precluding Sisters from attending "funerals of seculars"[105] and pointing out that "Sisters should not absent themselves from Community Exercises to entertain visitors".[106]

Similar tensions were experienced by other Sisters of St Joseph in integrating "secular" studies with their "spiritual" apostolate, and, for example, "being trapped in a choice between 'modern science' and medieval religious practices ... between staying

---

[102] Vacher, *Des régulières,* Session Six, p. 368.
[103] Letter, Father Woods to Sisters of St Joseph at Lochinvar, Australia, 9th September, 1887. Archives, Sisters of St Joseph of Lochinvar.
[104] "Chapters" are the policy-making meetings of the Congregation. They are attended by elected delegates of the Sisters and bears the highest authority for the Congregation.
[105] Chapter of the Sisters of St Joseph, 1881. Archives, Sisters of St Joseph, Sydney, Australia. A proviso was added, "Of course they attend those of priests or religious."
[106] Chapter of the Sisters of St Joseph, 1916. Archives, Sisters of St Joseph, Sydney, Australia.

with a patient or making it to prayers on time",[107] and so on. In effecting the teachings of Vatican II, Sisters of St Joseph have found themselves reclaiming their heritage where apostolic and charitable activities of the sisters flow from the consecration of their life to God. Apostolic action becomes the expression, the manifestation of the mystical life.

The description of a Sister of St Joseph entitled "The Legacy of Mother Rose" summarises the features of those seeking "God in the ordinary":

> How does one describe Mother Rose, who became a legend in her lifetime? The tall imposing figure standing for hours under the hot sun, shuttling up and down in city buses, shaking her head with impatience, patting a worker on the back and walking with her arms around the shoulder of village women, sharing jokes with her friends, playing the piano and singing like an angel, quick to get annoyed but just as quickly breaking out into a wonderful and unforgettable smile – these are the images that flash across our minds when we think of Mother. Her all embracing compassion extended even to thieves and criminals whom she refused to hand over to the bewildered police, firm in the hope of reforming them. Her indomitable courage that neither power nor position could bend and her charisma that won the hearts of the rich, the famous, the elite, as well as the poorest of the poor, have made her the adored Mother of thousands in Madurai (India).[108]

3.3 PART THREE: The spirit lives into the now

Dualism

How is the spirit of Joseph that finds "God in the ordinary" expressed in our time? Today, many people seek out spirituality not in the ordinary circumstances of life but in the occult, in the psychic or the exotic. There is a dualistic attitude to life.

---

[107] Coburn and Smith, *Spirited Lives,* pp. 202, 203.
[108] Unpublished paper, archives, Sisters St Joseph of Lyon, Winslow, Maine, USA.

Spirituality is on a different plain from one's interaction with the business world, for example.

Dualism also establishes a deep divide between daily life and religion, and even between spirituality and religion. We often hear it said, at least in the western world, "I'm spiritual but I'm not religious". For many, religion is dogma and rules. It is not integrated with daily life nor with spirituality. And yet there is a longing for this connection. David Ranson says:

> The ever increasing popularity of the New Age movement has taught us is that people, paradoxically, hunger for a sense of the sacred in life, for the mystique of life and for a new sense of connection with the earth. People desire that the 'natural' become enchanted once again.[109]

There is, then, a two-fold task for evangelisation today. One is to make connections between ordinary life and spirituality. The other is to connect spirituality and religion. If those who share the spirit of Joseph are to play an active role in awakening ourselves and our world to "God in the ordinary", then we must use the processes that form a conscious connection between people's approaches to daily life, spirituality and religion.

<u>Integrating spirituality and religion with daily life</u>
Ranson explains that, because spirituality is linked to consciousness, the same processes operate in both. Following the theories of Canadian philosopher, Bernard Lonergan, he identifies four "moments" in the thought-patterns of spirituality.[110] First, something catches our attention. It might be a piece of music, a beautiful scene, a terrifying happening. Something stirs us. He calls this moment, *"attending"*. The second moment is when we allow ourselves to deepen the experience. We give expression to it in some way – writing,

---

[109] David Ranson., *Across the Great Divide: Bridging Spirituality and Religion Today,* Sydney: St Pauls Publications, 2002. pp 43, 44.
[110] Ranson, *Across the Great Divide*, pp. 18–33.

painting, dancing, for example. This he calls the *"inquiring"* moment. Often, that is as far as many people take the experience. It is "personal". But it is foundational. Without it, much of "religion" can be barren or meaningless.

It is when we take our personal experience to the next level that we touch into "religion". We evaluate our experience against the collective wisdom of those who have gone before us, the deposit of faith. In this *"interpreting"* moment, we find religious meaning in, for example, the birth of a child, when we touch into an understanding of God who is total love. Alternatively, our personal experience throws light on our religious tradition. Against the experience of giving birth, a mother can "hear" God say:
> Can a woman forget her sucking child
> that she should have no compassion on the child of her womb?
> Even these may forget, yet I will not forget you.[111]

The final moment of the Cycle of Spirituality described by Ranson is the *"acting"* moment. In prayer, communal worship, ethical action and a lifestyle directed to compassionate justice, the cycle is completed: spirituality is integrated into life. In turn, this leads to further "moments", so that the movement begins again and the cycle continues. Against this model, the Cycle of Spirituality, we will now note different ways in which the spirit of Joseph finds "God in the ordinary" today.

In 1972, a group of Sisters from different Congregations of Sisters of St Joseph in France formed a community of "Worker Sisters" whose mission was to transpose into the modern era the ideals of the first Sisters – to be inserted into the world as the place of meeting God. These Sisters of today had *attended* to the beckoning of an awareness that in France, the Church had, in

---
[111] Isaiah 49:15.

general, been lost to the world of the worker. In the *inquiring* phase, they connected this fact to their own process of "finding their roots" as Sisters of St Joseph among the people. Their personal reflections were brought both to their own Congregations and to the wider Federation of Sisters of St Joseph, and *interpreted* in the context of experimentation then going on among the Sisters in response to Vatican II.

At first, the Sisters connected the proposed enterprise with the need to *bring* Christ to the workplace. They quickly realised, however, that Christ was already there – their role was to recognise him there.[112] "Would working in a factory be considered an apostolate?" they asked. Answers connected opportunities for pastoral ministry and engagement with workers against exploitation – was not this the place of the "double union"?[113] *Acting* brought the Sisters to the decision to form the Groupe Monde Ouvrier de la Fédération Saint Joseph and to put aside their professional qualifications in order to take on menial jobs among those barely touched by Church concern.

The cycle of *attending, inquiring, interpreting* and *acting* has been repeated over the years as the group reaches a different stage in its identity and mission. They have examined the limits of what they are able to accomplish and the further implications for mission of relationships they have made. Their experience has been one of following Christ who became human and, through living for others so that they might have life, meeting the God who is self-gift.[114] "This is our way of living the Incarnation, our apostolic Religious life," says one of the Sisters.[115]

---

[112] Groupe Monde Ouvrier de la Fédération Saint Joseph. "Engagées,Envoyées,Engagées dans un peuple." Reflection paper, May 2003. p. 12. Translation mine.
[113] Groupe Monde Ouvrier , "Engagées,Envoyées,Engagées", p. 10.
[114] Groupe Monde Ouvrier , "Engagées,Envoyées,Engagées", p. 6.
[115] Groupe Monde Ouvrier , "Engagées,Envoyées,Engagées", p. 14.

Similarly, Sisters from Rochester saw the gap between the ordinary world of the people they identified with as Josephite and that which media and popular stereotype has assigned them, quite apart from where the Spirit calls. After reflection with their community, two of them were authorised to open a Realty business (a real estate agency), to "serve low income buyers and sellers and to contribute our earnings to the Sisters of St Joseph of Rochester" [116] – although the clientele is now extended to those from every income level.

The same call to express the charism of finding God in the ordinary world of people's concerns has led some Sisters of St Joseph in Australia to explore ministry beyond Church-run organisations. In such cases, the salaries earned are handed on, after tax, to the Congregation, in order to fund ministries in poorer areas where stipends cannot be paid. A Congregational "Discernment Process" following the four phases ensures the connection of spirituality and action. Regular review is held with a Sisters' support group. Working with a government agency among a disadvantaged group, for example, one Sister was advised not to use the title, "Sister". It was not long, however, before one person asked, "Miss, are you a nun?" "Yes, I am. Does that bother you?" "No. But I thought you must have been. You treat us nicer than other people." Another has found that, while she must keep the boundaries of work responsibilities quite clear, staff come to her for personal advice on spiritual matters, even though they have stated they would never go near a church or priest. "It's a real John the Baptist role," said the Sister concerned. "You try to be the face of Christ and to meet him there where he's not recognised yet."

---

[116] From brochure, "Sheila Walsh Realty Inc."

An awareness of the alienation of youth to the organised Church led the Italian Province of the Sisters St Joseph of Chambéry to make ministry to youth a focus after a recent Chapter. Realising that the interpreting of their spirit into the language of youth needed to be done by younger Sisters, the Province handed over the project to such a group, giving them full responsibility for its shape and providing appropriate avenues of communication and accountability with leadership. The process of *attending, inquiring, interpreting* and *acting* has resulted in a new vigour within the Congregation, a sense of engagement with "real life" and great hope. New membership of the Sisterhood has resulted, even though this was in no way the aim of the project. "I was struck by the fact that these Sisters were 'normal' young people like me" said one woman, "and they made me realise that God is part of ordinary life."

Associates in Peru see themselves as "co-missionaries" with the Sisters, walking with their compatriots who have even less than themselves, ready to learn in inquiry from them and carrying that into the action of service in practical ways. A Sister's reflection on their experience recalls the Le Puy scene of the mid-1600s:

> As time went on, women's reflection groups expanded into centres for learning crafts that might be useful or relaxing. Sometimes (these have given) rise to cooperative efforts for the production of goods for sale to augment a little the meagre income. This can be carried out in a workshop situation or by working from home. Rewards are reaped slowly, with hard work and a tenacity of hope which women, and occasionally their husbands, bring to the enterprise.

Partnership with lay groups

Older Sisters of St Joseph are aware that partnership in mission with lay people must be developed in order to promote Joseph's spirit of "finding God in the ordinary" and "incarnating God's presence". "There were always lay people who worked closely with us," said one Sister. "We just didn't call them Associates.

I don't know about us sharing our spirituality though – we got them to work with us, not pray with us. Unless it was something like 'Pray for a special intention'. Maybe they thought we were the holy ones and their job was to do the work? But we always worked with them. We have to do that better now."

"Doing it better" will involve helping groups bring the cycle of *attending, inquiring, interpreting* and *acting* to bear on their daily lives. The characteristics which accompany the process of finding God in the ordinary – practicality, hard work, identification with the common people and thus egalitarianism, involvement in the local community and its concerns, and the integration of prayer and life in the "one movement", finding there the "double union" of ourselves with God and each other, all with a good dose of "common sense" – these will speak to our world. Members of the group of young people, "Josephite Community Aid", say the same thing in other words:

> We try to be generous in spite or our own poverty. Included in generosity is the spirit of practicality and hard work. There is a sense of seeing something that needs doing, assessing the situation, and then rolling up our sleeves and doing it. It is an 'earthy generosity' of being prepared to get our hands dirty. It is a 'practical holiness'.[117]

---

[117] JCA pamphlet, "Our Spirit".

Portrait of a Sister of St Joseph

Eyes open on a world both miserable and sinful
    but a world worked on by the Holy Spirit;

Eyes open and ears attentive to the sufferings of the world
    like St Paul to the pleas of the Macedonians (Acts 16:9);

Eyes open, ears attentive and spirit alert, never settled down,
    always in a holy disquietude, searching, in order
    to understand, to divine
    what God and the dear neighbour await from her today
    now, for the body and for the soul;

Eyes open, east attentive, spirit alert .... sleeves rolled up
    for ministry, without excluding the more humble,
    the less pleasing, the less noticeable;

Finally, in her face the reflection of the virtue
    "proper to our Congregation",
    continual joy of spirit.
    This is the quiet inner glow of the sister
    whose life in the service of Jesus Christ
    has been successful.

Marius Nepper SJ

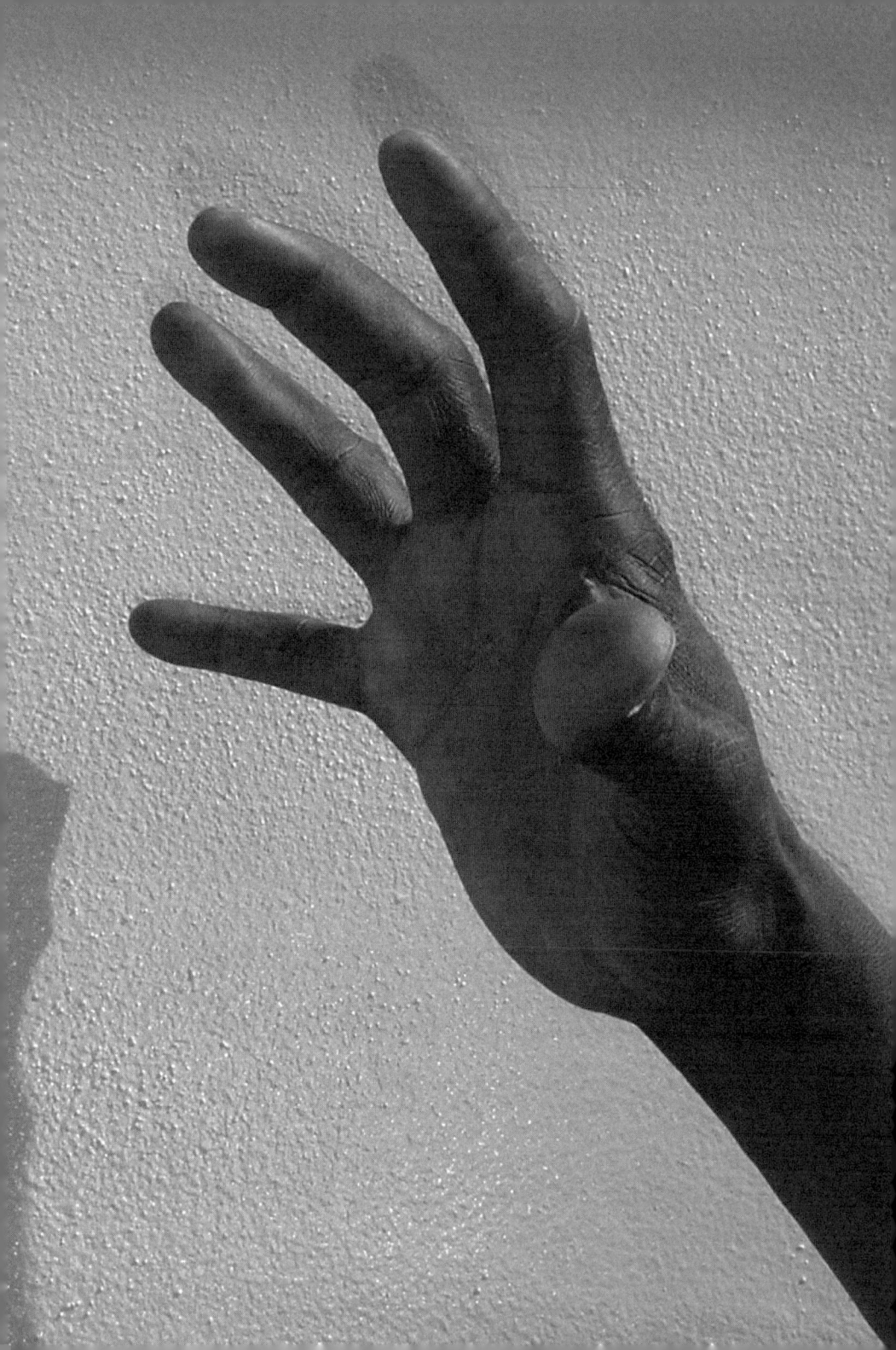

CHAPTER FOUR

The Spirit of Joseph ……

acts justly.

Now Joseph was a just man (Mt. 1:19).

4.1 PART ONE: The spirit is revealed

Justice and religion
When did it happen that people came to accept that war will be directed against innocent civilians? Wars have always had their non-combatant victims, but, in general, history describes them as taking place on "battlefields" where rules of warfare engaged the "skills" of soldiers trained for the purpose. Perhaps the dropping of the atomic bomb on the ordinary citizens of Japan in 1945 was a threshold point. Albert Einstein commented at the time: "The release of atomic power has changed everything except our way of thinking … the solution to this problem lies in the heart of mankind."[1]

If human beings are ever to find ways of resolving differences with each other peacefully, especially at the international level, the root causes of problems have to be addressed. Because these involve attitudes of justice, fair-mindedness and tolerance, Indian Jesuit Kuruvilla Pandikattu claims that religion is vitally involved:
> What truly touches the heart of the human person is religion! Religions, particularly the institutional varieties, have been responsible for promoting violence, hatred and inhuman behaviour toward the 'out-groups'. Without denying these

---

[1] Quoted in Kuruvilla Pandikattu SJ, "Spiritual Information for Integral Transformation", *Compass* Vol 37: Autumn 2003. p. 31.

tragic aspects of religions, we can assert that ... in the realm of values and world-views, religions have the source of knowledge to respond positively to the challenges posed by modern science (*and, I would add, economic theories*) and the inadequate world views fostered by it (*them*).[2]

Justice and Scripture

So what light can our religion throw on the question of justice? Not everyone accepts that religion and justice go together. And yet the theme of justice is constant throughout Scripture. Justice, according to writings of the Old Testament, is based on the relationship the Israelites have with God. If they conform and are faithful to the covenant God has established with them, and therefore to their obligations to the community of Israel, people are described as 'righteous' or 'just'.

Covenant justice is action resulting from "a relation of fellowship between partners".[3] This applies to relations between both humans among themselves and humans and God. To be just, according to Scripture, means to be free from any fault which would damage communion with each other. According to Isaiah, doing "justice" is going out towards the other to remove whatever is getting in the way of partnership.[4]

Two added notions of justice are found in Wisdom literature and in the Psalms. One is that we must go beyond the basic requirements of mere giving and taking between equals – for instance, between a trader and a customer in the exchange of goods for money. Instead, we are urged to practise sympathy and compassion toward those of lower status so that they can be treated as equals. Those who offend against what today we would call "social justice" are condemned:
    You have .. stripped the naked of their clothing,

---

[2] Pandikattu, "Spiritual Information for Integral Transformation", p. 31. Italics mine.
[3] Klaus Blerger, "Justice", in Karl Rahner ed., *The Concise Sacramentum Mundi*, Crossroad, NY, 1975. 788.
[4] Is 53:11.

> You have given no water to the weary to drink, and you have withheld bread from the hungry.
> The man with power possessed the land, and the favoured man dwelt in it.
> You have sent widows away empty, and the arms of the fatherless were crushed.[5]

The object of justice – fairness, mercy and generosity – is the stranger, the innocent, and especially the poor (the orphan and widow). "Speak up for those who cannot speak for themselves, defend the rights of those who have nothing. Speak up and judge fairly, and defend the rights of the poor and needy," says Proverbs.[6]

Marian Cowan CSJ[7] notes that, because of their experience of God and heightened awareness of sin, prophets became in themselves a sign of justice. "Many times the 'very life' of the prophet, for example, Hosea and Jeremiah, was the form that the message took," she says.[8] To be prophetic was to signify in one's life, work and teaching how and where the barriers to justice might be found. Prophets did not set themselves up to be so – hindsight enabled the community to see in their lives the word of God calling it to justice. False prophets, however, did claim God's authority, manipulating the signs for their own ends and identifying God with what was popular.

In particular, Old Testament writings assign works of justice to kings.[9] It is the task of royalty (we can substitute the word "government" in our day) to remove whatever in society gets in the way of subjects living their partnership with God and each

---

[5] Job 22:6-9
[6] Proverbs 31:8-9. See also Ps. 82:3, Jer 7:5-6, Is 1:17.
[7] The letters "CSJ" stand for "Congregation of St Joseph". Other initials used by different groups of Sisters of St Joseph are "SSJ" ("Sisters of ..") and "RSJ" ("Religious of ..").
[8] Marian Cowan. "Professional Prophets", Religious Education Congress, Feb 17, 1978. Reported in *The Denver Catholic Register*, Feb 22, 1978.
[9] 1Sam 24:18; 26:23; 2 Sam 8:15; 1 Kg 3:6; 10:9

other. So justice is an essential quality of the work proper to those entrusted with governing power.

Analogously, justice is attributed to God, since it is "the just one" who enables us to be in relationship with the divine. Isaiah applies the term in particular to the son of David who is to come – the "holy and righteous one"[10] will remove all barriers between humanity and God and will enable all peoples to live together in peace:
> The suckling child shall play over the hole of the asp
> And the weaned child shall put his hand on the adder's den.
> They shall not hurt or destroy in all my holy mountain,
> For the earth shall be full of the knowledge of the Lord.[11]

The just are pronounced blessed not by reason of individual acts of kindness but in view of their lives as a whole – their relationship with God and neighbour.

With the New Covenant, Paul claims, there is a change of focus. Instead of the source of justice being located in observance of the Law of Moses, it is now found in being in relationship with Christ. By his death, Christ has removed all barriers between us and God; his action of justice has made us just.[12] Therefore, Christians are to live "just" lives – in ways consistent with the new life of the Spirit that flows from Christ's saving work.[13]

In summary, then, Scripture describes justice as being at once ethical and religious. Justice is a gift of God and a response to the grace ("justice") of God. The early Fathers of the Church called on this understanding to claim that justice demands that we always work for the common good. Because everything we have has been received from God, who gives us life and talent to benefit from the gift of creation, we cannot claim anything as

---

[10] Is 11:1ff, Acts 3:14.
[11] Is 11:8-9.
[12] 2 Cor 5:21; Rom 5:16; Rom 14:7
[13] Rom 3:30, 1 Cor 6:11. In particular, James 1:27 cites "religion that is pure and undefiled" as including "social justice" – care of the orphans and widows.

being absolutely and exclusively our own. We are, then, required by justice to use our goods to aid the needy neighbour with whom we form one Body in Christ; through our actions the justice of God can then reach them.

Ancient philosophy also gives a religious flavour to justice. Plato relates it to the supreme good. He explains that everything that exists is essentially made to function in a way which comes directly from the form of the good. Things should be structured in such a way that they can fulfil their function. This applies to individuals and society. Injustice results if they deviate from acting in the way that makes themselves or others capable of performing their proper function.

<u>What is justice?</u>
Given this religious context, how do we define "justice"? The word is derived from the Latin "*ius*" which means a "right". Justice is concerned with rights, and the duties which correspond to those rights. A right is the power to do whatever is necessary to achieve the end or purpose for which we are destined. Each person has a moral claim to the means of carrying out this basic responsibility. Because people develop fully only in a social context, and because rights of individuals do impinge on others' rights, justice and its operation needs to take into account the reality of inevitable conflicts and the demands for harmonisation of rights. Social Justice deals with this question.

As opposed to moralism, which might urge unselfish love to address conflict, Social Justice sets up systems to orient society towards protection of rights. It is possible, for example, for individuals to be "moral" – kind, forgiving, patient, compassionate, etc., – but for society itself to be unjust. A prime instance is the system of slavery which operated for so long in our society.

It is important, too, to distinguish between "society" and "State" when we speak of Social Justice. The interaction of shared customs, laws and organisational elements such as politics, economics and religion that influence community relationships go to make up "society". The "State" is the centre of political power and organisation, be it of the whole body (the citizens) or of the institution which actually governs (the government). The primary purpose of the latter is to maintain order and security by means of law.[14] Through the government, the burdens and benefits of societal life are distributed so that the community can attain its function – e.g. the administration of taxes to ensure basic needs are met, such as housing, health and education.

The teachings of Vatican II, particularly in the documents "Church in the Modern World" and "Declaration on Religious Freedom", presume a notion of Social Justice that recognises the God-given dignity of the human person, the common good and the inviolability of conscience and freedom.[15]

But we cannot presume that all societies will base their systems of justice on Christian or Catholic principles. Philosophies with wide impact on world affairs such as those of the Age of Enlightenment, Marxist socialism and others, do not base themselves on religious notions of justice.

In his encyclical *Populorum Progressio,* Paul VI drew attention to the effects of the "spirit of capitalism" where the laws of economics become a focus in themselves, no longer dependent on nor serving the value of the human being or the norms of religion and social ethics.[16] Justice, in this climate, obeys the

---

[14] Encyclopaedia Britannica Vol 17, Hemingway Benton, USA, 1981. p. 609.
[15] Austin Flannery ed., *The Conciliar and Post Conciliar Documents of Vatican Council II,* Dublin: Dominican Publications, 1975. Ref. especially, *Church in the Modern World,* Nos. 12, 16, 17, 24, 26, 27, 29, 36.
[16] Paul VI, *Populorum Progressio,* art. 26.

conventions of negotiated contracts within the framework of the law of supply and demand.

Joseph and justice

Why, then, do Sisters of St Joseph all around the world feel compelled to enter into the struggle for justice? We are told in Matthew's Gospel that Joseph was a "just" man.[17] Anne Hennessy points out that in the context of his society, builders like Joseph travelled with their trade group from town to town to work. She is of the opinion that they were regarded as "just" "because these men could study the Law with various synagogue groups".[18] From their wide study of the Law of Moses, they knew what God's will was and therefore did not share the "uncleanliness" of ignorant groups such as shepherds.

In other words, Joseph was a man who lived according to Covenant justice. It is in this religious context of justice as right relationship with God and neighbour that those who share the spirit of Joseph find themselves.[19] Like Joseph, they are attentive to God's will in their lives. Because they see the will of God is for all peoples to live in communion with God and each other, they go out to do whatever is in their power to remove barriers to this ideal.

Instinctively, it would seem, people of different eras have associated Joseph with this justice that enables the reign of God to be established among us – that promotes the common good and recognises the dignity of all persons. For example, Leo XIII called on fallen nobility in late nineteenth-century Europe to see in Joseph an example of one who, though he could claim "royal

---

[17] Mt. 1:19.
[18] Hennessy, *In Search of a Patron,* p. 44.
[19] "Justice is a special Matthean emphasis ... and refers for the most part to the human response of obedience to the Father's will." Benedict Viviano, in Raymond Brown ed., *The New Jerome Biblical Commentary*, London: Geoffrey Chapman, 1989. p. 632.

blood", took his place alongside those who worked with their hands and whose right to sustenance was no less than his.[20] Similarly, in the traumatised world of rising atheistic communism, Pius XI insisted on the dignity of the worker, saying of Joseph:

> In a life of faithful performance of everyday duties he left an example for all those who must gain their bread by the toil of their hands. He won for himself the title of the Just, serving thus as a living model of that Christian justice which should reign in social life.[21]

Joseph and the justice of compassion

Our understanding of justice is extended, however, when we are presented with Joseph's response to dilemma. Faced with the fact that his betrothed, Mary, was pregnant not by him, he went beyond literal law to enable compassion in order to right the balance of relationships between them. The punishment for women found not to be virgins at the time of marriage, according to Deut. 22:20-21, was stoning. Louise Perrotta comments:

> Just how strictly this law was implemented in Joseph's day is unknown. However that may be, *something* unpleasant was clearly the norm for a woman in Mary's position – an unpleasantness Joseph was unwilling to inflict. A trial, perhaps (a procedure for a "trial by ordeal" of an adulterous wife is described in Numbers 5:11-31), or a public accusation of adultery through which a wronged husband might establish his own innocence and his right to keep the dowry.[22]

The Hebrew word for 'compassion' comes from the root *rhm,* as does the word for 'womb'. It is not by accident that compassion is associated with what is promotive of life, what nourishes it and protects it. Compassion demands a love which puts the other before self and that is willing to give of one's own life for

---

[20] Leo XIII, *Quamquam Pluries* (encyclical), Aug. 15, 1889.
[21] Pius XI, *Divini Redmptoris* (encyclical), March 19, 1937.
[22] Perrotta, *Saint Joseph,* pp. 33, 34.

the other to flourish. When we love "with passion",[23] we can easily put ourselves in the shoes of the other in order to feel with them and to reach out in love. A reflection on teachings of St Francis de Sales, whose spirituality had a strong influence on these French Sisters of St Joseph, describes compassion in these words:

> Compassionate love exemplifies our solidarity with others and especially makes us realise our common human vulnerability, our mutual interdependence and our need to be with those who are suffering. It makes us see the interconnectedness of our lives.[24]

Pope John Paul II calls the ability to temper a strict interpretation of legal justice with compassion an "inner justice".

> Precisely because of this inner justice, which in the last analysis coincides with love, Joseph does not decide to repudiate Mary, when he learns of her incipient pregnancy. He resolves to divorce her quietly, but the angel of the Lord asks him not to fear and to take her to himself.[25]

The inner justice of compassion restored the relationship between Joseph and his beloved. With Mary he would step into the mystery of God's workings. His Spirit-led action also enabled a larger restoration of relationships. The coming of the Messiah would usher in the reign of God,[26] making it possible for all to accept life in perfect relationship with God and each other. Through Jesus, we have the means of being part of God's reign and helping our world achieve it.

---

[23] The Latin word "com" which is part of the English "compassion", means "with".
[24] Alexander Pocetto, "Compassionate Love and Salesian Spirituality". http://2224.allencol.edu/~salesian/salesian.html.
[25] Zenit.org., Pope's Angelus Address on Fourth Sunday of Advent, Vatican City, Dec. 23, 2001.
[26] A. A. Sicari, "Joseph Justus" in *Atti del Primo Simposio Internazionale*, Roma: Libreria Editrice Murildo, 1971. p. 68.

It is in the Eucharist that the fullness of God's reign is announced, signified and foreshadowed. Jesus shared his table with the outcast and rejected. Sinners found acceptance and the poor were assured of God's favour. When we partake of the one Bread of Life, we come together, all equal, as one Body in Christ. The grace of God's justice can operate in and through us; no barriers remain between us and the God who unites us with each other.

4.2 PART TWO: The spirit unfolds.

Promoting justice in a world of systematised injustice
Seventeenth century Médaille and the six founders of the Sisters of St Joseph, and even nineteenth century Woods and Mary MacKillop, would not have applied the term "justice" to their efforts to bring a sense of dignity and worth to the disadvantaged. The recovery of the Biblical sense of the word is relatively recent in Catholic circles, with scripture scholars playing a prominent part in opening up to us the connection between justice and *communio* – union of God and neighbour. Previously, manuals of moral theology spoke only of legal and contractual justice – even social justice was a novelty.[27]

However, the Biblical notions of "doing justice" are precisely the focus of Médaille's constitutions, namely, to bring all into union with God and each other by aspiring "to provide for all the spiritual and temporal needs of the dear neighbour".[28] The *Rules of the Institute of St Joseph* written by Woods in 1867 likewise state that union with God ("they must belong

---

[27] The acknowledgement of Social Justice by Pope Leo XIII, *Rerum Novarum* 1890, was considered in its time to be an innovation.
[28] *Constitutions for the Little Congregation of the Daughters of St Joseph* p. 7.

completely to Him") and neighbour ("recognising in them... the person of .. Jesus") is the underlying "object" of their service.[29]

It would take a shift in social consciousness to change attitudes towards class and the conviction that God's Will assigned certain rights to the high-born which were not extended to peasantry.[30] So notions of justice in the seventeenth century did not envisage changing the system upon which this society was built. While the French Revolution incorporated notions of equality, its repercussions would take many years before they became part of general thinking.

In 1832, Julian Tenison Woods had been born into the upper class in England and had retained many of its attitudes of superiority, even though he was adamant that the Sisters' primary concern was service of the poor.[31] Mary MacKillop, born ten years later in Australia, was on the cusp of changing awareness. Well educated herself, tutored in the main by her father, she knew full well of the injustice of class-consciousness in an egalitarian country. A humiliating episode in which a family member of her employer snubbed her at a ball because she was "just an employee" was one that lived on in her memory. Marie Foale explains Mary's early resistance to Sisters teaching instrumental music:

> Her reasons were threefold. Firstly, she believed that a piano should have no place in a poor man's home as she knew of

---

[29] Woods' wording of the first section, "Objects of the Institute" lacks the systematisation of Médaille. Indeed, when Mary MacKillop took the Constitution to Rome for approval, it was judged "very imperfect and confused". Although the spirit and much of the wording of the first rule was handed down in the *Book of Instructions* for the Sisters, the actual Constitution was handed on by Cardinal Franchi of Propaganda to be re-written by Raymond Bianchi OP.

[30] That is not to say, of course, that such attitudes do not still exist – although the possession of wealth might now be the deciding factor, rather than notions of God's Will! Discrimination against people of different race or colour can be put into the same category.

[31] Was Julian influenced by the philanthropic ideals of his time? Benevolent societies and mission and aid societies typical of England during the years of his youth promoted a paternalistic view of society. The Marxist thesis also originated in England. But the idea that the poor should work with and for the poor without violence for their spiritual and material betterment was one that Julian picked up, I believe, in post-Revolution France. See Chapter 6.

cases where, in their anxiety to have their children learn to play a few tunes, 'poor, foolish parents' had allowed the children's real educational needs to suffer. Secondly, she did not want to have sisters performing or teaching instrumental music for, in her egalitarian institute comprised largely of working-class women, those able for this work might be held in higher regard by the people than those who could not do it and this, in turn, might give rise to `very dangerous distinctions' which would disturb the peace among the sisters. Thirdly, she was afraid that the sisters might give way to that tendency which she believed was innate `in more, if not all of us', to pay more attention to those who paid well for services received and to neglect the poor children for whose benefit the Institute had been founded.[32]

The purpose of Sisters coming together, both in Australia and earlier in France and countries to which they were missioned, was to be in and to build right relationships. Recalling the example of the community of the early Church where love of God in service of the poor marked out the disciples of Christ, Médaille had urged his Sisters, "My dear souls, make this example live again and so unite your hearts in that of Jesus that they are but one".[33]

Through their ministries, particularly in education, welfare and health care, Sisters helped remove the barriers that prevented the disadvantaged from taking their rightful place as children of God and world citizens. The Sisters were, then, agents of justice in helping restore the balance between those who had and those who did not. In serving the "dear neighbour", they promoted union with God and each other. In other words, no matter what class those Sisters came from themselves, they identified with the poor among whom they lived and built up "a relation of

---

[32] Foale, *The Josephite Story*, p. 129. In 1889, when economic conditions had changed for most Australian Catholics, the ruling against Sisters teaching instrumental music was lifted.
[33] Jean-Pierre Médaille, *Règlements of the Daughters of Saint Joseph*, trans. Sisters of St Joseph USA, Erie, 1973. p. 13.

fellowship between partners". This is a work of justice but also of compassion.

Unity and Reconciliation

In 1968 the Federation of Sisters of St Joseph in United States and Canada drew on the primitive documents of Father Médaille and the example of the Sisters who went before them to name their mission as "Unity and Reconciliation". The Federations in Europe have also named this orientation. The "double union" of God and humanity is both goal and task. Union is only achieved when, through God's grace, barriers have been removed through the process of reconciliation. Certainly, the term is applied to the work of Christ whose death and resurrection overcame the barrier of sin which blocks union with God and humanity. Baptised into the life of Christ and missioned to carry on this work today, those who share the spirit of "Joseph the just man" will be particularly involved in the enterprise.

"Unity and Reconciliation" can be identified also as an underlying, if unfocussed, theme in the ministries of the Sisters of St Joseph founded in Australia. Father Woods had named as the "Epistle of the Institute of St Joseph" an excerpt from the first letter of Peter which admonished,
> Finally, all of you, have unity of spirit, sympathy, love for one another, a tender heart and a humble mind. Do not repay evil for evil or abuse for abuse; but, on the contrary, repay with a blessing. It is for this that you were called – that you might inherit a blessing. …. For the eyes of the Lord are on the righteous, and his ears are open to their prayer.[34]

The effect of the Sisters' ministry promoted unity and reconciliation with God and each other. This is highlighted in an article written for the *Brisbane Courier* of December 17,

---

[34] The whole passage named by Woods is 1 Pet 3: 8-15, in a letter to the Lochinvar Sisters, Archives, Sisters of St Joseph of Lochinvar. See page 303.

1879 when the Sisters of St Joseph were forced to withdraw from Brisbane:

> As far as we can judge, religion in this city has never suffered a greater loss than it will in the departure of these good Sisters. They supplied gratuitous Catholic education in the only practical way, because, without humiliation to the recipients; they preserved the faith of hundreds with whom no minister of the Gospel ever came in contact; they rekindled it in hearts from which it had long died out; they tended the sick, they helped the needy, they comforted the afflicted, they lifted up the fallen, they brought back the erring to the paths of virtue; peace followed their footsteps into many a wretched home; they bound up many of the wounds from which society suffers in a city like this; in a word, they performed the most arduous and, ... often the most repulsive duties, with a zeal of which the world has but a feeble idea; and they did it all in the most unobtrusive manner with the scantiest resources, without distinction of creed or country, and without a murmur in the fact of numberless difficulties and even of discouragement from quarters whence it should least be expected.[35]

To be prophetic

In removing barriers to union, Sisters of St Joseph, like the prophets of old, became in their being, a sign of justice. The three vows have traditionally given to the Sisters an orientation which sets them on this path. While not setting out to be "prophets", their way of life is in direct contradiction to what can promote injustice in society.

The world of injustice manipulates wealth, relationships and power for self-serving ends. The alternative to this is a world which opens itself to God's reign of right relationships between God, humanity and all of creation – God's compassionate justice. Sandra Schneiders explains:

> By perpetual vows of consecrated celibacy, evangelical poverty, and prophetic obedience, (Religious) establish an

---

[35] The Sisters were forced to withdraw because Bishop James Quinn wished to impose diocesan government on them.

> alternate world which they live into being on a twenty-four hour a day basis, witnessing against the Prince of this World's version of a hopelessly divided human race and to a people whose hope springs from the Resurrection that universal shalom in the Reign of God is possible. They seek to announce in every culture and every age that the Savior of the World has come that all may have life and have it to the full (cf. Jn. 10:10).[36]

Elsewhere, Schneiders connects this prophetic stance directly with justice:

> There, on the margin, the prophet cries out in lament against the injustices of systems, whether ecclesiastical or civil, evokes the memory of God's plan for creation and the Church, and energizes hope to strive toward the Reign of God. ... Religious vows and Religious community life is itself a distancing or self-marginalization in relation to the world for the purpose of prophetic witness.[37]

Poverty: Through their vow of poverty, Sisters of St Joseph have, during hundreds of years of history, set themselves beside the marginalised, recognising them as their equals. Their time, talents and financial and spiritual resources, indeed their whole lives, have been put at the disposal of the least. As Father Woods had written for Sisters of St Joseph of the Sacred Heart, "We are Sisters of the poor, and let us on that account consider that our property belongs as much to the poor as to us".[38] While this might appear foolish to some, the vow of poverty is related to the baptismal commitment that all Christians share.

Christians are bound to God in hope, knowing God to be our final end. Full union, glimpsed weakly now in our relationships with God and each other, will, we believe, come to their ever-new, overflowing fulfilment in resurrected life. In fostering reconciling union with God and neighbour, those who share the

---

[36] Sandra Schneiders. "Religious Life in the Future", paper presented at Congress 2004, *With a Passion for Christ and Passion for Humanity*, UISG and USG, Rome.
[37] Sandra Schneiders. *Finding the Treasure*, New York: Paulist Press, 2000. pp. 226-227.
[38] *Book of Instructions:* "Of the Rule".

spirit of Joseph the just, enable hope to be deepened in our world and Church. The vow of poverty might be called a form of "consecrated hope", expressing this virtue in a prophetic way.

Availability for mission is one form the vow takes. Leaving what is familiar, depending on God's providence and devoting oneself entirely to the welfare of others in response to God's love demands detachment from what is of prime benefit to the self. "Some of us may have to go into new fields where we will meet strange faces and scenes, but these are not going to daunt us for our motto is, 'To do and to dare: to live and to die provided God's will be done and souls saved'," wrote Mother Antoinette Cuff in Kansas, to Sisters being sent on mission in 1919.[39]

However, as in all ministry, Sisters soon find out that they are the receivers rather than the givers. A Sister who spent time as a missionary in Guatemala explained that Jesus became real for her in the face of the poor. As they daily faced hunger, suffering, hardship and death, these people never gave up their hope in God. She was particularly inspired by one man who said,

> I have come to the conclusion that my destiny is death. If I remain passive, a conformist, and do nothing about the oppression and injustices we suffer, my wife, my children and I will die of starvation. If I fight and continue the struggle for liberation and change in our society, I will die of bullet wound – but I shall die with hopes of a better future for our children. Sisters, I am ready to lay down my life so that our people may one day know what it is to be liberated and live in a just society.[40]

Devoting resources to works of justice, another expression of the vow of poverty, requires considerable generosity on the part of Sisters. In 1995, the Sisters of St Joseph of Orange,

---

[39] Thomas, *Footprints on the Frontier,* p. 270.
[40] Smyth & Wicks, *Wisdom Raises Her Voice,* p. 182.

California, decided to dedicate part of their Motherhouse to a program for abused women to help them get their lives back together. "The Sisters decided to not only open up their hearts, but their home as well," says Sister Louise Ann, director of Bethany Residence. This sharing has a profound effect on the women. While there is screening of applicants and well-defined rules, the women are often overwhelmed by what is offered to them. "They sometimes cry when they see their rooms," Sister Louise Ann points out. "For many of these women, coming out of abusive marriages or a life torn apart by hardship, a simple thing like having their own room and bathroom seems like a dream come true." The program, scantily funded by Government, is practical, including skills training in communication, job interviews, life changes, counselling and budgeting. Sister Louise Ann sums up:

> At Bethany, our goal is to provide hope and support to these women. While they are here, we treat them with respect and dignity. We know we can't help everyone – that's not our goal. ... However, ... we can see we have made a difference in the lives of those we serve.[41]

Many other Sisters share a similar experience. At the 1993 International Gathering of Sisters of St Joseph in Le Puy, Sister Emma (Sisters of St Joseph of Lyon) described their involvement with those on the margins, particularly refugees:

> In Stockholm, (Sweden), the community had the use of two four-room apartments. One of the sisters had her bedroom in the second apartment, so we could offer hospitality to sisters, friends, or guests passing through. We gave up this arrangement to take in, for eight months, a family of Somalian refugees with three children. When this family was able to find housing though Social Service, we took in a Lebanese family with five children. The father was an Imam, ministering

---

[41] Information and quotations from personal interviews and from *Focus,* Fall 1999. pp. 2, 3.

to Muslims in Stockholm. The greatest challenge was helping others in the apartment building accept these strangers.[42]

Edwards says that "the place of the Spirit is the place where the humanity of the other is respected, in the space that allows the other to be the other".[43] The Spirit who called Joseph to justice continues to call us to give of ourselves so that others might know hope and their human dignity be recognised.

Chastity (Consecrated celibacy): Sister Kathleen Keating, Congregational Leader of the Sisters of St Joseph of Springfield from 1979 - 1987, once asked her Sisters, "Look at those to whom we minister. How can we change the *stranger* into a *neighbor*?"[44] The vow of chastity, or "consecrated love", is one way in which Sisters of St Joseph attempt to do this. Signifying the *universal* love of God,[45] the vow embraces especially the least in society in an assurance of worth. "We must go beyond our love for one another," Sister Kathleen continues, "to love all, to reconcile all, to reconcile neighbor with neighbor, and neighbor with God."[46]

The vow of chastity for Religious involves us in loving as God loves – with passion, no strings attached. It is compassionate love, a "feeling with" the other. Such compassion bridges gaps and is therefore a means by which justice, right relationships, is restored. The vignette offered by an interviewee is a good example, when she stepped between those who would treat with harshness a mentally disabled person throwing a tantrum because she didn't want mashed potatoes, but who calmed down when Sister offered her "hot icecream" instead.

---

[42] *Proceedings of the International Forum, Le Puy – Lyon, August 7-10, 1993,* An International Gathering of the Federations and Congregations of St Joseph, "Rooted to Bear Fruit." p. 30
[43] Edwards, *Breath of Life,* pp 89, 90.
[44] Consuelo Maria Aherne. *Joyous Service: The History of the Sisters of St Joseph of Springfield.* Chicopee, Massachusetts: Arthur Collier Jr, 1983. p. 239
[45] Complementary to the *exclusive* love that God has for each person, signified by marriage.
[46] Aherne, *Joyous Service,* p. 233.

By no means is this kind of loving exclusive to Religious, but the vow does signify that total self-gift is involved, the giving of one's whole life. Diane Bisson, in recording the experience of those who have served at the Sisters' Providence Centre in Toronto, Canada, reflects on compassion:

> Part of the mystery of compassion is that we are often more able to be compassionate to others when we are most in touch with our own vulnerability. When we are compassionate, we are "welcoming" of another person into our lives and into our hearts.[47]

The acknowledgement of weakness in not having the "answers" is what at least one of the Sisters remembers as being a salutary lesson for her.

> Our main focus is to be there and to be a presence there. Not to change them (the "street-women"), just to accept them as they come. ....
> In the beginning I had very mixed feelings. I thought it was just a band-aid and I felt there was something we ought to do to really help eliminate some of the problems. As I have spent more time there I have become aware that just being present, just being there for women coming in is a very important ministry. We do not always have to be doing.[48]

Efforts like those of the Sisters of St Joseph of Erie's Bethany House Ministry – founded "to provide a place of security, peace and safety where women, with or without children, can live while rebuilding their lives after adversity"[49] – are repeated in every country that hosts Sisters of St Joseph. A Sister volunteer for 'Hotline', realising "what little was available for women and children in the way of shelter and safe haven", felt like "the prophet Habakkuk in the Book of Daniel (14:33-36) ... God had somehow or other 'lifted me by the hair of my head' and placed me in those experiences where God knows I can make a difference in the life of others and in the life of the church." Her

---

[47] Diane Bisson. *Compassion Builds a House,* Toronto: Providence Centre, 2000. p. 9.
[48] Smyth & Wicks, *Wisdom Raises Her Voice,* pp. 67, 77.
[49] *Journeys* Vol 20, No 1, Winter 2002. p. 4.

response was to negotiate with the Congregation to begin "Community House for women and children".[50]

Supervised housing projects for mentally disabled adults, such as *Ain Karim* in South Australia, aim to restore the balance of dignity to those marginalised in our society. Attitudes brought to such projects need to be the same as encountered in the one-on-one relationship between a Sister and a troublesome pupil who, she found, came from a loveless background. "You like me, don't ya!" he said to her. "How do you know?" "I can tell!" "He needed affection," said the Sister. "This helped his self-respect."

Justice of compassion can hold in reverence the mildly retarded girl in care whom one interviewee was preparing for confession after she had "played up" and who remarked, "God forgives me. Are you going to forgive me?" Sister Helen Prejean CSJ is a well-known example of one who links justice and compassion, working with prison inmates to come to reconciliation and families of victims to healing through forgiveness. The Sisters of St Joseph of Boston treasure in corporate memory the story of one of their early Sisters visiting a dying former Superior General to whom she had caused much pain:

> Sister Camilla came, took Mother's hand and said, "Mother, for whatever hurt I caused you, I am sorry and I ask you to forgive me. God love you." She bent down and kissed Mother who returned a loving smile.[51]

The criterion of compassion is not acceptability but need. A Sister returning to France from the Ivory Coast described the fear and suffering engendered there because of "this dirty war". Her work among the suffering, sick and handicapped did not discriminate between friend and foe: her ministry was, she

---

[50] *Journeys* Vol 20, No 1, Spring/Summer 2003. p. 9.
[51] Sisters of St Joseph of Boston, "At the Dawn of a New Age" – A Forum Envisioning the Future of the Past, 1998. Chapter 3: p. 8 of 17.

considered, an apt expression of "double union", aiming for "peace and unity with Christian and Muslim".[52]

A woman who, as a widowed grandmother, joined the Sisters of St Joseph of Lyon in Maine, sums up this prophetic kind of loving:

> The Sister of St Joseph is not afraid to roll up her sleeves in solidarity with the poor and work for social justice that all 'may come to have the conditions of life to be fully human'. The mission of unity which each sister strives to achieve as much as she is able is a mission that I can commit myself to in an effort to bring it about in our broken world. ... The charism of unity is shared by all of the sisters. It evolves and takes shape in the context of the realities of everyday life and one in which each sister is accepted with her strengths and her weaknesses. The charism is lived with the people and it celebrates all life as important and deserving of love and respect.[53]

Obedience: Baptism bonds us in a faith relationship with a God who, we believe, calls us to full life and happiness in this life and the next. The vow of obedience – in this sense, "consecrated faith" – directs personal power towards enabling the will of God to be done in our own lives and in our world. In its corporate obedience, a Religious Congregation collectively devotes itself to standing against power-systems, religious and secular, that disempower the vulnerable for their own ends.

Obedience in the spirit of Joseph is attentive to the call of God in the power-plays of domination. Two episodes on opposite sides of the world illustrate this. When Mary MacKillop was deposed and banished by Bishop Reynolds in Adelaide in 1883, she was cut to the quick. She admitted to being tempted "to give up and seek a rest that up to this I have never got, either in

---

[52] *Savoie Mission Partage.* No 30, 2003. p 13.
[53] *Heartbeats,* Newsletter, Sisters of St Joseph of Lyon, Nov. 2002. p. 4.

the world or in religion".[54] However, as their foundress, Mary had rights that she now claimed:

> I want you, my dearest Sister, and my Council to thoroughly understand that as far as I can now gather, Dr Reynolds wants to break the Sisters in Adelaide off from me entirely and to form the Institute on a plan of his own. If this be his plan, ... don't let yourselves be intimidated. ... Think calmly over this and pray. Let us be united and we shall be strong. By far the greater part of the Sisters are faithful, and one united declaration of this and expression of confidence in their Mother General − (and for this one time I do claim it) − poor unworthy foundress, will greatly help and strengthen our cause.[55]

The second episode concerns another deposition − this time in 1934 of Mother Domitilla in Boston by Cardinal O'Connell. One of the Sisters responded, "We cannot let this happen. We cannot consent to this. This is not Mother Domitilla, this is not the Cardinal, this is <u>our</u> Community."[56] The Sisters needed to find some way of claiming their right to elect their superior, and they found it through a statement in Canon Law (which would then have been written in Latin and not readily available to Sisters). One of those required to kneel before the Cardinal and explain her resistance to his will described what then happened:

> I quoted Canon Law to support the request for an election. In an angry tone he told me, "Get up and get out." I left very quietly, but I was still near enough to hear the Cardinal say to one of his Monsignors, "They <u>will</u> have an election."[57]

The election, however, did not happen until six months later − time enough for the Cardinal to save face.

Working for justice is not only response to faith, but it is a necessary aspect of religion. David Ranson points out that

---

[54] Letter to Sister Monica (acting Superior), Sept. 26, 1884. Archives, Sisters of St Joseph, North Sydney.
[55] Letter to Sister Monica, September 26, 1884.
[56] Sisters of St Joseph of Boston, "At the Dawn of a New Age", Ch. 3: p. 7 of 17.
[57] "At the Dawn of a New Age", p. 8 of 17.

> the mystical dimension of religion needs, itself, to be in tension with a 'political' dimension. By 'political', I mean the capacity to effect change in society. By being truly 'political' – which is quite different from being partisan – religion retains its public character. It is not afforded the luxury of drifting into 'private reservations of the human spirit' but remains committed to working for the common good and for social transformation. Spiritual experience should never render us inert or blind to the needs and demands of others but rather, more attentive and more strategic in their regard.[58]

The response of one group of Sisters to the abuse of drug-lords took religion into the public arena in an unobtrusive way. The Sisters did, as an interviewee said, "what little we could. In our program, 'Bridge Over Troubled Waters', we went after runaways, make friends with them, had a medical van that went out at night, gave them a place to go to, attended to them, gave them food (peanut butter sandwiches – different groups of Sisters made them) and asked Sisters in our convents to take kids in for the night".

Two other Sisters told how they – a Maths/Science teacher and a cook – got involved in the Civil Rights movement of USA. The people they lived among were mainly migrants, needing practical help such as English lessons, clothing and furniture. However, a visit to a housing project introduced them to the realities of racial prejudice. They soon found themselves working with different Congregations and priests in advocacy, talking to politicians, helping parents to understand what was going on. Willingly they took part in protest marches and other efforts to give voice to the voiceless. The human face of real people took the question of justice beyond a "cause" to that of righting relationships.

It was at this time that Superiors General such as Sister Consuelo Maria of Philadelphia urged their Sisters, "Sisters, in

---

[58] Ranson, *Across the Great Divide,* p. 49.

light of the original vision of Father Médaille, I urge every Sister of St Joseph to plan to **ACT** (**A**ction-oriented, **C**oncerned about political issues, **T**rained through seminars, etc.) this year to make a difference, to make life better for someone, to rekindle hope in the world, to continue to be a healing presence in that world."[59] Sisters tell of meeting farmers boycotting supermarkets, helping them give out leaflets and sitting down with them while they told them their problems. At a march in support of oppressed farm workers in their dispute with grape growers in California, a younger Sister was approached by "an irate individual" accusing her of "Communistic sympathies".

> "I just bet your Superior doesn't know what you're doing," he accused, "and I'm going to let her know."
> "Well, if you want to do it now," the Sister said, "she's the white-haired lady over there," indicating Sister Frances' flashing coiffure.[60]

Times have changed since the 1970s, but the issues surrounding the abuse of political power are being expressed as urgently as ever". "How can we promote a culture of non-violence and be a prophetic voice among the dear neighbour?"[61] is the question being heard right around the world. The answer is multi-levelled, but involves the basic respect for human dignity shown by those who have shared the spirit of Joseph through the years. An old Sister told how she was in a State hospital at one time, visiting a former pupil with epilepsy (considered a mental illness in those days). He had a picture of the Sacred Heart on a cord around his neck. "Get that thing off," said the nurse. When a tussle ensued, the Sister suggested, "Let's ask him why he's wearing it." "He's my only friend," said the young man.

Maintaining the dignity of the poor has evoked wondrous creativity. "Tell Johnny I'd like him to do a message for me,"

---

[59] Message to Social Action Commission, 1974. Archives, Sisters of St Joseph of Philadelphia.
[60] Geagley, *A Compassionate Presence,* p. 242.
[61] Joan Duffy. "Healing Presence and the Dear Neighbor" *Soundings,* Vol 25, #1, 2003. p 3.

was a ploy adopted in many guises to ensure Johnny got some breakfast before starting school. One Sister as a child wondered why, however, hard she tried, she never got the prize of a piece of fruit for good work done. It was years later that she realised that the ones who "won" were from the poor end of town. She found out, too, that the "prize" was actually what her teacher had saved from her own breakfast.

A New Zealand Sister was renowned for scouting out people in need. A family where both parents had died was being cared for by their eldest sister, still in her teens. She was proud and did not want "charity". Sister Chanel was the only one able to "pop in for a cuppa" and somehow ensure the children had school uniforms and other necessities. "Those children all grew up well," says her friend, "and the boys are successful businessmen in the town today."

How many First Communion outfits have unobtrusively found their way into families unable to afford what others had? How many department stores had standing orders for whoever arrived with a "letter from Sister" to be outfitted "from the inside out" and the bill sent to the convent? Only in her 90s did the mother of one Sister tell her that the parcels she had grudgingly brought home from school as a child were supplies that had got them by in hard times. "During the Depression, most boarders couldn't pay fees" recalls an old Sister from Perthville, Australia. "People used to bring in a side of lamb or whatever, so we scraped through. We wanted the poor ones to feel equal to the wealthy ones." In one case a child arrived at boarding school with no clothes. Since the town was at a distance from the school, Sister rang the priest who was due to visit in a couple of days, asking him to buy some clothes and bring them with him. "Sure, what would a kid need clothes for, right out there in the bush?" was his reply.

These were great women whose works of justice arose in obedience to God's Will for the full life of all. Sister Ethelreda in Adelaide, who visited the jails after school and on weekends, is an example. She tutored a murderer for university English and it was found he had topped the State when exam results were announced. Sister Kieran is another. "One gentleman arrived at the back door," said a Sister in community with her at the time. "He looked like a swagman (it was during the Depression), but he asked if he could have a bath, and while he was having it, Kieran made him up a meal. We weren't as brave as she was, so we were frightened. She wasn't rash, but she was always respectful to people, no matter who they were. It turned out he was a priest travelling from his country parish to the city!"

Experience has taught Sisters of St Joseph that causes of injustice need to be addressed, as well as immediate help being given. The stance of obedience listens for God's call even where not expected. The "Sister Workers" in France happily join their efforts with other non-Church groups to deal with underlying issues of justice:

> We discover that the values of justice and relationship[62] are better present in this unbelieving world, in the world of those who think differently. We discover the importance of remaining open and respectful of the differences. A young unbelieving militant said to me: "You, like me, you work always for justice." ... Even if the language of the militants isn't "religious", for us it speaks, breathes the Gospel.[63]

Sisters in Australia have found the same, as they challenge government policies on behalf of the neighbour, East Timor (Timor L'Este). No longer under the rule of an invading country, this tiny nation is still struggling to have its sea-borders recognised and oil-rights acknowledged. Susan Connelly RSJ finds herself sharing the speakers platform with a "surprising" variety of groups in rallies around Australia, as she

---

[62] "fraternité".
[63] Groupe Monde Ouvrier, "Engagées,Envoyées,Engagées", p. 34.

unflinchingly proclaims the Christ who stands with the least. At the same time, she, and others working at the Mary MacKillop Institute for East Timorese Studies in Sydney, continue to form partnerships with groups in Australia and Timor L'Este to provide practical help, education and health care to one of the poorest nations in the world.

At both levels, – macro and micro – the work of justice involves engagement in the protection of rights at their systemic roots and also in equipping victims to address those issues themselves (for example, through education, or even through providing experience of human worth). Both aspects are complementary. In particular, the empowering of victims is one that many Sisters have felt within their competence. One shared her story:

> I was teaching in a very depressed mining area. The children had such a poor self-image that I felt I had to do something. So I trained them for the eisteddfods. We raised money for the bus to get the children to the city. They hadn't been there before. We had enough money over for an iceblock each. We actually won the eisteddfods. All these posh elocution teachers were asking me, "Sister, where did you get your letters?" "In Ireland", I answered. They were talking about degrees. Well, I learnt my ABC in Ireland! We had our photo in paper and everything. That did more for the children than any preaching could have. It was a practical recognition of their dignity.

Carmel Pilcher RSJ sees this Josephite spirit of justice exemplified in the Eucharist:

> If we gather with reverence, recognising the Christ in each other, celebrate the presence of Christ in Word and Sacrifice, then we cannot but be changed by what we experience. As we realise our obligation to fully participate we will also realise that living Eucharistically is more than for one hour of the week but spills over into our daily life. We will come to the holy table recognising that we are God's holy people, and the unity of the table will be reflected in the integrity that the Christian community will show to the world. The Christ of the altar will be recognised in the socially deprived, the physically impaired

and those on the fringes of our society. We Christians will be impelled to challenge structures and institutions that are unjust and corrupt and that ignore Christ in our own outcasts, be they the socially deprived or the refugee.[64]

Sisters of St Joseph and all who share the spirit of Joseph the just, give of themselves so that others might know hope; in love they change the *stranger* into a *neighbor;* and in faith they promote a culture of justice. This is what a newly-professed Sister found: "In my ministry to others and especially the poor, I ... discovered a treasure and came to know a group of women .. who rolled up their sleeves and became a presence for those who have no voice.[65] Bette Moslander CSJ sums up,

> We are on a frontier of vast need, desirous of fulfilling our destiny to be servants ... that others might have life. There are far fewer of us than the tasks demand, but enough to begin. The exploration into prophecy does not require large numbers, but large faith.[66]

4.3 PART THREE: The spirit lives into the now

Globalisation

Loreto Sister, Libby Rogerson, addressed a Conference in Melbourne Town Hall in 2003:

> Globalisation, whether we like it or not, is here to stay. If we want to be effective ministers then the globe is our mission field. Formation and study programmes for novices and seminarians must provide information about the issues that affect our globe – the dominance of transnational companies, the power of international finance institutions, what it means to belong to a global church.[67]

---

[64] Weekly Reflections for the Year of the Eucharist, Liturgy Office, Catholic Archdiocese of Sydney.
[65] *Soundings*, Vol 25, Summer 2003. p. 9.
[66] Bette Moslander. "Significant Moments in LCWR History 1950 – 1990", Leadership Conference of Women Religious, 2001. Cited in Ann Hoye SSJ, *Seasons of Nature and of Grace: History of the Sisters of St Joseph of Wheeling 1853 – 2003*, Sisters of St Joseph of Wheeling, 2002. p. 212.
[67] "Vocations and Future Church Ministry". Talk given October 21, 2003

For many Sisters of St Joseph, even thinking about having "the globe as our mission field" is exhausting! Effective in dealing with local issues, they consider themselves incapable of setting up against "transnational companies" or "finance institutions".

Yet "globalisation is a process, not an event," says Mark Raper SJ, "and it involves complex but interdependent networks".[68] If corporations can network for monetary gain, surely those whose focus is the establishment of God's reign of justice and peace can do so. It is in our ability to localise justice that we can be most effective on the global scene. With an awareness of the spirit of Joseph being shared around the world, structures of networking can reinforce the efforts of Sisters, Associates, co-workers and lay-groups as they express in their own area the justice of God's compassion.

It is this aspect of localisation, I think, that Pope John Paul II reminds us of when he calls for the humanising of globalisation, urging us towards a 'globalisation in solidarity, globalisation without marginalisation'.[69] Our work at local and regional level helps put a human face on God's compassion with those who suffer ill-effects of globalisation, such as the great numbers of people seeking asylum. We need not be overwhelmed by the multinationals whose resources present a seemingly formidable barrier to justice. The search for solutions to global problems needs to be local and regional, yes, but global networking can extend effectiveness, encourage solidarity and provide a counter-balance to trends that would ignore justice.

One of the means we have at our disposal for more effectively dealing with global issues is the non-government organisation, "The Congregations of St Joseph", a body set up by the Federation of Sisters of St Joseph in USA and Canada and now

---

[68] Mark Raper, "Globalisation and Human Solidarity" in *Compass,* Vol 37, 2003. p. 24.
[69] John Paul II, *World Day of Peace Message,* Jan 1, 1998, no. 3.

representing Sisters of St Joseph in every continent of the world. Its director, Carol Zinn CSJ, describes its mission:

> In General Consultative Status with ECOSOC (the Economic and Social Council of the United Nations), the NGO is a network of 14,000+ Sisters serving in 51 countries in the areas of education, healthcare, human rights, the eradication of poverty, women's concerns, environment, sustainable development, peace and security, children's concerns and economic justice. The activities of the NGO, "The Congregations of St. Joseph", include participation in the UN Commissions of Social Development, Sustainable Development, and Women; participation in UN-NGO committees of education, human rights, spirituality and global concerns, religious NGOs, social development, sustainable development, women, education of the girl child, trafficking, eradication of poverty, financing for development, working groups on HIV/AIDS, Iraq and Israel/Palestine; participation on various caucuses: earth values, values, peace education and sustainability.
>
> The NGO, "The Congregations of St. Joseph", works to join the voice and activity of the members throughout the world to the international arena at the UN. It also helps to further the work for the UN around the world by sharing information about the UN and its work for peace, justice, humanitarian aid, eradication of poverty, and sustainable development.

Through this body, Sisters of St Joseph have the opportunity to receive information from and make representation to the UN about whatever areas of concern they are involved in. They know firsthand the pain caused to enormous sections of populations everywhere, living in levels of poverty directly the result of unjust economic, judicial, educational and health systems. But knowing they share values and spirit with others who join them in their efforts, the Australian-New Zealand Federation of Sisters of St Joseph can boldly assert in their constitutions:

> Like Jesus we stand in solidarity with the poor.
> We, too, challenge oppressive structures and powerful institutions
> which deny justice and dignity
> to our sisters and brothers.[70]

It remains a task, however, to extend the sense of moral solidarity and to explore appropriate structures, building on those that already exist both with the UN NGO "Congregations of St Joseph" and with groups in national and international regions, to more obviously facilitate networking and enable the St Joseph Movement to pulse more vibrantly.

Furthering the spirit

When a "bright, politically involved young woman engaged to be married and well on her way to what .. American culture would consider a successful life" decided recently to join the Sisters of St Joseph, her friends were shocked. But it was in her studies and volunteer work with the Sisters that Deirdre learned that issues of social justice and injustice are about unity and reconciliation and the ongoing work of building right relationships. "During my time in Mississippi, direct service to the poor, involvement in public policy, and practice of the law came together for me in the prophetic nature of religious life," she said. For her it is a journey towards wholeness. "This is how I can best be who I am in relation to Jesus' calling."[71]

Religious Life as a Sister of St Joseph continues to signify in the way of the prophet, the will of God for justice. But Church mission is the task of the whole Church, and consecrated life stands alongside other forms of life in carrying out this mission. The focus of justice as an aspect of the Josephite spirit is one that Sisters of St Joseph highlight as they hand over

---

[70] *A Future and a Hope,* Constitutions of the Australian-New Zealand Federation of Sisters of St Joseph, approved Rome, March 19, 2000.
[71] *Soundings,* Vol 25, Summer 2003. p. 4.

management of ministries to lay co-workers, and nurture the living of the spirit on a number of fronts.

Sponsored ministries: The setting up of Boards to take responsibility for the running of institutions with ultimate responsibility remaining with the trustees, the Sisters, is now a well-established practice around the world. Different terminology is used in some countries – for example, "Incorporated Ministries" is the term generally adopted in Australia. A thorough education program in Josephite spirit and spirituality for Board members is always involved, since these elements form part of the patrimony that the Sisters entrust to their care. With a few exceptions, Canon Law at present restricts ownership of Church institutions to Religious Congregations (authorised to minister in a diocese by the bishop); research is currently being undertaken as to how, in the future, such ownership might encompass other groups. In the meantime, Sisters have found in some cases that the sponsoring of ministries actually increases their capacity to conduct such ministry. A small group of Sisters, such as the Sisters of St Joseph of Hamilton or the Sisters of St Joseph of Tipton, each with less than 90 members, can run numbers of large hospitals and other institutions with a professionalism that equals those of any for-profit scheme. Yet the spirit of Joseph persists: "Our goal is to emphasise life. Whether it is the life of a child at day care of the last days in the life of a senior, we will always focus on life and living life to the fullest with dignity, comfort and care."[72]

Inservice Training: As already noted in previous chapters, formation in the spiritual basis for works of justice within the tradition of St Joseph is not only recommended for those who work in its institutions but is obligatory. Unless, as Cardinal

---

[72] Advertising brochure, St Joseph's Lifecare Centre, Brantford, a Ministry of the Sisters of St Joseph of Hamilton.

Hume warned, the reign of God operates first of all in the heart of each person, "our efforts will remain generous and well-intentioned but not the work of the Holy Spirit".[73]

One Sister from Toronto reflected on her experience of anxiety about how values would be passed on, as hospital Sisters were replaced by laity.
> In the early 1990s a committee made up of a cross-section of employees ... was formed to name the operative values of the organization. ... The committee had a meeting and ... at the end of two hours they named five values. These are the operative values: human dignity, excellence, compassion, social responsibility and community of service. Those were the values those hospitals stood for .. and what the Sisters stood for. That was a wonderful experience. I was always struck by how quickly it happened, and by their conviction.[74]

Outreach: Many schools, hospitals and other institutions formerly managed by the Sisters and now handed on to lay leadership have established international outreach programs that facilitate networking and extend values of justice. Brochures of St Joseph's Health System, Hamilton, (Canada), describe the program they host in India and other countries:
> Our focus is on partnerships and solutions that the host country can sustain. We seek projects that complement work already underway, building the community's ability to care for itself. St Joseph's Health System is grounded in our healing mission to promote the dignity of all persons, especially the poor and marginalized, and to strive to alleviate the causes of poverty and oppression. While our mission is rooted in the Roman Catholic tradition, we work to make the world a better place for people of all faiths.
> Working side-by-side with health professionals at University Hospital, International Outreach ensures that supplies reach their intended destination and that equipment remains functional. Training sessions and the Residents Exchange

---

[73] Cardinal Basil Hume, source unknown.
[74] Smyth and Wicks, *Wisdom Raises Her Voice,* p. 173.

> Program equips doctors, nurses, and staff with knowledge and skills they can teach others.

Such practical, respectful service encourages attitudes of equality rather than paternalism. Rather than introduce a foreign solution to difficulties, it builds on local knowledge and expertise. Neither does it presume that what is available in one country will be found elsewhere. Exchange programs foster the ability to "stand in another's shoes". Inclusivity and collaboration with others in outreach schemes extends values of justice and hence the reign of God.

Similar structures in Australia promote partnership with communities of indigenous peoples and overseas groups. Through incorporated bodies such as St Joseph's Australian-Peruvian Mission Associates, for example, funds are raised and contacts made with parallel bodies in Peru to establish projects chosen by the people as of most benefit to their community. Sometimes these projects are on a relatively small scale – for example, constructing a sports field, enabling individuals to do training in basic medicines to run a subsidised medicine-dispensing operation, or to employ legal help to supplement Sisters' efforts to break through mounds of paper-work and consequent years of languishing in prison of people awaiting trial. Always, though, there is the realization that outreach is mutually enriching. Recently, Sisters working with indigenous groups reflected:

> We are now called to stand in solidarity with and move towards partnership with Indigenous Peoples... acknowledging that conversion is a process that touches our hearts and calls us to action to grow in right relationships with Aboriginal and Torres Strait Islander Peoples.[75]

In a non-structured way, the "Josephite Community Aid" volunteers involve local schools and groups to extend attitudes of justice in personalised outreach. Having met Jestina, a

---

[75] Sisters of St Joseph, *Review of Ministry with Australian Indigenous Peoples*, p.4, Appendix.

refugee from Sierra Leone, when they visited a block of flats in a socially-deprived area of Sydney, they learnt that her son, thought to be dead, was indeed alive. However, expensive procedures involving DNA tests and legal advice were needed in order to prove the mother-son relationship to the government. Schools and organisations were approached to help. Further assistance was needed for medical treatments and airfares. But in June 2004, Jestina was reunited with her son.
> The excitement when he came through the doors was unbelievable! The Sierra Leone community sang hymns of praise and thanksgiving all the way home in the bus. Jestina's comment was: "I'm so happy, I've got my life back."[76]

Changing cultures that promote injustice
Pope Paul VI advised, "If you want peace, work for justice."[77] But systems of injustice can be so entrenched that they form part of the culture that legitimises them. The practice of slavery is one example. Before it could be eradicated – at least in the western world – profound changes had to take place within the thought-patterns of society itself to render it unacceptable.

With the backing of the Sisters and of St Joseph's Hospital, Jack Glaser, Director of St Joseph's Center for Healthcare Reform in Orange, California, is mounting a public education campaign to change attitudes about health care in the United States. There, health care is not regarded as a common good nor a common right. It is linked to wealth, in turn dependent upon employment and income. The result, even with some level of *Medicare,* is that a high proportion of United States citizens, including around 11 million children, is excluded from the right to health protection.

To set about changing attitudes that will eventually result in reformed structures, Jack has employed the methodology of

---

[76] *Spreading the Spirit.* Josephite Community Aid Newsletter. Issue 29, Spring 2004. p. 4
[77] Paul VI, *World Day of Peace Message*, par. 197.

"FrameWorks", an institute with its headquarters in Washington DC, whose research helps change-advocates apply its findings to particular social issues. Catholic teaching about justice, as Jack points out, is "long on vision and short on how we get there"[78] – understandably so, since "how we get there" is often determined by cultural factors which can only be interpreted by the local, rather than the universal, church. As part of the "local church" and as an expression of the charism of St Joseph, Jack is playing his part in bringing biblical and moral principles to bear on the cultural consciousness of US society.

Jack recognises that there are two dimensions to promoting social change. The first is external and visible. An example of this would be the projects established by Sister Gretchen Shaffer from Sisters of St Joseph of Wheeling, when she set about responding "to needs for systemic change in a way that was also manageable".[79] Having become "mountain women" in a community called the "Knob" in Mingo County, West Virginia, Gretchen and her companion assisted in setting up a centre for empowerment in the Big Laurel Learning Center,

> seeking ways to develop community, to teach adults and children who are economically poor in an area so very rich in natural resources. Big Laurel is known for demonstrating and educating people about an alternative to land ownership. It supplies tools for analysing the social problem of powerlessness and its impact on a people and a culture.[80]

The second dimension is less visible – the underlying attitudes and values of a particular society. To address these, an analysis of the factors involved and the depth of commitment held by stakeholders is necessary. Some situations needing change will have few factors connected with them – for example, to change a school uniform involves a fairly shallow set of references – a

---

[78] Michael Culliton & Ann Neale *NETWORK*, A National Catholic Social Justice Lobby, Washington. DC, March/April 2004.
[79] Hoye, *Seasons of Nature and of Grace,* p. 202.
[80] Hoye, *Seasons of Nature and of Grace,* p. 203.

collection of reasons for the change, consultation with parents, involvement of pupils, decisions about implementation, etc. But other situations will be complex.

To change attitudes in the USA about the right to health will take, Jack considers, a "seismic shift" in people's thinking. The campaign to do this has involved four preparatory steps:
1. Jack has identified a number of institutions whose stake in keeping health care in the USA as it is, is high:
> These include banks, insurance companies, research institutions, government agencies, health care facilities, technology industry, universities, pharmaceutical corporations, advertising and marketing firms, for-profit health corporations, professional and trade organizations, etc. These institutions are large and rich. They have enormous political and cultural influence. They are interdependent and synergistic to a very high degree.[81]

2. He has analysed the "fiercely held" values and assumptions held by the USA public about health care.
3. In order to engender discussion across the country, he and his co-workers have set up alliances with other groups bent on social reform. Together they are setting up conversations among ordinary citizens.
4. Finally, the problems surrounding the question of health care in the country have been "re-framed" according to the methodology of "FrameWorks", in such a way that the solution becomes obvious to people at grass level.

Discussion points include the examination of underlying values, priorities and assumptions. "We have learned when people begin conversations on health care by first identifying their values, they seem to have a sharper eye for the inadequacies of the current system and a more positive assessment of reforms that could meet the basic health care needs of all,"[82] Jack says. The conversation is also framed in such a way as to help people

---

[81] Culliton & Neale, *NETWORK*
[82] Culliton & Neale, *NETWORK*

go beyond matters of finance to those which bring awareness of people's interdependence and the common good of society.

"If you want peace, work for justice"

The Mass of Reconciliation II has a beautiful preface which prays in part,

> In the midst of conflict and division,
> we know it is you
> who turn our minds to thoughts of peace.
> Your Spirit changes our hearts: enemies begin to speak to one another,
> those who are estranged join hands in friendship,
> and nations seek the way of peace together.
> Your Spirit is at work
> when understanding puts an end to strife,
> when hatred is quenched by mercy,
> and vengeance gives way to forgiveness.[83]

As those who share the spirit of Joseph work for justice and therefore for peace, they can learn from one another through networking and collaboration. So many of our number stand with those whose voices are silenced: trafficked women, asylum seekers, child soldiers. How can concerted efforts be made, for example, to change attitudes in countries whose governments are more and more adopting punitive, unjust measures in order to discourage refugees? If psychiatrists are finding that large numbers of detainees suffer trauma during incarceration, how can the problem be "re-framed" not to deal with "adequate treatment for mental illness" but rather with the treatment of all detainees and the length of time they are held in such institutions? What causes people to be so traumatised within these centres? Why are they put there? These and other injustices cry out for our attention.

The phrase "communion, peace and solidarity" used by Pope John Paul II in his letter for the Year of the Eucharist

---

[83] The English translation of *Eucharistic Prayers for Masses of Reconciliation*, ICEL, 1975.

summarises the task of those who work for justice. This is expressed, he says, in the Eucharist:

> The Eucharist is not merely an expression of communion in the Church's life; it is also a *project of solidarity* for all of humanity. In the celebration of the Eucharist the Church constantly renews her awareness of being a "sign and instrument" not only of intimate union with God but also of the unity of the whole human race. Each Mass, even when celebrated in obscurity or in isolation, always has a universal character. The Christian who takes part in the Eucharist learns to become a *promoter of communion, peace and solidarity* in every situation. More than ever, our troubled world, which began the new Millennium with the spectre of terrorism and the tragedy of war, demands that Christians learn to experience the Eucharist as *a great school of peace*, forming men and women who, at various levels of responsibility in social, cultural and political life, can become promoters of dialogue and communion.[84]

In the spirit of Joseph the just, we continue our interpretation of biblical and church teaching on justice at the local level while affirming our links with each other in a globalised world, knowing that the face of God's compassion is thereby portrayed and that the reign of God is further established among us.

---

[84] Apostolic Letter, *Mane Nobiscum Domine,* to the Bishops, Clergy and Faithful for the Year of the Eucharist, October 2004 – October 2005.

CHAPTER FIVE

The spirit of Joseph ......

brings together.

Joseph made his home in a town called Nazareth (Mt. 2:23).

5.1 PART ONE: The spirit is revealed

Communion
Sister Kathleen Keating from Springfield, USA, was sharing with her Sisters the condition of her ageing father who confused dream with reality. So he would regularly check with her whether events he described as having taken place in the Retirement Home had really happened. After he told her a story one day she asked him, "Was that a dream or was it real?" He answered, "Oh, no, it was real; everybody dreamed the same thing." "What an earth-shattering effect Sisters of St Joseph could have on society," Sister Kathleen concluded, "if we all dreamed the same dream and made it a reality!"[1]

The dream of God for creation is for communion. Human beings are born out of communion. The coming together in love of parents gives birth to the child. In turn, the child, born as an individual, finds in total vulnerability and dependency that life itself demands community, relationship. Coming to communion with others, and indeed, with the creation which nurtures our life, becomes our mission and our destiny. In death we return to the earth that has sustained us.

---
[1] Aherne, *Joyous Service,* p. 227.

Moreover, as Edwards points out, creation and all of life is itself born out of a communion – the communion of God. The "going-beyond-self" that is involved in human communion connects us with what is beyond – the divine, the Mystery.

> Creatures exist only because God, who is communion, enables them to be. Creation means that each creature exists at every moment in relationship to the divine Communion. All things exist from Communion.[2]

God as communion

Language for the Christian understanding of God as communion arose out of reflection about who Jesus Christ is with and for us. Christians recognised that God is communicated to us in the person of Christ. The Letter to the Hebrews, for example, identifies Jesus as the Son of God: "He reflects the glory of God and bears the very stamp of his nature, upholding the universe by his word of power."[3]

Christians experienced the life of God in the grace of the Spirit given through the Son. They shared the Spirit of Jesus. They were brought into union with God and each other through it. They were enlivened by it. God was revealed as Trinity.

In maintaining that the Christian experience of union with the Trinity is the *one* God and not *three,* Augustine made an analogy between what happens in human thought. He points out that there are three distinct elements in the process of thinking about an object – recalling the object, the mind's knowledge about that object, and the focusing of the mind on the object. While it is one mind, the elements are distinct. He likens the process to our remembering, knowing and loving God. We can make distinctions between the three elements, but they exist in relationship to each other.[4]

---

[2] Edwards, *Breath of Life,* p. 48.
[3] Hebrews 1:3.
[4] *http://www.newadvent.org/fathers/1301.htm* On the Trinity, Augustine, **Books 9, 10, 14, 15.**

In like manner, he says, God's communion is the relationship of three in one. Analogies limp, but the essential understanding of God as revealed by our experience of creator, saviour and sanctifier is of a Being-who-is-in-relationship. The nature of our God revealed is a God of communion. Thomas Aquinas described this understanding of God as the One who *is, outpoured* in the Son and continuously *spiralling in love* in the Spirit.

The well-known icon of Andrei Rublev[5] depicting the meeting of Abraham with the three angels[6] is a metaphor for the Christian understanding of Trinity and our meeting with God. The three figures are seated around a table set out for a banquet. *Hospitality* is an indicator of communion; God invites us into communion, to share at the table.

The figure on the left directs his gaze to the second, his hand raised in blessing; we recall the words of the Father in Matthew's Gospel, "This is my beloved Son, with whom I am well pleased; listen to him."[7] In turn, the second figure points to the third, whose whole mien links the two with the first, at the same time (since his arms lie loosely open) inviting the viewer to enter into the circle. "The Counsellor, the Holy Spirit, whom the Father will send in my name, he will teach you all things, and bring to your remembrance all that I have said to you."[8]

Each of the three figures has a staff – they are travellers, and even though they have the wings of angels, they walk the journey of life on this earth. The background objects indicate this journey. Behind the Spirit there is a rocky road. The Spirit is with us on our pilgrimage towards the tree situated behind the

---

[5] Andrei Rublev, was born around 1360 and worked in Moscow. He died in 1430 and is buried at the Andronikov Monastery in that same city.
[6] Genesis 18: 1-8.
[7] Mt. 17:5.
[8] John 14:26.

Son and spreading its branches, giving protection and shade. Because of the sacrifice of the Son (indicated by the dressed lamb within the chalice on the table), this tree is now the tree of life. The path continues towards a house with door and windows open, located behind the figure of the Father. "In my Father's house there are many rooms,"[9] Jesus had said. God invites us into the *intimacy* of household relationship. "See what love the Father has given us, that we should be called children of God; and so we are."[10] God watches for us at the window; the door is always open, no matter how far we wander.

The communion of the Body of Christ

The Acts of the Apostles presents the birth of the Church through the coming of the Spirit, whose first action is to form community.

> All the believers were one in heart and soul, and no one said that any of the things which they possessed were their own, but they had everything in common. ... There was not a needy person among them, for as many were possessors of lands or houses sold them, brought the proceeds of what was sold and laid it at the apostles' feet, and distribution was made to each as had need.[11]

Community came to be because of their common faith and their care of one another. The incarnation, death and resurrection of the Son had opened to all of humanity the possibility of union with God. But union with God is bestowed through being in union with neighbour. Those who do not love their brothers and sisters in Christ cannot say they love God.[12] Henri Nouwen says,

> Because all humanity has been taken up into God through the incarnation of the Word, finding the heart of God means finding all the people of God. There, a Christ in whom all

---

[9] John 14: 2
[10] 1 John 3: 1.
[11] Acts 4:32,34,35
[12] 1 John 4: 20.

people are not gathered together is not the true Christ. We who belong to Christ belong to all of humanity.[13]

The image of the Body of Christ was one used in the primitive Church to depict the relationship of Christians both with God in Christ and with each other. We are well familiar with the description of Paul urging Christians to contribute whatever gift they bring for the building up of the total body of Christ; through baptism they enter into the life of Christ and become one with him and hence with each other, so that even their sufferings are united with his and contribute to the new life won through the cross.[14]

Christian Community

In at least one case, however, I have heard of a lecturer in psychology using the notion of incorporation into Christ as an example of unhealthy substitution of another's persona in place of their own. Besides being in poor taste, such an assertion does come out of a culture of predominant individualism.

Individualism sees community or society simply as a collection of individuals, each understanding themselves as a unit and, while not ignoring the benefit of interaction, seeing their own fulfilment as of prime importance. A perverted self-love in this instance places no value on self-sacrifice for the good of the other. The self is the ultimate standard of value. The individualist would promote pluralism as the ideal of community. Co-operation, if voluntary, may be a good even though each person is responsible for him/herself, since the final result can be better for the self when undertaken with others. It is within this mindset that the "following of Christ" will be one of appearances – an unhealthy adoption of another persona, an

---

[13] John Garvey ed. *Circles of Love: Daily Readings with Henri J. M. Nouwen* London: Darton, Longman and Todd, 1988. p. 54.
[14] Rom. 12: 4-18; 1 Cor. 12: 4-30; Eph. 1: 22-23; 3: 6; 4: 25; 5:30; Col. 1: 24 et al.

imitation of Christ rather than a conscious living of the mystery of the incarnation within one's own life.

On the other hand, collectivism would hold that one's sense of self can only be obtained from interaction within the community. Mass-mindedness, with its inherent dangers, is one result of collectivism. Identity is given by the community. The primary goal of a collectivity is the good of the group – be it nation or church or commune. Everything else is subordinate to it. Therefore self-sacrifice is held up as an ideal whereby the benefit of others determines one's identity and worth. The ego is suppressed, since the needs of the society can take precedence over the needs of the individual, even without their free consent. The group absorbs rather than develops the individual.

Neither of these extremes lends itself to an adequate description of "community". But the term "community" is applied to many scenarios. Some people gather together because they have interests in common; there is benefit in combining forces in order to more successfully develop those interests. Is this a "community", or is it an "association"? Sharing goals and objectives is certainly one aspect of community, but is not the whole story.

Community involves the give and take of relating to one another. People experience community when, because they are attracted to each other, they form circles of friendship and mutual support that act as a buffer in times of hardship and provide nourishment for their own self-development. But is community simply a "society of friends"?

There are those who look to community to overcome their sense of isolation, the pain of loneliness. However, it is to be remembered that "loneliness" and "aloneness" are two different things. There will always be one way in which we are "alone". Coming to grips with this aspect of the human condition is part of the journey to self-acceptance. It is only when we have found our own value before God that we can be fully open to the impact of others in our lives. Or, as the psychologists say, our ego must be strong before we can surrender it to another. This journey may be made within community; however, like the journey of birth, or, indeed, death, it is one that demands we go alone into our centre in order to give ourselves over to the One who is always there with us.

What, then, is involved in forming Christian community? Does it go beyond the above notions of community? Again, the insights of Henri Nouwen throw light on the discussion.

> (Christian) Community is grounded in God, who calls us together, and not in the attractiveness of people to each other. There are many groups that have been formed to protect their own interests, to defend their own status, or to promote their own causes, but none of these is a Christian community. ... The mystery of community is precisely that it embraces *all* people, whatever their individual difference may be, and allows them to live together as brothers and sisters of Christ and sons and daughters of his heavenly Father.[15]

Christian community promotes neither individualism nor collectivism. Instead, in the interplay of relationships, in giving and receiving and, yes, in sacrifice, we both discover our own individuality, as Nouwen says, and can identify with and appreciate others,

> because it is God's glory itself that manifests itself in his people in an abundant variety of forms and styles. The uniqueness of our neighbors is not related to those idiosyncratic qualities that only they and nobody else have, but it is related to the fact that God's eternal beauty and love become visible in these unique, irreplaceable, finite human beings. It is exactly in the preciousness of the individual person that the eternal love of God is refracted and becomes the basis of a community of love.[16]

---

[15] Garvey, *Circles of Love*, p. 43.
[16] Garvey, *Circles of Love*, p. 19.

Joseph and community

Another work of art, Murillo's painting, the "Two Trinities"[17], recalls the 17th century devotion taken up in the rule of Médaille. As already noted, this devotion promoted union with the divine through incarnating in one's own life the fruits of this union given by the Spirit. The model of such living was the Holy Family. St Francis de Sales, for example, writes, "We may say that the Holy Family was a trinity on earth which in a certain way represented the Blessed Trinity itself."[18]

It is noteworthy, however, that Médaille, unlike Francis de Sales, chose as the aspect of the heavenly Trinity mirrored by Joseph, the unifying love of the Spirit.[19] "In honor of Saint Joseph their Patriarch," instructs Médaille, "they (the Sisters) will be one in the service of each other, and one in the service of the neighbour without distinction, for whom they will try to have cordial charity, as Saint Joseph had for his dear spouse and for the Savior Jesus."[20] Marcia Allen notes that, as a Jesuit, Médaille would have brought an Ignatian concept of service to bear on this instruction.

> For Ignatius and the Companions, service was the "wellspring" for their enthusiastic love for others. Service was that which revealed to them God's face and in serving they in turn unveiled God's glory, God's presence in the world around them. This was their peculiar mysticism. It was through serving that they found union with God. And union with God was always union with others.[21]

---

[17] Murillo was born in Spain in 1618 and died in 1682. His painting, "The Two Trinities", has the image of the Christ-child at the centre, intersecting the circle of Father and Spirit above and Mary and Joseph below. In its own way it depicts the Chalcedonian formula of the two natures of Christ.
[18] St Francis de Sales, Discourse 19. Quoted in Foley, *Saint Joseph*, p. 62.
[19] For Francis de Sales, the parallel to the Holy Spirit was Mary. Joseph's role was likened to the Father.
[20] *Règlements*, p. 5.
[21] Marcia Allen CSJ. "The Service of Cordial Charity – Joseph the Model", Unpublished paper, July 2003. p. 4.

Self-gift: For Joseph, service was the means by which the "double-union" with God and humanity was achieved since that service was directed to Jesus, the embodiment of the "double-union", God incarnate. For him, "community service" was not just an extra. It was integral to his identity. As co-provider, Joseph served his family-community. As father and husband, he would have devoted himself especially to the welfare of those with whose lives his was intimately entwined. Historically, the context for everyday interactions for him would have leant towards the "collectivist" model of community rather than the "individualistic" one.

> In Galilee during Joseph's lifetime, survival demanded that people live in groups, and a person's sense of identity derived from the group in which he or she was a member, usually the kinship group in which one was "embedded". The basic group was the extended family or household, which was a unit of both production and consumption. Kinship or lineage governed all other facets of life. The reputation of a family determined its members' social position: that is, their possible marriage or business alliances, the social functions they could attend, and the religious roles they could fulfil.[22]

As father of a family within the wider household community, Joseph would have met regularly with the men of his village to strategise for its welfare. He would also have served as doorkeeper for household and village. Hennessy explains,

> There are many indications from culture and archaeology of the importance that the common people of Palestine gave to decisions regarding involvement with and withdrawal from society beyond the household. ... Entrances to family property or to houses had rather elaborate doorsills and heavy doors that opened inward and were bolted from the inside. These spatial signs of limitations, along with religious practices promoting purity and separation, not only moderated contact with the world beyond the household and village, but also defined and strengthened the ties within these primary groups.[23]

---

[22] Hennessy, *In Search of a Patron,* p. 29.
[23] Hennessy, *In Search of a Patron,* p. 51.

"Joseph's family responsibilities," the author continues, "were played out in a public arena."[24] The self-giving, even self-sacrifice of service, carried out not for his own gain but for the life of the group, was both an expectation and a necessity.[25]

Bonding: What Joseph's emotional life was like we have no way of knowing. His role in salvation history, however, has led some to surmise that he would have experienced the basic human feelings that others in like situations share. Jacques Bossuet, a 17th century French orator, saw in the fact that, in choosing Joseph "to act as father to his son in this world", God, "as it were, charged Joseph's breast with some ray or spark of his own boundless love for his Son".[26] In a radio address in 1958, Pope Pius XII asserted, "Joseph showed Jesus all the natural love, all the affectionate solicitude, that a father's heart can know."[27] It was in his family that Jesus learnt what loving was. He came to know that God is love, a community of love. If, as faith-development theorists tells us, a child's first impressions of God are received from the relationships with one's parents, it is relevant to note that Jesus never uses the term of power, "Almighty", to refer to God, but instead uses the diminutive he would have addressed to Joseph, "Ab-ba"[28].

In whatever ways Joseph demonstrated his love for those dearest to him, we can assume they would have conformed to the norm for societies of the time and the roles they demanded. The prevailing family value in this Galilean society was family loyalty. The devotion of Joseph to his immediate and wider family would have reflected not the "emotionally-based love-myths that prevailed in the West in the nineteenth and twentieth

---

[24] Hennessy, *In Search of a Patron*, p. 50.
[25] Hennessy, *In Search of a Patron*, p 51.
[26] Bossuet, Jacques. Oeuvres Complètes, Sermon on St Joseph.
[27] Pius XII, Feb. 19th, 1958. Cited by Foley, *Saint Joseph*, p. 36.
[28] Hennessy makes the point that this term does not necessarily indicate "affection" in contemporary western terms; it was (and still is) a colloquial form of address used in the domestic situation by children and adults to their fathers. *In Search of a Patron*, p. 49.

centuries"[29] but commitment to further their honour and to care for their welfare.

It would have been important for Joseph to build bonds of solidarity between his family and others in the community, both for survival and identity. At a personal level, he would have met often, "perhaps daily, with other husbands and fathers to share the ups and downs of daily life".[30] Developing business contacts would have formed part of social interaction. Gatherings for Sabbath prayers, religious ceremonies, festivities and celebrations would have provided occasion for them to forge close ties with the group. Certainly, the Gospels tell us that this family was well known in the village and that the relatives of Jesus are closely identified with it.[31]

Hospitality: Jesus, it seems, loved parties – so much so, that he described heaven as one long party! A sign of the reign of God, he said, was the abundance, nourishment and festal cheer of a banquet. How many meal scenes are there in the Gospels? Was entertaining at meals a trait of the family of Joseph? Was this family renowned in Nazareth for their parties?

Known to be "just", Joseph, we can assert, observed the religious obligation of the Jew to home hospitality. This would have applied not only to close friends and family members, but also to the stranger, the poor and the needy. For Jews, hospitality was[32] a way of demonstrating compassion, recalling the time when they were strangers in Egypt. The notion was deeply embedded in their culture; extending hospitality added to a family's honour. The scene depicted by Rublev (referred to above) recalls the hospitality of Abraham (the "father of the Jews"), who, on seeing the three strangers approaching, rushes

---

[29] Hennessy, *In Search of a Patron*, p. 49.
[30] Hennessy, *In Search of a Patron,* p. 52.
[31] Mt. 13: 55; Mk 6:3; Lk 2: 39, 3: 23; Jn 1: 45.
[32] And still is!

out into the heat of the day to meet them. He personally waits on them, even though he is a rich man and has servants to do so. For Jews, Abraham's hospitality set a standard with which they were ever to be identified.

Early Christians were urged to adhere to this model of hospitality, as noted in the letter to the Hebrews: "Do not forget to entertain strangers, for by doing so, some people have entertained angels without knowing it."[33] "Offer hospitality to one another without grumbling,"[34] advises Peter. The primitive Church, following the example of Jesus, met over meals.[35] The risen Christ was encountered over meals.[36] Through the Eucharistic meal, union was established between the believing community and Christ himself.

Through his service of family and neighbour, through developing the bonds which held them together and through hospitality, Joseph anticipated the ushering in of the reign of God by Jesus, whereby barriers of separation have been removed and all of humanity is brought into one. Like the Holy Family, the Christian is called to be an icon of the Trinity, promoting life, giving of self and bringing all together in love.

Louise Perrotta describes Italian customs practised on the feast of St Joseph, where tables of special foods are set out in homes or town squares, the poor being especially well served by three people standing in for the Holy Family. Migrants to America have, in some areas, continued the tradition, setting up an altar in the saint's honour.

> The altars generally have three tiers to symbolize the Blessed Trinity. A statue of St Joseph and a statue or picture of the Holy Family are placed on the top tier and decorated with flowers, greenery and fruit. .. If the altar is set up on the eve

---

[33] Hebrews 13:2
[34] 1 Peter 4:9-10.
[35] Acts 2: 42–47 et al.
[36] Emmaus, Lk 24: 28-32; the Upper Room Lk 24: 41-43; Sea of Tiberius Jn 21: 9-19 et al.

of the feast, people often visit to pray and to leave petitions and donations for the poor. ... A braided loaf symbolises the staff of St Joseph. Other traditional foods are also found on the altars.[37]

Art has a way of saying in concise, dramatic form what many words can only attempt!

5.2 PART TWO: The spirit unfolds.

<u>Sisters of St Joseph as community</u>
"Médaille's vision," says Marcia Allen, "...of the early communities of women in the Massif Central, was that this dynamic called service is communal."[38] For Médaille, the concept of service being communal was contained in the very title, "Congregation of St Joseph", since it was the aspect of unifying love that he saw as characteristic of the saint. Therefore the sisters should be constantly reminded of their mission and character, simply by the use of their name.[39]

For Médaille, Trinitarian language spoke of God's nearness and the self-communication of God to humanity through Jesus, in the Holy Spirit. In his *Constitutions*, Médaille says,
> To state in summary the end of our very little Congregation of Saint Joseph, the sisters who are united in it will remember that their little community is consecrated to the very holy uncreated Trinity of God the Father, Son, and Holy Spirit, and to the created one of Jesus, Mary and Joseph.[40]

The vocation of the Sister of St. Joseph was then, as now, "to enter into this mystery, to welcome with all our being the life God gives, and with Christ, to live and work so that life may be

---

[37] Perrotta, *Saint Joseph,* pp. 104, 105.
[38] Allen, Notes of lecture, Concordia, July 2003, p. 10.
[39] Byrne, Notes of lecture, Concordia, June 2003.
[40] *Constitutions for the Little Congregation of the Daughters of St Joseph*, p. 15.

communicated, that humanity might be restored and healed."[41] "Trinity," Byrne says, "is a way of life."[42]

In particular, Médaille's parallel of the Spirit with Joseph spells out the orientation of building relationships that should characterise the Sisters. In his third summary clause of the *Constitutions*, he states,
> Thirdly, for the honor of God the Holy Spirit who is all love, they should so live that their little community can bear the name of congregation of the great love of God and that in all things and everywhere they make profession of the greatest love in practice.[43]

The parallel clause offers Joseph as the human exemplar of such love, its incarnation:
> Sixthly, for the honor of their very glorious Patriarch St. Joseph who was all charity for Jesus and for Mary, they will profess the most perfect union and charity possible among themselves and a very complete charity and compassion, according to God and to the directives of their little Institute, toward every kind of neighbor, all thanks to the sovereign help of grace without which we are nothing.[44]

The Eucharist was for Médaille a further example of how love in practice brings people together into a unity:
> Furthermore, my dear Daughter, this Blessed Sacrament is a mystery of union and perfectly accomplishes the union: In it Jesus hidden in the Host unites all creatures to himself and to God, his Father, and – think of the title "communion" – unites all the faithful among themselves by a "common union".
> May it please the Divine Goodness that we be able to contribute, feeble instruments though we be, to re-establishing this total union of souls in the Church, in God and with God.[45]

In time, however, the profound connection between consecration to the Trinity and the unifying purpose for which the Sisters of

---

[41] Byrne, "Re-conceiving Identity", p. 7.
[42] Byrne, "Re-conceiving Identity", p. 7.
[43] *Constitutions for the Little Congregation of the Daughters of St Joseph*, p. 15.
[44] *Constitutions for the Little Congregation of the Daughters of St Joseph*, p. 16.
[45] *The Eucharistic Letter*, pars. 42, 25.

St. Joseph had come together became blurred. As early as 1694 when the constitutions of the Sisters of St Joseph were first printed,[46] wording was changed in such a way as to indicate that the Sisters of St Joseph simply practised devotion to the Trinity and to the Holy Family.[47] By the 19th century, the implications of a theology of Trinity were, in the main, depersonalised and a matter of intellectual debate. This was the case for Julian Tenison Woods and Mary MacKillop, and for most of the Church until Vatican II.

For Mary and Julian (and many Sisters of St Joseph around the world at the time), God's compassionate love incarnated among us was represented through devotion to the Sacred Heart and to the Immaculate Heart of Mary. Devotion to St Joseph completed what they saw as "the model of the religious family, that of the family of Nazareth".[48] While the "unselfish love"[49] and service of Joseph were noted, his hiddenness, simplicity of life and commitment to God's Will were the virtues most often mentioned as deserving imitation. Certainly, the purpose of the Sisters was to "give themselves entirely to God" (come into union with God), and to "make God known and loved by others". St Joseph was, too, a model in the building of community,
> in the discharge of our external duties towards the children of our schools, the poor over whom we have charge, or in our separate relations towards one another in the religious community of which we are members.[50]

Overall, however, the primitive constitutions of the Sisters of St Joseph of the Sacred Heart lacked the Trinitarian focus of those written by Médaille. By now, too, as noted, revised

---

[46] As opposed to (hand-written) manuscripts.
[47] Byrne, "Reconceiving Identity", p. 6.
[48] Lyne, *Mary MacKillop,* p. 181.
[49] MacKillop, Mary. Circular letter to the Sisters for St Joseph's Day, 1890. Another phrase in the letter refers to Joseph's "total forgetfulness of self". Archives, Sisters of St Joseph, Sydney.
[50] Circular, same as above.

constitutions of other groups of Sisters of St Joseph also lacked the depth contained in those of their founder, even though the Trinity was still mentioned. However, charism is a living spirit; it is handed down through encounter with and memory of living persons, more so than in the printed word.[51] So it is that the charism of unifying love, recognised by Médaille in St Joseph and handed on through those sharing this Spirit, features in the stories of Sisters of St Joseph around the world.

Inclusivity
From the first, Vacher points out, the way of life of the Sisters caused them
> to be welcoming to all persons and manners of action which can contribute to advancing the Glory of God in serving the neighbor. All the levels of society can be a part of the little Congregation, in being recognized for their diversity, and accepted for what they are, thus contributing to the evangelization of their milieu. All the organizations of Christian life or action can be used. In working in this way for its double end of the holiness of the sisters and the holiness of service to every neighbor, the Little Design of Father Médaille receives its vocation of gathering in unity, the congregation itself and the world.[52]

In the new world of the Americas, the spirit of inclusivity soon became a feature of membership, as the six original missionaries from France were joined by women of Irish, German and other European backgrounds reflective of the ethnic "melting pot" of the USA and Canada. However, the acceptance of indigenous women into the Congregations was a much later development. Coburn and Smith comment:
> In 1892, Sisters Julia Littenecker and Monica Corrigan visited Mexico to discuss opening a school and to recruit Mexican women into the community. Although the CSJs were making

---

[51] With Vatican II, Sisters of St Joseph re-examined their original rules. The "printed word" of Médaille's primitive documents has provided for the Sisters whose roots lay in Le Puy a joyful recognition and revelation of what has lived on amongst them. The documents put words on the spirit of Joseph that has perdured.
[52] Vacher, *Des "régulières"*, Session Four, p. 161.

inroads in Arizona and California, ethnic prejudice and the impoverished circumstances limited their recruiting efforts in the Southwest. The Arizona novitiate became the home for six Hispanic novices, but Anglo parents, who did not appreciate the "foreign aspect and primitive conditions," sent their daughters east to St Louis for their novitiate. After fourteen years, having recruited only a handful of new vocations, the novitiate closed.[53]

It would be well into the 1900s before Sisters native to India, Africa and the Americas would enable the Sisters of St Joseph to be truly heterogenic within their own ranks.

Early membership of the Sisters of St Joseph of the Sacred Heart in Australia/New Zealand reflects the ethnic variety typical of the population of the two countries. However, the inner culture was predominantly Anglo-Irish. As yet, the Congregation has not been able to successfully incorporate Aboriginal and Maori candidates into their ranks; those who did enter in the 1950s and '60s eventually left, cultural differences proving too much for them. With Vatican II having raised awareness of the world to the necessity for inculturation, real efforts have been made to heighten sensitivity to this issue. The foundation in Peru has with joy received Peruvian members, and present overall membership includes women from Asia and the Pacific Islands.

The spirit of inclusivity, however, found particular application in ministry. Community-building efforts of the Sisters sought out the excluded and brought them into the group. The reason for the first mission of the Sisters in the USA was to minister to the deaf and the children of slaves. Mary MacKillop in Australia was drawn to those who stood on the edges of society. "These are the children we love," she said as she put her arms around one raggedy boy. In India, those excluded by the class system of that country earn the special care of the Sisters. At Fatima College in Madurai, young students from all castes eat

---

[53] Coburn & Smith, *Spirited Lives,* p. 90.

together. The Sisters see that it is their mission of unity that is the driving force behind their deliberate choice "to give place to the poor and exploited, especially to women and dalits"[54] (untouchables). In a village of Tamil Nadu, Sister Mary Manicka, Sister of St Joseph of Lyon, coordinates, with her team, 3,000 groups of women in her "ant-like" work of helping them claim their rights as community members.[55]

A spirit of inclusivity impels Sisters like the legendary Sister Thomasine in South Australia to embrace a cancer patient with hardly any face. It allows Sisters to feel at home with families whose practices of hygiene are less than the norm – where the visitor must first sweep aside clucking chickens from the table-space before being able to drink the proffered cup of tea. Inclusivity feels the anger of one young Sister unable to intervene as the Superior refused to take aboriginal boarders because white families would send their children away. In her old age, the Sister could say with satisfaction, "When I became a superior myself, I was able to take them!"

Inclusivity has led Sisters working in parishes to form support groups for divorced and separated, to find ways to include women who have had abortions and who have then cut themselves off from the Church community, to devise paraliturgies for parents of miscarried and aborted children to grieve and get in touch with the compassion of God, to reach those with mental illness and their carers, to bring in the refugee and the lonely. This spirit lives on in a Canadian Sister who explains, "At the young age of eighty-three I decided to retire from tutoring! Since moving to Morrow Park I have transferred my ministry from visiting "shut-ins" to phoning them and to writing to those who have difficulties in hearing. I call it my telephone ministry."[56]

---

[54] *Misi Synthèse,* No 20, Juillet–Octobre, 2000. p. 10. (Translation mine).
[55] *Misi Synthèse,* p. 10..
[56] Smyth & Wicks. *Wisdom Raises Her Voice,* p. 112

Hospitality

Closely allied to the spirit of inclusivity is that of hospitality. "There's nothing like Josephite hospitality!" is a phrase regularly heard in circles involving the Sisters. Jubilee celebrations, feastdays, professions, anniversaries – occasions for hospitality are never-ending. Bringing someone into your own home is indicative of bringing them into your heart. With the reclamation of spirit that has happened since Vatican II, Sisters have been able to extend home-hospitality to a far wider cross-section of people than in the past.

While the former etiquette rules of Religious had certain parts of convents closed off from lay-visitors, stories of the "spirit alive" in the experience of Sisters tell of the strength of the spirit of hospitality. One Sister told of how the parents of a certain family in the town were often "not able to cope". The Sisters would take in the children as temporary boarders. "We used to have Mass in the chapel and the twins would be in the room beside the chapel and they'd wake up and they'd have high recreation while we were having Mass. We had them there for three weeks at a time when the mother couldn't cope. .. They came on beautifully – they were lovely. I've got some nice photos of those children."

Prudence demanded discrimination, but Sisters were able to find ways of making sure those needing a good meal got it, and that lodging was found. One priest, with embarrassment, related that, in the 1940s, he set out from the convent after dinner but, on discovering he had left his hat behind, returned. There he found the Sisters at the table eating his scraps. There was not another skerrick of food in the house. His, however, was not a unique story.

The Sisters in Baden (USA) who opened their convent to refugees and have formed strong bonds of friendship with them; those who offered sanctuary to asylum seekers; those who welcome local groups to share facilities such as a swimming pool, meeting rooms and times of prayer – all these extend the hospitality of God into our world, in the manner of Joseph. In the past, right around the world, Sisters of St Joseph referred to the men who came knocking at the back door for "a bite to eat" as being "St Josephs". Not all of them, however, had the experience of one "St Joseph" in Concordia who was met by a harried Sister carving the meat right on meal-time. In broken English she meant to explain to him that she would attend to him later. Upon seeing her brandishing the carving knife and hearing the words, "I get you, I get you", he ran down the street as fast as he could!

Restoring unity
The ability to reconcile, which "Médaillan" Sisters of St Joseph have recognised as part of their mission of unity, is an aspect which characterises many of the Sisters' stories. Variations of what a Sister described in Philadelphia could be told everywhere Sisters have been. "During the summer vacation," she explained, "the diocese used to call on Sisters to take a census. Once while doing this I met a woman who told me she was excommunicated. 'Let's sit down and talk,' I said. She told me she had left the Church when a priest said that because her children were in a public school she would go to hell. 'The Church is as much yours as the pastor's,' I assured her. 'Go and talk to a priest-friend of mine.' I met her later and she was beaming with happiness. 'He said to me, "What a mistake!" and I felt like a terrible load was lifted off my shoulders!' I was just so happy she was reconciled."

When the Sisters of St Joseph opened three schools in Brisbane, Queensland, many children living near them transferred from a school run by the Sisters of Mercy. Bad blood could have ensued, since the Sisters of Mercy were operating under a government-funded scheme that depended on the number of enrolments. Mary MacKillop handled the situation by leading her Sisters in visiting the families involved, expressing admiration for the work of the Sisters of Mercy and persuading them to return their children to their school. "By October," says Gardiner, "the Mercies were directing vocations to the Josephites."[57]

Restoring unity through reconciliation calls for patience and understanding. One Sister told how, when she was a child, her father returned to the practice of his faith through the quiet influence of the Sisters. The one who taught her used to come to visit the family and often played a game of cards with her father. His comment to her later was, "They know where Jesus Christ is."

Another Sister was renowned for her ability to help couples sort out their problems. She would be called upon at all times, day and night, to intervene in domestic disputes. "Just putting them right" was her laconic remark on returning home. Sometimes, though, reconciliation can only take the form of comfort and acceptance of the inevitable. "We learnt from one another as young Sisters how to be for the people," recalled a Sister. "One night at 2 a.m. the doorbell rang and there were two pupils very upset. 'Come quickly,' they said. 'Mum is crying, because Daddy is living in a tent with another woman.' The Superior told me to get dressed, and we walked to the home with the children, and we all cried." "God's capacity for being with creatures," says Edwards, "God's capacity to love, God's capacity to feel with those who suffer, is *infinitely* beyond anything possible for human beings."[58]

---

[57] Gardiner, *Mary MacKillop,* p. 84.
[58] Edwards, *Breath of Life,* p. 113.

Inter-religious relations: Long before the words "ecumenism" or "inter-faith relations" were in current usage, Sisters of St Joseph have, with others, been agents of reconciliation with people of other faiths. Margaret Brennan points out that

> Women religious ... insisted on accepting people of other religions in their academies and hospitals, predating ecumenism, often the only visible sign of goodwill among the religions in an area; they picked up the pieces of failing social welfare systems by their work with orphans, immigrants, minorities and the urban poor. It is impossible to think of an American Church without them or of the evolution of American women without them.[59]

In 1856 the Sisters of St Joseph of Chambéry were the first Catholic Religious to go into Lutheran Scandinavia since the Reformation. They lived in Copenhagen, renting three small rooms in a basement next to a cemetery. Their unassuming ways gradually won over the people. A Danish province rapidly developed, extending to Germany, Norway, Sweden and Iceland. Today, the Spirituality Centres run by the Sisters serve people from all faiths. For example, a Danish Sister, Sr Emma, is regularly asked to facilitate meetings of the Lutheran church and give spiritual direction to its pastors. In 1920, Paul Claudel could write "Catholicism was brought back to Denmark, so to speak, by the Sisters of St Joseph of Chambéry."[60]

At the time of her excommunication in 1871, Mary MacKillop and her expelled Sisters were given housing by a Jewish man, Emanuel Solomon. He had already come to their aid some years before when they had had to give up their convent to the Dominican Sisters newly arrived from Ireland. The cottage they had then rented was so small some had had to sleep on the floor. When he heard of this, Emanuel Solomon had given them "the use of a nearby row of cottages rent free for as long as they

---

[59] Brennan, *Persistence of Vision*, pp. ii, iii.
[60] *Misi Synthèse*, p. 13

needed them".[61] Later, Mary wrote of her gratitude to this extraordinarily kind gentleman but thought it was no surprise, since "after all, St Joseph was a Jew".

Another story told of Mary MacKillop illustrates her ability to relate to and trust the goodness of each person, even if their faith background was officially hostile to Catholicism, as Presbyterianism then was:

> Cardinal Moran has asked her to run some Confirmation classes for adults six miles away. As there was no suitable place for this, she went out with Sister Irene one afternoon looking for somewhere. "We knew no one out there," said Irene, "but Mother saw a very pretentious looking mansion and said, 'They should have plenty of room.' I did not like the idea of asking, but Mother said we are doing God's work and He will help us." The people were Presbyterians, but for some months their large drawing room was used by a crowd of about thirty Catholic men and a couple of nuns, to whom every kindness was shown.[62]

Institutions run by the Sisters were well-known not to discriminate between people of different religions. In Colorado (USA), the *Georgetown Courier* wrote of a hospital run by the Sisters, "The makeup of the (hospital) committee speaks for itself and plainly shows that neither religious beliefs nor nationality enters into the matter in any way whatsoever."[63]

Especially in the teaching of music and business studies, Sisters around the world did much to break down bigotry, prejudice and fear between Catholics and those of other faiths. When the Sisters of St Joseph of Goulburn opened a school in Batlow (New South Wales) in 1923, a Protestant lad was, unknown to his parents, among the first enrolled. He had earned his sixpence school fee by milking the neighbour's cow.[64] An older

---

[61] Foale, *The Josephite Story*, p. 52.
[62] Gardiner, *Mary MacKillop*, p. 455.
[63] Coburn & Smith, *Spirited Lives*, p. 125.
[64] Glass and O'Grady, *Their Story*, p. 13.

Sister in Haunton, England, told how, upon "retirement" she joined a local Senior Citizens Club and was soon being sought out by those harmed by religious divisions. She found herself "working there full time" in her ministry of reconciliation. "Everyone needs a bit of love," was her comment.

<u>Being with</u>

Of all the attributes of the spirit of Sisters of St Joseph, the most frequently cited is, I find, the ability to be present with others. Marcia Allen claims this as being of the essence of the Josephite spirit. "Truly being present and allowing others to be present fully, accepting them as they are, saying yes to their fullest life, entering into the dialogue of life around us with them, really <u>with</u> them, is the service we're about."[65] The constitutions of the Federation of Sisters of St Joseph in Australia/New Zealand says,

> We live close to people in mutual service,
> offering and receiving compassion, challenge and hope
> as we walk together in the ordinariness of daily life.[66]

Stories preserved by the Sisters of St Joseph of Buffalo tell of early days in Dunkirk near Lake Erie. The orphanage there was in constant need of funds, and locals would arrange picnics and other outings both as social occasions and as money-raisers.

> The groups who arranged the picnics judged their success by the number of Sisters who attended. These affairs brought the Sisters close to the people. Here and there one would see the older Sisters in some shady spot engaged in confidential talk with one who needed consolation or advice.[67]

Visiting the families of students, the sick, and those in straightened circumstances has been an integral part of the Sisters' ministry. For some Congregations, this practice was stopped after the imposition of the 1918 code of canon law. One

---

[65] Allen, Notes of lecture, July 2003.
[66] *A Future and a Hope,* p.12.
[67] Sister M. Immaculata, *Like a Swarm of Bees,* p. 153.

old Sister in Canada remembers when she was first professed being told by another in community: "When I was a young Sister we met the boats (bringing migrants to be settled). That's who we really are. We'll be back there some day." Would not the same Sister now be pleased to know of Sisters of St Joseph carrying out a chaplaincy role to sailors of cargo ships today – their interest and presence being a rare sign of hope to homesick, often-abused and spiritually-starved men and women as they enter a strange port and country?

"Being with" makes real the presence of God with us in our human condition. "The Spirit is the companion to each creature, loving it into being and opening up a future for it in God," says Edwards.[68] Older Sisters remember that, as children, they used to "walk down the road with the Sisters as they visited shop owners and pupils' parents". "Sisters would be at basketball, barracking for their students, and parents would have a yarn with them there on the courts," said one. "Some women had no-one else to talk to." "When I was born, the Sisters came to see my mother," said another. "The Sisters were the darlings of the town. 'I couldn't live here without those Sisters,' you'd hear people say."

The Sisters' egalitarian attitudes did much to endear them to the people. "I used to help Sister fill up the inkwells before school," recalls one past pupil. At the time she did not see anything extraordinary in the fact that Sister filled them *with* her. But others who came from schools run by different Religious Congregations often noted the fact that this Sister would pick up the broom and sweep the floor *with* the students, that she polished the Church brass *with* them, that she did the drains and took on whatever needed to be done *with* the helpers she engaged.

---

[68] Edwards, *Breath of Life*, p. 114.

The mutuality that is part of community can only be built in an environment of "being with". In Wales, the Sisters recall a much-loved member who used to stay with the gypsies in the caravans. She went to their conventions and joined in their activities, not in a patronising way but because she really loved the people. In USA the Sisters' attendance at pow-wows won over the preliminary resistance of a local indigenous tribe to education, so much so that the tribe leader eventually became the principal of the school when the Sisters felt they should withdraw. It was no surprise to Sisters of St Joseph, known for being *with* the people in outback Australia, that when they pulled into a station on their train journey to Cloncurry, Queensland, a man should emerge from a tin hut and hand up to them a bundle of newspaper in which there was bush corn beef – "Me missus thought you'd be hungry," he said.

Similarly, Sisters got to know the people and their needs by living in community among them in a Trailer Park in Montgomery, USA. Sisters in Australia, living in caravans in remote Aboriginal communities are present to these people. Brazilian Sisters have joined their Sisters in France to live with the poor and displaced in high-rise flats: "Each, according to their ability, has taken on different works – visiting the sick, working with youth and migrants, preparing prayer services."[69] In Peru, among the people in the invasion areas[70] of Lima or in the Andes, Sisters "trust that the message we are giving is that we want to be with them in their daily struggles". How else can God's compassionate love be communicated?

Presence: Being at one *with* cannot be faked. It must come from an inner disposition of presence with and to the other.

---

[69] *Message Aux Amis*, Soeurs de Saint Joseph de Chambéry, Province de France, Dec. 2002. p. 4. (Translation mine).
[70] Former haciendas that has been taken over by the Peruvian refugees fleeing violence or seeking economic security in the city.

Sisters of St Joseph of Orange could say of a greatly-loved former Superior General, Sr Frances Dunn,

> As a leader, at St Joseph Hospital and in our religious community, Sister Frances had an open door policy. She was there to listen to people's needs and problems. She responded with a straightforward honesty. There was no beating around the bush.[71].

Attentiveness to others indicates for them the receptivity of God. Being present to God's openness to us is the basis of contemplation. God's presence in the other is acknowledged when I give my attention totally to them. Because union with the neighbour and union with God is the one movement, Sisters of St Joseph try to express this fact in service of God *in* the neighbour. Some groups of Religious, for example, the Monks and Nuns of Jerusalem so popular in France, express service *and* prayer through their daily regimen of working at a factory or professional job for half the day and then returning to the monastery, donning robes and chanting the Office for the other half. Young people flock to these services. The balance of prayer and work is symbolised; being present to God *and* being present to the other is given visible expression.

For the Sister of St Joseph however, being present to God *in* the other demands habits of contemplation that must acknowledge, own and celebrate the way in which God's Spirit breathes *in* the daily experiences of our lives. Mary MacKillop wrote to Monsignor Kirby in 1873, "I must tell you that from early childhood, as far back as I can remember, (God) gave me such a sense of His watchful presence that I would feel myself reproved for my smallest faults."[72] Habits of being "present" to God throughout the day have been practised by Sisters throughout history. The term "practical mystic" has been used in reference to many a Sister of St Joseph. Again, it cannot be a pretence. The Sister who at 32 years of age had a stroke that put her in a

---

[71] *Focus*, Fall 1999. Sisters of St Joseph of Orange, California. p. 7
[72] Letter to Mons. Kirby, Ascension Thursday, 1873. Archives, Sisters of St Joseph, Sydney.

wheelchair for the rest of her life and who holds the life of each person in reverence before her knows that she then encounters God. The one who meets her, too, knows that the sense of presence in this encounter is of Presence Itself.

Of course, being present to God in the focussed "place apart" such as the prayer room or chapel, the hundreds of Spirituality Centres conducted by Sisters of St Joseph around the world, the ashrams such as the Ashram Saint-Joseph at Pachmarhi in Madaya Pradesh, India, in Church liturgy and in community prayer, is a necessary aspect of our lives. These are expressions of communal faith. They tell us that the God we know is a God of community. These external events and signs help extend and anticipate the reign of God where full communion will be attained. Sister Veronica Lonergan in Melbourne, reflected on her last assignment in a city school before "retirement": "At first I missed the close parish relationships I had hitherto experienced – I had not realised what strong bonding takes place between parents and teachers when one lives in close proximity, and kneels frequently with them in worship in the parish church sharing their joys and sorrows as fellow community members."[73] An awareness of God's presence within the community leads us into the community that is God.

This was the awareness of the group of old Sisters in Adelaide who sat each afternoon on the convent verandah waiting for the "school Sisters" to arrive back and tell them what had happened during the day. These "great pray-ers" would spend much of their time in the chapel, gathering the concerns of the world in consciousness and placing them before the Love that embraces all. God's presence *with* us was a living awareness for the hospital chaplain who bent over a dying indigent as he confessed that he had murdered and who could readily assure

---

[73] Veronica Lonergan RSJ, *I Sought and I Found*, Catholic Regional College, North Keilor, 2002. p. 6.

him, "Yes, God has forgiven you!", sprinkling him with Holy Water as he smiled and died. It is the developing awareness of novices in India who, for a few days each year, live with Catholic families to pray with them and be with them in their occupations and difficulties.[74] The term used in John's Gospel to indicate the Spirit who is *with,* is "Paraclete", meaning "one called alongside of".[75]

Kindness
The word "gentleness" used by both Médaille and Woods in reference to the approach of Sisters to service of the neighbour has, in some instances, been misunderstood to indicate sentimentality, leniency or self-depreciation. In its original context, however, it has the association of "kindness". This was the term that was constantly used in reference to the spirit shown by Sisters of St Joseph in the past. The strength of "kindness" is contained in the notion of "kinship" that underlies its meaning. Kindness is a response to those whom we regard as our own "kind", our "kin". In the making of community, kindness binds us to one another.

Acts of kindness on the part of Sisters in the past have built up the kinship community of God's love. It has been a practical kindness that spoke to the times. A service often mentioned around the world was the Sisters' availability to lay out the dead. In a past age, this was a kindness that touched into necessity but that seems strange to us now.

Sisters who, during the Depression and after the Second World War, begged and made cocoa or soup for children before school; who knitted baby-clothes for every newborn in the parish; who, like Mary MacKillop on hearing of the death of a mother next door, took in the children until other care could be obtained for

---

[74] *Misi Synthèse,* No 20, Juillet – Octobre, 2000. p. 10.
[75] Edwards, *Breath of Life,* p. 74. The word "Paraclete" can be translated as "advocate", "helper", "witness" or "comforter".

them; Sisters who brought a smile, sometimes a small gift and always a recognition of dignity to the strugglers, the sick and those in prison – these built up bonds that linked people to one another. "You be good to my boys," Sister Jeanne Marie used to say to the prison wardens.

Kindness fosters an environment of reconciliation. When a frightened, angry boy ran away from home in a town of Pennsylvania, the Sisters became aware that he was hiding in their coal shoot under the chapel. Having informed the parents, one of the Sisters persuaded them to leave him there until he was ready to come out. This he did after two days, able by then to face his issues and telling the Sisters he could hear them praying for him and that this had helped calm him.

Stories of kindness are remembered and handed on as part of the heritage of the Sisters of St Joseph: the music teacher who prepared a bowl of hot water for children to warm their hands on cold, frosty mornings; the teacher who would get cross if no-one had lit the school fire before classes – "Those children have walked to school. They deserve to come to a warm place!"; the one who asked a boy to stay back after school when she knew the family had no food – the other children thought he was "getting into trouble" but it was the only thing she could think of so as not to show him up for being poor; others who would give boxes of food as "wages" to lads they asked to wash windows, or mothers to do ironing.

Sisters have tried to encourage a spirit of kindness in others. Speaking of her ministry with women in Nazareth House, Toronto, a Sister explains,

> We try to provide an environment where there is community building and where we can foster life, where love and compassion are fostered so that people can grow. If the women are in an environment where they feel accepted and

received, then the lights go on and we can help them help themselves.[76]

Another Sister in Framingham told how she asked students to volunteer to accompany a migrant Italian child to and from school each day in the hope that friendships would be formed. On the first day only one had grudgingly agreed to do so. The next day the whole class volunteered. Why? When the two had arrived home on the previous day, the grateful mother had given them a glass of vino to warm them up!

Kindness engenders kindness. In the same breath, stories of the kindness of Sisters are coupled with those of the kindness of people to them. "We would never have survived if it hadn't been for the kindness of the people" is a world-wide refrain. "It was so wonderful to arrive at the station after the school holidays and to see children there on the platform waiting for you," says one. "We would arrive at the convent and someone would have left a box of vegies there at the back door" remembers another. In one place, parishioners arranged for dinner to be sent up from the hotel for a week to save the Sisters time as they prepared for the new year of school. "There was a flood in Inglewood (Queensland) while we were away," recalls a Sister. "When we got back, we found our clothes all freshly washed on the line. The people had gone through the convent and cleaned it out before we came." "When we left at Christmas time," another reflects, "the whole town would turn out to say goodbye. They would cry to see the Sisters going."

Relating

Particularly in times of crisis, the ability to relate, to bring a human face into otherwise frightening circumstances, is one that has created bonds between Sisters and those they served. During the Flu Epidemic of 1918, the response of Sisters was the same everywhere. They opened their convents and schools

---

[76] Smyth and Wicks, *Wisdom Raises Her Voice,* p. 75.

as hospitals, they donned masks and nursed the people in their homes, they mourned with those who had lost loved ones, they died themselves. Whether it was in Auckland or Dublin, Boston or Eureka (California), the sight of Sisters, bearing the insignia of the Red Cross and armed "with a kit containing camphor and sweet oil castor oil and mustard plasters"[77] as they tended the ill was a familiar one. The reflection of the Sisters of St Joseph of Orange in later years would have echoed around the world, recalling not only the healing of bodies but the healing of relationships:

> The face-to-face exposure to the Sisters greatly impressed the Eurekans. There was a significant rise in Church attendance as many fallen away or "lukewarm" Catholics were brought back to the sacraments by the example of the Sisters. A more pragmatic effect was the alleviation of much bigotry towards the Sisters. ... Soon the Sisters were publicly hailed for their care and compassion, widely praised in newspapers and political circles.[78]

Compassion: Relating with compassion looks through the eyes of another. It has led Sisters, as in Goulburn, to accept a bag of carrots, a box of grapes or a couple of pumpkins in lieu of school-money when families have been struggling financially. It led a Mary MacKillop to say to an orphan boy confessing to stealing a bun, "Go and tell Sister that I asked her to give you another one". A Sister Cuthbert, with "love oozing out of her", would declare to a busybody reporting novices for taking fruit from the orchard, "Go out of my sight. If you were 16 years of age and hungry, you'd eat more than crab-apples!" A postulant, just arrived from home and very nervous, dropped and broke a new plate, never used, when setting the table. "Never mind, dear," said the superior, "It's done good service."

Compassion has enabled Sisters to say, "We loved the people at Tumberumba. They were in the same boat as we were." It has

---

[77] Geagley, *A Compassionate Presence,* p. 107.
[78] Geagley, *A Compassionate Presence,* p. 108.

enabled true friendship to be born: "Mum would go to see Sister when she went into the town. They were happy together." To a Sister described as "prayerful, friendly, understanding and kind", a mother did not hesitate to give the baby to hold while she went to Communion. Compassionate relating has stood by families in sorrow and hardship:

> Sister Zita Fleming gave me back my life. A few years ago, my darling son died of AIDS. Sister Zita Fleming from the Office of AIDS Ministry, one of the most powerful ministries in the archdiocese, saved my life and that of our six other children and my husband. They kept us together as a family, taught us how to live again by giving, by staying in touch with God, by remaining part of the community, by falling in love with the Sisters of St Joseph, really.[79]

Mutuality: In the primitive *Règlements*, Médaille instructs the Sisters that they should be "one in the service of each other"[80] as well as in service of the neighbour. "Mutuality," says Evelyn Woodward, "is the capacity to receive with respect and understanding the reality of another, and to offer to the other .. our own reality without pretence, game-playing, indirectness or manipulation."[81] Mutuality involves accepting or receiving the other with respect. It can grow into friendship. It begins with whatever self-disclosure is appropriate for the level of relating. Since faith is what impels mission and is the basic bond for Religious, Médaille's rule included the self-disclosure of faith by timetabling into the Sister's schedule a daily sharing with each other of the fruits of their meditation.

In the years between Médaille's time and ours, religion has gone through an era where it was regarded a private thing. Even today it is difficult to get Sisters to share faith with each other in community. Public "saying" of prayers is acceptable, but the

---

[79] *At the Dawn of a New Age*, Appendix 2, p. 2 of 7.
[80] *Règlements*, p. 5.
[81] Woodward, Evelyn RSJ, *Poets, Prophets & Pragmatists: A New Challenge to Religious Life*, Victoria (Australia): Collins Dove, 1987. p. 46.

level of self-disclosure in such exercises can be nil. Sisters have tended to identify other aspects of life together in their reflections about what has fostered a spirit of mutuality in the building of community.

"We've always supported one another in our ministry," says one interviewee. "You only had to say you needed help in teaching a subject and Sisters would bend over backwards to share their tips and give you whatever aids you needed." "Our Sisters always write to each other for feastdays." "During holidays we had great fun together. We would put on concerts and dress up. We'd play tricks on each other." "Vacation time was when we could be ourselves and relax together and renew friendships." "We always knew one another's families well and would visit them together. We were all one big family, really."

In his teaching on the Eucharist, Augustine urges us to "be what we see on the altar and receive what we are – Christ's Body".[82] Bringing people together into community is an integral part of the mission of those who share the spirit of Joseph. In his practice of building community, Joseph played a vital part in making it possible for all human beings to be united in love with the divinity through Christ, "who humbled himself to share in our humanity".[83] The communion of the Body of Christ signifies and effects the reign of God:
> In the tradition of the Sisters of St Joseph
> we visibly symbolize and effectively realize
> Christ's compassionate presence
> to critical needs for unity and reconciliation.[84]

---

[82] St Augustine of Hippo, Sermon 272.
[83] *The Roman Missal*, ICEL, 1973.
[84] Statement of Sisters of St Joseph of Orange, Chapter, 1986. Quoted in Geagley, *A Compassionate Presence*, p. 271.

5.3 PART THREE: The spirit lives into the now

"Being With" today
When Joan Healy RSJ ventured into Cambodia after the fall of Pol Pot, she saw her role as one of encouraging and lending support to local leaders in healing the effects of trauma in their communities. One of these leaders was Meas Nee who, in his book *Towards Restoring Life*, describes first the breakdown of trust and spirit of the village peoples with the imposition of Khmer Rouge rule, and then the gradual re-weaving of the basket of community life "slowly and gradually, but only by those who will take the time to stay close to the village people and build trust with them."[85]

In a totally different culture, the "Sister Workers" group in France brings a similar awareness to their presence among labourers alienated for generations from the Church. They see that the restoring of relationships can only begin by "being with".

> "To be with" – our first Sisters opened the way, in the mid 17th century. Having been put on that road by Jean Pierre Médaille, didn't we succeed where Francis de Sales had failed?[86] ... In order to "be with", it is necessary to start by "living with"; to leave the institutions, to insert yourselves into populated quarters in small communities ... To "be with" it's necessary to "work with". Most of us therefore have left our comfortable professional lives where we had recognition, appreciation as teachers or nurses.[87]

"Being with" calls not only for physical presence. It involves also an openness to the other, an ability to respect and admire them. This is what a group of postulants of North India found

---

[85] Meas Nee. Joan Healy, listener and scribe. *Towards Restoring Life,* Phnom Penh: JSRC, 1995. p. 46.
[86] Groupe Monde Ouvrier, "Engagées,Envoyées,Engagées", p. 14.
[87] Groupe Monde Ouvrier , "Engagées,Envoyées,Engagées", p. 10

when, as part of their formation, they lived for a time in a village where there are only 15 Christian families:

> We stayed in a little house and slept 16 together, in one single room deprived of usual facilities. On the village square the people, pigs and cows circulated. We had to boil the water because it was impure. To bathe, we went to the river. ... We've been truly enriched by the simple manner in which the people live and by their values; sensitivity, service, sharing, generosity, courage, kindness and attentiveness.[88]

As one of the Sisters living among the people in Peru reflected, they could only "be with" if they learnt from these people and allowed themselves to be directed by them:

> We are too few and too inexperienced in the culture to establish schools, hospitals, refuges, or community legal aid centres. That suggests that the Lord of the harvest does not have institutions in mind. God has, however blessed our concerns and desires to help by showing us, through the people around us, how best we can serve. From among those around us come people who want to work with us, and moreover, to encourage us towards what will benefit others most.

In the crime-ridden areas of Santa Ana, California, self-help projects need the witness and input of a community:

> These ministries could not function as effectively without the contributions of lay Partners in Mission. By working together, cooperatively, more can be done for those in need.. ... These are people whose hearts and minds reflect the charism of our Community. We want to develop relationships to help us better serve our neighbours.[89]

Maria Sullivan RSJ, founder of "Josephite Community Aid", sees also that "being with" is the way those who share the spirit of Joseph encounter Jesus:

> Of course, we have to work to bring about the structural change which will resolve the inequalities. But let us do this

---

[88] *Misi Synthèse,* No 20, Juillet – Octobre, 2000. p. 10.
[89] *Focus*, Fall 1999. p. 8.

> from a position of immersion: from that place where we are privileged to walk side-by-side with those who are able to most clearly reveal Jesus to us.[90]

All of the above examples indicate the ongoing gifting by the Spirit to those who identify with the way of Joseph in Church mission today. It is the same Spirit which led a gathering of Sisters in Boston in 2002 to express "their desire to be in solidarity with victims of clergy sexual abuse, ... with those who are struggling with their confusion and feelings of betrayal".[91] The spirit of Joseph that urges us to "be with" is what Evelyn Woodward calls a spirit of empathy, a consequence of the Incarnation whereby God may be described as not so much breaking into human life as being totally receptive to humanity, allowing it to impact even on divinity Itself.

> An incarnational spirituality implies a desire to become as all people are in the sense of entering their lives with an openness to their stories, encouraging the living out and completion of those stories, indicating sometimes that there are new directions possible, walking along new pathways with them encountering the same difficulties in the landscape."[92]

Building Community in a changing world

However, in a changing world, some feel they no longer know how to "be with". They find it difficult to identify with a world whose values seem quite alien to those they grew up with. Timothy Radcliffe identifies the causes of these recent shifts:

> What we have seen over the last years is the corrosive effect of a new and simpler model of society, for we have all found ourselves members of the global market, buying and selling, being bought and sold. The basic institutions of civil society that sustained the professions and vocations have lost much of their authority and independence. Like everything else, they must submit to market forces. In England, even a

---

[90] *Spreading the Spirit.* Josephite Community Aid Newsletter. Issue 29, Spring 2004. p. 2.
[91] *Soundings,* Vo. 24, Summer 2002. p. 6.
[92] Woodward, *Poets, Prophets & Pragmatists,* p. 93.

football team exists now less to play football than to make a profit.[93]

With the collapse of structures that gave shape and identity to ordinary people in their place of employment, in locations of financial security and in predictable ways of being in relationship with others, people have lost confidence in commitment and so struggle with notions of giving themselves to another without guarantee. A culture of individualism does not nourish attitudes of "being with". For survival, focus has to be on one's own welfare or on that of one's immediate family. Why give yourself in empathy to another?

Yet there is in the human psyche a longing for community. It is the only way human beings can become who they are. The sight of young people in constant contact with friends through internet, email, mobile phones and text messaging may raise issues for some (*Is their social world being limited to the few they know instead of remaining open to new encounters? Can they bear to relate face-to-face?*), but this "most connected of any generation"[94] genuinely seeks community. To the search, many bring a generosity of spirit and sense of commitment that flies in the face of individualism.

Some Religious, however, fear that their type of community belongs to a different age. How can it offer to young people in this new world what they are looking for? Religious Life, as well as the whole Church, has suffered from the same confusions of change as the rest of society. The reshaping of identity that had to happen after the call for adaptation by Pius XII and Vatican II has not yet found definite expression. Nineteenth century confidence in the power of institutions to remedy social ills and to provide religious and life solutions has

---

[93] Timothy Radcliffe. *Sing a New Song*, Dublin: Dominican Publications, 1999. p. 193.
[94] Libby Rogerson. Address, Vocations Conference, Melbourne. p. 1. Quoting Hugh MacKay.

now ended in disillusionment. Do the mindsets of institutionalism still operate in present structures of Religious Life? Are Religious able to form the bonds among themselves that are necessary for community-building today? Some would say not:

> If community is what draws the young to religious life, it is the difficulty of community life that makes so many give up. We aspire to communion and yet it is so painful to live.[95]

In one way, the situation faced by Meas Nee in the rebuilding of Cambodia is replicated around the world. The shattering of communities by global forces is one that must be approached with delicacy and care. Those who share the spirit of Joseph, oriented towards bringing into unity through ministries that restore dignity and effect reconciliation, bring a vital gift to the task of forming community.

The venture, though, must be a "seamless garment". Living community as Sisters, Associates, co-workers and lay-groups cannot be separated from ministry efforts to create community in society. As Médaille said, love of each other must be as much a part of our ministry as loving service of the neighbour. Expressions of such community may take different forms. Community members of Josephite Community Aid "are spread geographically, but live together in the spirit that is JCA".[96] The foundational tradition of the Sisters of St Joseph has been to live in small groups, among those with whom they minister. For a variety of reasons including the needs of ministry, some Sisters now live alone. How they express "community" with other Sisters is often through frequent "community occasions" such as weekends of prayer, shared reflection, celebrations and communal discernment. The challenge remains, though, to "be what we are" – the community of the "Body of Christ", entering

---

[95] Radcliffe, *Sing a New Song*, p. 224.
[96] JCA booklet, section "How We Live".

into and expressing our union with God and each other through the way we live.

Establishing relationships of mutuality: Meas Nee speaks about the need first of all to "restore the confidence trust of individual people, of families, and of whole communities".[97] This is done through providing opportunity for people to tell their story and to be heard. Blaming, he points out, does not help. In Religious communities, the faith of Sisters has endured the chaos of a changing world – these are survivors. Who listens to their faith? Who encourages it and builds on it? We can only do it for each other. Times for reflecting together on Scripture or on the experiences of life – the process of theological reflection and sharing "the state of the heart" – are built into timetables of most communities of Sisters today. What Radcliffe says of Dominicans we can say of ourselves:

> For most of us, especially many who are entering the Order today, it is not enough just to recite the Psalms together. We need to share the faith that brought us to the Order and which sustains us now. ... Perhaps we can only do this tentatively, shyly, but even so we may offer our brothers and sisters 'the bread of life and the water of heaven'.[98]

The integrity of those who have left Religious Life needs also to be listened to and revered. Efforts now being made by Sisters to hold reunions of past members will continue to be important, both to acknowledge the bonds that brought us together in the first place and to find new ways of going into the future as partners in mission. In Rochester, for example, a group of former members has come together, calling themselves "The Collaborators" and establishing three goals for themselves: 1) to be a link, reaching out to former members, and building reconciliation and support as needed; 2) to participate with the Sisters as appropriate, as they undertake a process of

---

[97] Nee, *Towards Restoring Life,* p. 47.
[98] Radcliffe, *Sing a New Song,* p. 131.

refounding; 3) to give input to the Congregation as to how society "reads" their efforts to be present to the neighbour.

"The challenge of community", says Sachs, "is the overcoming of all that impedes love."[99] Building relationships of mutuality, where love breaks through personal and social barriers, can be challenging for some, especially where, for example, a culture of teacher-pupil relationships has infiltrated into community life. Instead of relating mutually as adults, present members can, in this environment, treat newcomers as "students", having to be "taught"; their experience is not valued and their contribution to future possibilities is not sought, let alone respected and honoured. It sometimes takes years for these "newcomers" to "prove" themselves and be accepted as full members of the community. Receptivity of another in mutuality requires instead an openness to the new, the acceptance of difference and a willingness to respond to the other.

An "environment of mutuality" is not the same as a "mutual admiration society". Certainly, as Associate Helen noted after the events of September 11, 2001, being connected to people who share one's own convictions can make "a more complete person".[100] But mutuality also sustains differences. Timothy Radcliffe tells of a novice's disillusionment with the selfishness, fragility and sinfulness of community members.
> The novice master replied to hum, "I am delighted to hear that you no longer admire us. Now there is a chance that you might come to love us." The redemptive mystery of God's love is to be seen not in a community of spiritual heroes, but of brothers or sisters, who encourage each other on the journey to the Kingdom with hope and mercy.[101]

---

[99] Sachs, John R. *The Christian Vision of Humanity*, Collegeville: The Liturgical Press, 1991. p. 38.
[100] *Soundings*, Vol 24, Summer 2002. p. 5.
[101] Radcliffe, *Sing a New Song*, p.144.

Mutuality is built up through sharing the stories that are appropriate for the type of community envisaged. Communities of Sisters and lay groups relate at the level of faith, bound in the love of Christ in others; families must develop bonds of conjugal and familial love; co-workers are linked at both a professional and mission-oriented level. For those who identify with the spirit of Joseph in any of these settings, the advice of Meas Nee has something to say to us:

> In the beginning, simply try to make the people feel at home with you. Join in with them. Don't be stressed with projects. Slowly. Sit under the shadow of the trees with the families and listen to them. Sit in the cool of the night. Don't feel ashamed that you waste time. You are gradually learning to understand people's strengths, people's problems, people's feelings. Spend time to talk with them. It is a matter of (re)building spirit, life and relationships.[102]

Being communities for mission: A characteristic of Sisters of St Joseph everywhere is that we are communities on mission.

> The fact that we are apostolic religious
> with a particular mission in the Church
> has always determined
> the nature of our communities.[103]

We are sent on mission by our community; whatever our apostolate, our community is with us. "We are out there, in the parish of the classroom, for them on their behalf, representing them."[104] In fact, the forming of communities is part of our mission. Community is sign and instrument of our union with the Divine Communion, the goal of every apostolate. It expresses what the Church is, the Body of Christ. "We who experience the redemptive self-communication of God, who are in the process of divinisation, also make present, through our presence, the saving, self-communicating mystery of God."[105]

---

[102] Nee, *Towards Restoring Life,* p. 48.
[103] *Constitutions of the Sisters of St Joseph of the Sacred Heart*, Ch. V, par. 19.
[104] Radcliffe, *Sing a New Song,* p. 130.
[105] Byrne, "Re-conceiving Identity", p. 7.

So it is that, whether we are Religious or lay, community building is integral to the mission of those who share the spirit of Joseph. Somewhere I have read, "To serve the poor alone is not a sufficient reason to live in community; they could be served without living that way." The quotation is true, insofar as "living under the same roof" is taken to mean "community". However, the term means much more than that. To serve the poor automatically establishes community, at least in its primitive form, since the aim of all service is to enable the bonds of Christ's love to take shape among us. The "Holy Spirit of Love", renewing the face of the earth in us, unites us in love and makes us into a community.[106]

Evelyn Woodward quotes a reflection on the interplay between community and mission:
> I need to belong here. That means that I want people to notice I'm around and *how* I am when I'm around, and I want to offer the same attention to the others. On the other hand, I don't think we ought to sit around discussing and theorizing about ourselves in ways that separate us from the poor and the wounded and the suffering. I'd like to think that the quality of our life together gives us drive and urgency, and that it's safe to reach out because there's a place to reach out from.[107]

This is what Helen Prejean CSJ has found. When asked recently about where she gains personal support for what could be a very lonely mission of advocating against the death penalty, Helen could cite many groups around the world who form community with her in effort and belief. These groups surround, as it were, her own community of Sisters of St Joseph who mission her and sustain her. Her mission of reconciliation is shared by those who contribute to it in a host of different ways. The impact of that mission is reflected in the words of Erie Associate, Stephanie:
> After meeting Sister Helen I understood what the SSJ charism in action means. Sister Helen lives the charism in how she

---

[106] Byrne, "Re-conceiving Identity", p. 7.
[107] Woodward, *Poets, Prophets & Pragmatists,* pp. 61, 62.

> works with both inmates – to help them reach a point of reconciliation – and victims and their families to reach a point of forgiveness.[108]

Stephanie goes on to quote Debbie Morris, a victim befriended by Helen, who states in the last line of her book, "Justice didn't do a thing to heal me. Forgiveness did." "What a powerful message", she says.[109]

Joseph was gifted in a special way to signify and effect the reign of God among us through the creation of community. In hospitality, service and love he played a vital part in the incarnation of God's visible presence among us, entering our world, being enfleshed in our homes and our hearts. We who share Joseph's spirit are likewise invited "to become one with God, to be children of God, to live not as strangers at the table, but as God's intimate family, to receive and share this unimaginable outpouring of Love".[110] Pope John Paul II reminds us of God's hospitality:

> There is no doubt that the most evident dimension of the Eucharist is that it is a *meal*. The Eucharist was born, on the evening of Holy Thursday, in the setting of the Passover meal. *Being a meal* is part of its very structure. "Take, eat... Then he took a cup and... gave it to them, saying: Drink from it, all of you" *(Mt 26:26, 27)*. As such, it expresses the communion which God wishes to establish with us and which we ourselves must build with one another.[111]

---

[108] *Journeys* Vol 20, No 1, Winter 2002. p. 10.
[109] *Jounreys,* Winter 2002. p. 10.
[110] Byrne, "Re-conceiving Identity", p. 7.
[111] Apostolic Letter, *Nobiscum Domine,* par 15.

Spirituality from Père Médaille

Sr Ann Teresa, SSJ (Annecy)

To love God and neighbour, our Founder's orientation
To love all others his aspiration,
By Double and Total Union in integration
For Union, Communion and Reconciliation.

O infinite love, all pure and all transcending
Love of our triune God, the three in one
Love of the Father and the Son, each for the other
O'erflowing in the Person of the Holy Spirit.

O greatest love, all pure and all-transcending
Lowly I bow before your hallowed throne,
Humble and child-like, living for the other,
Fill me to the full, to the brim, to overflowing.

O perfect love, all pure and all-transcending,
Love of our God, the blessed Trinity,
O steadfast love, my shield and my protection
True and unswerving love from God's own heart.

From Time and Eternity,
Marie de Montfort SSJ ed,
p. 20.

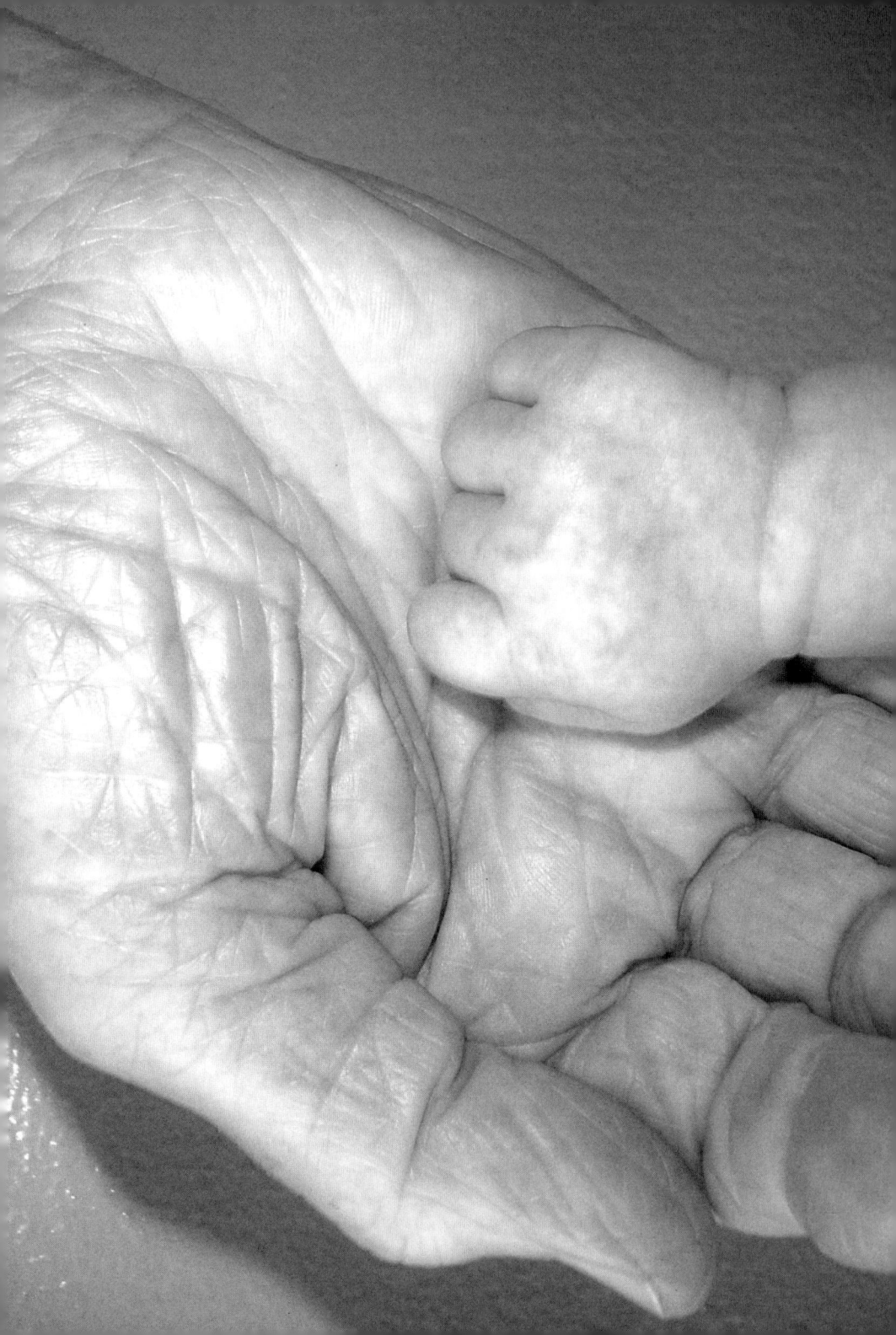

CHAPTER SIX

The spirit of Joseph ......

walks humbly.

The shepherds went with haste, and found Mary and Joseph, and the child lying in the manger. (Lk. 2:16)

6.1 PART ONE: The spirit is revealed

<u>We come from the earth</u>
A gathering of Sisters in the South Australian Province of the Sisters of St Joseph of the Sacred Heart was addressed some years ago by an Aboriginal woman stolen from her home as a young child according to government policy of the time and given to white foster parents to raise. In tears, the Sisters listened as Mona, now married with a family of her own and a respected lecturer in a Teachers College, told of her search for her birth mother and of going back to her own "country". There she was shown the place where she had been born, a red sandhill. Her response was intuitive; throwing herself down, she was birthed again as, wailing, she burrowed into the ground and tossed the fine sand all over her body.

It is not by accident that the words "humus" and "human" have the same root. Our connectedness as human beings with the earth, something our biblical ancestors were well aware of, is supported by scientific knowledge and confirmed by anthropological studies of all societies. While sacramental theology and practice has preserved this connection, at least notionally, within the Christian tradition, it is only recently that a spirituality of interconnectedness with the whole of creation has been reclaimed by Christians. What we detect in the spirituality of Jesus who identified himself with water, who likened himself to the wheat grain, who saw in the world around him the word of the Father and had the ears to hear it; what Irenaeus knew as he set out for martyrdom to be ground by lions' teeth into the bread of sacrifice; what the medievals, Francis of Assisi, the German mystics and Julian of Norwich experienced as they contemplated the presence of God among us, we now receive as treasured legacy on the Christian pilgrimage of life.

Associated with understandings of "humus" and "human" are two other aspects of our being, "humility" and "humour". In fact, so intertwined are humility and humour that they tend to exist together in the one person, and when one is absent, so is the other. When humility is replaced by pride, humour easily becomes cynicism. Sarcasm and self-sufficiency make good companions. Egoism and ridicule belong together.

Humus
In a retreat exercise years ago, I asked people to share their experience of where they find God. A farmer's response was memorable: "Every time I stand in the paddock and hold a clod of earth in my hand," he said, "I am in touch with God."

The debate about whether Scripture encourages the exploitation of the environment or whether, on the other hand, it actually emphasises the interconnectedness of creation, has occupied many Biblical scholars, theologians and scientists in recent times. Reams have been written about the word in Genesis 1:28 often translated as "dominion": does it mean "having power over" the rest of creation, or does it mean "governance" in the tradition of kings who were expected to care for and protect their weakest subjects? We can glean from the creation stories of Scripture an awareness that all living creatures are "kin, all created from clay and the breath of life from God"[112]. Edwards says this fact gives us direction:

> An important foundation for ecological theology is the conviction that the Spirit of God is creatively and lovingly present to all creatures, and present as the *power-in-relation* in our interconnected planetary life. The earth, then, has a sacramental character: it symbolises the divine that is present in it.[113]

Beauty in the natural world speaks of God. Through the unfolding of nature we are led to wonder and awe. Even in harshness, it leads us into mystery; it calls us to go beyond ourselves. We learn about virtue from land, plants and animals – patience, endurance, generosity, courage, trust, surrender. We see connectedness and interdependence at work in this world of nature. We see, too, its death-throes when lines of connection are broken, through pollution and destruction and exploitation of its gifts.

Ecological theology calls for ecological morality. This means that care and protection of the earth is to be seen as a sacred trust. Our environment must have inherent value rather than being regarded merely as a social and economic resource. We have responsibility for the long-term effects of our usage of earth's resources, since the connectedness of human beings to the rest of creation is a fact of life and death. This world, like the human being, is born in and destined for relationship with its maker. "Creation itself will be set free from its bondage to decay and obtain the glorious liberty of the children of God,"[114] says Paul. Like a mother in labour, the earth "groans in travail"[115] until it comes into unity with God who is community. <u>Human</u>

---

[112] Norman Habel. "Design, Diversity and Dominion: Biodiversity and Job", in Denis Edwards and Mark Worthing eds. *Biodiversity & Ecology: An Interdisciplinary Challenge.* Adelaide: ATF Press, 2004.
[113] Edwards, *Breath of Life*, p. 128.
[114] Rom. 8:21.
[115] Rom. 8:22.

The creature made of earth, the human, is, like the natural world, a revelation of God. Described in Genesis as "image of God", the *adam* is made from *adamah* – "dust" – and breathed into life by God. Early Christian writers saw that sin (biblically described in Genesis Ch. 3) desecrated the image of God in the original creation of humanity. It was Christ, the perfect image of God, who renewed, restored and re-established the possibility of that relationship. In this context, Jesus Christ is seen as the perfect human, the counter to the first *adam*. Irenaeus uses this argument: "He (Jesus) commenced afresh the long line of human beings, and furnished us, in a brief, comprehensive manner, with salvation; so that what we had lost in Adam – namely, to be according to the image and likeness of God – that we might recover in Christ Jesus."[116]

The human being is a God-animated body, a body-spirit, born out of and into relationship with God and co-relationship with others. Genesis' double account of the creation of man and woman emphasises the aspect of their recognition of "flesh of my flesh"[117]; their bodies indicate who they are – complementary and interdependent, in relationship with one another.

However, Platonic philosophy's splitting of body and soul and the description of humans as "embodied souls" took root among early Christians, replacing in popular consciousness the biblical fusion of body-soul. Even though Thomas Aquinas in the 13th century maintained that "the body is wholly the body of the soul, while the soul is essentially embodied (and yet immortal – with a permanent relationship to the body and matter)"[118], various heresies throughout history have tried to deny the place

---

[116] St Irenaeus of Lyon, *Adversus Haereses* (Book III, Chapter 18), http://www.newadvent.org/fathers/0103318.htm
[117] Gen. 2:23.
[118] Jörg Splett. "Body" in Karl Rahner ed., *Encyclopedia of Theology: the Concise Sacramentum Mundi*, N. Y: Crossroad, 1975. p. 159. Thomas followed Aristotle's thought.

of the body as an essential component in human nature. What was important to them was the soul – the body was just a casing, to be thrown away.

In modern times, this dualistic outlook was reinforced by Descartes and other European philosophers. For a person to ignore the interplay of body and spirit, despising the body, even punishing it, has been taken as a sign of "sanctity" by many. But, as Splett points out, psychological and biological studies now illustrate the "unity of soul and body" and "do not allow of a clear division between the two components".[119] We *have* bodies and at the same time we *are* bodies. In our bodies, we, body-soul, are opened out to others and to our environment; in our bodies, we, body-soul, express who we are and become who we are. We are connected to the rest of creation through our "dust-ness", but also in our total being, body-soul, we image and communicate with the divine.

An incarnational theology recognises that our growing into God's love freely given to us, grace, does not only apply to the soul but to our whole being, both as social creatures and as individuals. "Holiness" is "wholeness". It is in our bodiliness, says Radcliffe "that God comes to meet and redeem us, becoming a human being of flesh and blood like us."[120] Radcliffe sees this having particular application to the Eucharist:
> We discover what it means for us to be bodily in that climax of Jesus' life, when he gives his body to us: "This is my body, given for you." Here we see that the body is not just a lump of flesh, as bag of muscles, blood and fat. The Eucharist shows us the vocation of our human bodies: to become gifts to each other, the possibility of communion.[121]

Humility

---
[119] Splett, "Body", p. 159.
[120] Radcliffe, *Sing a New Song*, p. 141.
[121] Radcliffe, *Sing a New Song*, p. 141.

When images like Dickens' Uriah Heep spring to mind on hearing the word "humility", it is no wonder that being humble has such a bad press! In a list of desirable qualities of character today, humility would hardly rate a mention.

Yet if we take the trouble to rid the word of its overlays, it can reveal an exciting range of possibilities. Humility acknowledges our humanity. It recognises who we are – not gods, not animals or other created forms. But it also reminds us that we and all created things are interdependent. Humility shows us that we exist in relationship to the divine and to the rest of creation. It is natural, then, Edwards reminds us, that we should involve created things in expressing our relationship with God:

> The experience of God's presence in creation and the experience of the radical otherness of creation can lead to worship and thanksgiving. In eucharistic liturgies, we bring the gifts of creation to the table and invoke the Spirit over them, praying that they might be sacramentally taken up into the divine communion, thus anticipating the final communion of all things in God.[122]

Before God we stand in humility – we are humans. But that does not mean that we deny who we are. While there is an obvious connection in meaning between "humility" and "humiliation", the latter word carries with it associations of not only being made humble, but of being shamed and made less than human. Especially in the context of modern warfare and treatment of prisoners or asylum seekers, it carries with it accusations of injustice and cruelty.

Wilfully subjecting people to humiliation goes against God's reign of justice. But, within the confines of justice, coming to reconciliation in everyday relationships is sometimes only be achieved by lowering oneself, being prepared to be humiliated, in order to meet the other. "Get off your high horse!" people

---

[122] Edwards, *Breath of Life,* p. 116.

say. Jesus carried this one step further. By associating himself with those treated unjustly, by becoming "a worm and no man"[123], Jesus brought God's reconciling love into the world of alienation. Edwards points out,

> What is unique about Jesus is not simply incarnation itself but the *kind* of incarnation we find in Jesus – Jesus is found like a slave, among the poor, the victims, and the oppressed. Jesus expresses God's covenant with the poor of the world.[124]

How do we describe the humble person, in the healthy sense of the word? With Jesus, the ideal human, as a model, we can say the humble person is "human". Therefore compassion, acceptance of the other, flexibility and the ability to discern the needs of the person before strictures of law will mark those who are humble, as he was.

Greatness and humility, they say, go together. Great leaders do not feel compelled to blow their own trumpet. Their authority is not imposed; rather it engages the personal authority of those they lead. Humility in a leader wins hearts and minds; it engenders trust; it binds people together.

Those who are humble allow themselves to learn from another. "Their capacity for interdependence", says Donna Markham, "bespeaks their comfort in trusting the collective wisdom of the group."[125] Respect for the dignity and expertise of others enables them to work collaboratively. At the same time, they are true enough to themselves to be able to approach the other with confidence, not being threatened by gifts different from their own, able to rejoice in the opportunity to combine personal skills with those complimentary to theirs.

---

[123] Ps. 22:6
[124] Edwards, *Breath of Life,* p. 63.
[125] Donna Markham. *Spiritlinking Leadership,* N. Y: Paulist Press, 1999. p. 133.

Commitment to the truth characterises the humble person. Humility is truth. Those who are humble do not surround themselves with masks, hiding from themselves or others what is really going on. Wisdom, having learnt truth, is simple. It goes to the heart of things. Legend tells us that when St John was an old man, he summarised the entire Gospel in three simple words, "Love one another!" Those who arrive at the simplicity of truth do not go blindly into reaction against loss of esteem or forces beyond their control. They invite feedback and make it safe enough for truth, including criticism and advice, to be expressed in that feedback. Duplicity of speech and pretence have no part in their lives.

Humility carries with it a certain vulnerability. In other words, it recognises that we are not self-sufficient. "Walking humbly with our God" means that we can never become our own gods. We are in relation to the Other; we are naked before the Other who knows us to the core. This does not mean we are doormats, before God or anyone else. Rather, humility acknowledges we must empty ourselves of all the false "selves" we tend to adopt and allow God to reveal the true self, at one with God, to emerge. I owe it to my creator to be that self, humbly and without guile. "The glory of God", said Ignatius of Antioch, "is the human fully alive."

Those who are humble are in touch enough with their own inner selves to allow for mistakes and to know the difference between what can be tolerated and what crosses boundaries of common sense or human decency. Mistakes do not have to be covered up; they can be levers for new growth, not only in others but in the self. So patience with one's own imperfections and the courage to try again after failure and humiliation allow them to maintain an inner hope that gets them through the valleys of life.

Humour

It takes a sense of humour to cope with mistakes, especially when they are made by oneself. Shakespeare uses the comic to show the absurdity of humans setting themselves up as little gods. His fools are the wise ones. They can tell the truth and tap into issues that others hide from. Façades are stripped away and perspectives given that reveal motives and draw attention to hidden agenda. In today's world, cartoonists often fulfil the fools' function. Through humour, and sometimes pathos, they shed light on the human condition and offer a more authentic way of looking at the world and its challenges.

Humour requires an openness to surprise. It is, then, an aspect of contemplation. Being open to the action of God in prayer and daily life means that we must let go of control and self-idolatry. Hughes applies the same concepts to meditation on the life of Christ:

> When people begin to use their imagination on Gospel scenes, they are often surprised at the Christ they meet. To some, he seems much more ordinary than they would have expected, others are surprised or even shocked by the Christ they find, like the man who saw a Christ playing the clown and doing cartwheels. Surprise can be a sign that we are encountering the living Christ, image of the God of surprises.[126]

Humour breaks down barriers between people and brings them together. They can appreciate the self that becomes transparent in the shared experience of being surprised by a story, illustration or incident. Humour taps into another side of the person. Especially in relation to the self, it frees us of taking ourselves too seriously. We can let go of the judgement or condemnation of others. We allow ourselves to be "human".

---

[126] Hughes, *The God of Surprises*, p. 112.

Closely connected with humour is the ability to play. Relaxation is necessary for healthy life. "In this day and age," says Donna Markham, "it is an accepted given that taking time for physical care and rejuvenation is a proven antidote for high stress levels."[127] Radcliffe says to take this time is a mark of wisdom:

> Wisdom danced in the presence of God while she made the world. St Thomas says that the contemplation of the wise person is like play, because it is pleasurable and because it is done for its own sake, like a dance. 'Unmitigated seriousness betokens a lack of virtue, because it wholly despises play which is as necessary for a good human life as is rest.'[128]

Humour helps us deal with the paradoxes and contradictions of life. Often these lead us into mystery. We cannot earn the thing of beauty; we cannot fathom the incomprehensible nor the awesome. But through them, character is formed and the seemingly infinite capacity of the human for encounter with the "Other" leads us to even greater depths. What we learn as humans, as humus, in humility and with humour, is that all is grace.

<u>Joseph walked humbly</u>
In a reflection for Christmas some years ago, Australian sociologist and columnist, Hugh Mackay, wrote in a local newspaper:

> Until Christianity came along, humility was regarded as something of a weakness, even a pathology. In the classical tradition, the cardinal virtues were justice, prudence, temperance and fortitude; the Christian tradition added faith, hope and (crucially) charity to the list. In defining our responsibility for the welfare of those less fortunate than ourselves - the sick, the poor, the bereaved, the disadvantaged - Christianity emphasised the need for self-sacrifice, modesty and humility.
>
> To Christians, the crucifixion of Jesus is the ultimate symbol of humility, but Christmas is a reminder of the humble

---

[127] Markham, *Spiritlinking Leadership,* p. 126.
[128] Radcliffe, *Sing a New Song,* p. 159. Quoting Thomas Aquinas, *Eth ad Nic* iv ib 854.

circumstances of his birth, as well: no room in the inn, Mary and Joseph consigned to a stable, the newborn baby laid in a manger. That familiar story is easy to romanticise in carols and on slick greeting cards, but the reality must have been rather grim for all concerned. In fact, if there's an "inner meaning" of the Christmas story, it is probably that greatness is born in humility, disadvantage can be an advantage, and inspiration may spring from the most unpromising circumstances.[129]

Joseph's greatness – born in humility: What can be said of the Christmas tableau as a whole can be said of Jesus, Mary and Joseph individually. In the poverty of the manger – an animal's feeding trough – Joseph walked with God enfleshed as a baby, totally dependant, weak and limited. According to the Gospel story, Joseph received the wise ones from the east, prepared to kneel before a child. The wise men had learnt a new wisdom, not from King Herod, whose power rested in violence, but from recognising that joy indicates God's presence: "When they saw the star, they rejoiced exceedingly with great joy; and going into the house they saw the child with Mary his mother, and they fell down and worshipped him."[130]

Since we have no direct record of Joseph's character, the notion of Joseph's humility can only be surmised from the scant information we have. Joseph is a background figure in the story of salvation. Yet his role is crucial. Through him, the Davidic line of Jesus is established and legalised. To allow the Incarnation event to take place, Joseph does not demand prominence. Shannon and Russell reflect on Joseph's stance of humility:

> Being in the "limelight" isn't always necessary for making great things happen. The person in the background, the invisible volunteer, the crewmember backstage, the last one to leave the kitchen, are often the essential link to a successful venture or a famous person's success. The

---

[129] Mackay, Hugh. "The Case for Humility", *Sydney Morning Herald*, Opinion column, Dec. 21, 2002.
[130] Mt 2: 10.

"unsung" heroes and heroines are most often the enablers of great happenings while remaining in the shadows or behind the curtain.[131]

Perrotta draws from the same observation that Joseph's holiness "had more in common with the ordinary daisy than the showy orchid" and that this "makes for a devotion that centers on the safe path of attentiveness and receptivity to the hidden workings of grace."[132] The "inner meaning" of the stable scene is, indeed, that "greatness is born in humility". The presence of the shepherds reminds us that King David himself was a shepherd. These ignorant, lowly ones are those to whom the Good News is first announced. God shows preference for the ones without status in the society of the time. Those who are at home with their humanity, who do not have to hide it with the trappings of wealth and power, are the ones who can "walk humbly with their God".

Joseph and the earth: Anne Hennessy paints for us a picture of what would have been Joseph's relationship with the land:
> Most peasants were farmers, a role that they regarded as a sacred task and duty passed on from previous generations. They were emotionally close to the land; they treasured it, and their lives were governed by its produce and by the seasons. The people lived in harmony with the land in the common endeavour of praising the Creator. Theirs was not the mentality of dominance, control, or the re-direction of natural resources. The value system of these farmers was rooted in tradition, which they considered sacred; religion was integral to their lives and inseparable from familial identity. "Agriculture was both a livelihood and an identity."[133]

---

[131] Shannon & Russell, *The Just One*, p. 19.
[132] Perrotta, *Saint Joseph*, p. 132.
[133] Hennessy, *In Search of a Patron*, p. 40. Quoting Douglas Edwards. "First Century Urban/Rural Relations in Lower Galilee: Exploring the Archaeological and Literary Evidence." In *Society of Biblical Literature Seminar Papers 1988*, edited by Lee T. Levine, 53-74. N. Y: Jewish Theological Seminary of America, 1992.

As tradesman and farmer, working in hard substances and gleaning a living from the soil, Joseph's interaction with the created world would have been varied. Jesus referred to rocky outcrops and poor fertility in his parables. Did the land tilled by Joseph contain the types of soil that yielded grain, "some a hundredfold, some sixty, some thirty"?[134] Did he spend days on end clearing stones and leading flocks to better pasture? How did he read the seasons? Certainly, the ability to recognise their signs was passed on to Jesus.[135]

In whatever ways Joseph conducted his daily affairs, the important point for us is that the Jewish attitude of living in harmony with the land was part of "the common endeavour of praising the Creator". Stewardship of the earth was a way of worshipping and acknowledging God. It accepted that all of creation is gift but that human involvement in its care is an act of partnership with God.

Joseph and Divine Providence: This relationship of interdependence, one that Joseph would have shared, has fostered throughout history a trust in Divine Providence. Some stories that have come down to us give the impression that the one who trusts God is passive, and that out of nothing, God provides. My understanding is one, rather, of the active interdependence of creation. Divine Providence accommodates the life of all, in the give and take of co-existence. The Catechism of the Catholic Church says:

> The sun and moon, the cedar and the little flower, the eagle and the sparrow: the spectacle of their countless diversities and inequalities tells us that no creature is self-sufficient. Creatures exist only in dependence on each other, to complete each other, in the service of each other.[136]

---

[134] Mt. 13: 8.
[135] For example, Mt. 16: 2-3.
[136] *Catechism of the Catholic Church,* New York: Doubleday, 1995. #340.

The response of humanity to Divine Providence is thanksgiving. In the Jewish-Christian tradition, the stance of gratitude has been expressed by the consecration of fruits of the earth in worship of God. Thus Joseph and Mary presented the offering of the poor, two turtle doves, to symbolise dedication at the birth of Jesus. Celebrations of harvest festivals, Passover meals, purity observances and Sabbath rituals also involved interaction with material objects to signify their religious intention. Human beings engage the rest of creation with them in worship.

Trust in Divine Providence saves us from the anxiety of needing to hoard excessive amounts of provisions and wealth for ourselves to the detriment of others. For centuries, Joseph has been held up in the Church as a model for those who live simply. A sense of partnership with a God who makes provision for all repels greed, exploitation, and what Mary Jo Leddy calls the "insatiable demands" of consumer culture today: "To say 'it is enough' ... becomes an act of gratitude."[137]

The humble Joseph, dependant on God's Providence, is one, though unique, among the "cloud of witnesses"[138] who like him have responded to the call to walk humbly with God along the human pilgrimage of life. In doing so, they have found their oneness with the earth and all creation; they have learned wholeness, simplicity and the freedom of trust; they have entered into that fruitful Love that unites all in its embrace.

6.2 PART TWO: The spirit unfolds.

<u>Sisters of St Joseph and humility</u>
Médaille had urged his Sisters that their little group should be known as the "Congregation of God's great love." For him,

---

[137] Mary Jo Leddy. *Radical Gratitude*. New York: Orbis, 2002. pp.157-8.
[138] Heb. 12:1

Joseph was an incarnation of love. But it was a love that is totally self-giving, for the good of the other. In other words, the way Sisters were to love was in humble service of the other. Of the 100 maxims that Médaille wrote for his Sisters as a guide for their manner of service, 25 of them, it has been noted, are devoted to humility.[139]

Médaille understood humility as a means to an end. Self-emptying for him was getting rid of whatever prevents us from becoming fully the person God has made us to be – a person who images God, in whom the work of Christ and the grace of the Spirit can operate freely. He saw the Eucharist as a perfect example of this; his instructions to the Sisters as a whole can be applied to the individual:

> Our dear Institute must be all humility and profess in everything to cherish and choose what is more humble; for this is the way that the most lowly, the most profound, and the most complete humility is manifested. Thus it should be all modesty, gentleness, candor and simplicity, wholly interior and spiritually alive; in a word, empty of self and empty of everything and completely filled with Jesus and God, ... I can only say of this fullness that it operates in such a way that the infinite Being of God and Jesus, intimately present, seems to vivify the body and soul of an insignificant nobody, and to cause her to be nourished by the holiness of an Infinite God. Now, my dear Daughter, is not all this found in a marvelous manner in the Holy Eucharist? What more humble than our dear Jesus in this mystery! What more modest, more mild and gentle, more simple and candid, more full of God and empty of everything else! There, my dear Sister, is the model of the spirit of our Institute.[140]

Humility, expressed in an unassuming manner and in service of the other so that their dignity might be recognised, did characterise the Sisters of St Joseph from the start. So much so, that it was five years before the civic dignitaries of Le Puy

---

[139] Coburn & Smith, *Spirited Lives*, p. 23.
[140] *The Eucharistic Letter,* pars. 26–29.

found out that it was a group of Sisters who were managing the hôpital, a short distance away from their offices. Full of indignation and determination to get rid of Sisters who would surely be a drain on town finances, they descended on the hôpital, only to find that the thriving little ribbon and lace-making business being run there was providing income to the area![141] Vacher says of the Institute of the Sisters of St Joseph:

> Its inherited littleness is one of the sources of its life. This nothing that becomes dynamic, this dynamic of nothingness is, without a doubt, one of its most basic characteristics.[142]

For Mary MacKillop and Julian Tenison Woods in the 1860s, hiddenness and humility were likewise characteristic of the spirit of St Joseph. The first rule instructs the Sisters:

> They must be poor, humble, and consider themselves the least among all religious orders, studying to keep themselves and their lives hidden in God as the life of St. Joseph was. They must give place and preference to the religious of every other Order, and their highest ambition must be to remain unknown and poor.[143]

Woods' description, however, reflects an understanding of self-emptying different from that of Médaille; it focuses on itself as a value, and is understood as a "virtue" exemplified by Joseph rather than a tool enabling full growth as a gifted human being into Christ. Nevertheless, the glory of God is still its aim; what is advocated is that Sisters should avoid making themselves into their own little gods:

> Let us love to be unknown, and we shall only be so by concealing ourselves as much as possible from all but God. Let us rarely or never speak of ourselves or of our own actions. If we must do so, we should be careful not to make what we said or did appear in too favourable a light. It is very destructive to humility to want to know the opinion of others about ourselves or our work. We wound the Sacred Heart

---

[141] Byrne, Notes of lecture, 2003.
[142] Vacher, *Des "régulières"*, Session Four, p. 164.
[143] *Rules of the Institute of St Joseph*. Adelaide, 1867. Archives, Sisters of St Joseph, Sydney.

also by thinking or saying that we have done anything, as if God were not the beginning, the end, and the efficient cause of everything.[144]

For Mary and Julian, Joseph's humility was his most notable virtue. Mary wrote to her Sisters:
> We know that St Joseph was humble and hidden. Does it become a child of his to desire worldly notice? Does it become her to talk much of herself, or make a noise about any little thing God deigns to accept at her hands? Yet are we always as humble, as retiring, as modest as a child of the lowly St Joseph should be?[145]

The Eucharist provided a further model of such humility, as the *Book of Instructions* pointed out:
> We have in our convents an example of a perfect religious, and let us carefully study it. Our Blessed Lord, for love of our souls, dwells with us .... He has given up everything.... He is humble, for what annihilation is more perfect in God than to appear here as bread, which is lifted about from place to place, and in all things subject to His creatures.[146]

The influence of French piety did mean that in their daily lives, Sisters of St Joseph everywhere, especially in the nineteenth century, adopted certain monastic disciplinary practices aimed at developing attitudes of humility, such as kissing the floor, kneeling to a superior or to the community to ask for their prayers, and such like. For the time, such practices were deemed appropriate. They were taken for granted in a culture that gained great spiritual nourishment from writings like the "Imitation of Christ", a book composed in the fifteenth century by Thomas à Kempis, and to which Ignatius Loyola, for one, acknowledged a debt of influence.[147] However, with its emphasis on avoiding temptation and fighting against the sinfulness of the world, this little classic gives a negative

---

[144] *Book of Instructions*, "Of Humility".
[145] St Joseph's Day circular, March 1893. Archives, Sisters of St Joseph, Sydney.
[146] *Book of Instructions*, "Of the Blessed Eucharist".
[147] Thomas a Kempis (1380-1471) was a Dutch monk whose writings, deeply steeped in scripture, gave Catholics, and especially Religious, guidance well into the twentieth century.

impression of the human pilgrimage, even though, with analysis, the author's observations do reveal an acute awareness of human nature. On example suffices:

> This is the greatest wisdom -- to seek the kingdom of heaven through contempt of the world. It is vanity, therefore, to seek and trust in riches that perish. It is vanity also to court honor and to be puffed up with pride. It is vanity to follow the lusts of the body and to desire things for which severe punishment later must come. It is vanity to wish for long life and to care little about a well-spent life. It is vanity to be concerned with the present only and not to make provision for things to come. It is vanity to love what passes quickly and not to look ahead where eternal joy abides.[148]

Despite the influence of such condemnatory emphases, the stories that form part of the heritage of Sisters of St Joseph show an overwhelmingly commonsense attitude to humility. At the same time, these stories paint the picture of Sisters being in the background, not seeking notice. On the occasion of her Silver Jubilee in 1882, the great pioneer of Sisters of St Joseph in USA, Mother Stanislaus Leary, was embarrassed to find that the priest had broadcast the event and that quite a large crowd had gathered at the Church for Mass. The *Ontario Messenger* carried the story:

> Indeed had it been known to the people of the surrounding country that such a celebration was to take place, the church could hot have contained more than a fraction of the numbers that would have been present to give expression to the respect and regard which they have always held and still hold for her. But her humility prevented this; few, if any, knew of it outside the town itself. It was concealed even from the clergy for the same reason, none of whom were apprised of it save three, and two of these were present in the sanctuary merely in time for the Mass.[149]

Another Mother General, realising that her Sisters wanted to re-elect her even though she had served in office for many years,

---

[148] *Imitation of Christ*, Book One, Chapter 1.
[149] Thomas, *Footprints on the Frontier,* p. 93.

went on a prolonged train trip to avoid being nominated during the election process. "It was time the Sisters put their faith in someone else," was her explanation.

In the main, the Sisters' attitude of humility was expressed in the practice of egalitarianism and service. Gardiner writes of Mary MacKillop who accompanied a group of Sisters to Brisbane in 1870:
> As well as being responsible for the whole mission, she herself taught in the schools and helped in the house with the rest. She gave instructions to the First Communion children, and washed their feet in imitation of Christ washing the feet of his disciples – a scene that left a lasting impression on those who saw it.[150]

Older Sisters in Orange, California, remember their founder, Mother Bernard, as a woman who never demanded from the Sisters anything she didn't do. "There was nothing beneath her," one Sister said. "She would lug bags of feed for the birds herself. During recreation, she would really relax and have fun." Another Sister described a past Mother-General: "People would gather around her. She always had a bag of sweets for the children. There she was with her big boots unlaced, but totally herself."

When speaking of Sisters who had the "true spirit of a Sister of St Joseph", interviewees invariably cited the example of those recognised for their (healthy) humility. "The children who were closest to her were the ones with the least academic ability," noted one. "She would spend her own time with them." "When I met the Vicar-General recently," said another, "the one he asked after was Sister Philomena who spent her whole life peeling potatoes." "When Sister Ignatius, who was a very powerful teacher, found out she had mis-judged a child, she knelt down and apologised to him," recalled a Sister from

---

[150] Gardiner, *Mary MacKillop,* p. 83.

Wales. "True Sisters of St Joseph aren't hoity-toity. They are open to people. If we love people, we will always find a way to help them. We should receive them as if they were our own family."

Being humble does not save anyone from the pain of humiliation. In the 1870s when Sisters in the USA had lay-sisters, Bishop Timon of Rochester had promised a lay-sister he would give her the habit of a choir-sister, but either forgot or ignored the promise. Noting that the Bishops wanted lay-sisters to work for the orphans, Margaret Brennan records the bitter words of the Sister involved:

> I am broken down from fifteen years hard and heavy work, from Dunkirk to Canadaigua, doing the baking and washing for the sisters and the orphans ... but the hardest cross for me is to be despised and disrespected because for the love of God and my neighbour. I have taken the lowest place ... religion exalted them and degraded and lowered me.[151]

This Sister had many companions in having to cope with injustice and indignity – a Mother Martha of Hamilton (Canada), deposed from office and banished because, when under lay supervision, some high-spirited children had dressed up in priests' vestments while the Sisters were away; a Sister Mary de Chantal who replied to the man who spat in her hand when she was begging alms for the orphans, "That is for me, now give me something for the Lord's poor"; a Mary MacKillop, accused of being a drunkard (having been prescribed a tablespoon of brandy by her doctors for crippling period pain), and who wrote:

> God knows I had the shame and humiliation of often taking stimulants, and of knowing that I was kept up by such, when I should otherwise have sunk and not been able for any duty, but far better to have yielded and to have given up than to

---

[151] Brennan, *Persistence of Vision*, p. 41.

have this shame and sorrow brought upon me by the false tongues of those I loved.[152]

As their history shows, the humility of Sisters of St Joseph has often had the effect of making others feel humiliated. This was the case in the Vienne community in the late seventeenth century:

> Powerful influences had caused some aristocratic subjects to be accepted as members, and they wanted the prestige of being "regular". They wished to live in fairly large groups serving institutions, but to dwell in a cloistered part of the building with a grill and turn, to recite the Divine Office, and to wear a train and buckles on their shoes. The Bishop of Vienne, their ecclesiastical superior, concurred in their request."[153]

The Sisters of St Joseph in Australia "were very aware of their colonial origins and the consequent lack of contact with traditional religious orders."[154] They (and others) referred to Congregations from overseas as "<u>real</u> nuns". When the Dominicans came to Adelaide and took over the Franklin Street convent and school, the Josephites felt that "at last they could observe a group from an ancient religious order, giving them a measure by which they could judge their own experimental way of life, which they were trying to adapt to the needs of a pioneer colony while retaining the external characteristics of religious orders already in existence."[155] However, for aristocrats like Archdeacon Russell, who had a partition erected in the school dividing fee-paying students from those unable to pay (the Sisters removed the partition), these Sisters of St Joseph "who went about the streets visiting the shops and the markets with

---

[152] Letter to Sr Monica Philips, 26 September 1884. Archives, Sisters of St Joseph, Sydney.
[153] Therese Vacher. *Letting in Joy by Looking to our Past,* précis excerpted from *Des Régulières dans le Siecle*, trans. Sr Francis Cecilia English. p. 13.
[154] Marie Crowley. *Women of the Vale: Perthville Josephites, 1872 – 1972,* Richmond (Victoria): Spectrum, 2002. p. 36.
[155] Margaret Schiemer RSJ. "Josephite Spirituality: Integrating the Tradition". A Research Project undertaken as part of a Degree in Theology and towards a Major in Christian Spirituality at Catholic Theological Union, Hunters Hill, NSW. Unpublished. 1987. p. 12.

their begging-bags, were an embarrassment."[156] It was he who later played a major part in the events leading to Mary's excommunication.

Truth: In her autobiography, Therese of Lisieux talks about the simplicity which attributes to God the gifts of character and personality that make up the self, and the "false-humility" which would deny any quality connected with the self. That the founders of the Sisters of St Joseph urged humility is undeniable. However, self-abnegation is not the same thing as self-obliteration. A spirit of simplicity and truth receives as gift the talents and aptitudes we have. Médaille urged his Sisters to credit the Holy Spirit with "the honor resulting from the success of your good actions."[157] Mary MacKillop encouraged her Sisters to take on whatever position or responsibility was called for in the service of others: "In imitation, then, of our great Patron, ... let us avoid excusing ourselves from any office on the plea of our unworthiness."[158] Truth is found in humility; humility is truth.

A feature of the Sisters of St Joseph who branched out from Le Puy was that they were not afraid to develop their own talents for the sake of the mission. Of the six women who formed the first community in 1650, only one had been able to read and write. Yet by the end of the century, members of the Sisterhood had equipped themselves to undertake a wide range of apostolates, from education to social welfare and nursing, and management of trade centres. "In the whole group of houses of St Joseph, one finds ... a rather great diversity of tasks according to the regions and the needs of the populations: for example, the making of medicines ..., the function of a surgeon as at Grenoble, the upkeep of churches, ... and the instruction of

---

[156] Gardiner, *Mary MacKillop,* p. 280.
[157] Maxim 15.
[158] St Joseph's Day circular, March 1893. Archives, Sisters of St Joseph, Sydney.

new converts in the protestant regions."[159] Without fear they responded to the urging of Médaille, "Live out your life with one desire only: to be always what God wants you to be, in nature, grace and glory, for time and for eternity."[160]

The mid-1800s saw a great expansion of the Sisters of St Joseph in the new world of the Americas. There they quickly established schools, hospitals and universities. However, while they educated themselves in order to meet the needs of those they served, they often became anonymous in the process. Cultural influences played a big part in this:

> Women religious, socialized from childhood in appropriate female behavior, received a double dose of instructions on humility, self-sacrifice, and passivity, since these behaviors were expected and reinforced in both patriarchal secular society and within the context of religious life. ... For nuns this meant avoiding "singularity" or the appearance of standing out in any way. .. Special talents were to be hidden to avoid pride or any temptation to receive individual accolades for activities.[161]

The same cultural influences meant that the work of Sisters was often taken for granted. Commenting on Médaille's maxim, "Rejoice more when in the eyes of the world it appears that His glory is promoted by others rather than by yourself"[162], Coburn and Smith note the following:

> In effect this prescribed avoidance of recognition gave male clerics permission to ignore sisters' efforts and at times take credit for their achievements. A good nun would not challenge such expectations. Struggling with religious hierarchy, male privilege, and patriarchal interference, women religious had to appear to acquiesce or remain detached while attempting to control their institutions, maintain their community's autonomy,

---

[159] Vacher, *Des "régulières"*, Session 5, p. 272.
[160] Maxim 73.
[161] Coburn & Smith, *Spirited Lives*, p. 80.
[162] Maxim 25.

or even receive simple acknowledgement and recompense for their services.[163]

This ambiguity between truth and a cultural mis-interpretation of humility was managed with difficulty. In Australia, Father Woods was thrown by the directness of Mary MacKillop in questioning his wisdom about the way he was dealing with certain Sisters; Bishop Sheil took as "impudence" and "disobedience" her explanation that, even though he had the right, she could not accept for herself his proposed changes to the Congregation. To be assertive and to say things as they are while trying to maintain an environment of dialogue and respect takes both courage and confidence.

There have been innumerable occasions when Sisters of St Joseph have had to manage this ambiguity. For example, when the primary schools in Annecy, France, were secularised in 1881 and the Religious teachers dismissed, Mother Louise threatened to withdraw the nursing Sisters from the hospital in protest. Having been prevailed upon by the city dignitaries she relented, but laid down conditions upon which the Sisters were assured of a salary, acceptable working conditions and security of employment. "The Mayor undertook to see that the Council raised no opposition."[164]

Sometimes Sisters have compensated for anonymity by over-achievement in their own studies or in those of their students. The scholarship system in Australia that operated for most of the twentieth century meant that gifted children from poor backgrounds had educational opportunities far beyond family means. Many Sisters of St Joseph were outstanding in the coaching they gave to students; they became legends in their own right, since so many of their pupils, even those of average ability, won scholarships and acquired social success. However,

---

[163] Coburn & Smith, *Spirited Lives,* p. 81.
[164] Bourne, *His Mercy is From Age to Age,* p. 136.

the resulting competition among Sisters as to who "won" most scholarships could make for the very divisions in community that instructions on humility had aimed to avoid. "Some Sisters were more equal than others," was one interviewee's wry comment.

More often than not, though, the pressure for excellence was for the sake of those the Sisters served. A constant refrain among Sisters recalling the past is, "I really loved those children!" "We loved the people!" "I loved being in that place!" At their best, Sisters of St Joseph have spent themselves as did St Joseph in love for the other. While competition did on occasion exist among themselves, at the same time they were outstandingly generous in helping each other in studies, lesson preparation, methodology and moral support.

Poverty prevented some Congregations from providing ongoing tertiary education for Sisters, especially in Australia/New Zealand where universities were State-run and entirely secular until the 1990s. Other Congregations took it as a matter of course that university education would be the norm, even at a time when it was a rare thing for women. Karen Kennelly quotes from an oral history interview, recalling the encouragement given to Sisters on the faculty of St Catherine's College (St Paul, Minnesota) to achieve:

> Sister Antonia's insistence on reaching for high standards was freeing rather than oppressive. To the sisters sent off to earn degrees at Oxford, she gave "no instructions regarding what to do or not to do." Just "be sure to see everything." Occasionally she sent them extra money and counselled them to have a treat, to get themselves a bathing suit and enjoy an ocean swim incognito, to use their vacation periods for travel on the continent as well as in England. She was capable, too, of empathy with the teaching sister whose opportunities for collegiate training were limited. When she became aware that some teachers were prevented from attending summer school

by the poverty of their local convents, she "took hold of the situation" and got them there.[165]

Humility does not preclude Sisters from being trained as doctors or university professors, but neither does it set up grades of distinction that would value the contribution of one Sister's work against another. Throughout the history of the Congregations, Sisters of St Joseph have directed their abilities to serve those in need. In doing so, they have broken new ground and have dared to take up responsibilities of leadership, at the same time avoiding such direct recognition and public acclaim that would deflect attention from their missionary purpose. In recognising the truth of our own nothingness before God, we are yet convinced that God uses our insignificance for great things if we but open ourselves in surrender to God's power in us.

Humanness: One interviewee related that as a little child she thought Sisters came down from heaven every morning and went back at night. "I loved to smell them," she said. It did not take her long, of course, to find out that these Sisters were human, very much so. It is the aspect of humanity that characterises a Sister of St Joseph.

A Sister from Baden wrote of her encounter with these "humans":
> I had been in Catholic school my whole life, but this was so different. These Sisters were so different. They seemed like human beings! They laughed with us, they cried with us, they even occasionally had a beer with us! They welcomed us into their lives and homes. Even more incredibly – they had people who were my age .. lots of them!
> Some of these young sisters became friends of mine, and slowly I began to feel a kinship with these women that felt like

---

[165] Karen Kennelly CSJ, "Women Religious, the Intellectual Life, and Anti-Intellectualism: History and Present Situation. In Puzon, Bridget OSU, ed. *Women Religious and Intellectual Life: The North American Achievement*, San Francisco: International Scholars Publications, 1996. p. 56. Sister Antonia was the then President of the College.

it "tied a cord around my heart, and led me to a place I would not have gone." ... I feel at home here. I experience this Congregation as a group of women who are always lovers first. I sense that there are no limits on who is the "dear neighbor" – all people are dear to you.

In Philadelphia a college graduate recalled with gratitude the wonderful human being who was their Dean of Studies. In the rebellious 1970s, a group of friends, against every rule, smoked for weeks behind a tree:

Just when we felt secure in our life of sin, the AXE fell. In a voice which seemed quite normal, and even affectionate, Sister requested that we stop by her home room after class. Naturally, we complied, thinking that she was in need of our companionship. As we gathered around the desk conversing about the hockey game we had lost and other ordinary topics, our blood suddenly turned to ice. While speaking about sportsmanship, Sister deliberately placed one cigarette butt after another on the desk without making any reference to them at all. Changing neither her tone nor her expression, she destroyed our secret world in two minutes flat. Almost inaudibly, but firmly, came her oft-used sentence, "Dearies, don't let it happen again."

The obituary of a Sister in Concordia records:

When Eva decided to enter religious life, there was a question of which community to choose. That the Sisters of St Joseph were permitted to visit their parents periodically was the dominating factor for choosing to come to Concordia even though the distance (from home) was so much greater.

It has been common to Sisters of St Joseph worldwide that their lives were able to break through many of the restrictions of institutionalism and monastic practices. In South Australia, at a time when novices of other Congregations lived in isolation from family, the Novice Mistress is remembered for her ability to "bend the rules" in order to do the humane thing. On at least one occasion she accompanied a novice to visit her dying mother, and both stayed overnight in the family home until the woman died. During the Depression years, a Sister in Port

Lincoln heard that her mother in Quorn, a driving distance even today of around eight hours, was dying and asking for her. Quickly the community arranged for her to be taken by boat to a town near her destination; from there she caught a bus to Quorn and days later returned to find the boat owner still waiting for her.[166]

Such humanity was not always shown, and some Sisters suffered greatly from unresolved grief and inhuman expectations (for instance, when a principal entered the classroom, took a Sister aside and said, "Dear, a telegram just came to say your father has died. Now, get back to your class!").

But these were aberrations of the spirit of Joseph; the true spirit is demonstrated by the Sister who taught at a Minimum Security Prison for boys. Years later, an ex-inmate introduced his girlfriend to her. "This woman saved my life, "he said. "I was ready to put a belt around my neck. She smiled at me and made me feel as though life was worth living." Or by the Sisters who, when a large fire broke out in the block next door late one cold night, got out of bed, dressed and made hot coffee which they served to the firemen. "This act endeared them to the people and did much to break down the hostile attitude of some of the non-Catholics."[167]

Reflecting God's image in our humanness has involved for Sisters an openness to the other and a willingness to show warmth. A politician in California distributed publicity leaflets about his career, and included one that described school days

---

[166] Similar stories are found everywhere. Sister Virginia Ann Gardner from Erie, for example, relates how as a novice she was allowed to visit her sick mother. "Slowly I came to realize our congregation seemed one with a heart. In truth there were areas in which charity or sometimes even expediency dictated that it bend rules much as Jesus had done in his public life. (St Paul would say love eclipsed law)." Gardner, Virginia Ann SSJ, *Let It Be*, Erie: Sisters of St Joseph, 1998. p. 32.

[167] Mary Cornelia Sullivan SSJ. *This Little Family: History of the American Province 1885 – 1910*. Vol. 1, Unpublished volumes, Archives, Sisters of St Joseph of Chambéry, West Hartford, Ct., 1956. p. 20.

and the Sister who taught him. "She let me know I was likeable," he wrote. Other people remember "human" Sisters who made each person feel important; "She always made mention of special things someone might have done, no matter how trivial." "You didn't have to be clever. She believed in you, no matter what." "Did you realise there wasn't a pupil in your class who didn't love you?" one ex-student asked a Sister. "That's because I loved them", she mused.

In the first year of teaching boys and girls, Sister Virginia Ann's inclination to act humanly was strengthened by a Sister who advised her, when she found a pupil's pornographic drawings, "Don't make the boy feel smaller than he will when confronted with these drawings; instead give him a talk about how he is dealing with the parts of the wonderful human body God created; we can always treat them with respect or we can give in to baser instincts. Everyone has that choice to make." Virginia Ann acted on that advice, treating the situation as she would any infraction and not as a capital offence. "I have always remembered Sister's counsel," she reflects, "and though this all happened more that half a century ago, I still pray for that student."[168]

Those able to show humanity are whole people, able to separate the mis-deed from the person – "She would tell you off, but she didn't keep up grudges." They are not afraid to do the kind deed. When a Sister had had a bad day at school, she noticed that the Principal, who happened to cook the meal that night, produced a rainbow cake for desert – "She knew it was my favourite." "Sister really related to you as a human being, not as a 'junior Sister'". "She would cry with you." One interviewee described her years of struggle with a girl, "tough as nails", as she tried to inculcate in her some sense of self-respect. The only hint of success was when the family informed her they were

---

[168] Gardner, *Let It Be,* p. 31.

moving. "This may be a dump, but it's the best dump in town," was the girl's verdict as she sobbed in Sister's arms.

Other interview snapshots of the spirit of humanity are of Sisters minding the children of stressed-out mothers; of a Mother General whose diary entries include, "Took a child to the dentist"; of a Sister holding an alcoholic woman with tremors for nearly two hours, having responded to the distress of her husband and retarded son; of the community who answered the door to a woman running from her husband who had a gun and (with no police in the town) invited her to stay in the convent that night; of the Sister who lay dying and who announced, "Jesus, you're no good. Go and get your mother!"

Trust in Divine Providence: Material poverty has been the lot of most Sisters of St Joseph. Their experience of "Divine Providence" has been real and imminent because of this. They have had to rely on God's loving care, since there was nothing else they could do. Stories abound of Sisters desperately placing notes of petition at the foot of a statue of St Joseph. "This is your project," said one Superior General. "I need £300 before 3 o'clock, otherwise the workmen won't have their wages." She went back to her office to open the mail; the last letter was from a man whom the Sisters had helped years before and who was now in a position to pay what he owed, £500. A Sister in Canada recalls when she was sent to open a hospital in a former hotel. There was nothing there, not even bed-pans. Having been told by her Superior not to borrow money, she said to St Joseph, "If you want the hospital, it's yours." Without money, it came into existence – beds and equipment at no cost from a hospital being renovated; donations out of the blue; free service by doctors.

Médaille had written, "(Sisters) will live in complete abandonment of themselves to divine providence with no desire of fixed plan, with a perfect acquiescence and a gentle placing of self into the very holy will of God in whatever occurs."[169] In his *Eucharistic Letter*, he urges the Sisters to allow "Divine Providence to guide us as a gentle mother who truly knows our needs and who by her very nature rears children lovingly nestled at her breast."[170] Reflecting on her life, an older Sister saw this pattern as she described her work among refugees:

> Most of the refugees were coming out of Africa, people of colour, highly educated professionals. All spoke some English. If they did not speak English they spoke French, and I wondered if God knew I would be in a situation in which I would need French when I had planned my sabbatical studies at St Pierre et Miquilon and in Lyons, France. So it was a blessing for me.[171]

Julian Tenison Woods had written to the Sisters at Lochinvar, "You are meant to give an example of the poverty and simplicity of the Holy Family, and your life will be a failure and a mockery if your heart be not full of its spirit."[172] Sister Columcille wrote in 1891:

> (Father Julian) wished that those Religious Institutes which he founded should look upon poverty as their greatest riches, since poverty means nothing else but confidence in God, reliance on him and faith in his promises instead of trusting in earthly things... He wished the Sisters also to be poor so that their services might always be available to poor places, which would lose the benefit of religious teachers unless they could be obtained at a very small cost.[173]

"Don't enter the Sisters of St Joseph," urged one mother. "They're the poorest order in the Church." Sisters tell of the first "convent" in the goldfields of Western Australia – three tents, two for sleeping and one for a kitchen. This was later "upgraded" to a shed made of wood and iron – in desert country,

---

[169] *Constitutions for the Little Congregation of the Daughters of St Joseph.*
[170] *The Eucharistic Letter,* par. 8.
[171] Smyth & Wicks, *Wisdom Raises Her Voice,* p. 88.
[172] Letter, September 9th, 1887. Archives, Sisters of St Joseph, Lochinvar.
[173] Archives, Sisters of St Joseph, Newport, Tasmania.

with extremes of heat and cold.[174] Other Sisters speak of opening convents where they had to sit on fruit cases for chairs and where they took turns to use the cutlery. Putting newspaper between sheets for blankets was not an uncommon measure. In German Hill (Australia), Sisters slept in a stable by night and moved their beds out into a small shed to make room for school each day.[175] Sisters in India, founding a new community in a neglected and poverty-stricken area, "were lodged in a derelict building and had to open umbrellas above their beds."[176] The 1880s saw Mother Antoinette Cuff (Concordia) and a companion travelling by lumber wagon on weekends, having taught all week, to beg money for their school. Sometimes they stayed overnight with some farm family, on occasion having to sit up all night because the bed was black with bed bugs. "We suffered much from poverty,"[177] wrote Mother Stanislaus, as could many another Sister of St Joseph. Themselves poor, they looked after the poor and shared whatever they had.

Sisters of St Joseph include in their at homeness with the poor, a care to "make do" with what is, and a realisation that none of us is self-sufficient. Recycling is not a new thing in Josephite circles! People look with envy at antiques that have been part of convent furniture for over a hundred years. But alongside the chair that might now be valuable could be a library shelf made from planks of wood that happened to be lying outside. An infant teacher in Sydney, Sister Alphonse, was renowned in her time for her innovative methods and ability to teach classes of a hundred and more children to such effect that lecturers and tutors from State-based universities brought student-teachers to observe her at work:

> Most of our equipment had to be home-made, as there was not much available in commercial aids, what there was, was

---

[174] This oral account is corroborated by Marie Foale. *The Josephites Go West,* Fremantle: Univ. of Notre Dame Press, 1995. p. 47.
[175] Crowley, *Women of the Vale,* p. 39.
[176] Bourne, *His Mercy is From Age to Age,* p. 79.
[177] Thomas, *Footprints on the Frontier,* p. 132.

> expensive, and funds were always low. To have a well-equipped and interesting classroom meant I was always busy collecting scrap junk and spending hours making and renewing aids. I overcame some problems with art and craft by seeking the help of parents who came after school hours for training, until a considerable support-group in making equipment had been built up. Working with large classes was hard work, ... and we had ... only a love of teaching, and a creative mind which, I realise, is a God-given gift. Teaching outsize classes was possible, lots of fun and satisfying, because with your hand in God's, nothing is impossible.[178]

Mary MacKillop drew from Bethlehem-Joseph's inability to provide out of his own resources for those he loved, a consciousness of our dependence on "Divine Providence". This was a mark of her spirituality that permeated her whole life. Sisters of St Joseph who during the Depression years were absolutely dependent on God's providence for survival, live on today in the spirit of those who likewise must trust, in an age of uncertainty especially about our own future, in God's ongoing care for our world and Church. "The will of God will never lead you to where His grace cannot keep you," quoted one interviewee.

Earthiness: You will find the phrase "roll-your-sleeves-up-women" written in the languages of every country in which Sisters of St Joseph minister. Through the association of St Joseph with the Incarnation, Sisters of St Joseph have an identification with the land and a pragmatism that acknowledges God's love revealed in hard work and the ordinariness of the everyday. "Josephite life not a transplanting ground for weeping willows!" a Superior General is quoted as saying.

As Julian Tenison Woods noticed during his stay in France in the early 1850s, Sisters of St Joseph were at one with farmers

---

[178] Kathleen Burford RSJ. *Unfurrowed Fields: A Josephite Story, NSW 1872 – 1972,* Sydney: Sisters of St Joseph, 1991. pp. 249, 250.

and townspeople. Particularly by their willingness to work hard, they were able to relate to those who, in Australian terms, are the "battlers" in life. Sisters in Eureka, California, who taught all day and in the evening dug the foundations for a hospital were not unique among Sisters of St Joseph. Neither was the Sister who told of visiting a hassled mother and completing the ironing for her before leaving.

In Woods' case, the earthy spirit of Joseph led him to an awareness of connectedness to the rest of creation. In scientific circles, his appreciation of the natural world won him universal respect. "He once wrote that his love for science was second only to his regard for the priesthood and its duties."[179] A hundred years before the Green Movement came into being, he was advocating for the legislated protection of forests, lest, "peerless and priceless as they once were", they be but "things of the past."[180] To a newspaper he wrote:

> Every rock, every leaf, every insect has something beautiful, nay wonderful to tell ... a perfect fairy land of beauty will open to the gaze at every step. The flowers will unveil the hidden secrets of their beauty; the stones reveal their crystalline structure, and the tiniest insect display wonders of mechanism ... All new, all varied, all instructive, and all tending to raise the mind to higher and nobler conceptions of what creation does to declare the glory of its author.[181]

Likewise, the attitude of those who share the spirit of the earthy St Joseph are those who can identify with Sister Maria Margarita Jimnez who died in Orange, California, in 2003. She recalls in her memoirs being a child who "takes time to see and 'wonder' at everything". She describes one such incident:

> I remember looking at an ant crawling on the ground over dirt, stones and into the grasses. I got down on my stomach and

---

[179] Schiemer, "Josephite Spirituality".
[180] Woods, J.E.T. "Tasmanian Forests: Their Botany and Economical Value." Cited by Anne Player RSJ, "Julian Tenison Woods, Scientist, 1832 – 1889." *Journal and Proceedings of the Royal Society of New South Wales*. Vol 122, 1989, Parts 3, 4. p. 113.
[181] Woods, Julian Tenison. "Notes Made in North Australia", *Sydney Mail*, July 17, 1880.

watched it, and then I remember pretending I was that little ant seeing through its eyes. Suddenly, the dirt became a vast desert and the stones became mountains and the grasses became a jungle! It was a delightful experience. .. I had discovered a whole new world thru the eyes of one of God's little creatures.[182]

At the time of the beatification of Mary MacKillop in 1995, many writers, artists and other social commentators, Christian or not, acknowledged that Josephite spirituality illustrates the "earthy" spirit of Australia. They saw Mary as an icon of the land. Those who joined her took up the banner:

> Brown clad they came, these women of the soil;
> Free they were from Convention's crippling bonds
> Mobile, like the Spirit of the Great South Land
> Ready to brave its dust and heat and drought
> To live the people's lives
> To follow to Australia's farthest posts
> Her isolated poor.[183]

Humour: If the ability to laugh at oneself is an indication of humility, then Sisters of St Joseph certainly have this virtue. One Sister told how, as a young woman, she would walk past the convent and hear the Sisters talking and laughing while they were gardening. "They just seemed so happy, I wanted to be with them," she said. Stories of "making our own fun"; of dressing up as "country cousins" and being received into the parlour by the superior before being found out[184]; of a Thanksgiving goose "jumping out of the pan"; of a dog licking the word "Welcome" off the cake baked for a visiting Superior General; of a city postulant being sent to milk a cow at the country convent and, on managing to get only half a cupful, walking home slowly in the rain so that the level of milk would increase – all these and more are the heritage of Sisters of St Joseph.

---

[182] Necrology, Sister Maria Margarita Jimenez. Archives, Sisters of St Joseph, Orange.
[183] White, Patricia RSJ, Poem, "An Icon for Australia". Archives, Sisters of St Joseph, Sydney.
[184] *Focus*, Winter, 2002. p. 7.

In 1883, Mary MacKillop received a letter from Sister Calasanctius describing their journey by ship to New Zealand: "Sister Raymond was so dreadfully seasick that I believe she will turn *schismatic* sooner than cross the Southern Ocean again."[185] In 1864, the Sisters travelled in mufti to England because of Protestant opposition, but were advised by a Visitation Sister to abandon the outfits "well in advance of the Deluge"– "You will be insulted quite enough."[186] A French-speaking Sister in the United States was showing visitors around the hospital when she was asked where the restroom[187] was. "Oh, we don't have any," was the reply. "But we have two porches. You can use those for rest." Another Sister fresh out from Ireland was asked by her kindergarten pupil if he could go to the restroom. "Rest room!" she said. "I'd like to know anyone who needs a rest more than me!" In Western Australia a Sister got the children to form a guard of honour, anticipating the visit of the Abbot. The parish priest arrived alone, carrying the rabbit he had told her he would bring to show the class.

We treasure vignettes of a Sister phoning the police to come and kill a billygoat so that they could retrieve the £1 note that it had eaten; of another making a dive for a naughty pupil when her heel went through the white-ant eaten floor and, not being able to move, saying with as much dignity as she could muster, "Just as well I can control myself!"; of a community coping with the "ten plagues of Hillston" – searing heat, dust-storms, floods, mud "which set like concrete", mice in their millions, possums stealing fruit from the kitchen table, swarms of grasshoppers, corkscrew grass, bushfires and flies – all with a nonchalance that would have put Pharaoh to shame.[188] Then there is the Sister who, hearing that a poor woman recluse had lost her dog and was grieving, arranged to have another dog, a bitch, given to

---

[185] Power, *Sisters of St Joseph of the Sacred Heart*, p. 14.
[186] Bourne, *His Mercy is From Age to Age,* p. 106.
[187] An American euphemism for "toilet".
[188] Burford, *Unfurrowed Fields,* pp. 251–253.

her. She was amused to hear later that when male dogs came around, the woman would come out with a big stick and shout at them, "Go away!! This is the sister's dog!" "I was sorry the poor dog was assigned to the vow of chastity", the Sister commented.[189]

In 1953, Sister Maura Ann of Erie reflected on Joseph, the man who had walked humbly with his God:

> In St Peter's Cathedral there is an exquisite marble statue of St Joseph. It does not stand out under the blaze of the sanctuary lights but back in the shadow of the High Altar. Somehow or other, to me, this exemplifies the life and the work of the Sisters of Saint Joseph. I do not know whether the placing of his statue was done with anything specific in mind, but I like to think that, had the choosing been his, this is the very spot St Joseph would have chosen for himself. And can his daughters improve on that?[190]

Daughters of St Joseph and ordinary people who "do their bit" towards extending God's reign, and who bring harmony into a world contending with the effects of human sinfulness – these are the people through whom the spirit given to Joseph lives on. Not all of them are recognised. Some of them avoid publicity at all costs. The case of Sister Mary O'Leary, named in the Australia Day Honours List in 2003, is, however, a little extreme!

> Mary, who had died a few months earlier following an accident, had never liked the limelight, but carried it a bit too far in order to dodge this lot! It seemed characteristically Josephite that our only medal recipient should be such a hidden and unassuming worker for the poor – and further, that she shouldn't even be around to accept it.[191]

---

[189] Marina Norris RSJ. "A Kiwi with a Variation", unpublished reflection paper, p. 24.
[190] Archives, Sisters of St Joseph, Erie.
[191] *Perthville Josephites Keeping in Touch with Friends and Associates*, December 2003, p. 1.

6.3 PART THREE: The spirit lives into the now

<u>Walking in Humility</u>
Walking with our God in humility and trust at the present time is a counter-cultural thing to do. In a world of insecurity and fear, where the scramble to survive in a constantly-changing business world rewards self-promotion, competition and even dishonesty, humility can certainly be seen as a "weakness".[192]

The "Worker Sisters" in France have experienced this, as, laying aside their professional privileges, they have found themselves powerless in a world based on status. Denise reflects:
> Yesterday I was teaching, I was someone. Today with a scrubbing brush in my hand, my little blue bonnet on my head, no-one is interested in me. The doctor who reigns in the clinic crushed my fingers without seeing me when he was climbing the stairs. It was a powerful experience. Who am I? What game am I playing?[193]

In a sense, Sisters of St Joseph corporately experience this "weakness" or vulnerability. With attitudes changing towards the role and value of Religious Life especially in the western world, the privileged position they enjoyed in Church and society is no longer assumed. Sister Virginia Ann reflects on the comment of a lay woman made in 1969:
> "I read this article about sisters," she said, "It claimed you have done your job so well, you are no longer needed. It must be wonderful to feel so successful, so fulfilled!" ... Thirty years later I have achieved enough humility to admit I don't know what God intends; I need to grow into that wisdom. However, at present, I agree with people who say religious life in the future will change and emerge as something very different – much smaller. But it will survive.[194]

---

[192] Mackay, op. cit.
[193] Groupe Monde Ouvrier, "Engagées,Envoyées,Engagées", pp. 13, 14.
[194] Gardner, *Let It Be,* pp. 184 - 187.

In the meantime, in setting up structures of partnership with laypeople who share the spirit, the Sisters are enriched, and also assured that they are nurturing the charism as it evolves for a new world. For instance, there are many Sisters now who involve others in giving body-massage to women prisoners, to people in economically poor areas, to the aged or to those on retreats. God reaches out through human touch. The Sisters of St Joseph of Hamilton can take pride in the fact that a holistic understanding of the human being persists through the commitment of their Health System "to caring for the whole person: body, mind and spirit." The testimony of Lynda describes how this care worked out in practice for her dying mother:

> "There was never any hesitation to go the extra mile," Lynda recalls. This included bringing daily communion to Helen on days when she couldn't go to the chapel herself, providing an air mattress to help ease bed sores, and, during the last month, making it possible for Lynda and her four siblings to be at their mother's bedside 24 hours a day.[195]

Associates have identified with the spirit that stands by those who are regarded as the least. Peruvian Associates of the Sisters of St Joseph of London (Ontario) are partnered by the groups in Canada who support them and communicate with them. Associates of Sisters of St Joseph of Perthville (Australia) have adopted a school in East Timor, one of the poorest nations in the world.

The dignity of the human being is upheld by Associates who "help one another to recognize and appreciate her/his particular interests, skills, talents, and gifts which are currently being used or are waiting to be developed."[196] The new Associate who was attracted by Sisters who were "real people" and who wants to "reflect their work and spiritual nature" in his own lay life is

---

[195] Advertising brochure, St Joseph's Villa, Dundas, a Ministry of the Sisters of St Joseph of Hamilton.
[196] Handbook, *Agregés of the Sisters of St Joseph of Rochester:* Goal 3. p. 11.

tapping into the gift of "being human".[197] This is an integral part of the legacy that Sisters of St Joseph have inherited and that is vital for Church mission today.

Trusting in Divine Providence

> Don't ask me where the money came from for JCA (Josephite Community Aid). We started in 1986 with absolutely nothing and with no way to pay our bills. People came to hear that the young volunteers in JCA worked directly with people who are very poor. I was the treasurer and I worried at first. Maria (Sister Maria Sullivan) would always say: "Don't worry – God will provide." I think Fr Julian Woods and Blessed Mary MacKillop had a great belief like this. And God did provide, through the goodness of people. One time, we had only $320 left in our account (this was about ten years after we started JCA) and by then we had expenses of more than $200 a week, so I felt I had to call an extraordinary meeting of the Management Committee. We talked about the situation and we prayed. The money started coming in the next day (not from anyone at the meeting) and it continues to come. I am a banker and I have no idea how you would describe the surety of JCA, especially in the beginning. I can hardly say to the bank: "God will provide"!! But God has provided and I'm sure God will provide while ever the ministry is with the people who are really poor.

This is the reflection of Joe Leto, member of the Management Committee of Josephite Community Aid in Sydney. His story is an echo of similar stories recording the experience of past and present Sisters of St Joseph. In Peru today, a Sister recalled that, particularly when they first arrived in the country, they had no recourse but to depend on God's Providence:

> In searching for ways to address what we perceived as urgent needs, we in Peru often had to "make do" or "substitute", recalling how things were done before we had the gadgetry of today. Often in beginnings, there is nowhere to bring people together. The sisters, in these circumstances, would perhaps obtain permission to commence in frail structures made of sheets of bamboo matting, the public meeting place of the

---

[197] *Soundings*, Vol. 20, Winter 2002. p. 9.

young settlement, or even in the tiny space of a similar private "home". In neither case could materials be left stored in such places. Everything has to be carried there and back each time. .. What an inconvenience it is when the photocopier breaks down! or the power goes off. Lack of multiple copies of books and other resources, had us trying to remember what ingredients are needed to make a jelly pad, to save bussing into the city, and the half an hour or more each way. Now we have a copier, and the electricity to work it. Experience in providing oneself with teaching aids in the days when our schools had no government assistance, was valuable in devising a stock of materials for encouraging children's creativity: we saved every carton, tin and wrapping to become houses, boats, towers, trucks and fantasy things, and hauled them with us along with glue and paint.

In an uncertain world, trust in Divine Providence is needed now, more than ever. That calls for a spirit of generosity – being ready to risk, living "out of an awareness of God's gifts and (responding) by always courageously choosing to live what I will discern to be the most loving response to each circumstance as it presents itself".[198]

Being earthy

The earthiness of the spirit of Joseph calls us to integrate all aspects of our lives and to be aware of our connectedness. When Judy became an Associate, she recognised this call: "Joining the CSJ Associates and being with women – formally and informally – who have a deep love of life and share it in down to earth ways is, for Judy, a kind of 'homecoming'."[199]

In a number of instances, Sisters have taken on in recent years ministries that directly express an ecological spirituality. Sister Janet Fraser in Toronto speaks of one such ministry:

---

[198] Claire Olivier CSJ. *Responding to the Maxims: A Spirituality Revisited,* Orange: Sisters of St Joseph of Orange, 1995. p. 5.
[199] *Soundings,* Vol. 24 #5, Summer 2002. p. 7.

> Cherish the Earth ministry grew from a wonderful experience of God ... an awareness of God in all of creation. Once we see that we are part of this ongoing evolution of creation, we are part of the earth, then we realize we have to live in relationship, not detached and above, thinking that we can do anything we want to do to the earth. ... I think it is for us to witness new ways of doing things that are really healing for us and healing for the earth.[200]

Sally Marsh SSJ writes songs and stories celebrating the presence of God in all creation. She has dedicated one of her beautifully-illustrated children's books to her parents:

> As the first people of earth in my life, you prepared me to live and love as a member of humanity. You taught me to respect, care for, and appreciate the beauty of all living creatures, all growing things, of water, rocks, stars and the sun, as a member of the entire Earth family. You encouraged me to use my five senses and my heart to reach out as a member of the universe.[201]

In Australia, Carmel Crameri RSJ and others are engaged in a project sponsored by six religious congregations in Victoria called EarthSong. They promote earth literacy and ethical living that acknowledges the sacredness of place and the interconnectedness of all life. Further north in Queensland, Sisters of St Joseph, Mary-Ann Casanova and Rose Schlick, run an Eco Education Centre for education, spirituality and hospitality. The building designs, material selection, energy requirements, water harvesting and recycling programs plus the planting of local indigenous flora are all directed to demonstrate the values upon which the venture is based. It is noteworthy that they have drawn on the botanical surveys made by Julian Tenison Woods in Queensland over a hundred years ago to inform their choice of plants. Having already collaborated with the Queensland Bishops in preparing a kit to support their pastoral letter about the Great Barrier Reef, Mary-Ann and

---

[200] Smyth and Wicks, *Wisdom Raises Her Voice,* p. 110.
[201] Sally Marsh, SSJ. *Hugh Manatee and the People of Earth*, Holyoke: Sisters of St Joseph of Springfield.

Rose hope (as do Carmel and other Sisters) to facilitate a wider acceptance and understanding of the spirituality of ecology among those who identify with the spirit of Joseph.

In a recent Lenten reflection, theologian Tony Kelly CSsR points to the one who, along the road to Emmaus, showed how the Christian walks humbly with God and provides for that journey:

> Let's remember that the eucharist, the Christian prayer par excellence, is quite a very earthy matter. It uses the grain and the grapes that have grown in our land. This presupposes the fertile soil, the rain and sunshine, the cycle of seasons, and the skill and care of farmers and bakers, vine-growers and wine-makers. Men and women have worked with nature to produce this food and drink for our nourishment and celebration.
>
> In the eucharist, the Holy Spirit transforms what nature has produced and what human beings have made into the sacrament of the Lord's real presence. The eucharist, then, celebrates our communion in the greatest gifts of God coming to us through what nature provides and human work has produced. This sacrament does not take us out of this world, but makes us belong to it in deeper reverence and responsibility. It 'earths' us, so to speak, in the mystery of creation.
>
> The real presence of Jesus on the altar opens our eyes to the creative presence of God in all creation. It invites us to contemplation, to see the whole world as the vast temple of God, as an all-nurturing 'mother earth'. What a profound mystery nature must be if it figures so essentially in this and the other sacraments.[202]

---

[202] Kelly, Tony. "Time to Mark an Ecological Lent", *Catholic Leader*, Feb. 20th, 2005. p. 9.

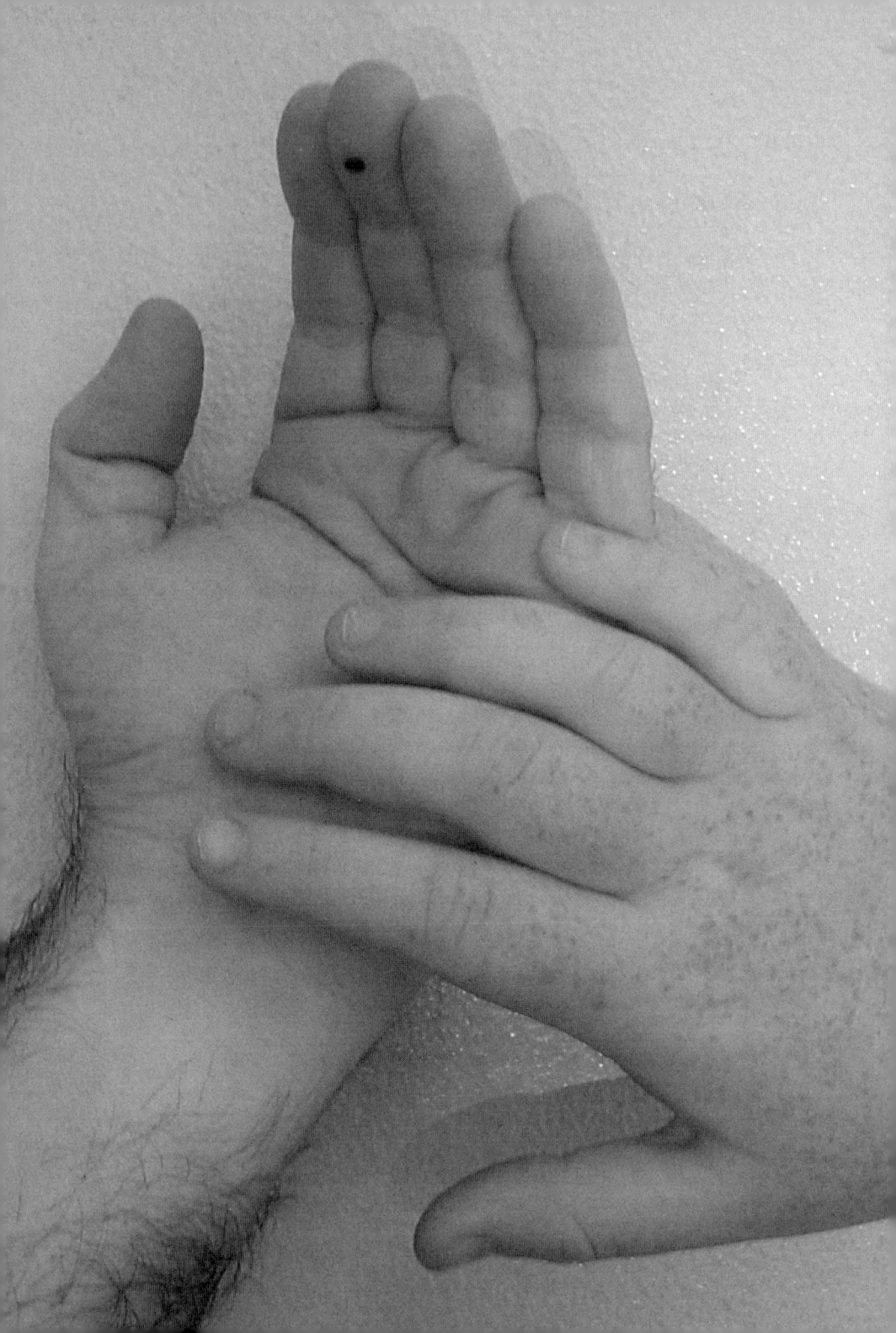

CHAPTER SEVEN

The spirit of Joseph ......

engages pain.

Look, your father and I have been searching in great anxiety. (Lk. 2:48)

7.1 PART ONE: The spirit is revealed

<u>The place of pain</u>
"God so loved the world", we are told, "that he gave his only Son, that whoever believes in him should not perish but have eternal life."[1] Another way of saying it is that God is outpouring love. But the mystery of self-gift or self-emptying and its associated pain is something unexplored by most of us. In our heads we know that suffering can produce strength and new life. We hold up images of trees blackened by bushfires and sprouting the tiny, delicate shoots of green. Mothers expose themselves to the pangs of giving birth. We quote Jesus, "unless the grain of wheat die…" We believe in the Resurrection. Yet we never lose our fear of pain. We cringe from thoughts of "crucifying" the ego so that full life and real love might emerge.

At the same time, we admire those who overcome this fear. In a powerful account of engaging pain for the life of the other, a young woman from Josephite Community Aid tells her story:
> Sometimes you have to question if maybe you're the one who is mad. I was in the bushes in a little park off the main street of a country town. .. I was flapping my arms, running around

---

[1] John 3:16

and saying 'shoo, shoo' very loudly. All the while, my friend watched on.

I had met her several years before when she jumped in front of a truck and I, impulsively, jumped after her. The truck clipped the back of my jacket as I shoved her aside. A strange friendship had developed from there. An odd reciprocity. She had learned to read and grew marginally more socialised. I learned about having a chronic mental illness, following her on the Ferris wheel of stability and health, sliding off medication, bellying out in a screaming, psychotic, delusional, suicidal, homicidal rage. One memorable midnight phone call started with (deleting the expletives), "I'm locked in my house, I'm gonna stab my mother and the cops wanna talk to you." The cops did wanna talk to me. Mostly about how I was the best person to calm her down and avert matricide. I had followed her through hospitalisation, drugged eyes and slurred speech, through violence that left me battered and bruised, through moments where visitors or nurses mistook me for a patient and tried to teach me about God, or about taking my medication.

A little crowd was gathering now, to watch the lunatic raving in the bushes. Eventually, my friend gave the signal. The monsters were gone. I'd chased them all away. Finally, with them gone, she could calm down and stop screaming. We took a moment to compose ourselves, smiled at the crowd, and wandered on, hand in hand.[2]

Living out death and resurrection is a journey begun at birth. We go through it in the daily give and take of life, in small ways and big. Mental and physical pain can take us into places we do not want to be. There is no way we can trivialise this part of our lives. It has always been with us, and people have always struggled with it. It is a theme that permeates Scripture. From the account of sin in Genesis, through to figures like Job who had to yield in submission to the mystery, through to the crucifixion itself, the question "Why?" is still asked.

---

[2] Ruth Townley, JCA.

It is understandable that this is the question asked about suffering. It makes things easier to bear if we know the reason for it. If we can be assured of success, we will go through whatever it takes to achieve the end we aim for. The discipline demanded of athletes, performers and scholars is not questioned by our society, but is taken for granted. People are willing to work long hours to produce crops; they will sacrifice life-savings for an operation to prevent the death of their child; they will risk their own lives to rescue a loved one from danger.

The anguish comes when there is no "why". No philosophising can explain away domestic violence or murder or the road accident caused by the stupor of drunkenness or drugs. Racial hatred making a deranged choice of victim; vindictiveness harbouring resentment for years and taking revenge in vicious, willful ways; envy plotting the downfall of those whose gifts threaten and who have achieved; none of these evils can be glossed over with pious thoughts or platitudes. Bad things do happen to good people. Some people do seem to have the odds stacked against them.

But faith tells us that we do not live in a random universe of chance. We believe that there is justice, and that life is not just about the survival of the fittest. Suffering, undeniably part of life, does, eventually, have meaning, we believe. There is a "why". However, when the purpose of suffering is unclear; when it seems pointless, unjust and malevolent, we struggle with allowing it to be. We can't align a loving God with such futility and malevolence. The tsunamis of life, the horrors of terrorism, the trauma of the oppressed and abused, and the undeserved suffering of war victims fill us with anguish. Why should the innocent be subjected to such pain?

These age-old questions will always be with us. To them we can only bring the wisdom of our own experience and that of those who have gone before us. From these resources we can engage pain in our journey into full life. We can learn from those whose bravery overwhelms us. The courage of the little boy dying of leukemia and yet able to show concern for the grief of his parents, care for the welfare of his brothers and sister, and generosity to others in need (giving his books and toys to children less well-off than he), inspires us to take on a perspective about what really counts in life. Suffering, we learn, need not break the human spirit. Indeed, the grace of God can use the suffering itself to form character and to work for our good.

This does not mean we negate suffering. Anger, confusion and raw grief need to be expressed as we cope with the reality of pain. The psalmist who complains to God about the unfairness of life, who calls out for comfort and who bargains with God in an effort to put off ill-health and the threat of death surely encourages us to do the same. It is only in hindsight that we can say, "God is our refuge and strength, an ever-present help in trouble."[3]

Engaging pain calls us also to respond with compassion, as, we believe, God does, to suffering. This extends to ourselves as much as to others. We face our own brokenness with patience, allowing ourselves to be only who we are. Compassion for others will urge us to respond to their suffering with practical help in whatever form is appropriate. We don't have answers, but we have presence – be it presence of waiting, or of moral support or of action. Job's friends did well until they opened their mouths, trying to explain what he must have done to deserve such suffering.[4] For such deep pain, a silent "being with" was the only thing needed. At the same time, while compassion does not require us to solve others' problems for them or to stand in their stead, we need to be active in doing

---

[3] Ps. 46:1
[4] Job Ch. 4 et al.

what we can to prevent pain. Jesus' hand of healing reaches into our times through us. His voice, indignant at the hypocrisy of law-enforcers blocking the touch of God's compassionate love, needs our voice now to point out injustice and to protect the rights of those who are silenced.

For Christians, the ultimate sign of self-emptying for the life of the other is the cross. Even in outline, with the vertical meeting the horizontal, the cross symbolises for us the contradiction of life and death. An instrument of death, it has become the symbol of new life, of liberation from death. Australian writer, Ted Mason, comments on this symbol:

> The Cross of Jesus means embracing suffering to do away with suffering; it can be a very painful way of living out the truth. Cross bearers will be found in the struggle to bring dignity to the humiliated, justice to the oppressed, equality to the disadvantaged, unity where there is division and compassion to the suffering. When we oppose oppression, there will always be pain, maybe conflict, but something new will be born. The path of freedom is the Way of the Cross, and we are called to live out this truth in spite of the difficulties. New life begins when we have the courage to overcome our own fear and apathy and seek genuine communion with those in poverty, in pain or in deep need. Our genuine love and care for our fellow human beings brings us into communion with Abba, through Jesus, in the Spirit. This extraordinary communion will always result in Resurrection.[5]

"The Spirit of God," says Edwards, "transforms the brutal and wicked act of crucifixion into an event that brings healing and liberation".[6] At each celebration of the Eucharist we pray that the Spirit will similarly transform the work and sufferings of the community symbolised in the gifts of bread and wine. These are the gifts which, through the power of the Spirit, will "become

---

[5] Ted Mason. "He Is Risen - You Will Meet Him In Galilee", *Online Catholics*, http://www.onlinecatholics.com.au/issue44/commessay2.php
[6] Edwards, *Breath of Life*, p. 83.

the body and blood of Jesus Christ our Lord".[7] "This is my body which is for you....This cup is the new covenant in my blood."[8] The cross on Calvary became "sacrifice", that is, "something made holy". Our celebration of the Eucharist takes us into that event; the total self-gift of the Son is made present to us. We enter into communion with a Love that conquers death and enables us to embrace new life.

<u>Joseph engaged pain</u>
As one whose life was given over to enabling the reign of God to be revealed among us, Joseph knew the pain involved in self-emptying. However, the gospel accounts only hint of what outpouring love meant for him. The anxiety referred to by Jesus' mother at the loss of Jesus in the temple is one such example. Anne Hennessy calls this passage of the gospel "most paradoxical":

> To Joseph's relatives and friends, "losing" one's son while on pilgrimage would indicate either laxness on the part of a parent or disobedience on the part of a child. This situation, for all the suffering it caused, could easily have been misinterpreted by others as Joseph's failure to control "his" son. On the other hand, in this same Temple scene, the young Jesus causes amazement because of the wisdom of his questions and discourse. Since Joseph was the acknowledged "father" and thus the religious educator of this young boy, Jesus' behaviour would have brought honor to Joseph.[9]

While acknowledging the latter point regarding honour, loss is loss, and so the overall experience described by the gospel story would have been one of deep anguish. The suffering of being misjudged and condemned is, besides, a lonely one. Most groups are impatient of explanations and, even in the case of calumny, do not allow self-defence. They call it "paranoia" or

---

[7] "Eucharistic Prayer IV", *The Roman Missal,* ICEL, 1973.
[8] 1 Cor. 11: 24-25.
[9] Hennessy, *In Search of a Patron,* p. 55.

"defensiveness". Joseph would have known this loneliness, not only in the temple scene, but in his inability to justify the choices he made throughout life. To go against family norms in making the pregnant Mary his wife would have incurred the disapproval of relatives and friends. In societies bound by laws of kinship, there is little chance of keeping secrets. His reputation would have been at stake when he chose what he perceived as God's will, abandoning established relationships to go into Egypt. "Joseph experienced the desolation and the consolation of choosing between God and society, between group tradition and following his God."[10]

The events which led to the flight into Egypt would not have been Joseph's only experience of coping with danger. Survival in the first century was a somewhat precarious affair. The alliance between Rome and the Herodian kings was violent and oppressive. The accession to power of King Herod the Great in the mid-first century BCE, for example, was marked by Roman soldiers slaughtering "thousands of local people on Mount Tabor."[11] After Herod died in 4 BCE, Judea came under the rule of his son Archelaus, whom Joseph feared so much that he did not go back to Bethlehem. Crucifixions and executions were continuous from immediately after his accession to the throne until his banishment in 6 CE. Meanwhile, another son, Herod Antipas, was made ruler of Galilee where an uprising in Sepphoris, close to Nazareth, resulted in "the enslavement of many of its citizens and the burning of several satellite villages."[12] Was Nazareth threatened at this time? Did rape and pillaging touch the lives of Joseph's family there?

Under such rule, impoverishment was the lot of farmers and labourers who occupied the lowest social levels. "In first-century Palestine, all peasants were oppressed by heavy taxation

---

[10] Hennessy, *In Search of a Patron*, p. 56.
[11] Hennessy, *In Search of a Patron*, p. 34.
[12] Hennessy, *In Search of a Patron*, p. 34.

in currency, goods and services (which could take the form of forced labor)."[13] Food shortages would not have been unknown. Besides being at the mercy of tax collectors, they would have been subject to nature's whims as farmers are today, where bad weather, pests and disease can wipe out crops in an instant.

In the building flurry particularly of Herod Antipas, bureaucrats enriched themselves in the tax trade, ensuring labour and moneys for construction works as well as collecting taxes on behalf of the Roman invaders. Further psychological suffering was the result. "Galilean peasants were torn because the very families toward whom they felt civic and religious loyalty were those who oppressed them by secular and religious taxation, including donation of their best produce, and by being absentee landlords who left them at the mercy of stewards and other middle men."[14] The presence of Herodian and Roman troops in towns and villages would also have been a continual affront to them.

If Joseph did, indeed, work as a building labourer in Sepphoris, he would have had to work under foreign supervision, since the use of Roman facades and other decorative structures in the new cities involved building techniques quite different from those with which Jews were familiar. "Joseph, as other Palestinians hired or coerced into the work force, had to labor under Romans or Roman-paid architects and engineers as well as Herodian supervisors (synonymous with 'traitors' to loyal Israelites)".[15] The suffering involved in all of this would have been exacerbated by the dangers involved in the work itself, and injury and deaths did result; Jesus' reference to a building

---

[13] Hennessy, *In Search of a Patron,* p. 29.
[14] Hennessy, *In Search of a Patron,*, p. 37. Quoting Sean Freyne. *Galilee, Jesus and the Gospel: Literary Approaches and Historical Investigations,* Philadelphia, PA: Fortress, 1988. pp. 199–211.
[15] Hennessy, *In Search of a Patron,* p. 45.

accident that happened in Jerusalem as recorded in Luke 13: 4 would not have been a one-off event.[16]

Joseph's life was a hard one, where encounter with pain was all too present. His sufferings were physical and emotional. The disparaging remark made by Nathaniel, "Can anything good come out of Nazareth?"[17] gives an indication of the contempt in which people from this backwater were held. It was against a setting of financial and political oppression where disruption, hardship and struggle were daily realities, where religious and social ambiguities confronted the ordinary person and where survival itself could not be taken for granted, that Joseph lived a life of single-hearted devotion to God in the tradition of the great patriarchs. Out of the contradictions of his life and its confrontation with pain was nurtured the model for life in communion with a God "who brings life from defeat and death".[18] "Joseph," says Anne Hennessy, "pre-figured that availability to God's designs which would characterize Jesus' formation of his disciples".[19]

7.2 PART TWO: The spirit unfolds.

Self-emptying

Self-giving, or self-emptying so that God's designs might be carried out through us, is a theme that has permeated the spirituality of Sisters of St Joseph from the time of Médaille. In the *Eucharistic Letter* Médaille reminded the Sisters that they should be "empty of self and empty of everything" in order that they might be "spiritually alive".[20] The aim of this self-giving was to bring life to the other: "For it seems to me that 'our little

---

[16] Lk 13:4, "Or those eighteen upon whom the tower in Siloam fell and killed them, do you think that they were worse offenders than all the others who dwelt in Jerusalem?"
[17] Jn. 1:46.
[18] Edwards, *Breath of Life*, p. 58.
[19] Hennessy, *In Search of a Patron*, p. 56.
[20] *The Eucharistic Letter*, par. 26.

nothing' has for its end to procure a great perfection of souls rather than simply their salvation".[21] For Médaille, as for Scripture, the word "perfection" meant "fullness".[22] What was being aimed for was "fullness of life" for others – not simply "saving their souls".

As pointed out by Mason, bringing "dignity to the humiliated, justice to the oppressed, equality to the disadvantaged, unity where there is division and compassion to the suffering"[23] is not done without cost. Giving of self for the fullness of life of others, itself a sign of God's reign, will inevitably involve suffering, conflict and pain. Right from the beginning, this has been the experience of Sisters of St Joseph. In a letter written by Father Médaille to Sister Fayole, superior of Saint-Didier, we read, "I am pained to see you bearing crosses. You have them everywhere. .. The order that providence has established for the birth and progress of good works is sown with crosses."[24]

Médaille himself suffered sorely from being cut off by his Jesuit superiors from the work he had founded. He complained of not getting letters from the Sisters: "I would have been comforted to learn some news of your Congregation, but the good God did not wish it".[25] He suffered from ill-health and shortly before his death, Vacher comments, he endured a "stripping of the heart"[26] reflective of the "complete stripping of self" which, he had said, was necessary in order to dispose oneself toward total union with God.[27]

---

[21] *The Eucharistic Letter,* par. 32.
[22] For example, when Matthew 5:48 says, "You, therefore, must be perfect, as your heavenly Father is perfect", he does so in the context of God's love being indiscriminately extended both to those who are faithful and those who are unfaithful. Therefore, the admonition asks us to love with the same indiscriminate fullness as God does.
[23] See reference 5 in this chapter.
[24] Vacher, *Des régulières,* Session 4, p. 159.
[25] Vacher, *Des régulières,* Session 4, p. 159.
[26] Vacher, *Des régulières,* Session 4, p. 159.
[27] Maxim 100.

Times of intense suffering have tested the character of the Sisterhood of St Joseph. During the fearful years of the French Revolution, at least five Sisters were guillotined. One of them, Marie Garnier (Sister St Julien), 38 years old, had avoided arrest by hiding in a cavity in the wall of the house in which the members of the family and two other Sisters had been arrested. From there she had fled to the woods where she remained all night, praying. She considered what she had done was cowardly and so, at dawn, she emerged from her sanctuary and gave herself up to the commissioners, who, it is said, were amazed at such courage but nevertheless condemned her to death along with the others.[28]

In subsequent months, Mother Saint John Fontbonne and her sister were also imprisoned and marked for execution, saved only by the assassination of Robespierre. Savage takes up the story:

> Mother Saint John could rarely be induced, in later years, to speak of this period of her life, of the eleven months of suffering which she and her companions endured in damp cells, deprived of every physical comfort, and above all of the consolations of religion, Mass and the Sacraments. Her aged father, bowed with years and grief, frequently walked twelve miles to bring them wholesome food and to plead for their release. They had little hope of being permitted to leave the prison, and daily held themselves in readiness for death, not knowing when they would be summoned to the scaffold. Announcement was at length made to them one evening in mid-summer, 1794, that their execution would take place the following day. The night was spent by them in final preparation for their approaching end. When morning dawned, and the great doors of their dungeon swung open, the disappointment was great to find that freedom and not death was waiting for them.[29]

---

[28] Byrne, Notes of lecture, June 2003.
[29] Savage, *The Congregation of the Sisters of St Joseph of Carondelet*, p. 13.

There is a particular suffering that comes from being humiliated. Mother St John was not exempt from this. She had re-founded the Sisters of St Joseph in 1807, and in 1838 could look back on the establishment of more than two hundred houses in the diocese of Lyon, plus branches in Bourg, Chambéry and Carondelet (USA). Her own feeling was that, as she was now going on eighty years old, it was time for her to relinquish her position as Mother General. Another Sister, Mother Sacred Heart, possessed good leadership qualities and was favoured by the archbishop.

> To facilitate the election of Mother Sacred Heart and to eliminate any strain her own presence might occasion, Mother St John set out for Paris, secretly and unaccompanied, intending to make a retreat there. However, her design was frustrated when – her absence soon discovered – she was overtaken on the road and forced to agree that she would return to Lyons when her retreat ended. In her absence the Chapter was convened and she was one again elected superior general.[30]

Mother St John accepted the decision of the Sisters and resumed duties. But within the year, the archbishop, without warning, demanded that Mother St John resign to make way for his choice. This she did graciously and Mother Sacred Heart became the second superior general. But this story of "tangled cross-purposes clouded with suffering and humiliation"[31] carries with it an experience of disrespect and abuse – "being used" – that many a Sister of St Joseph has shared.

Under the Southern Cross
At her Religious Profession in Adelaide, South Australia, in August 1867, Mary MacKillop adopted the name "Mary of the Cross". Although she had wished for the title, "of the Sacred

---

[30] Emily Joseph Daly. "Genesis of a Congregation" in *Sisters of St Joseph of Carondelet,* St Louis: Herder Book Co., 1966. pp. 47–48.
[31] Daly, "Genesis of a Congregation", p. 47.

Heart", Father Woods had persuaded her that "the Cross" was more appropriate:
> How is it that whenever I leave you, I find you as I pass by, at the foot of the cross, always trying to escape, and yet always brought back to the same old hilltop with a dark and cloudy sky and dreary view all round. Well, then, cling to it, Mary, since it is God's will and very clearly so too, and you will sanctify yourself better there than even in a convent, though these are big words.[32]

At her profession she could, then, write to her mother,
> The Cross is my portion – it is also my sweet rest and support. I could not be happy without my cross – I would not lay it down for all the world could give. With the Cross I am happy, but without it I would be lost.[33]

The basis of Mary's approach to suffering was the firm belief that God's love would never let anything happen that would not be for the ultimate good of herself or others. Moreover, through the cross, Jesus had accomplished the redemption of humanity from the power of sin. The cross was integral to his mission. Therefore, in sharing the cross, Mary could be sure that she was close to Jesus: "It is under the cross that I love to be with Him".[34]

In the notes of retreats she gave her Sisters and in her own meditations and writings, there is strong evidence that Mary's understanding of the cross was that of the French School of Spirituality which, in the 19th century, was virtually universal. Australia was served by Irish and English priests, many of whom had either been educated in French seminaries (as was Father Woods), or were taught by those who had. The French School, of which Bérulle was representative, emphasised the gap that existed between the all holy God and humanity, so inclined to sin and therefore far from God. Sinful humanity, it

---

[32] Julian to Mary, June 30, 1865. Archives, Sisters of St Joseph, Sydney.
[33] Mary to her mother, February 26, 1872.
[34] Mary to Monsignor Kirby, 1873. Archives, Sisters of St Joseph, Sydney.

was considered, "needs to offer a suitable sacrifice to God in atonement and adoration, but is unable to do so".[35] It is only Christ, fully divine and fully human, who could offer this perfect sacrifice, himself, and who could, then, offer true worship. Bérulle saw that adoration and "absolute self-giving" were key to Jesus' life and therefore to all Christian life:

> The goal of Christian living is to make one's own those dispositions in the heart of Jesus. Therefore, the complete surrender of the creature to the Creator, the perfect adoration of the believer before God, can only be achieved by a complete adherence to Christ who embodies in himself the very essence of such surrender and adoration. .. Bérulle preached a deep, total renunciation of self that is at the same time and adherence to Christ and a being possessed by him.[36]

Through entering into the "dispositions in the heart of Jesus", Mary MacKillop could, like Jesus in Gethsemane, anticipate suffering, feeling dread but at the same time be confident that God's love would uphold her. Over a year before her excommunication and the dispersion of the Sisters, she must have felt that things were not going well back home in Adelaide, as she wrote from Brisbane:

> Should our poor schools be taken from us, should our Institute even be suppressed, ah no, our courage, our calm trust in the Sacred Heart would only grow stronger, for we would know that when the storm had passed away, St Joseph would again assemble his children to work once more and more sweetly than ever in the cause of the Sacred Heart.[37]

However anticipated, the actual excommunication was an overwhelming experience of the cross for Mary, just 29 years old. Many events had led up to the situation. One of the factors was jealousy. Father Woods was an enthusiastic visionary,

---

[35] David Walker. "The French Influence", *The Australasian Catholic Record,* Vol LV, No 1, 1978. p. 30.
[36] Walker, "The French Influence", p. 30.
[37] From a statement, probably not circulated, written in August, 1870. Archives, Sisters of St Joseph, Sydney.

multi-talented and occupying a position of trust in the Adelaide diocese. However, some priests thought him a "deluded fanatic".[38] Since Woods at the time when these accusations were strongest was overworked, in financial debt and verging on a mental breakdown, their prognosis was not far from the truth. During 1870, Mary was away in Brisbane, Bishop Sheil was in Rome and two of the Sisters, encouraged by Father Woods, were claiming to have satanic and heavenly visions, thus earning the scorn of those who suspected this new Sisterhood anyway.

Two incidents brought things to a head. When the priest-friend of arch-enemy Father Horan was expelled from the diocese, having been reported for "scandalous conduct" with the children of a Josephite school, Horan swore to "get even". The second was when one of the "visionaries" rifled the convent tabernacle and left drops of blood on the altar cloth. In the months following his return to Adelaide in 1871, the Bishop upbraided Father Woods and approved a request that he should leave the diocese for an indefinite period to preach missions. Advised by Horan, Bishop Sheil then set about changing the rule of the Sisters of St Joseph. Mary had by now returned to Adelaide, and, even though she recognised the Bishop's right to set up what would be a new sisterhood, explained that she would not be part of it. Horan's distortion of messages to and from the bishop was not unrelated to the immediate series of events which culminated in Mary's excommunication "for disobedience and rebellion".[39]

The lifting of the sentence five months later came at great personal cost to Mary. Although she had been comforted by the ministrations of the Jesuits who gave her shelter and arranged that she attend Mass and received Communion while hidden in the Church attic, she had known the humiliation of innuendo,

---

[38] Gardiner, *Mary MacKillop,* p. 85.
[39] Gardiner, *Mary MacKillop,* p. 104.

gossip and mistrust. Bishop Sheil died and the Sisters were reinstated (although depleted in number), but Father Woods was banned from directing the Sisters and Mary eventually lost his friendship. This was the pain of love. From this standpoint, Mary could urge her Sisters to find meaning in their suffering: "Sisters, let us refuse nothing to God's love. He humbled Himself and suffered for us, let us be glad to show Him we are willing to suffer whatever he deigns to ask of us".[40]

Engagement with pain was also keenly felt by Father Woods. Self-emptying for him had been a guiding conviction:

> We are but instruments in the hands of God, and must never act as if we were more. A musician takes a flute which has nothing in it, and of itself produces no sound. He(/She) breathes into it and the sound which issues he(she) modifies by the keys he(she) touches. This is an imperfect image of the way God uses us.[41]

But despite his clear understanding of surrender, Julian struggled with being overlooked and with not being held in the esteem he regarded as his due. He was hesitant to go back to Adelaide at the time of the excommunication, as he had left there under a cloud, owing money and physically and mentally unwell. He complained to Bishop Sheil at the time:

> My children are dispersed and under the cruellest of the heaviest punishments that could be inflicted upon them – the Convent deserted – schools destroyed, the charitable institutions .. broken up – and contention and strife on every side. .. I have been publicly and painfully deposed from my office by having these things done and with unusual severity during my absence.[42]

One of the greatest disappointments for Father Woods was the rejection by Rome of his ideal of poverty for the Sisters. He had wished them to own no property at all; they were always to be

---

[40] Mary to the Sisters, 18 September 1906. Archives, Sisters of St Joseph, Sydney.
[41] *Book of Instructions,* "Interior Peace". Text uses masculine gender only.
[42] Julian Tenison Woods to Bishop Sheil, 5 November 1871. Archives, Archdiocese of Adelaide.

subject to the generosity of the diocese for housing. The Constitution re-written by Roman authorities had prescribed that Sisters should own at least a central house; there would not always be an Emmanuel Solomon to give them shelter in emergencies. But Julian's reflection was bitter:

> It has been almost a death blow to me to see the poverty and simplicity of the Institute of St Joseph destroyed and that without my being able to say a word in its defence. I can never get used to that and it makes me sick with sorrow whenever I think of it.[43]

Of fragile mental state, Julian fluctuated between seeming acceptance of his dismissal as director of the Sisters to one of blame and resentment. He felt he had been betrayed by Mary and supplanted by the Jesuits: "I always thought that the result of too exclusive a direction by the Fathers of the Society would be a change in the spirit of the Institute and would eventually turn it aside from that for which I originally designed it".[44]

Nevertheless, he was to go on for many years working zealously and effectively among the Australian people, giving missions and writing important scientific works. His relationships with hierarchy continued to cause problems to the end. He founded another religious institute, the Sisters of Perpetual Adoration, gave instruction to diocesan Sisters of St Joseph, and spent his last days in Sydney being cared for by a group of women who, as Mary MacKillop did to the last, revered him as good and holy man.[45] Margaret Press describes his final cross:

> With swollen limbs, aching head, searing pain in both eyes and overpowering physical weakness, he was reduced to the state of abject nothingness about which he had so often

---

[43] Gardiner, *Mary MacKillop,* p. 183.
[44] Gardiner, *Mary MacKillop*, p. 184.
[45] Mary wrote to the Sisters at his death in 1889, "I ask you, my dearest Sisters, one and all – those who knew him personally and those who have only heard of him – to remember that he dearly love the Institute and that he wished to see the Sisters humble and full of charity towards each other. We must try to honour his memory by imitating his virtues." Archives, Sisters of St Joseph, Sydney.

preached; the stripping to the bone of a disciple to leave himself open to the loving, castigating hand of God. His death on the feast of the Rosary in October 1889 came after two years of catharsis, in which he had one by one let go the pursuits most dear to him. He had followed to the letter the precept he had written to both the Sisters of St Joseph and the Sisters of Perpetual Adoration: "... we must love to be hidden, and not to shrink from being despised, and go on in our own simple way, trusting in God."[46]

The cross – an ongoing foundational image
With foundations such as these, it is no wonder that the histories of all branches of Sisters of St Joseph are littered with stories of encounter with the cross. This was the experience of Mother Stanislaus Leary, founder of a number of diocesan groups of Sisters of St Joseph. She, too, had her problems with visionaries. Having established the Congregation at Canandaigua (now Rochester), she found herself in the 1880s in conflict with a novice who claimed to have visions of the Virgin Mary, supported by paranormal disturbances. Her confessor believed her, and when Mother Stanislaus wanted to dismiss the novice who, she judged, was deluded, he took the matter to the bishop. Months of wrangling ensued. Finally the novice did leave, but not without deep division being caused in the community. "Mother Stanislaus had, it seems, taken too much authority to herself, had influenced others to go against the judgment of a priest".[47] This was but one of the incidents which would make the cross for Mother Stanislaus a leitmotif, as recorded in a comment made at her death: "Though much of her life had been spent beneath the shadow of the cross, it was, nevertheless, a life singularly blest in its accomplishments".[48]

---

[46] Press, Margaret RSJ. *Julian Tenison Woods: 'Father Founder'*, North Blackburn, Victoria: Collins Dove, 1994. pp. 226, 227.
[47] Brennan, *Persistence of Vision,* p. 95.
[48] Brennan, *Persistence of Vision,* p. 151.

Mother Bernard Gosslin, founder of the Sisters of St Joseph of Orange, used to like to talk of the Passion, it is said, "but never got around to the Resurrection".[49] She, like other founders, had to struggle with the pain of financial stress, tragic deaths of young Sisters and the difficulties of communication with church authorities. She felt rejected when her successor as Superior General, Mother Francis Lirette, appointed her to houses far from the Motherhouse, obviously so that she would not influence Sisters living there under a new regime. By the time of her death in 1956, though, the community embraced and revered this woman, "alert and happy in her final years".[50]

With the renewal of Vatican II, the legacy of the cross took new forms, as Sisters struggled to discern the signs of the times and adapt rules to cope with unfolding demands. Sister Alice Anita, Superior General of the Sisters of St Joseph of Philadelphia, was aware that, while many Sisters would take up the challenges with zeal, some good women who had with great sacrifice conformed to a strict interpretation of former rules would feel betrayed. For this group who had been her "greatest strength", she had deep concern. Of those "enthusiastic persons who have not been touched by the pain of change and joyfully work toward the processing of our goals," she asked compassion and patience. The process of renewal, she warned, would reflect the dying and rising of Jesus: "All of these human emotions are the ingredients of the full Paschal Mystery we are experiencing".[51]

The "return to the spirit of the founder" has involved, so Sisters have found, the self-emptying described in Philippians II. "There we read of Jesus emptying himself, giving up even the appearance of his divinity to become one with all human

---

[49] Geagley, *A Compassionate Presence*, p. 75.
[50] Geagley, *A Compassionate Presence*, p. 207.
[51] Foreword, *Father, We Are Called, A History of the Corporate Renewal Movement in the Congregation of the Sisters of St Joseph,* Chestnut Hill, Philadelphia. p. iii.

beings".[52] In the day to day service of others, Sisters have given of themselves, believing that God's love overcomes all evil and leads us to fullness of life.

Experience of the Cross
Suffering for the sake of mission: For some, suffering has been like a searing fire, actually encountered in at least three recorded instances in the histories of Congregations: Evian (France) in 1858[53], Troy (New York), and Chicago where the 1871 fire destroyed whole streets, and hundreds of people lost their lives. But in each of the scenarios, the lives of children, symbols of hope, were saved by the Sisters. In the Chicago event, the Sisters fled the orphanage, carrying the babies and giving older children charge of smaller ones. As they led their procession down the Chicago roads, they saw people desperately jumping out of burning buildings to their deaths. When the fleeing driver of a team of horses threatened to run down the children, Mother Mary Joseph "stepped up and took the horses by the bridle, while he continued to beat them".[54] Luckily, other bystanders restrained the driver and the Sisters and children got across the road.

While tragedy may strike anywhere, those who volunteered for overseas missions were fully aware that they were thereby exposing themselves to danger. When the Sisters were sent from Lyon to St Louis in 1836, there was no guarantee that they would survive the crossing of the Atlantic. Indeed, the voyage was threatened by a severe storm and sickness among the passengers. Two other Sisters who arrived four months late next year had been given up in everyone's mind as having been lost at sea. The excitement of the Sisters of St Joseph of Chambéry in sending missionaries to Brazil in 1858 was tempered by the death at sea of the leader of the group of six, before they even

---

[52] Gardner, *Let It Be*. p. 188.
[53] Gardner, *Let It Be*. p. 87.
[54] Coburn & Smith, *Spirited Lives,* p. 208.

reached their destination. She was only 27 years old. Later, in 1896, another group from Moûtiers was to have the same experience; they arrived in the south of Brazil bearing the dead body of their superior.[55]

For Sister pioneers, suffering for the sake of mission was an expectation. Sisters who went to St Paul, Minnesota, in 1851, faced "privations of the most severe kind":

> We had a small stove on the first floor – the pipe of which was set upright through the roof, around this opening we could count the stars; the rain storms were frequent. When the rain poured down through the roof, we (like the man in the gospel) would take up our beds and walk, but only to rest in the water on the second floor. As there was only one well in the place, and this was generally locked, we often had a long wait for our coffee in the morning.[56]

The 1901 opening of the Broadmeadows Babies Home for foundlings in Melbourne, Victoria, offered similar stresses for the Sisters. Mary MacKillop noted that "altogether the cross is attending the work".[57] Lack of money, running water, lighting, heating and other "ordinary conveniences" made the Sisters work extraordinarily difficult.

During the Second World War, Sisters of St Joseph of Orange in the Solomons shared the primitive conditions and fear of the local people when the Japanese invaded the islands. With a priest and a Marist Sister executed and others taken prisoner, the Sisters realised that, as caucasians, they had to escape. The account of their epic journey to freedom, where local people and co-missionaries constantly put themselves at risk to save them, did make footage for a TV series (even if the celluloid version was quite fanciful), but nothing can take from the trauma and bravery involved.

---

[55] *Misi Synthèse* p. 21
[56] Coburn & Smith, *Spirited Lives,* p. 100.
[57] Joan Ryan. *A Seed is Sown*, Melbourne: Advent Business Forms, 1992. p. 82.

As late as 1951, Sisters in Bhubaneswar, India, had to survive under extremely primitive conditions when they opened a school there.[58] Interviewees in Australia recalled having to live on the veranda of an outback school when the convent burnt down; people had gathered together whatever underclothing they could for them – otherwise they had nothing but what they stood up in. Others described wading knee deep through flood waters from the convent to the school, bearing a Primus stove and a loaf of bread, their only food for four days until help reached them. From their perch in the school they watched cattle, household furniture and trees being swept away by the floods. The local policeman, when warning the townspeople to flee before the oncoming waters, had forgotten about the Sisters!

Sorrow has accompanied the ministrations of Sisters. One told of a Sister haunted to her dying day by the remembrance of a little girl burnt to death when she was treating head lice with kerosene, the remedy of the day, and the girl's hair caught on fire from a candle nearby. Another Sister said she had been told of the similar trauma of those who, going out each day to do what they could for "the poor sufferers" of the 1918 'flu epidemic, had seen horrors they never forgot.

Hostility from those to whom Sisters have dedicated their lives is another commonly-experienced cross. Mary MacKillop, writing about the early days of the Institute, quoted a newspaper commentary on their experience:
> The non-Catholic portion of the community were not altogether pleased with the innovation, but the positive hostility of the Catholics themselves to the new order was remarkable. It was not openly manifested, but the new nuns were treated with neglect. The Catholic people were in general, familiar with no religious orders who moved about the streets. Their idea of nuns were confined to cloistered religieuses, ... who were never seen outside the precincts of

---

[58] Bourne, *His Mercy is From Age to Age,* p. 223.

their convents. In fact the new nuns were looked down upon, and it took some time to disperse this prejudice.[59]

In 1886, Sisters of St Joseph of Carondelet responded to a request from the Indian Chief of Fort Yuma in Arizona to open a school there. (An inducement must have been his promise "not to punish them with forty lashes ... when they got drunk"![60]) The physical privations of the mission were, however, made all the more difficult by the "prejudice and the hostility of a small group of the Indians",[61] which continued until they were forced out by government policy in 1900.

When the Sisters came from Eureka, California, to Orange in 1922, a cross of a different kind awaited them:

> Members of the Ku Klux Klan, wearing white sheets, burned a cross in Orange Plaza to protest the Sisters' presence. Mother Bernard, ever practical, marched into town and informed the town leaders that if the anti-Catholic behaviour did not stop (and the cross was not removed), the Sisters would take their considerable business away from Orange. Fearing loss of revenue, the town fathers did the prudent thing. The cross came down, the Klan was relegated to obscurity, and the Sisters were free to begin their new lives in southern California.[62].

Self-denial has been taken as part and parcel of serving as a Sister of St Joseph. A Sister who had ministered all her life as a nurse, could have been a concert pianist when she entered. Asked about having to give up this dream, she replied, "Our gifts are used for the good of others, not for our own self-glory". Other Sisters have found themselves assigned to duties or areas they have found repugnant. While Canon Law had always provided for representation being made to superiors in such

---

[59] MacKillop, Mary. *Julian Tenison Woods: A Life,* introduced & annotated by Margaret Press RSJ, Melbourne: Harper Collins, 1997. p. 127.
[60] "Fort Yuma", unpublished booklet produced by Sisters of St Joseph of Carondelet. p. 1.
[61] "Fort Yuma", p. 7.
[62] *Focus,* Summer, 2002. p 5.

cases, authoritarian leaders were not always renowned for an ability to listen or take these difficulties into account. One Sister struggled with being sent to a town in which she felt rejected and homesick:

> I often wondered what he (Jesus) had invited me to "see" during this section of my journey. In my search I stumbled, and the consequent ache in my heart led to an empty feeling within me. Gradually, he led me to realise that I needed to experience "emptiness" before he could fill me with the fullness of his love.[63]

In their readiness to suffer for the sake of mission, Sisters have aligned themselves with Jesus in giving his life for the life of all.

Persecution: Physical hardships endured for the sake of the Gospel are one thing. Open persecution, often directed at the emotions, is another. This was the lot of the Sisters of St Joseph of Annecy when, under great financial straits, they began their Wales mission in 1865. A rumour was started that the Sisters had come to make Catholics out of the Protestants, and defamation of their characters was spread abroad. They were represented as being witches; the people, it was stated by Mother Athanase, had been told that, "Short of taking their lives, they deserve anything else we may do to them".[64]

In Townsville, Queensland, in the 1870s, a parish priest seemed to gain personal satisfaction from publicly humiliating the Sisters from the pulpit. When he accused one of the Sisters of teaching heresy which was not the case, the local Sisters first of all confronted the priest who just abused them, and then when the newspapers began to take up the case, Mary MacKillop wrote to the Bishop who promised an enquiry but did nothing. In a cowardly way, he instead defended the priest, "very anxious to excuse him at the Sisters' expense".[65] Mary withdrew the Sisters from the parish.

---

[63] Lonergan, *I Sought and I Found*, p. 3.
[64] Bourne, *His Mercy is From Age to Age,* p. 107.
[65] Gardiner, *Mary MacKillop,* p. 216.

Often against the wishes of the local people, the administration in France gradually laicised the schools from 1880 on. Local authorities used harassment to try to drive out the Sisters when the people refused to send their children to the commune school. A law was passed limiting the number of postulants entering religious life; the Sisters refused to take up an offer to increase this number "on condition they paid a tax for this privilege".[66] In 1904 a law imposing further conditions of its Act of Secularisation[67] formally declared that "teaching of every grade and every kind is forbidden in France to the congregations". Over 14,000 schools were closed in France that year, with profound effects on the life and ministry of thousands of Religious.[68] Sisters of St Joseph were among the Congregations so affected. Their response was two-fold – to branch out further into mission areas such as India and Africa, and to do what they could operating in secular dress as "Mademoiselle X".

Petty persecution has been a constant companion in the lives of many Sisters. In one town, the Parish Priest collected and kept all the school money. The Sisters resorted to selling little cakes to the students at lunch time to get money to survive. Another Sister felt unable to defend her name among parishioners when a curate (i.e. a junior priest), jealous of her success, spread the rumour that she had failed as a teacher and had therefore been assigned to work in a parish. Dubious practices have been adopted by some priests to rid themselves of Sisters they found too confronting. The experience of Mary MacKillop, that "the Bishop is not one who will admit that a woman has a right to differ from him in opinion",[69] is one that has been repeated in many a scenario.

---

[66] Bourne, *His Mercy is From Age to Age,* p. 138.
[67] Whereby the government guarantees "neutral", non-religious services to citizens.
[68] This law was revoked in 1940 during the Vichy regime.
[69] Letter to Fr Woods, 3 December 1871. Archives, Sisters of St Joseph, Sydney.

Betrayal: Perhaps the sharpest sorrow we experience is when those who are our own are its cause. Gardiner tells of an incident that must have been particularly hurtful to Mary MacKillop, since one of her own Sisters contrived against her:

> There was a bill for boots and no money to pay it. Sister Clare went to the Archdeacon (Father Russell) and they plotted to get the boot merchant to summons Mother Mary so that when she did not pay she would be sent to gaol. But Father Thomas Lee overheard them from the nearby waiting room at the Bishop's House. He made straight for Macclesfield (where Mary was staying) and saw to it that Mary was put in a buggy and driven over the (State) border (from where she could not be summonsed). "I don't mind," she said, "it was not for myself but for my Sisters. I could not let them go without boots. St Joseph will provide."[70]

Around the same time, Mother Stanislaus Leary, then at Rochester, approached her close friend, Bishop McQuaid, regarding her dismissal from St Mary's Orphan Asylum by the priest on the Board there. She had not only founded the institution but had managed it successfully for over 16 years. To be suspected by the priest of impropriety was more than she could bear. However, what now proved more painful was the lack of support she received from the Bishop; eventually he was to withdraw his friendship. When he informed her that he planned to replace her as Superior, Mother Stanislaus drew on her faith to assure the Sisters she would bear the change "with resignation and conformity to God's will",[71] but at the same time, it seems, expressed her anger to her former friend. His reply to her non-extant letter is carefully worded, ending with the words, "Begging God to be with you." Brennan comments on this fact:

> The "Begging God to be with you" is almost-tender, almost-vulnerable, almost-regretful. Their correspondence from this day on is laced with restrained pain like this – the pain of friends who are no longer friends, trying to speak to each

---

[70] Gardiner, *Mary MacKillop*, p. 281.
[71] Brennan, *Persistence of Vision*, p. 102.

other, unable to bridge the new space between them, unable to penetrate the stony silence that marks their relationship. They continued to wound each other: he with authoritarian high-handedness, innuendo, scolding, cold disregard for her feelings; she with stubbornness, refusal to disappear quietly, thinly disguised defiance, verbal barbs and (she knew this drove him wild), constantly changing her mind and plans. The rift was irreparable.[72]

Mother Stanislaus' experience was reflective of what had previously taken place in Australia between Mary MacKillop and Julian Tenison Woods. Mary's efforts to heal relations after her return from Rome with a new Constitution was met with ambivalence by Woods. He would declare that they would remain friends, but then Mary would discover he had spread untrue facts about her and the part she had played in Rome's rejection of his rule. He tried to persuade Sisters to leave the Sisters of St Joseph to found other Congregations under him. Hurt and astounded that he could do such a thing, Mary wrote honestly to him, stating the truth and begging him to get advice from trustworthy friends who could help him regain perspective. Julian cut off all correspondence with Mary. Grieving, she wrote to Sister Josephine, one of her friends:

> Ah Sister, if he would only tell me *the truth* and not let me hear these things from others. Forgive me for complaining – I am so disappointed to the heart in him. Our poor, poor Father, may God help him and save him ere he goes too far.[73]

Before his death, Julian grudgingly agreed to receive visits and gifts of strawberries from Mary, but their relationship was never the same. For some years, groups of Sisters likened the split between Mary and Julian to a "divorce"; there was some estrangement between the different Congregations, and it took many years before Sisters found, to their delight, that a common spirit had survived the pain of separation.

---

[72] Brennan, *Persistence of Vision,* p. 101.
[73] Letter to Sister Josephine, 25 June 1875.

Mother Alexine Gosselin of the Sisters of St Joseph of La Grange found herself, too, the victim of disunity in the community and the betrayal of her own Sisters when Archbishop Mundelein demanded her resignation. A number of factors had led up to this. One was the entry into the community in 1916 of her recently-widowed mother. Alexine did not encourage this, fearing it would cause problems to the community, but the Archbishop over-ruled her and gave his permission. Financial problems and the fact that racist lines divided the community – "those Sisters who were behind her (Mother Alexine) were French; those who wanted her out were Irish"[74] – culminated in Alexine's resignation and a period of exile for her and her mother from the community. Her diary entry at the time reflects her suffering:

> To me, to resign in order to avoid annoyance or trouble is a cowardly act, but I had to put all my principles aside and submit. I have ever since wondered what crime of disedification I could be guilty of that I should, without warning, be deposed and not given a chance to finish my term of superior-ship which expires one year from this August. Ever the worst of criminals has a right to a trial by civil authorities. He knows for what he is being punished, yet is given a chance to vindicate himself.[75]

The kiss of Judas bears a particularly bitter pain. Engaging pain as did Joseph, Sisters who have known this kind of sorrow have survived only in complete confidence that out of death God brings life.

Identification with those who suffer: For the sake of mission, Sisters have shared the sufferings of those they serve. In the 1914-18 war, temporary hospitals were set up in convents causing inconvenience and want, such as at the Motherhouse in Annecy.[76] In India, in 1918, the year of the "great 'flu", Sisters

---

[74] Geagley, *A Compassionate Presence,* p. 102.
[75] Geagley, *A Compassionate Presence,* pp. 102, 103.
[76] Bourne, *His Mercy is From Age to Age,* p. 160.

suffered as well from the effects of plague, cholera and famine. The "General Strike" of 1926 saw Sisters in England and all over the world living extremely frugal lives in order to care for the hundreds of starving and malnourished families among whom they lived.

In "foreign missions" and "home missions", petty jealousies and bad communication often resulted in a real confrontation with the cross. Loneliness and fear were daily realities when one was far from home, where wild animals raided villages, where rebel forces might attack at any time, or where annoyances such as children hiding in trees rather than attending school made life frustrating for those whose only wish was to serve.

Identification of Sisters with those who suffer has long been presumed in Catholic circles. One interviewee told of walking one night with a companion along a country road. A man rushed to the fence as they passed his house. "Sisters, I knew you'd come", he said, "Mum has just died". Especially in days before State Social Services, families in grief would bring children to the local convent for the Sisters to care for until relatives could take them. "We always seemed to have underage children to wash, bathe, feed and clothe, because their mother had died", said one old Sister.

Some of these Sisters, sharing the grief of others, were not able at the time to take account of their own feelings. This, they now realise, was a distortion of the understanding of self-forgetfulness or conforming to God's will enjoined on them by the teachings of their founders. Sister Virginia Ann Gardner lost both her parents shortly after she entered the Sisters of St Joseph of Erie. She wrote later, "It would be 40 years before I went through the pent-up grief I should have honoured back in the mid-1940s".[77]

---

[77] Gardner, *Let It Be,* p. 42.

An ability to be with those who suffer has led many Sisters to undertake a ministry of hospital chaplaincy. One interviewee touchingly writes of her experience:

> Many through their sickness reflect the suffering of Christ; they, like Him, feel humiliated, rejected and stripped of everything that gives life meaning. At times while reflecting on such experiences I would recall the oft-repeated words of Mary MacKillop: "Work on humbly with the means God places at your disposal." Or "Beware of self mixing with the work of God". I was also made aware that there is more to chaplaincy than just professionalism. Isn't it more important to be there to feel the trembling hands of a little eight year old girl who was brutally raped? Isn't conversing with an old Aboriginal man – a king in his own right – yet without a kingdom? Isn't calming the fears of a woman who has had a kidney transplant? Isn't being with a twenty year old lady born with a grotesque deformity, whose mother couldn't love her and whose father was utterly ashamed and embarrassed, and hear her say, "Thank you Sister, for loving me"? These are the people on our hillsides, hungry for our bread, not for silver or gold, but who measure life by the love that is expended on others. These are they who have walked with me on a healing journey and made me feel tall each time I stooped to touch their pain and brokenness, and with whom I became their fellow traveller, meeting Christ at every bedside.

In the 1970s when a strike was staged in Philadelphia by the nurses in a Nursing Home run by the State (no longer in existence), Sisters responded to a request by the Cardinal to see what they could do about unattended patients at the home. Having agreed to sign papers that their intent was purely humanitarian and not political (since they would have to cross the picket lines), the Sisters went to the home, to find patients in the most dire conditions. It was a ward made up of diabetic patients: some were blind, others were single or double amputees. The Sisters bathed and dressed them, and their presence was such that the Methodist Chaplain remarked that the patients had received more care in that space of time than they had over a year! Such identification with those who suffer is captured in an incident where a Sister was staying with relatives in Queensland. Her young niece observed her kissing the crucifix as she took it from the chord around her neck before going to bed. "Why do you kiss that?" she asked. "Because I love him", was the reply.

Misuse of power: Faulty communication can be the root cause of much unnecessary pain. The stories behind the division of Sisters of St Joseph both in Northern America and Australia into separate systems of governance were based on an understanding of church law that was in the flux of change. Prior to the 1860s, Sisters who had pontifical approval could serve in more than one diocese, but the "ecclesiastical superior" of the group was still the bishop in whose diocese the Motherhouse was located.

However, this was now being changed, and the role of "ecclesiastical superior" eliminated. Right at the beginning of the decade, on the cusp of the change, Sister delegates met in St Louis to discuss and vote on adopting general government, requiring pontifical approval. But several bishops forbade Sisters in their dioceses to attend.

> Male clerics' resistance reflected opposition to the archbishop to what they understood to be a loss of power. Not only did they not want the archbishop of St Louis to have any authority over them, they strongly resisted a female superior general who would have anything to say about sisters or institutions in their dioceses.[78]

The result for the Sisters was the severing of houses from the motherhouse in St Louis, breaking up of friendships and ties of ministry and resentment about decisions over which Sisters had no control.

Similarly in Australia, when Bishop Quinn returned to Bathurst in 1874 and found that the Sisters had renewed their vows according to the new Constitution given to Mary MacKillop by

---

[78] Coburn & Smith, *Spirited Lives*, p. 58.

Rome, he was extremely angry. The priest who had encouraged the Sisters to do so ran for cover. He asked Mary to say nothing of his involvement, and so Quinn assumed Mary had "deliberately arranged for a priest who was uninformed of the situation to receive the sisters' vows".[79] The cause of his angst, however, was probably based on a misunderstanding of what pontifical approval meant for Religious Congregations. More than ten years later, Bishop Quinn, it would seem, was ignorant of the changes to law that had taken place. His fear that, with Sisters of St Joseph having pontifical approval, the Bishop of Adelaide would have superior authority over Sisters serving in his diocese, led him to set about forming his own diocesan Congregation.

Resistance to having a "female superior general" was, too, part of Bishop Quinn's problem. In his appeal to Rome against central government for the Sisters of St Joseph in Australia with Mary MacKillop at its head, he objected to what he regarded as scandalous behaviour for a woman: "I now ask, will the Sacred Congregation allow this running about of a nun, sometimes accompanied, sometimes alone, sometimes by day and sometimes by night, from one colony to another or from one end of the Diocese to the other in the public conveyances of the colony, to be turned into a system by placing the community in the several dioceses of Australia under Sister Mary?"[80]

Bourne speaks about the disregard of some Bishops for the Sisters' rule when it suited them. As a protection against this, many Congregations of Sisters of St Joseph, including Annecy, sought papal approbation, giving them a universal status rather than a diocesan one and thus more able to safeguard the charism of their Congregation. In the political and religious context of

---

[79] Crowley, *Women of the Vale,* p. 50. Crowley explains that Quinn's prior experience in Ireland with Sisters of Mercy and the difficulties of communication between Rome and Australia would have led him to make the assumptions upon which he acted.
[80] Crowley, *Women of the Vale,* p. 58.

late 19th century France, Mother Anne Marie advised the Sisters, this was necessary:

> These are bad times. A storm of revolution may arise, and if it does, what would become of our Congregation? Besides, I might be succeeded by those who would wish to change the Rule, as has happened elsewhere. In this time of persecution we need stability".[81]

The sufferings caused by the abuse of power are complex, since in church circles there are usually other issues at stake. Sisters have often found themselves compromising to bullying and unjust commands so as to avoid scandal or to deflect negative consequences for others. When Cardinal Moran informed Mary MacKillop that Propaganda[82] in Rome had judged her recent re-election as Superior General as invalid, and appointed the more compliant Mother Bernard Walsh in her stead, Mary had to endure once again what she called the "painful ordeal" of being misjudged. The Sisters had been advised at the Chapter that, since the constitutions by which she had been elected were only six years old, another term of six years of leadership by Mary was in order. Mary herself had pointed out that, taking the foundation years into account, she had served for more than twelve. The Sisters had resolved to write to Rome to ask that, as foundress, she should be appointed for life, but it would seem that letters of bishops unwilling to agree to central governance, influenced the decision of Propaganda. It is ironic that Moran, having chosen Mother Bernard, an indecisive woman but "popular with the Bishops",[83] then waived the constitutions to place her in power for three terms.[84]

---

[81] Bourne, *His Mercy is From Age to Age,* p. 143.
[82] Propaganda Fide was the Roman "Congregation" or Vatican Department that exercised control over church affairs in mission territories. At that time, Australia was considered a "missionary country".
[83] Gardiner, *Mary MacKillop,* p. 348.
[84] The same thing had happened in the case of Mother Stanislaus' replacement, Mother Agnes Hines. Her appointment "was supposed to have begun a regularization of terms of office", but she remained in office for 39 years! Brennan notes, "It was not the rule McQuaid was concerned about, but the future usefulness and survival of the community in the diocese". (Brennan, *Persistence of Vision,* p. 102.)

All of this did not take place without frustration and ambiguous feelings on the part of Mary MacKillop. At the time of Mother Bernard's re-appointment, she wrote to her brother, Donald MacKillop SJ:

> I have not said to anyone else what I have said to you about her unfitness. My duty is clearly to uphold her and with God's help I will. Look upon this as an unburdening of my mind, and take it for what it is worth. I do not willingly dwell on these things, and with all my heart I pray God to keep me from admitting them to any of my sisters.[85]

We live in a world of paradox, and coming to terms with this fact has made up a major part of engagement with pain on the Christian journey even today. While we may challenge the circumstances that gave rise to Sisters in the past ignoring "individual needs and identity in favour of community identity and cohesion",[86] we hold close to their belief that the inevitable pain of life can be joined to the sufferings of Christ for the life of the world. As one Sisters recalled her Congregational Leader saying when, in fairly recent years, one of their number in a prominent position left to marry a priest, "we are all clay in the hands of the master-potter, and times of hurt, anger and confusion are simply stages we go through as the clay changes its shape. Our call is to be stalwart through it all".

Laying down one's life: It is when we "go into the valley of death," says Radcliffe, that we "show our belief in the God who raises the dead".[87] Mary Jo Leddy makes the same point:

> To say that God is the point of our being is also to say that the point of our lives extends far beyond death. As once we were created out of nothingness, so once again we will be recreated out of the nothingness of death.[88]

---

[85] Letter to Donald MacKillop, S.J., 1897.
[86] Coburn & Smith, *Spirited Lives,* p. 95.
[87] Radcliffe, *Sing a New Song,* p. 222.
[88] Leddy, *Radical Gratitude, p.* 138.

In 1691, when the armies of Louis XIV passed through the town of Gap in France, an epidemic struck the troops and they were placed in the tiny hospital of the Sisters of St Joseph there. As a result of caring for them, all the nursing Sisters died. There is record that other Sisters were sent to replace them.[89] The point of their lives and their deaths was the same – we are made for communion with God who raises and sustains us.

In Copenhagen there is an impressive monument showing Sisters of St Joseph of Chambéry shielding with their bodies those of little children. The image commemorates the bombardment that took place during World War II in 1945. Eighty-six children and eleven Sisters from the Joan of Arc school were killed.[90] What they knew in the total giving of self, Sisters today also know. In the war-zone of the Congo, Sisters in recent years slept for a month with their papers under their pillows in case they should have to flee. The combatants were only 3 kilometres away. "The reason that prevented us from going," the Sisters said, "was the necessity to share the difficult life of the people".[91]

There is pathos in the story of self-giving of Sisters in China. One of the first acts of the communist government that came into power in the late 1940s was to expel foreign missionaries. Their number included Sisters of St Joseph of Baden who had been in the country since 1920. However, a Chinese Sister, Therese-Joseph Lung, wasn't able to follow. She was released from her vows, and subsequently opened a dispensary in a rural zone, evangelising the population and baptising in secret. At the beginning of the 1980s, when certain religious freedoms were granted, she was at last able to write to the Sisters at Baden: "I am your Chinese sister. I had to leave the Congregation, but my heart is with you always. I've remained faithful to my vows. I

---

[89] Coburn & Smith, *Spirited Lives*, p. 27.
[90] *Misi Synthèse*, p. 13.
[91] *Misi Synthèse*, p 16.

thank the Lord who, by his grace, has permitted me to surmount so many struggles and sufferings".[92] In 1983, the Superior General, Sister Donna-Maria, went to China to meet with her. Always watched by police, they weren't able to speak freely, but they succeeded at last in having a brief conversation in her room. Sister Therese-Joseph wished to renew her vows before her. Not able to get a passport to USA, this living martyr died at Nanjing in July, 1994.

Irene McCormack RSJ is buried in Huasa Huasi, a remote potato-growing village in the Peruvian Andes. Even though the area was dangerous, she and her companion had continued to minister there when the priests had left. She reflected on that special time:

> As we in our little Christian communities, high up in the Andes, gather in memory of Jesus, there is no power or authority on earth that can convince me that Jesus is not personally present. I feel grateful that these months on end, without the 'official Mass', and in a culture where I'm experiencing new symbols, have gifted me with a new appreciation of the Eucharist.[93]

On May 21, 1991, Irene was executed by the *Sendero Luminoso*, along with four village leaders. Her crime, it seems, was her part in the distribution of food to starving people during the blow-out of inflation in Peru. The editor of a book in tribute to Irene described the events, culminating in her execution:

> Irene is made to lie face-down. Fifteen minutes later, at around 8 pm, she has been tried – found guilty ... of feeding the poor ... and is shot dead.[94]

As Sisters of St Joseph of the Sacred Heart around the world, family and friends tried to make sense of Irene's death, the whole of Australia, it seemed, was caught by the mystery of life

---

[92] *Misi Synthèse*, p 23.
[93] Margaret Le Breton RSJ, ed. *Irene: A Tribute to Sr Irene McCormack.*, Smithfield (Sydney): Alken Press, 1992. p. 96. Quoting circular sent by Irene to Sisters and friends in Australia.
[94] Le Breton, *Irene*, p. 23.

given for the other. TV, radio and print coverage was nationwide. Newspaper editorials took up the themes of empowering the poor, of the value of dedication and the prophetic witness of Irene's death.[95] The Catholic newspaper of Western Australia, Irene's home State, commented,

> Sister Irene's Christian heroism is not in her violent death, in which she had no choice, but in her decision that she and tens of thousands of like minded men and women would make their lives a practical gospel to lift up the poorest of God's people, no matter what the price.[96]

Speeches were given in Parliament in her honour, paying tribute to her and the dedication of all Sisters of St Joseph: "I believe strongly that by her losing her life in this far flung place she has actually achieved a great deal".[97] Her cousin, Archbishop Frank Little, spoke of her at a commemorative Mass as being "permanently planted amongst the people for whom she gave her life".[98] In a series of drawings, a Peruvian Associate and friend illustrated the meaning she gave to Irene's martyrdom:

> You are the seed which will grow.
> You are a messenger of Life, Peace and Forgiveness.[99]

A final comment has Irene say, "I want to unite all people in Your peace and love".[100] Paradoxically, Irene's martyrdom did provide occasion for a new awareness of unity. Sisters of St Joseph of the Sacred Heart, like other Sisters of St Joseph the world over who experience corporate sorrow, can make the following words their own:

> For all of us the event was a two-edged sword: an immeasurable grief bringing with it a powerful sense of unity. If we were shaken to our foundations, we were at the same time strengthened by a new bond, a new appreciation of the

---

[95] "Dangerous lives of dedicated people", *The Australian,* May 24, 1991.
[96] *The Record,* May 30, 1991.
[97] Le Breton, *Irene,* p. 47. Quoting Member for Warren, Mr Omodei, Western Australian Parliament.
[98] Homily of commemorative Mass.
[99] Le Breton, *Irene,* p. 91.
[100] Le Breton, *Irene,* p. 63.

> goodness and compassion we felt from each other, of the importance of friendship.[101]

Uniting all peoples into God's reign of peace and love is the goal of every Sister of St Joseph. To this end, their lives are poured out. This is done in major ways as in martyrdom and in small ways, in the daily living out of the cross. The former devotion of making reparation for others' sins gave many Sisters the strength to carry on through difficult times. "I denied myself strong drink for those who drank too much," said one old Sister recalling practices of the past. "When I got into trouble," remembered another, "I would picture Jesus on the way to Calvary and say to myself, 'Put your toe in your boot and keep on walking'." That these Sisters should pray the following prayer is in character:

> Heart of Jesus, desire of the everlasting hills, fill my heart with a yearning for your presence. As the years pile up and the realisation comes to me that there is much more time behind me than before, I ask you to increase this yearning, so that death, for me, will be just a fulfilment of this longing.[102]

Mary MacKillop had written to her Sisters,

> We have come here at the call of our God to learn to die to ourselves, and to live only in doing His ever-blessed will. ... to be cheerfully faithful to the duties of our state; seeking no rest, no reward here but the joy of doing His Holy Will, and by our perfect suffering, by our unselfish suffering, by our humble perseverance in the discharge of the duties of our holy rule – giving at last to His long waiting and most loving Heart the true service it has so much yearned for at our hands.[103]

Mother Stanislaus Leary had written in her diary:

---

[101] Margaret Brennan SSJ, Unpublished paper, "Side by Side", p. 31. Quotation, Sister Jamesine, Congregational Leader of the Sisters of St Joseph of Rochester in the 1970s. In her book, *Comunidad para el Mund,*.Mary McGlone likewise describes the loss of one of their Sisters, Gabriel Joseph Gussin, in the earthquake of 1970, as a time of profound conversion and commitment for the rest of the community.
[102] Lonergan, *I Sought and I Found*, p. 15.
[103] Circular to Sisters, March 19, 1893.

> Every heart has its grief, every house has its skeleton, every character is marred with weakness and imperfection. All these aimless conflicts of our minds are unanswered longing of our hearts, and should lead us to rejoice the more in the divine mystery assurance that a time is coming when night shall melt into noon and the mystery shall be clothed with glory.[104]

These two women, so familiar with the cross, spelled out in their writings and lives the meaning of humanity's engagement with pain. It is one that is integral to the charism of St Joseph. It is expressed each time we celebrate the Eucharist and share its mystery with others. As one Sister wrote:

> I feel privileged to lead a spirituality group in the Psychiatric Unit where I also bring Holy Communion to the patients. Here are some of the most broken and vulnerable members of the Body of Christ. "This is my Body" under the appearance of Joel, Alicia, Alex. .. Upon entering the patient's room I am aware that this is holy ground. I experience a deep sense of God's presence in the sacramental encounter with the patient. In this spirit of faith, I try to be with the patient wherever he or she is.[105]

7.3 PART THREE: The spirit lives into the now.

Giving of self

The Eucharist, as the above reflection notes, has wide implications for us. It goes beyond ritual to involving us in a self-giving that takes us into the world's suffering. Frank Andersen reminds us of this:

> And when we are offered the Blood of Christ, what is it that we are about to drink? We are prepared to drink the sufferings of *today's* Christ. We blood ourselves in a sacred commitment to the contemporary Covenant task: to create of ourselves, 'a holy nation, a royal priesthood, a people set apart'.[106]

---

[104] Brennan, *Persistence of Vision*, p. 147.
[105] Lillian McDonald SSJ. "Reflecting on the Chaplain's Role", *Soundings,* Vol 26 #1, Fall 2003. p. 7.
[106] Frank Andersen. "The Long Journey Home", EJ Cuskelly Memorial Lecture, *Compass*, Vol 8, Spring, 2004. p. 9.

Today, the willingness to give of self for the life of others continues to testify to God's outpouring love. Every age must express in the language of its day what this testimony will look like. A former Congregational Leader of the Sisters of St Joseph of Annecy was anxious that Médaille's notion of self-emptying be understood in African culture. While on visitation to West Africa, she asked the novices to interpret his teaching on self-emptying using African imagery. When she returned some days later, the novices, without any words, sat her down and set before her the dried, polished shell of a gourd full of cold water and invited her to drink. It was then that they explained to her what they had done. Having picked the gourd from the field, they had scraped out the dung-coloured flesh from the inside and put it in the sun to dry. Careful treatment had made of the shell a thing of beauty, worthy of bearing refreshment, pure, cool water, life-giving for any guest. In the same way, they said, Sisters of St Joseph are asked to rid themselves of whatever prevents them from becoming an effective means of God's love being communicated to others. "Never," said the Congregational Leader, "had I seen Médaille's teaching explained more clearly".

In India, Hindu nationalism has, in recent years, taken the form of the persecution of Christians, seen as a foreign presence.[107] Sisters of St Joseph there do, in fact, risk their lives when they encourage those of the lowest classes to recognise their human dignity. Charges are easily fabricated against Sisters who work effectively among the poor. When women from the lowest classes approached the well of the high classes to collect water, since theirs had dried up, blame was laid on a Sister who ministered in the community. She was accused of inciting rebellion and threatened with imprisonment. "Each day priests are killed, religious violated, churches destroyed," another Sister

---

[107] Many Sisters of St Joseph, in fact, come from an area of India where Christianity has been established for nearly 2,000 years.

points out. "Pray that we can face up to martyrdom if God so asks us".[108]

All over the world, the call to self-emptying impels Sisters and all who share the spirit of Joseph to be with those who suffer. Whether it is in Hope Hall, a school for slow learners in Santa Ana (California), or in Port Augusta, South Australia, where asylum seekers are detained under inhumane conditions in the Baxter Centre; in the invasion areas of Lima or the war-torn nations of Africa; in the anonymous deserts of Arabia or outside the military School of the Americas[109]; all around the globe, there are those who engage pain in order to be the "face of Jesus in the neighbourhood".

An Australian, non-denominational program, developed and sponsored by the Mary MacKillop Foundation, has adapted the work of psychologist J. William Worden in supporting young people and adults to manage grief consequent to death, separation or divorce. *Seasons for Growth* employs a group-based, educative process that "provides the opportunity for each participant to integrate, at his/her developmental level, the appropriate knowledge, skills and attitudes to understand and to cope with loss and grief".[110] The network of Sisters and lay partners trained in running the program extends the spirit of Joseph that stands with the suffering around the world.

The handbook of the Associates of Sisters of St Joseph of Baden encourages members to find freedom of heart in the "courageous surrender of self-seeking, of all that is opposed to grace, of anything that would be an obstacle to the perfect love of God

---

[108] *Misi Synthèse,* p. 10.
[109] Sister Rita Steinhagen, at the age of 70 years, spent 6 months in prison for having protested the School of the Americas training of Latin-American militaries in methods of repression. Her protest, made with others, consisted of twice jumping over the forbidden zone surrounding the area. *Misi Synthèse,* p. 19.
[110] *Seasons for Growth* website, http://www.goodgrief.org.au.

and neighbor".[111] Perhaps this freedom is illustrated most effectively by the reflection of Josephite Community Aid member, Ruth Townley, on her return from visiting the Baxter Detention Centre. Self-emptying such as she describes takes the form of being present to the sufferings of others. She has entitled her reflection, "Birdman":

> He tells me, on the first occasion we meet, that the guards call him the Birdman. Any bird with a broken wing he will return to health, gently, lovingly. Currently, when he sleeps, a honeyeater nestles into his chest and, on waking, it hops after him to the shower and washes itself next to him.
>
> I look around the compound, bleached by searing desert heat, and shift my focus from the rows of razor wire to the Mars-like vista beyond. To these men, it is barren and unforgiving. The honeyeaters are not the only winged creatures damaged here. The difference is, the birds can return to health and fly away.
>
> Later, I fly away, loud music and anger for the long trip back to Adelaide. In my mind is an image of the Birdman, rejected and isolated, whose eyes shift from liquid care, to downcast sorrow, to gleaming mischief as he tells me how he, the Iranian, must not kill the Australian flies, for fear of reprisal from Australian guards.
>
> Briefly my anger lifts as I remember my promise, in parting, to return next week and in the weeks after that. An unlikely forum for friendship, but a forum nonetheless.[112]

---

[111] "In Union". *Sharing the Spirit,* CSJ Association, Sisters of St Joseph, Baden.
[112] Ruth Townley, JCA, (after visiting Baxter Detention Centre while working in the Josephite Spirituality Centre, Adelaide, in 2004).

Julian Tenison Woods'
Epistle of the Institute of St Joseph

1 Pet 3: 8-15

All of you, have unity of spirit, sympathy, love for one another, a tender hear, and a humble mind. Do not repay evil for evil or abuse for abuse; but, on the contrary, repay with a blessing. It is for this that you were called – that you might inherit a blessing. For

> *'Those who desire life*
> > *and desire to see good days,*
> *let them keep their tongues from evil*
> > *and their lips from speaking deceit;*
> *let them turn away from evil and do good;*
> > *let them seek peace and pursue it.*
> *For the eyes of the Lord are on the righteous,*
> > *and his ears are open to their prayer.*
> *But the face of the Lord is against those who do evil.'*

Now who will harm you if you are eager to do what is good? But even if you do suffer for doing what is right, you are blessed. Do not fear what they fear, and do not be intimidated, but in your hearts sanctify Christ as Lord.

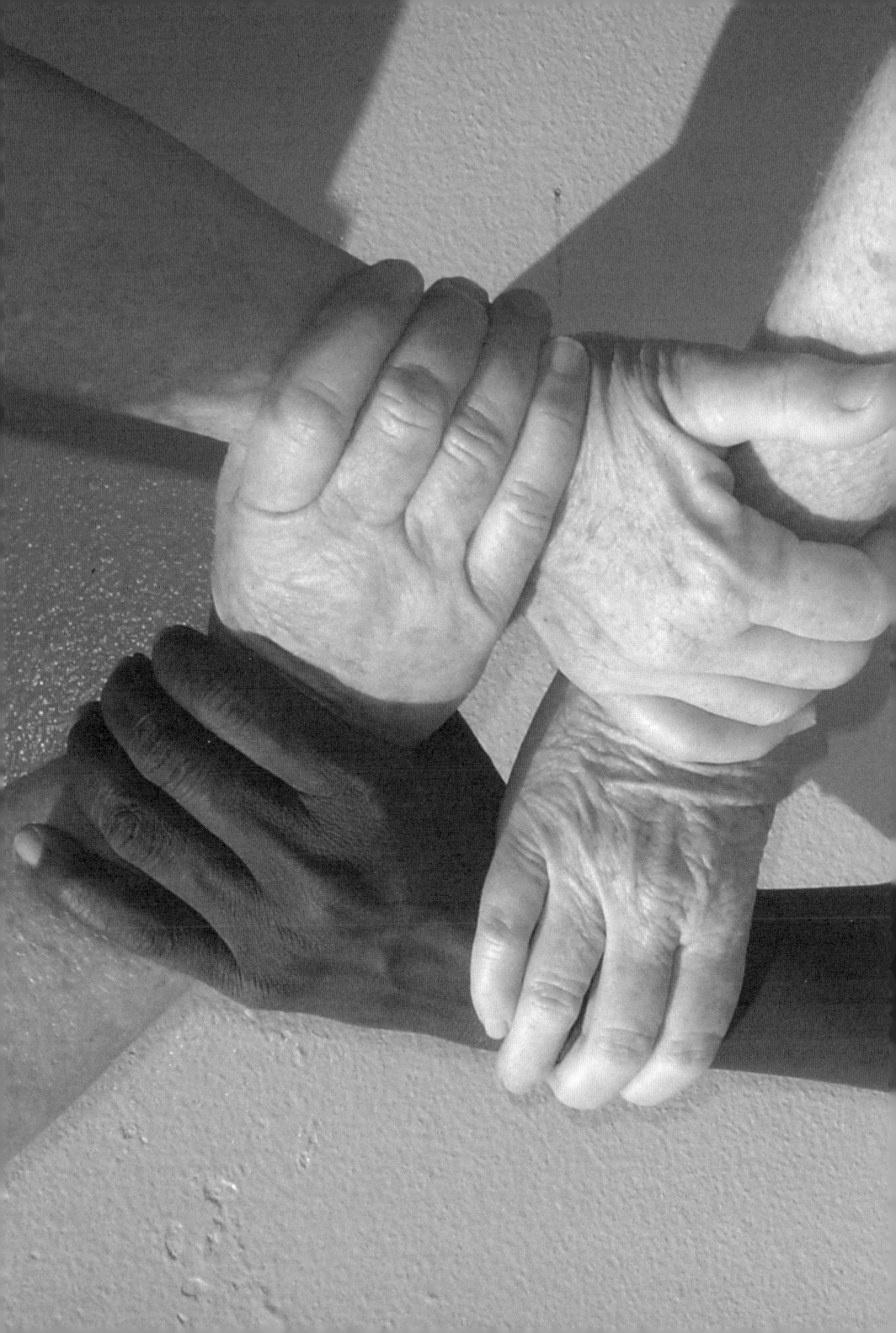

CHAPTER EIGHT

The spirit of Joseph ......

leavens Church.

You shall call his name Jesus, for he will save his people from their sins. (Mt. 1:21)

8.1 PART ONE: The spirit is revealed

The Church is Catholic:
In a collection of faith stories, Kate Engelbrecht tells of her journey to conversion:

> Why did I become a Catholic? Because I love imagery and poetry, I love metaphor, paradox and mystery. I love music and the smell of incense. I love flickering candles and the cool touch of holy water. I love to feel glimpses of a union with that reality we call God. I love good liturgies and powerful rituals that lift me to another level of consciousness. I became a Catholic because I love a life of sensations. And I stay a Catholic, because knowing this about myself, I need the discipline that comes with belonging to a tradition and a community which challenges me not to become a hostage to a life of the senses. I'm a Catholic because Catholics know that discipleship is rigorous and that we are called to face the truth of our lives, called to pick up our cross and die daily to counterfeit ways of being who we are. I'm Catholic because I love it that this community of broken, wounded people calls me to commit to relationships that matter, calls me to engage my conscience and to be fit to be available for communion with others.[1]

---

[1] Kate Englebrecht. "You're Not a Catholic Are You, My Dear?", *Why I am Still a Catholic: Stories of Faith & Belief,* Melbourne: David Lovell, 2003. p. 10.

As a noun, the word *Catholic* tells us who we are. When Kate became a Catholic, she first of all declared something about herself as a human being. As a sensate, vibrant woman, she looked to Catholicism for meaning. She found in this tradition both direction and purpose, taking her beyond the now to the ultimate. This it did in drawing her into graced union with the "reality we call God". For her, becoming Catholic was a gift. It gave her the forum which enabled her to express discipleship of Jesus whom she, like all Christians, recognised as the embodiment of God's will for bringing all peoples to salvation, into intimate relationship with God. She found this forum in the community, a forerunner and sign of union with God and each other, forming the body through which Christ continues to bring reconciliation to the world.

The word *Catholic* is also an adjective. It comes from the Greek *katholikos*, meaning "universal" or "of the whole". Until the divisions between the Churches of the eastern and the western Mediterranean, the term was used simply to describe a mark of Christianity. It denoted the unity within the diversity of the Churches. Early Christians could distinguish between those Church communities who were *catholic* (who were in union with "the whole"), and those who were *sectarian* (cut off by heresy and schism). The term was also used to describe the variety that marks the one Church. In its membership it included all classes of people endowed with differing gifts and could encompass diverse expressions of the one faith.[2]

After the East-West schism of the eleventh century, the word began to be associated with division. Those Churches which

---

[2] St Cyril of Jerusalem, who died in 386 CE, said, "The Church is called 'Catholic' because it extends through all the world; ... because it teaches universally and without omission all the doctrines which ought to come to human knowledge; ... because it brings under the sway of true religion all classes of people, rulers and subjects, learned and ignorant; and because it universally treats and cures every type of sin ... and possesses in itself every kind of virtue which can be named ... and spiritual gifts of every kind". *Catechetical Lectures,* 18, n. 23. Cited by McBrien, *Catholicism,* San Francisco: Harper, 1994. p. 4.

remained in union with the Roman papacy were eventually described as "Catholic" and those which broke relations took the name "Orthodox" (from the Greek for "right teaching"). With the Protestant Reformation in the sixteenth century, the word "Catholic" took on the sense of a "denomination" of Christianity. Used to describe *Catholic Christians,* the adjective signified *dis*-unity rather than the bonds of unity in faith between diversified peoples.

While the penny catechism had always listed catholicity as one of the marks of the Church referring to its universality, it was Vatican II that alerted us to appreciate once again the full meaning of the word as including diversity in unity. It thereby invited us to respond to the gift of who we are as Catholic, and also to the task we are given – to signify and effect union with God and each other while maintaining plurality in culture and identity. Can, then, the word *Catholic* be a verb?

In the sense that the teachings of Vatican II call us to express unity in diversity, it can be: those who are *Catholic* are called to act. The document, *Lumen Gentium,* points out that God, "having created one human family, decreed that his scattered children should be gathered into one people".[3] The Church, as the Pilgrim People of God, "received the mission of proclaiming and establishing among all peoples the kingdom of Christ and of God", since it is, "on earth, the seed and the beginning of that kingdom".[4]

A particular task of those who are *Catholic* is to be reconcilers. Sullivan says: "The church, as the body of him through whom

---

[3] Francis Sullivan. *The Church We Believe In,* New York, Paulist Press, 1988. p. 88. Referring to *Lumen Gentium* par. 13.
[4] *Lumen Gentium,* par. 5.

God was pleased to reconcile all things to himself, cannot fail to offer this reconciliation to people of all races and cultures."[5]

Perhaps the most obvious arena for reconciliation is that of Christianity itself. "The divisions among Christians," says the *Decree on Ecumenism*, "prevent the Church from realising the fullness of catholicity proper to it in those of its children who, though joined to it by baptism, are yet separated from full communion with it."[6] Citing the universal love of God of which Christ is the sign, the *Declaration on the Relation of the Church to non-Christian Religions* points out, too, that union with God is not possible unless we show love to one another, no matter what the faith background.[7] Living in harmony and respect, acknowledging and reverencing the image of God in each other, is demanded of those called to be reconcilers among all peoples.

The Church is Communion

Kate Engelbrecht's journey into Catholicism invited her, as she said, to commit to those relationships that we call "communion". A consequence of catholicity is that diversity is brought into unity – those who are scattered are made one. For the Christian, to be "saved" means to be brought into union with God through sharing the life of Christ bestowed by the Spirit. But we are not saved as individuals alone. Union with God is found through being brought into union with others. Baptism incorporates us into the Body of Christ. We are part of a people. Tillard points out that "the life that is

---

[5] Sullivan, *The Church We Believe In,* p. 92. Through Jesus, we believe, all of creation is reconciled with God: "In him, all the fullness of God was pleased to dwell, and through him to reconcile to himself all things, whether on earth or in heaven, making peace by the blood of his cross." (Col 1:19, 20). Jesus is "universal".
[6] *Unitatis Redintegratio,* Par. 4. (Gender-specific nouns and pronouns used in Flannery's translation changed).
[7] *Nostra Aetate,* par. 5, citing 1 Jn 4:8 – "They who do not love do not know God; for God is love".

reconciled with God is led with others, and this by its very nature".[8]

During the decades immediately preceding Vatican II, Pius XII, through his teaching on the Mystical Body of Christ, had placed emphasis on the (Catholic) Church's unity with Christ and the participation of all in its mission. In hindsight, we can see that this was to prove to be foundational to the Council's renewed and deeper awareness that between *all* who are baptised into Christ there is a bond of union.[9] The Council also recognised that the Church must demonstrate this union: "The Church, in Christ, is in the nature of sacrament – a sign and instrument, that is, of communion with God and of unity among all peoples."[10]

> Central to the church's mission in and to the world is its own living of *communio*[11] as fully as possible. The better it does the latter, the more effectively it accomplishes the former. Therefore, whatever contributes to the church's ordering and living its life of communion can be seen, not necessarily as turning inward and away from the world, but rather as ways in which the church sharpens its ability to be a visible and credible sign in the world of the way God wishes the whole of humanity to live.[12]

If it is God's will that all peoples live in communion, and if the Church is to be sign and instrument of this, then separation and disunion militate against what the Church is and does. Again,

---

[8] J. M. R. Tillard, trans. Madeleine Beaumont. *Flesh of the Church, Flesh of Christ: At the Source of the Ecclesiology of Communion,* Collegeville, Minnesota: Liturgical Press, 2001. p. 6.

[9] The Council recognised that the Church of Christ is somehow "present and operative" in Protestant denominations separated from the Catholic Church (see Sullivan, *The Church We Believe In",* p. 63). It recognised also "real though imperfect communion where there is not full theological or juridical communion" (Sullivan, p. 64).

[10] *Lumen Gentium,* par. 1

[11] *Communio* is the Latin form of the Greek *koinonia,* the bonds of communion that join the baptised with Christ and each other. Paul makes frequent reference to *koinonia* in his letters. The term "communion" had, for some hundreds of years until Vatican II, only been used in English to refer to the Sacrament of the Eucharist. To see that this union, which the Eucharist signifies and enacts, extends into daily life, and to use the term "communion" to describe that union, is an unfamiliar leap for some people.

[12] H Richard McCord, "Participation by Laity in Church Life and Mission", *Chicago Studies* 39 (2000). p. 50.

it becomes the task of the baptised to be reconcilers, both within the Church's own ranks and with those in our neighbourhood. In this way the Eucharist becomes real to us. As Pope John Paul II pointed out, the "special closeness which comes about in Eucharistic 'communion' cannot be adequately understood or fully experienced apart from ecclesial (Church) communion."[13]

It is in the Eucharist that the Church assembles together to express its identity as the Body of Christ. St Augustine gives us a powerful illustration of this in one of his sermons:
> So if you want to understand the body of Christ, listen to the Apostle telling the faithful, "Now you are the body of Christ and individual members of it" (1 Cor 12:27). So if it's you that are the body of Christ and its members, it's the mystery meaning you that has been placed on the Lord's table; what you receive is the mystery that means you. It is to what you are that you reply Amen, and by so replying, you express your assent. What you hear, you see, is the body of Christ, and you answer, Amen. So be a member of the body of Christ, in order to make that Amen true.[14]

Tillard concludes, "The moment of the greatest intimacy with the Lord – since one becomes his body – is also that of the greatest solidarity with others."[15]

The Church is Local

The place where we are brought into the communion of Christ's Body is the local church. What is local church? In a world familiar with bureaucracies, an image popularly used of the Roman Catholic Church is of a company with its headquarters in Rome and branches, or local churches, in the dioceses. This, in fact, is what the Church is *not*. Local churches are not branches of a universal Church centred in Rome. They are parish or faith communities gathered around their bishop, thereby making the

---

[13] *Mane Nobiscum Domine*, October 2004. par. 20.
[14] Augustine, Sermon 272. Cited by Tillard, p. 42.
[15] Tillard, *Flesh of the Church, Flesh of Christ*, p. 28.

universal Church present. Not only that, but their life is the life of the universal Church. The Council says that "it is in these (local churches) and formed out of them that the one and unique Catholic Church exists".[16] The fullness of Church is there at the local level, as is signified when the community gathers for Eucharist.

If local churches are not branches, neither are they independent bodies. Tillard comments on the teachings of Paul with regard to the local and universal Church:
> For Paul, the church of God is not a collection of autonomous churches, their coexistence simply neighborliness. It is the communion of these churches. Later on, Ephesians will say of the church *as such* that it is the body of Christ, a body made up of members united among themselves and, likewise, of communities united among themselves.[17]

For most people, the communion of the Church needs to be experienced in the local parish. This is their primary community. One parishioner explains what this means to him:
> The parish is the place where people can give something. For some, it's money. Some give their personal gifts. You may be an accountant or a doctor, a builder or an electrician. You can all do something. What you can offer is time rather than money. ... There are lots of people who are screaming to belong to a community, but for one reason or another – they feel guilty and excluded from the church. And they're *not* excluded! Parish is about knocking down the barriers. We have to say: there are greater sinners inside the church than outside. Come and join the sinners!"[18]

---

[16] *Lumen Gentium,* par. 23.

[17] Tillard, *Flesh of the Church, Flesh of Christ*, p. 13. It is also important to note that communities which make up the local church of the diocese are brought into unity with Christ around the figure of the bishop. In turn, that local church stands in relationship with other local churches around their bishops and in particular with the Bishop of Rome, symbol of unity for the universal church. "The Roman Pontiff, as the successor of Peter, is the perpetual and visible source and foundation of the unity both of the bishops and of the whole company of the faithful" (*Lumen Gentium,* par. 23).

[18] "Come and Join the Sinners", *Tui Motu,* June 2004. p. 19.

For this parishioner, the parish provides a forum for reaching out to "sinners" and using one's gifts for the building up of the community. Love, forgiveness and reconciliation are practised here. It is in the parish or faith community, gathered in spirit around the bishop signifying Christ, that the baptised come together to worship. Here they learn to be disciples of Christ. They encounter Christ in the gathering and in word and sacrament. From here they are sent out on mission, in their homes and neighbourhoods, their work-place or spheres of influence. As a gathering of people coming from all walks of life, reflecting the plurality of society, they signify and express the communion of all creation in Christ.

The Communion of Saints
Being in communion, then, is at the heart of being *Catholic*. We are initiated at Baptism into the body of Christ and are therefore connected to each other. This connection, with Christ and each other, is forever; it goes beyond death into eternity. It is called "The Communion of Saints".

The bonds that unite Christians as Church or "Body of Christ" bring with them obligations. On earth, in our living of community, we care for each other and sustain one another's faith in prayer and support. Again, this does not end at death. Just as the resurrected Jesus intercedes for us "at the right hand of God",[19] so also the "cloud of witnesses" who have gone before us in faith[20] hold the rest of the Church in prayer. Pope Paul VI, in his document *Credo of the People of God*, puts it this way: "We believe in the communion of all the faithful of Christ, those who are pilgrims on earth, the dead who are attaining their purification, and the blessed in heaven, all together forming one Church; and we believe that in this communion the merciful

---
[19] Rom. 8:34.
[20] Heb. 12:1

love of God and His saints is ever listening to our prayers, as Jesus told us: Ask and you will receive."[21]

Sometimes the intercession of those who have gone before us in faith is presented in magical terms. "Never known to fail" prayers are offered; prayer chains are passed from one to the other. The saints are described as "mediators with the one Mediator, Christ". Somehow they are supposed to "twist God's arm" for us. They are pictured as being a tool for us to get control of God. Superstition can flourish with this type of thinking. At the same time, we cannot assume that all who speak in such terms are being superstitious. When dealing with mystery, we do take recourse to imagery that is familiar to us. We try to put our words on what we do not know but we do experience – that the bonds between those unified in Christ extend beyond death and are active in our lives. However inadequate the imagery, the aim of prayer made through the intercession of the saints is that we might enter, with them, into that disposition of heart that is open to God's grace, freely given to us by an all-loving creator. This, as we have seen, was the disposition of Joseph, for whom God's will was his.

Joseph as Patron of the Church

It is in the context of the Communion of Saints that Joseph is addressed as "Patron of the universal Church". This title was chosen by Pius IX in 1870, and the reasons for doing so commemorated in the 1989 apostolic exhortation of Pope John Paul II, *Redemptoris Custos* (*Guardian of the Redeemer*). "This just man," the Pope said, "who bore within himself the entire heritage of the old covenant, was also brought into the 'beginning' of the new and eternal covenant in Jesus Christ."[22]

---

[21] Proclaimed by Pope Paul VI on June 30, 1968.
[22] *Redemptoris Custos,* par. 34.

Through his part in the Incarnation, Joseph offers to the Church the model of a "humble, mature way of serving and of 'taking part' in the plan of salvation".[23] So, too, members of the Church should find the part they are to play in enabling God's salvation to reach others. Just as Joseph was guardian of that Love which potentially unites all humans in God, so he is guardian of the Body of Christ which continues his mission. ("If I were a Roman Catholic theologian," said the Lutheran Karl Barth, "I would lift St Joseph up. He took care of the Child; he takes care of the Church."[24])

"Salvation, which comes through the humanity of Jesus," John Paul II noted, "is realised in actions which are an everyday part of family life."[25] A significant duty for Joseph, the everyday father, was to name the child "Jesus", which means "Yahweh saves".[26] "This is the only name in which there is salvation (cf. Acts 4:12)".[27]

It is appropriate, the Pope pointed out, that Joseph's memory should be recalled in our celebrations of the Eucharist. He (with Mary), "fed him whom the faithful must eat as the bread of eternal life".[28] The Pope, then, prayed that, as part of the Communion of Saints, Joseph would, through intercession and example, be a means by which the Spirit would gift the Church today with renewed vigour in proclaiming the Gospel.

> The Second Vatican Council made all of us sensitive once again to the "great things which God has done," and to that "economy of salvation" of which St. Joseph was a special minister. Commending ourselves, then, to the protection of him to whose custody God "entrusted his greatest and most

---

[23] *Redemptoris Custos*, par. 1.
[24] Perrotta, *Saint Joseph*, p. 135.
[25] *Redemptoris Custos*, par. 8.
[26] Perrotta, *Saint Joseph*, "'Jesus' represents a shortened form of the Hebrew 'Joshua', whose original meaning was 'Yahweh helps.' But it eventually came to be interpreted, 'Yahweh saves'". p. 36.
[27] *Redemptoris Custos*, par. 12.
[28] *Redemptoris Custos*, par. 16.

precious treasures," let us at the same time learn from him how to be servants of the "economy of salvation."[29]

Joseph and Collegiality

Some people see implications in the fact that, when he convoked the Second Vatican Council, Pope John XXIII "concretely related St Joseph to the collegiality of the Church by naming him patron of Vatican Council II, collegiality at work in the Church".[30] The spirit of Joseph, they say, is one of collegiality. Collegiality, as an expression of the communion of Churches, describes the relationship of bishops to each other as they meet in ecumenical councils, synods and episcopal conferences. Decisions made at these gatherings are informed by attitudes of co-responsibility and participation, by collaboration and consultation.[31] Such qualities come from openness to the Spirit, continually at work in our world.

As successors to the Apostles, the bishops as a college, in union with the successor of Peter, the Roman Pontiff, "represent the whole Church in a bond of peace, love and unity".[32] So collegiality describes Church leadership not in monarchical terms but as a group in a relationship of communion, arising out of and in service of the Church, "a people brought into unity from the unity of the Father, the Son and the Holy Spirit".[33]

Why did John XXIII associate Joseph with collegiality? He explained that, just as Joseph held an obscure and hidden role in the gospels and in Church history, so did the understanding of

---

[29] *Redemptoris Custos,* par. 32.
[30] *The Josephite Harvest*, Vol 82, No 3 June 1970. p. 8. Pope John XXIII officially convoked the Council in December 1961. He had announced his decision the year before and on March 19, 1961, wrote an apostolic letter outlining reasons for the Church's regard for Joseph and his patronage of the Council.
[31] For example, *Lumen Gentium,* par 25, points out that the Roman Pontiff and bishops "apply themselves with zeal to the work of enquiring by every suitable means into (this) revelation and of giving apt expression to its contents".
[32] *Lumen Gentium,* par. 23.
[33] *Lumen Gentium,* par. 4.

collegiality. Collegiality was foundational to the Church, yet its visible practice was overshadowed quite early in Church history by pyramidal structures. Apart from ecumenical councils, there eventually came to be few occasions where it was seen to function. "As it has taken a long time for the understanding of collegiality," said Pope John, "therefore, we have chosen St Joseph as the patron of the Council."[34]

The Holy Spirit, to whose promptings Joseph was ever alert, has led the Church to reclaim that the principles of collegiality are needed to express communion for our time. These principles have been applied, at the urging of the Council, to all areas of Church life – attitudes to authority, to the use of power, to relationships between priests and bishop, between priests and parishioners, and between those who hold any position of leadership in Church bodies and those they serve. Structures such as councils of priests, deaneries (where priests from different parishes meet to build communion), parish pastoral councils and diocesan councils have all been formed in order to express the reality of communion, both at local and wider, universal level.

Openness to the Spirit invites participation; it greets all the baptised as being co-responsible for mission; it trusts collaboration; it welcomes and authorises the charismatic element of Church life[35] and, in obedience, listens to God's voice speaking in consultation and in reading the signs of the times. Its attitudes to power are those of service. As Edwards says:

---

[34] John Joseph Cardinal Wright. "St Joseph and Collegiality", *San Giuseppe, Nei Primi Quindici Secoli della Chiesa,* Roma: Libera Editrice Murialdo, 1971. p. 10. "(Another) reason why Pope John chose St Joseph as patron of collegiality," says Wright, "is because of his silence and serenity in the pursuit of God's will. As part of his call to the Council, Pope John writes: 'St Joseph has little to say but he lives intensely. He never backs away from any call the will of God imposes on him. .. He gives example of openness to the voice of God'. ... He is a man of faith." pp. 10, 11.
[35] *Lumen Gentium,* par 12.

> Dominating power is excluded from the Christian community. In First Corinthians, Paul tells the community that he did not approach them in a superior way but in humility: "I decided to know nothing among you except Jesus Christ, and him crucified" (I Cor 2:1).[36]

These are the qualities Pope John XXIII recognised in St Joseph and for which he called upon his patronage. These are the qualities those who share the spirit given to Joseph, then, seek to express in their lives. As disciples of Christ on mission, they are leaven in the *local* Church or faith community, calling it to be *catholic* in maintaining the different gifts given to it by the Spirit, acting as *reconcilers* to build *communion* and choosing expressions of relationship that speak of co-responsibility, collaboration and service.

8.2 PART TWO: The spirit unfolds.

<u>Bringing into Communion</u>
In the *Eucharistic Letter,* Médaille had prayed for the Sisters, "God grant that we may be able to contribute as weak instruments, to the re-establishment in the Church of this total union of souls in God and with God."[37] At the time he was writing, great efforts were being made to bring Protestants back to the Catholic Church. Indeed, the "home missions" on which Médaille himself was engaged were directed to this end, as well as to instruction of Catholics in the practice of their faith. The unity of the Church had been severed. In a quiet, unobtrusive way, the Sisters of St Joseph were to help remedy that by being both model and instrument of unity. "Their love should be accompanied by so great a union that all those who see them can say that they have only one heart and one soul, as was said of

---

[36] Edwards, *Breath of Life*, p. 108.
[37] *The Eucharistic Letter*, par. 25.

the christians of the primitive church,"[38] stated their *Constitutions*.

Threat to the unity of the Church was the concern, too, of Mary MacKillop and Julian Tenison Woods in the 1860s. Mary wrote in a pamphlet to Roman authorities explaining the situation in Australia:

> These poor are for the most part emigrants from the British Isles, or other parts of Europe, or the children of such who, settled in scattered bands all over the colonies, have been brought up with little or no knowledge of their holy religion, and in perhaps nine cases out of ten, are the offspring of mixed marriages. ... Too often led away by the influence around them, some are afraid of losing the favour of their Protestant employers. Catholic wives dread to oppose their Protestant husbands. Catholic husbands are in their turn equally timid, or shamefully indifferent.[39]

In combating what she called "these evils", Mary saw the "early religious orders of the Church" as a model. Through total dependence on God, Mary, like them, could "make a kind of reparation to God for the little confidence" shown in Providence, and thus enter into union with God in service of neighbour.[40] In community and in the apostolate, Woods urged, Sisters should exemplify that union among themselves:

> We are all dear to our Father, and if we wish to continue so, must love those He loves. We must love and bear with each other as He bears with us.[41]

Urging the Sisters to "hunger for the divine food of the Blessed Eucharist", Woods commented, "We can live upon it, and should live principally by it – that is to say, we must consider our spiritual life as supported by this means".[42] The spiritual

---

[38] *Constitutions for the Little Congregation of the Daughters of St Joseph*, p. 35.
[39] *Necessity for the Institute*.
[40] Mary to Bishop Sheil, September 10, 1871. "My confessor," Mary continued, "at one time thought I would have to go to France ere I could meet with what I desired."
[41] *Book of Instructions*, "Of Unity and Charity".
[42] *Book of Instructions*, "Holy Communion".

life finds its fulfilment, as Médaille pointed out, in being brought into that communion with God and each other of which the Eucharist is sign and instrument: "Jesus ... unites all creatures to himself and to God, his Father, and ... unites all the faithful among themselves by a "common union".[43]

Thus, in their foundations, Sisters of St Joseph were set on a path of "re-establishing Church" by living communion and bringing others into communion with God and each other. For them the Eucharist was means and end of this union. "So great a privilege," commented Woods, "will have to be purchased with a great many persecutions and afflictions."[44] Such was to be the case, as Sisters of St Joseph lived out in their local situations what we term today the *communio* of the Church.

Re-establishing the local Church
The foundation of the Sisters of St Joseph in Le Puy took place at a time of great fervour and ferment in the Catholic Church of France. Around the little villages of the Auvergne, Sisters of St Joseph became well-known for the practical ways in which they carried out their apostolic role. In their care of the poor and suffering, in catechetical instruction and in forming lay women to work with them, they enabled the love of Christ, and thus the Church's mission, to reach into the daily lives of ordinary people. Many Sisters, we know, set about restoring dignity to churches vandalised during the Wars of Religion, by cleaning and decorating them and repairing furnishings and vestments.[45]

We might take this last fact as symbolic. Sisters of St Joseph were like St Francis of Assisi who had first responded to Christ's words, "Repair my house" by a literal rebuilding of St Damian's. The Sisters of St Joseph were to make a major, if

---

[43] *The Eucharistic Letter*, par. 21.
[44] *Book of Instructions*, "Holy Communion". In this section, Woods was referring to his advice that Sisters should receive Holy Communion frequently.
[45] Byrne, Notes of lectures, Concordia, June 2003.

unheralded, contribution to the life of the Church after the traumas of the Reformation and years of ignorance and wretchedness. They were, as Church, to be agents of reconciliation.

"Being Church" has been a mark that has driven Sisters, for good or ill, to continue often in the face of great odds to stay with the situation of the local Church and to find Christ there. Sometimes the missionary scene has been favourable; we are told of one Sister, Mère Carlotte de Vinols of Craponne, France, whose giving of retreats and spiritual talks was very popular:

> Some priests also came when she gave the exercises in public. Ordinarily she mounted the pulpit so that the crowd could hear her, because the crowd was so numerous that the church could scarcely hold them all. Under these circumstances, the ecclesial superiors witnessed publicly to the esteem they had for her, in allowing her to give the Benediction of the Blessed Sacrament every day in the sisters' church. Ordinarily this special grace was given only when a priest was giving the retreat, never when it was the superior of a small community.[46]

This was in the 1770s!

After the Revolution, Mother St Jeanne Fontbonne also found herself re-establishing the life and mission of the Church at local level through the Sisterhood. She was called to "create and unify"[47] – to reach out in new ways for the mission and to bring the scattered back into unity. In 1809, only two years after their re-establishment, she sent three Sisters to Sury at the request of the parish priest. Unprepared for their coming, the parishioners were determined not to lose "their Sisters". There was a stable nearby and its owner was willing to house his horse elsewhere.

---

[46] Vacher, *Des régulières,* Session Five, pp. 261, 262. Mère de Vinols was also renowned for her work among the poor. For her, "the manner of giving service was as important as the services themselves. The poor who were ashamed to beg had her preference. She procured for them all possible relief and she gave them words of consolation when she could not help them in their bodily needs". p. 263.

[47] De Brouwer & Cie, *Mère Saint Jean Fontbonne*, p. 208.

Would the Sisters mind living there? It was too like the Bethlehem story to say "No"; the Sisters set themselves up in these quarters to share the lives of parishioners as they found ways to build again the community so wounded by the Revolution years.[48] This was a pattern that would be repeated throughout the world.

In the United States, Sisters were likewise to signify and shape Church community through their impact on local populations.
> Consistently outnumbering priests and male religious, sisters were everywhere, serving as visible symbols, spiritual educators, and active caregivers of the church, particularly in the nineteenth century when Catholics in more isolated settings rarely saw a priest. The CSJs' daily activities took them into homes, schools, hospitals, orphanages, and other settings that formed a support network spanning the country.[49]

The Sisters of St Joseph of Chambéry who had reintroduced Catholicism into Denmark in 1856 were likewise reconciling agents as, through unassuming presence, making no distinction between rich and poor, they built up "an atmosphere of hope and trust that enabled some persons to be converted, some to return to the faith".[50] Again, in the "de-christianised parish" of Gouraya, Algeria, the Sisters of St Joseph were asked in 1884 "to revive the faith" by opening schools "to evangelise the young people who could in turn become apostles in their families".[51]

In the country towns of Australia and New Zealand, the Sisters of St Joseph, as Mary MacKillop pointed out, were sometimes the only sign of official Church that the people knew:
> The Sisters' work being in a manner a missionary one, its spirit leads them to go to far-away country places where they

---

[48] De Brouwer & Cie, *Mère Saint Jean Fontbonne,* pp. 156, 157.
[49] Coburn and Smith, *Spirited Lives,* p. 222.
[50] Louis Marie Silvestre SSJ. *Sisters of Saint Joseph of Chambéry, 1650 – 1985,* Rome: Sisters of St Joseph, 1985. p. 40.
[51] Silvestre, *Sisters of Saint Joseph of Chambéry,* p. 53.

> may be deprived not only of daily Mass but often of Sunday Mass as well. In such cases they gather the children and adults together, saying with them the Rosary, or reading the Mass prayers, and so keeping them up to the proper observance of Sunday.[52]

"This was a 'Church'," observes Lyne, "that was to be built through the relationships people have with one another."[53] "We identify with the local Church. That's part of being Josephite," said one interviewee. "Sometimes we've been people's only hope for the Church," claimed another. "In that place (an isolated town) where the priest, when he came, was so hard and rude, they needed to know about God's compassion. We tried to do that for them."

Sisters told of teaching converts to Catholicism after the evening meal; of visiting hospitals and gaols at weekends; of helping out on cake stalls to raise money for the parish, and like activities. "I was taught always to have an interest in the people of the parish beyond school and music," recalled one. "We always went to whatever was on in the parish." "When that canon law came in that we weren't allowed to talk to people outside the church, it was a terribly hard time," commented another. "That wasn't Josephite! We belong to the people!"[54]

Power Structures
Bishops: Within the structure of the institutional Church, it has never been presumed that Sisters of St Joseph, as Congregations, should self-authorise for official ministry. While all, by baptism, are called to mission, the organisation of ministries by which services are carried out in the name of the Church does require local bishops to oversee their good ordering. This fact in

---

[52] Mary MacKillop, "The History of the Congregation (1866 – 1900)". Unpublished paper, Archives, Sisters of St Joseph, Sydney.
[53] Daniel Lyne, *Mary MacKillop, Made in Australia,* Sydney: Mary MacKillop Secretariat, 1994. p. 8.
[54] This interpretation of an article in the 1918 code was enforced in some Congregations during the 1940s and was one that was commented on numerous times by interviewees.

no way diminishes the responsibility of each person to *be* Church – to be the face of Christ, the hands and feet of Christ, to our world. Neither does it play down the obligation of bishops to be open to, recognise and encourage the workings of the Spirit in individuals and groups within the Church.

"The development of the little houses of Saint Joseph could not have been done without the support of the bishops," says Vacher.[55] "Sometimes this approval was only a let-them-alone kind of situation," she points out.[56] On the other hand, positive encouragement was given by other bishops, including, of course, Bishop de Maupas.

History accounts of Sisters of St Joseph are full of stories where the support of Bishops nurtured the sense of belonging in the local Church that is natural for Sisters of St Joseph. However, this was often dependant on the ability of superiors not to threaten. If they were content to be "Father's helpers", carrying out orders with no questions asked, things could go smoothly. "As long as they were getting good work out of you at little cost to themselves, it was all right, but let there be any trouble or difficulty and it was all the other way,"[57] is one comment that would have been repeated around the world. That a woman should dialogue with a bishop or priest, or disagree with policies or decisions, was rarely accepted. Margaret Brennan records words of Bishop McQuaid:

> Now you sisters can never dream of aspiring to anything like the position of the priest. Whoever made that choice it was not man; it was God. .. Your merit depends in great abundance in cooperating with the priests in the work they have in saving souls, ... especially... the instruction of the young. ... Go on with the good work, helpers of the clergy.[58]

---

[55] Vacher, *Des régulières,* Session 4, p. 136.
[56] Vacher, *Des régulières,* Session 4, p. 136.
[57] Thorpe, *Mary MacKillop,* p. 244. Comment made in 1926 by Sister Hyacinth Quinlan, founder of the Sisters of St Joseph of Bathurst.
[58] Brennan, *Persistence of Vision,* p. 130.

"Strong women" inevitably found themselves at odds with Church authorities. Yet sometimes, even though they suffered from the abuse of power on the part of bishops, it was this very abuse that resulted in the spread of the Congregations. Mother Agnes Spencer was one such woman. Having been recognised by her superiors as "a woman of strong personality, great tact and ability", she was not pliable enough for Bishop Timon in Buffalo, and eventually, after humiliations from him, left the diocese to found the Sisters in Erie. "Mother Agnes Spencer's story is hardly unique in the 19th century American Church," says Brennan. "In fact, it was just such disagreement with bishops (often about property; always about power) that caused new foundations to spring up all over the country."[59]

So it was to prove with the Sisters of St Joseph of the Sacred Heart in Australia. When she was expelled from Adelaide, Mary was received in Sydney, and the house donated to her eventually became the Motherhouse. Because of the greater population, accessibility and wealth of Sydney, the Congregation was to grow at a rate there that would not have been possible in Adelaide. However, even though Archbishop Moran encouraged and stood by her,[60] it is probable that he was influenced by fellow-Irish bishops in supporting her removal from office, in order "to placate the bishops with regard to a woman who had a bad record for resisting attacks on her Institute's rights."[61]

Mary MacKillop's "resistance" was based on her clarity about the legal relationship of bishop and religious superior.[62] When

---

[59] Brennan, *Persistence of Vision,* p. 16.
[60] In 1884, he wrote to Propaganda that he was impressed by Mary, seeing her as "a well-educated person with much ability". He also told her she could "rest assured that he would do everything in his power to promote and consolidate the Order of the Sisters of St Joseph which had already borne abundant fruit in Australia." (Thorpe, *Mary MacKillop,* p. 169)
[61] Gardiner, *Mary MacKillop,* p. 326, 327.
[62] In a letter to Monsignor Kirby, November 18, 1873, she wrote: "The General Superior ... has to see that her Sisters in a remote province are as carefully attentive to their various duties

Bishop James Quinn threatened that he would get the police if she visited her own Sisters in Brisbane, she wrote: "Of course I did not mind his threats but told him I would do my duty."[63] Bishop Quinn was hoping to wean the Sisters away from central governance (which was the rule under which they had made their vows). In a sermon of November 30, 1879, he made his point clear: "It is impossible for me to accept the government of a woman or to have a community of nuns governed by a lady from Adelaide. I won't allow any woman to make a disturbance in my Diocese."[64]

Mary was well aware that some bishops abused their power, but her total faith in the Church as being God's instrument of salvation caused her to distinguish between the office and the human being who held it. Even in cases of blatant injustice, she would not allow criticism to be voiced, since to focus on the failings of the man would take from what he represented. It puzzled her that those who held such office would be wanting in conversion. At the time of the excommunication in 1871, knowing herself and others to be victims of jealousies and lies, she wrote to Father Woods:

> Oh Father, Bishops and priests have an awful power – and terrible in the sight of God must it be if that be abused. Why is not God thought more of, and the opinions of men less, and

---

in the way prescribed by their Rule as those who are near at hand, and in all this, instead of interfering with the authority of any particular Bishop, her place is rather to uphold his, and to be herself, in so far as her duties in his diocese require, as one of the least of his children. It is only in extreme cases where a Bishop might require of those in his diocese something contrary to this Rule, ... that the authority of the General Superior can in any way interfere with that of the Bishop. In all others, the provincial of each diocese carries on the arrangements of that diocese subject to the Bishop, consulting in all things his views, and bound to yield him the most ready obedience in all things which do not interfere with the first duty of the Rule."

[63] Gardiner, *Mary MacKillop,* p. 210.

[64] Lyne, *Mary MacKillop,* p. 147. James Quinn was vociferous of his condemnation of Mary, accusing her of being "young, sentimental, colonial (that is, born in Australia), of non-Irish stock, female, the daughter of a bankrupt colonial seminarian, a former excommunicate, a strong personality, obstinate, ambitious, based in Adelaide and controlled from there, influenced by Jesuits, a friend of Archbishop Vaughan" (who was English) (Gardiner, *Mary MacKillop,* p. 229).

> why are numberless souls forever lost through the faintheartedness of those whose duty it is to sacrifice personal feeling and try to save them by applying remedies to the evils that are effecting their ruin?[65]

That power should be for service was not a concept commonly expressed at the time, especially in regard to women. Crowley says of Bishop Matthew Quinn, for example: "Steeped in the Irish tradition, trained for the priesthood in Rome and entrenched in Roman and society's view of women, the only leadership he understood was that built on total, unquestioned authority."[66]

In the case of some diocesan Congregations, this authority was to touch Sisters' lives in minute detail. Interviewees told of one bishop who, in the 1920s, forbade the Sisters to read newspapers because they contained advertisements for corsets and bras! Others described bishops' involvement in the purchasing of underwear and visits to the doctor.[67] In an outback diocese a priest was renowned for his abusive behaviour to women religious. The bishop sent him to a parish where Sisters of St Joseph were teaching, because he knew they would not complain.

Under such regimes, as in other institutions at the time, members could actually be grateful if treated with benign behaviour. Sisters in one diocese would look forward to a visit of the bishop because it meant they were accorded a sleep-in of one hour. He could declare a holiday from school, if he wished. Sometimes he even arranged for the Sisters to be shown a movie! For adults to be kept in such a state of suspended

---

[65] Letter to Woods, 21 November 1871. Archives, Sisters of St Joseph, Sydney.
[66] Crowley, *Women of the Vale*, p. 61.
[67] For instance, a novice mistress was dismissed by the bishop of Bathurst because she had taken a seriously ill novice to a Sydney doctor for treatment, having presumed his permission to do so but finding on her return he had not given it because he did not know the nature of the illness. Crowley, *Women of the Vale*, p. 135.

childhood seems inconceivable to us today. However, it was a pattern repeated in other scenarios. Within the power structure of convent life itself, attitudes to authority of superiors was likewise dependent. In wider society, unmarried women living with parents were subject to similar expectations of submission. Women who ran large schools and hospitals, who had university doctorates, whose experience of life touched reality, could only have coped by living life on two levels. Where religious obedience is equated with systems of co-dependency, abuse of power is a constant possibility.

There were bishops, of course, who did treat Sisters with dignity and respect. They were not afraid to work in partnership with superiors and to relate adult to adult. In advance of Vatican II, they realised that systems of dependency in which people are at the mercy of the use or abuse of power by another are basically anti-gospel. In her letters, Mary MacKillop generally refers to such bishops as "friends" – "The Bishop of Rockhampton has just left, ... He is a dear, true friend."[68] We are reminded of the relationship Jesus named as characteristic of that between himself and his disciples: "No longer do I call you servants, ... I have called you friends, for all that I have heard from my Father I have made known to you."[69]

Priests: The Sisters of St Joseph were born into a world that held priesthood in the highest honour. The Bérullian School of French Spirituality had focussed particularly on the priesthood of Christ:
> The concept of priest embodies the theme of adoration, self-giving, and complete abandonment, particularly in the case of Christ, where the sacrifice offered by him as priest is his very self. Priesthood and sacrifice lie at the very heart of Bérulle's perception of the Christian mystery, ... This emphasis led to a

---

[68] Circular, November 16, 1885. Archives, Sisters of St Joseph, Sydney.
[69] Jn. 15: 15.

> very special reverence for the priest within the Christian community.[70]

In the nineteenth century, this attitude was further embedded in religious circles by the centralist structures agreed to in 1801 by Rome as Napoleon's condition for the official re-introduction of the Church in France. The medieval Church had already operated on pyramidal notions of power, trickling down from top to bottom. Uniformity and institutionalism now being promoted in industrialised Europe confirmed these tendencies, with easy application to religious structures. In this world, "reverence" becomes attached to the position rather than to what priesthood signifies. No longer does it stand purely for self-giving and sacrifice. Instead it becomes ambiguous – the spiritual signification remains, but is overlaid by authority based simply on the fact of ordination. In societies where the priest was often the only one with literacy skills, this situation was exacerbated even further.

It was on the spiritual significance of priesthood that Mary MacKillop based her regard for those who held the office. According to the understanding of the time, it was the priest who was "another Christ" – "*alter Christus*". That a priest should act in a way that belied Christ was incomprehensible to her:

> You know how I venerate the priestly character, therefore you can understand what I have suffered since I had to admit that a priest was deliberately in the wrong. I have been able to find excuse for everything but that, not for my own sake, but for the sake of the sacred character of him who could say what was not true. Had the truth been told to the Bishop, would these scandals have come? I forgive him; I forgive all who have had any part in these matters, and so do we all.[71]

---

[70] Walker, "The French Influence", pp. 30, 31.
[71] Letter to Father Woods, October 30, 1871. Archives, Sisters of St Joseph, Sydney.

To those priests who showed compassion and who were ready to suffer in the cause of right she was grateful: "They have proved themselves sincere and fearless friends."[72] Throughout her life, she set up a strong network of priest-friends upon whom she could rely for support and advice. Thus were laid in Australia the same foundations of support for priests that was an identifying characteristic of other Sisters of St Joseph whose roots lay in Le Puy.[73]

This was so, even though Sisters had first-hand experience of what can only be termed outrageous actions on the part of some priests. Many of these incidents have already been referred to. In one parish the people were well aware that the school moneys were being taken each week by the priest and the Sisters were barely surviving. However, the people were forbidden by the priest to give meat, eggs or other produce to them. When the Sisters went to the city for retreat, they would come back to find things missing from the chapel and other parts of the convent. "We put up with a lot of abuse from priests," said one old Sister. "But we always went back. The people were attached to us, you see."

Despite such experiences, many Sisters have hastened to explain that priests who behaved like this were in some cases mentally ill or under great pressure. Sister Evangeline Thomas quotes Mother Stanislaus Leary and her companions when they travelled to Newton, Kansas, to found the Congregation there in 1883:

---

[72] Letter to her mother, November 22, 1871.
[73] When Cardinal Gilroy re-opened the Cause of Mary MacKillop in 1951, having found papers refuting the charge of drunkenness, the Congregational leaders of the time urged him not to proceed "if the exoneration of Mother Mary would bring discredit on Archbishop Reynolds or any of his priests". The Cardinal recognised here the spirit of Mary: "She never said a word against bishop or priest involved in the calumny, and left this spirit among her sisters." Kathleen Burford RSJ, "Mary MacKillop's Cause and the Sisters of St Joseph", unpublished paper, 2005.

> "The priest, Father Swemberg, has shown marked unkindness toward us. We were not even allowed to arrange our house to our own liking without his dictation. One act of kindness from him we have not received." In her charity, however, she continued: "Still he is a good pious man but has been so long used to roughing it among the Indians no doubt that he has lost all feeling for kindness. In our isolated and unprotected position we feel this very much. ... We often became discouraged enough to break up the mission, but when we considered the wants of the poor children here and how much they would lose we cheered up and continued the good work."[74]

Being able to live with ambiguity, knowing that one's service was of God, not the priest, has enabled Sisters of St Joseph to earn the reputation of being what might be termed an alternative face of the local Church. For them, the Church was God's instrument for salvation – for union with God and each other. They came to realise that priests were sinners like everyone else, but they were still instruments of God. Thus all around the world, especially in isolated areas, Sisters' support of priests became legendary. Sometimes their loyalty was eventually shown to have been misplaced, as, for example, when evidence later proved that children were being abused. Given the times, even if accusation was made, it would have been rare for Sisters or other adults to believe it.

In many instances, the Sisters were the only ones lonely and depressed priests could turn to.[75] In nearly every group interviewed came the refrain, "We would stay up Saturday nights until 10 p.m. playing cards with Father so that he would be sober for Sunday Mass" (the hotels closed at 10 p.m.).

---

[74] Thomas, *Footprints on the Frontier*, p. 134. With the division of the diocese, two Congregations, Sisters of St Joseph of Concordia and Wichita, resulted.

[75] Of Mother Francis Lirette, Sisters of St Joseph of Orange, for example, it was said, "She took care of priests like they were children. If one of them had imbibed too much and was afraid to go home to his parish house, he needed only to appear at the Motherhouse door. Mother Francis herself would give him a room and allow him to sober up with no lectures and no remonstrating glances." Geagley, *A Compassionate Presence*, p. 153.

"Father would come up to the convent to work around the place to keep himself out of the presbytery, because he knew he would only drink himself silly once he got there." "We used to have him over for evening meals to save him from having to go to the hotel for them." "We would play cards to keep the priest away from the hospital – from the nurses up there." "Sometimes there would be a phone call late at night. 'Meet me under the lemon tree,' Father would say. So two of us would get up, boil the kettle and make him tea, and stay with him until he was feeling all right again. Then we would have to get up early again in the morning to attend to the boarders before teaching all day in school." One community used to play cards with the priest in a room whose window opened out on to the street. The Sisters were reported to the bishop by a scandalised parishioner who, when passing by, heard "a man" shout out from inside, "You've trumped me bloomin' ace!"

Very often, the relationship of Sisters with priests was of co-workers and "chief helpers". The invitation by the Bishop of Clifton, Wales, for the Sisters of St Joseph of Annecy to come to his diocese in 1864, was made on the recommendation of Captain Dewell who considered the Sisters "necessary to the support of the priests' work".[76] One Sister told of a priest asking her and her companion to witness the wedding of a very pregnant woman and a Protestant man. "In those days they weren't allowed to get married in the church," she said. "The woman's parents had thrown her out, so Father got us to help him prepare a party for them, and we had a lovely ceremony and a happy time."

Other Sisters spoke of the priest asking them to sew buttons on his shirts; "Father was getting old and his suit was often grubby, so we used to get it from him each week to clean it up." "Father was ill, but wouldn't go to hospital. So we cleared out the music

---

[76] Bourne, *His Mercy is From Age to Age,* p. 90.

room, and nursed him there until he recovered." "Nothing was ever too good for the priests." "We were always there for the priest. He'd drop in for a cuppa whenever he felt like it." "I think our Sisters saved many a priest. We would look after them." "In one place the priest was very hard, but he was around a lot, so we couldn't talk about our difficulties very well. We would call him 'Marge' whenever we referred to him so that if he did overhear us, he wouldn't know we were talking about him."

Stories where Sisters remembered with fondness the sense of camaraderie and brotherliness with priests are treasured. "Father was always good to us Sisters," many Sisters said. Small acts of thoughtfulness – such as taking the Sisters for a drive in the days when they did not have cars, including them in parish outings, acknowledging their contribution to the life of the parish – set up relationships that were mutually beneficial.

The self-sacrifice and dedication of priests they have worked with have given Sisters hope. They have rejoiced when their efforts to form local community have been met with equal zeal on the part of the priest. Many a Sister could identify with those in Suain, Papua New Guinea, when the priest died: "The parish, for which he had a great love, had been shaped by his presence for six years and the sisters had been fortunate in gaining so much from his experience."[77] Sister Virginia Ann Gardner tells of the inspiration she gained from one priest:

> Totally unaware of his influence on my prayer-life, a priest who struggles with alcohol addiction taught me a new meaning of faith. I had limited faith too much to the intellectual ("I believe in God"). In his homilies, Father expanded faith to include relationship with God. Without alluding to his addiction, it became clear that it was his very

---

[77] Crowley, *Women of the Vale*, p. 197.

dependency on the strength of God that was making perfect his weakness.[78]

Convent Life: If power structures within the Church were open to abuse, so too were those that operated within religious life itself. Geagley notes, "In the hierarchical structure of religious life, exceptionally strong and persuasive individuals made themselves into centers of gravity; power was concentrated in the hands of a few.[79] Relationships between superiors and community members could promote infantile behaviours unless checks were put in place to encourage attitudes of co-responsibility and mature response. Media stereotypes of Sisters being addressed as "children" or "little ones" by the "Mother Superior" had at least some basis in past practice.[80]

External factors played a part in entrenching attitudes of conformity among sisters. For instance, the promulgation of the Code of Canon Law in 1917-18 placed extra pressures on major superiors:

> Every five years superiors of Catholic sisterhoods had to submit responses to a detailed Vatican questionnaire, which measured how well the community was following the new canon law. Innovation, risk taking, and responding to the contemporary needs of the people, which were trademarks of the sisterhoods prior to 1920, were discouraged in favour of rigidity, uniformity, regulation, and following the "letter of the law." The vow of obedience became the over-riding concern.[81]

As the only option open to women who wished to work full-time in ministry, religious life assumed a position within the Church somewhere between lay and clerical life. Brennan notes,

---

[78] Gardner, *Let It Be,* p. 123.
[79] Geagley, *A Compassionate Presence, p. 121.*
[80] In the Sisters of St Joseph of the Sacred Heart, the superior of the convent was called the "Little Sister" in an effort to emphasise that the rank of the superior was one of service, not power over others. However, in time, the title "Little Sister" became one denoting comparative power, or, at least, prestige!
[81] Coburn & Smith, *Spirited Lives,* p. 224.

"Curiously, choosing a life of submission brought (Sisters) a certain power, a chance to have some influence in the society and in the Church; leaving the world offered opportunities to travel it more widely than they might have if they had married; renouncing marriage gave them a freedom to meet men as peers, at least in their work.[82] They were visible symbols, but rarely gave voice to issues outside of their professional ministry.

Relations with different Congregations was often competitive during these years, as frequently referred to by interviewees. "We didn't talk to each other, even when we attended the same meetings." "My sister was in another Congregation, and we hardly ever saw one another." "We felt the other Congregations looked down on us. We were the 'least' (and at times we were proud of it!)." "There would be vying for pupils by the Religious running the different schools."

It was primarily in addressing the reforms advocated by Pius XII that Sisters from all Congregations began the journey of reclaiming their founding purpose. Vatican II pushed them farther along that journey. Sisters of St Joseph were to find, to their delight, that the vision that had given rise to their founding was to find its echo in the understanding of Church promoted by Vatican II. They would recognise in the call to communion with God and neighbour, necessary for a full understanding of Eucharist, their own focus of mission. This vision would call for structures that would support it in ways that speak to our changed world.

---

[82] Brennan, *Persistence of Vision*, p. 59.

8.3 PART THREE: The spirit lives into the now.

<u>Mission to *communio*</u>

To form communion is at the heart of Church mission. It is also at the heart of the mission of Sisters of St Joseph. The rule composed by Médaille, with its central image of the "two trinities", is oriented towards achieving the "double union" of God and neighbour. Those who trace their roots to Le Puy can, then, draw on this rule to claim:

> Our mission then (350 years ago) was the same as it is today – unity of neighbour with neighbour and neighbour with God. The difference lies only in our response to the needs of our day and the time in which we live.[83]

When Sisters of St Joseph of the Sacred Heart reflect on their identity as being "with" the people, being "at the heart of Church", being "at one" with the poor, they find the same orientation. The founding Sisters aimed to bring to others "the message of ... human dignity and of Christ's saving love, symbolised ... by the Sacred Heart".[84] It is this love that brings us into communion with God and each other. To be open to and promote communion with God and neighbour is the fundamental mission of Sisters of St Joseph.

It is also the mission of all who share the spirit of Joseph. That this mission is so identified with the core of Church mission has been a conundrum for some. "What do we do that is different from anyone else?" they ask. Perhaps the answer does not lie in *what* but *how*. The particular charism or gift given by the Spirit to those who share the spirit of Joseph sets us out on a *way* of serving that has been outlined in this book. *Where* this service or ministry is carried out reflects both the universal (or catholic) nature of the gift and its characteristic application to ministry in the local Church.

---

[83] Sr Mary Theno, *Journeys,* Vol 20, No 1, Spring/Summer 2003. p. 6.
[84] "Founding Charism", *Constitutions, Sisters of St Joseph of the Sacred Heart,* p. 4.

Expressing *communio* in relationships

Most people today have lived most of their lives in the post-Vatican II Church. The Council's portrayal of the Church as the People of God has been the one we have grown up with and the one that motivates us to mission. A vital insight of the Council was that the Church is the sacrament of Christ.[85] In other words, it is each member, not just the ordained priest, who is the *alter Christus,* "another Christ". "Christ, our redeemer and high priest," says the *Catechism of the Catholic Church,* "continues the work of our redemption in, with, and through his Church."[86] The gift of the Spirit to those who share Joseph's way is to help build the new world envisioned by Christ: "That they may all be one."[87] In our being signs and instruments through which the compassionate love of Christ is given to the least, his saving work continues.

Associates: In fostering the movement of Associates, Sisters of St Joseph have not merely called upon the foundational practice of the Le Puy Sisters who shared spiritual formation with members of confraternities, but they have entered into a relationship with the lay Church of today that expresses the common mission of all the baptised. Associates take advantage of opportunities for spiritual development, and in recognising the charism they have been gifted with, discern how to use it for mission in their own sphere of influence.

To express unity in charism, many Associates join Sisters of St Joseph in gatherings for prayer, celebrations, retreats, and sometimes appropriate sessions of their meetings and Chapters. As they take on their own leadership structures, they invite

---

[85] *Lumen Gentium* par. 1.
[86] *Catechism of the Catholic Church,* # 1069. The reference is to Christ acting in the Church's liturgy. However, as the Catechism goes on to note, "In the New Testament the word 'liturgy' refers not only to the celebration of divine worship but also to the proclamation of the Gospel and to active charity. In all of these situations it is a question of the service of God and neighbour." CCC # 1070.
[87] Jn. 17:21

Sisters to share the same kinds of occasions also with them. Much remains to be done, however, with regard to establishing these structures. The relationship being fostered is partnership. The contribution of Associates to the lives of Sisters and vice versa is already recognised as being mutually beneficial. "Unity in diversity" is acknowledged when the different ways of living the charism of Joseph inform and support one another.

Other lay groups: Other lay groups such as co-workers with Sisters, volunteers, members of management boards and groups with whom they form an alliance also build up *communio* among God's People. In New Zealand, for example, a Christian ecumenical group of lay women, the Athena Women's Collective, found their Mission Statement was almost identical to that of the Sisters of St Joseph of Wanganui. Under the umbrella of the Sisters of St Joseph, they have now formed a Charitable Trust, and are currently looking to enter into a deeper relationship with the Sisters. Together, the two groups are exploring their common spiritual base and want to continue dialogue about ongoing partnership. Barbara Cowan RSJ says:

> A key feature of this experience is that neither group is "joining" the other. The link is hoped to give birth to a new reality that emerges from the spirituality of the Athena women and the Sisters, each nourishing the other.

Benefactors have always held a particular place in the hearts of Sisters of St Joseph. Without them, many of the achievements of the Sisters would not have been possible. With modern technology, the moral links between these "partners in ministry" and the Sisters are able to take more concrete form through exchange and dialogue in newsletters and personal involvement.

New forms of partnership in ministry have seen Sisters of St Joseph in Australia enter into agreements with other groups whose resources complement theirs and with whom a common goal can be achieved. For example, they have formed a consortium with other Religious and universities involved in sending volunteers to developing countries. Gathering with PALMS (the Australian Catholic volunteering organisation), the consortium works together to match volunteers to suitable placements, prepare them for the cultural crossing, and support them while overseas and during re-entry at the conclusion of the placement.

At their Province Chapter, the Sisters in Auckland, New Zealand, resolved to focus on the wellbeing of children at risk. A woman, authorised by Kauri Trust, approached the Sisters. She needed support, a house, and resources to begin a residential and educational program to assist and educate young girls who had dropped out of school, or with serious behavioural issues, and often living on the street. The result of her approach is a very effective collaborative program, "The Beautiful Daughters", where young girls on the streets are given options for safety, education and dignity previously denied them.

Networking with other groups and in local neighbourhoods extends communion among those whose contact with official Church is minimal. "Being the face of God in the ordinary" is a form of evangelisation that mirrors God's entering our human condition in the Incarnation. In itself, it is message. The Sisters of St Joseph Neighborhood Network in Erie, for example, touches the lives of the marginalised and also involves a host of other agencies in thus preparing the way for communion.[88]

The searching of some lay men and women around the world to express the charism of Joseph in new modes of consecration invites Sisters to open themselves to collaboration and encouragement. In Italy, for example, three consecrated lay-people – from Turin, Novare and Rome, have turned to Sisters of St Joseph for accompaniment in their discernment. One of

---

[88] "A Move in the Right Direction", *Journeys,* Winter 2002, p. 12.

these has recently gone to Brazil as a missionary with the Sisters there.[89] While they may not yet have made formal commitment or "consecration", other groups of women have entered into similar arrangements, living with Sisters for a defined time, sometimes accepting only a Sister's salary while working with them. What will grow from this?

In Turin, too, certain families who, over the years, have built up a relationship of friendship with the Sisters, now form community with them. They pray with them, spend time with them in meditation and on retreats, and engage in the hospitality ministry with them.[90] Whether or not such ventures will lead to another structured form of living in the spirit of Joseph is yet to be seen.

Sisters of St Joseph: In the lives of Sisters of St Joseph themselves, the expression of communion is being addressed at various levels. Their aim, to be sign and instrument of God's unifying love in a world torn by division and violence seems, to some, to be an impossibility. "It's hard enough to be in communication with one another, let alone live in communion!" claimed one Sister. An article in a publication of the French Federation of Sisters of St Joseph offers an insight into this practicality: "We discover, day by day, that the source of unity is not in ourselves but that it comes from Christ."[91] In other words, it is only in living out our faith together that our efforts are transformed by the Love who overcomes all division. Our lives, blessed and broken, become means for communion; Eucharist is lived.

True to the collegial spirit of Joseph, Sisters have adopted government structures that call for co-responsibility, participation, collaboration and consultation. Chapter

---

[89] *Misi Synthèse*, p. 11.
[90] *Misi Synthèse*, p. 5.
[91] "Construire le monde nouveau", *Comme un grain de Sénevé*, p. 24. My paraphrase.

preparation, processes and implementation are carried out in a communal way. "Open Chapters" to which all members are invited are held when possible. Two-way communication is encouraged. Several vehicles of communication, e.g. video conferencing, are used to ensure good, open communication from leadership and within provinces.

In relationships with other Congregations, efforts have been made all over the world to invert the competition of the past and to collaborate wherever possible. Circles of communion are thus established. In Erie, for example, this fact is cause for joy:
> One of our newest ministries is a collaborative project sponsored by our three local congregations of women religious, Benedictine, Mercy, SSJ. A program for women in need, it is the first time we have ventured to work in totally shared ministry.[92]

Exchanging personnel among different Congregations for particular works is also now common. In Adelaide, some welfare works originally begun by Sisters of St Joseph had been handed over to Sisters of Mercy and Daughters of Charity when they came to the archdiocese. Now, Sisters of St Joseph are working in these areas once again, side by side with the Sisters of the other Congregations. Sister Veronica Lonergan experienced a new sense of communion when she found herself the only Religious among lay staff in a Catholic school:
> Though all worked harmoniously together, I found it quite different from working with members of my own Congregation. It offered a good example of the universality of the Church and I know I am the richer for having been part of it.[93]

In a world of mergers and takeovers, some groups of Sisters of St Joseph find that, for the sake of ongoing mission, they must look to forming closer relationships with others who share the same purpose and charism. So, for instance, six Congregations,

---
[92] Gardner, *Let it Be,* p. 188.
[93] Lonergan, *I Sought and I Found,* p. 6.

four of them branches of Le Puy, have amalgamated, forming one new Institute of Sisters of St Joseph. In doing so, they have found themselves coming together in a bond of unity that has brought renewal to all concerned. Together they can be and do what was not possible separately. In dying to the localised identity previously theirs, they have rediscovered the deeper identity of what it means to be a Sister of St Joseph.

They and other groups of Sisters looking at "reconfiguring" find that they now experience *communio* at a deeper level. In looking at their common mission, relationships and founding histories, they are drawn by a deep awareness of shared spirit, cutting through divisions of culture and local concerns. They give witness to the bigger union that is the destiny of us all. They model the communion they preach.

Ordained Ministers: The catholicity of Church celebrates unity in diversity. The different gifts of its members are given so that Christ's mission of bringing all of creation into communion with God may be accomplished. There is inter-relationship between these gifts. They complement one another. The gift of the bishop's leadership expresses in sacramental form the presence of Christ in the Church, teaching, caring and worshipping. Priests, gathered around the bishop, enable that presence of Christ to nurture God's people so that, together, the whole Church can carry out its mission. The gifts of clerical service are vital for the Church.

It is with this awareness that those who share the spirit of Joseph carry forward their traditional support of ordained ministry. In our times, however, some past ways of doing this are seen to be inappropriate. For instance, it is now realised that the covering up of behaviours of dysfunctional priests (or other Church personnel) actually increases the very scandal it was trying to avoid. The long-term effects of sexual and psychological abuse are now known. To condone or ignore actions that cause such harm is to be implicated in injustice and sin, carried out in the name of Christ. Therefore, bullying, disrespect and disregard of women or of any person by Church ministers, let alone criminal behaviour, are challenged – out of love and regard for the position they hold.

It is well known that the actions of the few have placed a heavy burden on the shoulders of faithful and dedicated bishops and priests who form the great majority. As already noted, groups of Sisters of St Joseph and Associates hear in this fact an ongoing call to offer support and models of partnership with those who are ordained to Church ministry. Such partnership uses power for service. It is a leadership that engages the power of others for a common cause. It is "power *with*", not "power *over*".

Relationships of friendship, where the ordained, those in religious life and those in lay life collaborate, remain open to the promptings of the Spirit and invite participation, will be true to the spirit of Joseph, patron of the Church, patron of collegiality. The cost of liberating those alienated from God was the cross. If Church structures at present deny God's freedom to the marginalised, their change will demand the same gift of self. Issues around the use of power, social justice, the status of women and those barred from full participation in Church life, can only be addressed by personal conversion and witness to life in communion as proclaimed by Jesus.

This is the ideal. In the real world, of course, sin does operate. Thus the role of the reconciler is more important than ever. In whatever ways are possible, those called to express the communion of all creatures with God and each other need to bring whatever practical skills are needed to the task of repairing the flawed situation of Church *communio*. The doggedness that engages pain, characteristic of the spirit of Joseph, has enabled our forebears to do so in the past; it will continue to do so in the future.

Nancy O'Connor CSJ was an example of this. She epitomised the spirit of Joseph that reconciles, that relates in friendship, that calls people into communion and that acts as leaven in the local Church. At her funeral, Bishop Brown of Orange, California, was able to say: "For me, she will always be remembered as a gift to our Church, our congregation and to me personally."[94]

The St Joseph Movement

We live in a world torn by deep divisions – between rich and poor, the powerful and impotent. Even in democracies, people find they have little or no voice. They enjoy freedom, yet they live in fear lest others pose a threat to those freedoms. Barriers are put up to keep people out. Punitive measures are taken to ensure protection of power. In a world of unlimited communication, relationships break down to a degree never known before. We marvel when the camera takes us into the bowels of the earth and lets us climb to its greatest heights, yet the same earth writhes in agony as greed leaves it raped and abused. Where food is abundant, people starve. Where material goods choke our shelves, suicide, oppression and hopelessness also abound. Medical knowledge prolongs life and says we are invincible, yet war, violence and indifference destroy life every day.

From the situation of division and its consequences, says Carol Zinn, a number of hungers arise[95] In a world divided, people long for unity. Where isolationism tries to protect possessions and sovereignty, people seek interdependence. Oppressive policies are imposed in efforts to maintain power over others, yet the cry for justice keens loudly. A world that offers too much information leaves a vacuum of wisdom. In a broken world, people seek wholeness and healing. In an arrogant world where self-sufficiency is honoured, there is a yearning for

---

[94] *The Orange County-Register*, Aug 9, 2004.
[95] Carol Zinn SSJ made the points cited in this paragraph in an address to Sisters of St Joseph gathered in the heartland region of USA, May 29, 2004.

respect, recognition and connection. Society is governed by the values of materialism, and yet the search for the sacred, for mysticism, is stronger than ever.

Against every evil, God provides the gifts needed for its antidote. To answer every hunger, God gives what will sustain. The natural world has taught us this. Our histories have demonstrated it. In the Church, Sicari reminds us, we name these gifts charisms, whereby "the Spirit *marks certain of the baptized,* makes them fall in love with Christ *in a special way, gathers* them in a spiritual homeland, assigns them particular tasks for the building up of the Church, and educates them with the *pedagogical persuasiveness* that characterizes the charism".[96] In our times, those who find their homeland in the spirit of Joseph are especially challenged to hear the cries being made and the hungers being expressed.

For the charism of Joseph, it seems, has been given for our times. To answer division, we have our Eucharistic way of living, bringing people together into unity, expressing in our being and action the communion of all creation and God.[97] To break through the boundaries of isolationism and fear, we have the model of the Trinitarian life that has provided the framework and reference point for Sisters of St Joseph branched from Le Puy, and whose spirit was reflected in the foundation of Sisters of St Joseph of the Sacred Heart. The inter-relationships of the persons of the Trinity and its imaging in the community of the Holy Family invite us to live the "double union" in relationship with God *in* inclusive service of every kind of neighbour.

Oppressive power and the cry for just relationships are answered by those who share Joseph's spirit in solidarity with those who suffer, those pushed to the margins and for whom dignity of life

---

[96] Sicari, "Ecclesial Movements", p. 293. Italics are his.
[97] In this and the next two paragraphs I again take up the points made by Carol Zinn and also those I have made in preceding chapters.

is being denied. The healing of reconciliation and compassion is offered to those who are broken and who hunger for wholeness. Hospitality welcomes, with humility, reverence and a sense of interconnectedness, the God-given gifts of creation; it delights in the diversity of cultures and personalities that enrich our lives; it receives with joy the new and the stranger.

In a materialistic world, the charism of Joseph recognises in the ordinary, the presence of God among us. It points to the sacred in daily life. It glimpses, in relationships formed, the love of One who is total self-gift. The wisdom for which ignorance yearns is offered, as Joseph teaches us to listen with a disciple's ear and to discern, with openness to the Spirit, the will of God in our lives.

If the forces of evil operate on a global scale, so, too, do the workings of the Spirit. It remains a task for us today, though, to raise consciousness as to where the movement of the Spirit is leading us. For over three hundred years, the charism of Joseph has been expressed in the form of life of Sisters of St Joseph. In the founding of these Congregations, the charism was given a forum from which it could develop and operate.

But the charism is a gift that has been distributed on a far wider scale than the Sisterhoods. And especially today, it needs to take on visible form that enables it to be an effective instrument against forces that are well organised and very powerful. The spirit of Joseph might be hidden, but so are bees and white ants (termites). Yet these creatures of God are renowned for their organisation! And they are effective!

What needs to be explored is how the charism of Joseph might be recognised as being distributed among the People of God as a whole. How do we give it a more visible forum among laity? What concrete shapes might partnerships between lay, religious and ordained take? How can we build a sense of world-wide solidarity between those who gather around this charism? These are questions that need urgent attention if the Church is to be truly enlivened by the gift the Spirit has given us.

As a *way* of living the Gospel or of being Church, the charism of Joseph enables us, lay, religious and cleric, to do what Joseph did – to play our part in incarnating the great and compassionate love of God among us. In this way, through the action of the Spirit, our world will be brought into the communion for which God longs and for which we are destined.

A final story might illustrate how the spirit of Joseph lives on into our time. It is told by Donna Mealing from Josephite Community Aid (JCA), a full-time volunteer in 1992.

The day I met Jesus

As a volunteer of JCA we had a community house that had an 'open house' policy to those in need. On one particular and not so unordinary day when I was in the kitchen doing some everyday things, the doorbell rang – as it always did! There outside with arms outstretched to reach either side of the doorway was an ordinary man. A youngish looking man with neat dark hair, probably the same age as myself. He blurted out with passion "I am he, I am the saviour of the world, Jesus Christ". My immediate reaction was dumbfounded silence. Suddenly I was forced to be the one to make the next move. So I blurted back "Hi I'm Donna, would you like to come in?" We had an extremely in-depth discussion about a whole host of things over coffee and soon he left. He blew in, had a chat and blew out again as quickly as he came. I thought him to be a man that needed a great deal of people's kindness and I saw he had some real issues in front of him to tackle. I pondered on all this for a while, and upon reflection began remembering the passage from the bible..."When I was hungry, you gave me to eat. When I was thirsty you gave me to drink." Considering as a Christian we believe that Jesus is in all of us, maybe he was just really OUT THERE on that day. Was it Jesus I saw? Did I experience the most amazing thing ever? It's something I will never ever forget. I remember it like yesterday and I can still picture that gentleman's face. I feel very lucky to have met such a man.

EPILOGUE

The previous pages describe what I have observed as the characteristics of those who have been graced with the spirit of Joseph. In the bonds of this spirit they form a movement, a community, that tells our world of God's Great and Compassionate Love. This love breaks through the boundaries of fear to risk all; it finds God in ordinary practicality; it acts justly and brings people into unity; it walks humbly in earthiness and endures to the end; the spirit of Joseph is for mission, calling the Church to be sign and instrument of God's reign among us.

It is important to acknowledge that not all those who enter into this movement show these characteristics all of the time. The experience of failings in our own lives and among our companions speaks all too loudly against the assertion that all Sisters of St Joseph have shown compassion; that all Associates reach out to the marginalized, that a life of simplicity is a feature of each one of us.

Stories to the contrary abound, even in early histories. In Sauxillanges, France, for example, the Sisters understandably resisted mixing the sick poor and the orphans in the hôpital, preferring to tend the former in their homes. When the hôpital's patron insisted that a man suffering from a "repugnant disease" be admitted, the Sisters are reputed to have punched the patient in the nose and forced him out into the street, saying "they would rather die than have this illness in their house".[813]

Similarly Thérèse Vacher describes the tensions resulting from struggles between Sisters of St Joseph and city

---

[813] Byrne, "French Roots of a Women's Movement", pp. 131-133.

authorities in 1723 Vienne. The tensions may have been in reaction to the Sisters' assertiveness; that women should have the rights they were claiming would have posed a threat to men of the time. On the other hand, complaints may not have been without foundation. Whether based on fact or not, records list the grievances of rectors and administrators of the hospital against the sisters:

> They were negligent in carrying out the orders of the doctors. The two sisters who were in charge of the school taught some young girls from the city to read and write, but not the poor girls. ... As for their manner of living, the sisters no longer took their meals with the poor and sick at the hospital. ... They held many receptions ... for their friends and relatives and others of their congregation, their drivers, at the expense of the above mentioned hospital.[814]

Other surviving documentation leads Vacher to conclude that during the eighteenth century there was a gradual withdrawal of the Sisters from the kind of spirituality that expressed in one movement union with God and neighbour. Even though the Sisters' virtues are still alluded to, "one no longer feels the same nearness to the people".[815]

More recent and even contemporary stories from all over the world tell of abusive teachers, unfeeling nurses, cold, inhuman responses to individual need – the full gamut of human sinfulness is ours.[816]

---

[814] Vacher, *Des "régulières"*, p 232. Whereas most documentation regarding groups of Sisters of St Joseph in France was lost during the Revolution, that at Vienne has, in the main, survived.
[815] Vacher, *Des "régulières"*, p 370.
[816] This cannot be denied. It is well to note, however, the point made by Coburn and Smith that the image of Sisters in general has suffered distortion through lack of public voice, the crediting of the local pastor or bishop with achievements of the Sisters and "twentieth-century stereotypes (which) have buried the nuns' major accomplishments in either negative caricatures of rigid, ruler-wielding drones or in romantic and syrupy discourse describing passive and self-sacrificing martyrs." *Spirited Lives*, p. 223

As with all groups, each foundation of the Sisters of St Joseph as a body has gone through the organisational stages of enthusiastic beginnings, rapid growth demanding uniformity, maturity favouring conformity and decline with options for extinction or rebirth. The emotional impacts of these stages on the group are not to be discounted.

Neither is the internal culture that, in many cases, lent itself to institutionalism. Some of the complaints alleging cruelty have been met with incomprehension by older Sisters who, sometimes victims themselves, thought they were doing "the right thing" according to the standards of the day. Again, in times when, in order to respond to the expectations of mission, Sisters were presented with classes of 100+ children, when timetables had them nursing day and night without a break, when abuse by Church hierarchy placed them in impossible positions – all of these factors and more have contributed on occasion to a suppression of the spirit that is ours.[817]

But where do those who share the spirit of Joseph recognise their true selves? It is in the lives of the thousands of Sisters of St Joseph who have, with courage, endurance, practical commonsense and great love, given witness to the grace of this spirit. It is in the ordinary, faithful lay people who have lived it out in care of the neighbour, largely ignored but playing a vital part in the Spirit's forming us into the community of God's great, compassionate love.

So for every contradiction among those who associate with the spirit of Joseph, there are multiple positive experiences

---

[817] The reminiscences recorded in Coburn & Smith, *Spirited Lives,* p. 135, of a Sister teaching in the parish school all day, then teaching adults until 10 o'clock at night, "Then we had to do our washing and ironing on Saturday and take our turn to sit up with Mother Philomene every night until she died" could be those of Sisters of St Joseph around the world.

of what truly accords with it. We "recognise" it when we see it. We are drawn by it. We reverence it in its new burgeoning in the hope that what the Spirit is doing among us will flourish into a movement, a great river of grace.

Denis Edwards says that
> to be faithful to the Spirit, the church will need not only to respond to the hunger for spirituality, for Christian unity, and for church renewal, but also to play its part, both within the church and without, in the interrelated movements concerned with justice, gender, and ecology.[818]

As a contribution to Church mission, those who live the spirit of Joseph have a unique contribution to make to this quest. In partnership – lay, religious and ordained – we can be instruments through whom the Spirit brings about union with God and all peoples. I pray the reflections in this book might play a small part in this.

I thank all who have helped in the producing of this book. Josepha Clancy CSJ who edited the text knows how much I have valued her work and encouragement. To Margaret Press RSJ, Karen Kennelly CSJ and Joe Sobb SJ I give warm thanks for their reading of the text and their comments. The wonderful portrait of Joseph painted by Ann Steenbergen RSJ that is portrayed on the cover of this book speaks for itself – thank you so much, Ann. To Caroline Jones, Renée Stevens, Jack Glaser, Yvonne Tobin RPA and Frs Gerard Kelly, Denis Edwards, Steve Bliss OFM, Jeff Foale CP and Gerard Gleeson who gave occasional advice and feedback I am very grateful. Through emails and conversation, Sisters of St Joseph around the world – Marie Foale, Genevieve Ryan, Margaret Kenny, Sue Pollard, Carmel Crameri, Colleen O'Sullivan, Mary-Ann Casanova,

---

[818] Edwards, *Breath of Life*, p. 91.

Maria Sullivan, Barbara Cowan, Katherine Gray, Jane Morrissey, Ricarda Vincent, Marty McEntee, Sharon Costello, Patricia Byrne, Monica Hartnett, Margaret Kane, Kathy McCluskey, Therese Meunier, Catherine Steffens, Carol Zinn and Simone Saugues – have all played some part in enabling these pages to come together. To Peta Maley and Natalie Gordon, who assisted with indexing and final editing, I say a sincere thank you. My community – Claire Burgess and Benedetta Bennett – have not only fed back to me their impressions of chapters, but have also supported me by doing the little acts of kindness that keep one going.

Especially I thank the Congregational leadership of our own Sisters – Katrina Brill, Monica Cavanagh, Joan Healy, Pat Malone and Sheila McCreanor – whose vision, generosity, foresight and funding made it possible for me to contribute this work to our Congregation's pursuing of the Chapter decision to explore links of communion with other Sisters of St Joseph around the world and with other groups who share the charism of Joseph. To the Sisters in leadership and in communities, and especially the archivists, of the various Congregations of Sisters of St Joseph in Australia, New Zealand, USA, Canada, England, Ireland, France and Italy who offered me hospitality and made their resources available to me, I offer sincere thanks.

Two sayings have just caught my eye. One is from Gandhi: "Model what you're trying to achieve." The other is from the Australian cartoonist, Leunig: "God help us to live slowly; to move simply; to look softly; to allow emptiness; to let the heart create for us. Amen."

List of Primitive Documents Used in Text

Documents of Sisters of St Joseph, founded by Jean-Pierre Medaille, Françoise Eyraud, Clauda Chastel, Marguerite Burdier, Anna Chalayer, Anna Vey and Anna Brun, Le Puy, France, Oct. 15, 1650:

Constitutions for the Little Congregation of the Daughters of St Joseph
>Second Revised Translation, Research Team, July 1979. Edited 1984.

Maxims of Perfection, Jean-Pierre Medaille SJ, 1672.
>Translation, Research Team, under the direction of M. Nepper, SJ. Commissioned by the Federation, Sisters of Sr Joseph, USA. 1979.

Règelements of the Daughters of St Joseph
>Translation, Research Team, under the direction of M. Nepper, SJ. Commissioned by the Federation, Sisters of Sr Joseph, USA. 1973.

The Eucharistic Letter, Jean-Pierre Medaille SJ.
>Translation InterCongregational Research Team, Federation of the Sisters of St Joseph, USA, 1973.

Documents of Sisters of St Joseph of the Sacred Heart, founded by Julian Tenison Woods and Mary MacKillop, Penola, South Australia, March 19, 1866:

A Book of Instructions (for the use of the Sisters of St Joseph of the Sacred Heart. (*Explanation of the Rule and Constitution of the Sisters of St Joseph)*
>Written by Fr Woods and printed under the two different titles by Mary MacKillop and the Diocesan Sisters of St Joseph.

Memoirs, Julian Tenison Woods.
>Dictated to and transcribed by Miss Anne Bulger at Elizabeth St, Sydney, between 1887 and 1889. Unfinished Manuscript, Archives, Sisters of St Joseph, Sydney.

Rules of the Institute of St Joseph
>First rule, written by Fr Woods, October, 1867. Archives, Sisters of St Joseph.

The Necessity for the Institute, Mary MacKillop.
>Pamphlet written in 1873, London. Archives, Sisters of St Joseph.

Congregational Newsletters and Publications Used in Text

Comme un grain de Sénevé : Les Sœurs de Saint Joseph,
        Publication of Epinay-sur-Seine (France): Editions Cif, 1982

Connections: Newletter, Sisters of St Joseph of Orange

Focus: Periodical, Sisters of St Joseph of Orange, California

Josephite Harvest: Periodical of the Fathers & Brothers of the Society of St Joseph

Journeys: Periodical, Sisters of St Joseph of Northwestern Pennsylvania (Erie)

Keeping in Touch with Friends and Associates: Newsletter, Sisters of St Joseph of Perthville

Le Règne de Dieu Periodical, Sisters of St Joseph of Lyon

Message Aux Amis: Newsletter, Soeurs de Saint Joseph de Chambéry, Province de France

Misi Synthèse: Catholic Church Periodical, France.

Our Spirit: Booklet, Josephite Community Aid

Savoie Mission Partage: Catholic Mission Periodical, France

Soundings: Periodical, Sisters of St Joseph of Boston

Spreading the Spirit: Josephite Community Aid Newsletter

That Life Mary Flow: Newsletter, Sisters of St Joseph of Lyon, Maine Province.

* Note: Permission granted to the author by Sisters of St Joseph of Toronto to use extracts from
Elizabeth Smyth and Linda Wicks, *Wisdom Raises Her Voice,* Toronto: Sisters of St Joseph, 2001 and
Diane Bisson, *Compassion Builds a House,* Toronto: Providence Centre, 2000.

Index of Scripture References

Reference	Page	Reference	Page	Reference	Page
Gen 2:7	2	Mt 13:8	229	Rom 8:34	312
Gen 2:23	220	Mt 16:2-3	229	Rom 10:8	5
Gen18:1-8	173	Mt 17:5	173	Rom 12:4-18	175
Lev Ch19	98	Mk 5:36	43	Rom 13:10	88
Deut. 6:4-5	97	Mk 6:3	94, 182	Rom 14:7	134
Deut 22:20-21	138	Mk 10:44	76	1Cor1: 22-25	85
1Sam24:18	133	Lk 2:16	217	1Cor 6:11	134
1Sam26:23	133	Lk 2:39	182	1Cor7:32-34	4
2Sam8:15	133	Lk 2:48	261	1Cor11:24-25	266
1Kg 3:6	133	Lk 3:23	182	1Cor 12	76
1Kg 10:9	133	Lk 4:16	97	1Cor12:4-30	175
Job Ch4	264	Lk 5:10	43	2Cor 3:3	2
Job22:6-9	133	Lk 13:4	269	2Cor 5:21	134
Ps 22:6	223	Lk15:11-32	3	Gal 2:20	6
Ps 40:4	85	Lk24:28-32	182	Gal 3:19	88
Ps 46:1	264	Lk24:41-43	182	Eph1:22-23	175
Ps 82:3	133	Jn 1:45	182	Eph 2:22	5
Prov31:8-9	133	Jn 1:46	269	Eph 3:6	175
Is 1:17	133	Jn 3:16	261	Eph 3:17	5
Is 11:1ff	134	Jn 4:7	87	Eph 4:25	175
Is 11:8-9	134	Jn 14:2	174	Eph 5:30	175
Is 42:9	45	Jn 14:26	173	Phil 2:13	5
Is 49:15	124	Jn 14:27	43	Col 1:19,20	307
Is 53:11	132	Jn 15:15	327	Col 1:24	175
Is 65:17	45	Jn16:21-23	3	1 Thess 2:13	5
Jer 7:5-6	133	Jn 17:21	336	Heb 1:3	173
Jer 23:28	5	Jn21:9-19	182	Heb 12:1	230, 312
Mt 1:19	131, 137	Acts2:42-47	182	Heb 13:2	182
Mt 1:20	1, 44	Acts 3:14	134	Jas1:27	134
Mt1:20-23	5	Acts 16:9	129	1Pet2: 9-10	76
Mt 1:21	305	Acts4:32,34,35	174	1 Pet 3: 8-15	303
Mt 2:10	227	Acts27:24	43	1Pet 4: 9-10	182
Mt 2:13	41	Rom 3:30	134	1Jn 3:1	174
Mt 2:23	171	Rom 5:5	5	1Jn Ch4	88
Mt 8:26	43	Rom 5:16	133	1Jn 4: 8	308
Mt 13:5	94	Rom 8:21	88, 219	1Jn 4:18	43
Mt 13:55	87, 182	Rom 8:22	219	1Jn 4: 20	174

Index of Names, Places and Subjects

A Kempis, Thomas 233
Abandonment 676, 246, 327
Aboriginal Australians 81, 108, 164, 187, 188, 196, 217, 290
Abuse 62, 83, 106, 143, 146, 152, 154, 195, 207, 263, 272, 284, 293, 324-327, 329, 330, 333, 342, 343, 348
Act of Secularisation 56, 285
Adaptability 8, 20, 53, 55, 67, 74, 81, 83, 208, 237, 279
Adelaide, (arch)diocese of 21, 22, 24, 56, 62, 64, 68, 69, 111, 151, 155, 198, 237, 272-276, 292, 302, 324, 325, 340
Adelong 114
Adoration 274, 327
Agregées 16, 33, 255
Aherne, Consuelo Maria 148, 153
Ain Karim, South Australia 149
Alacoque, Margaret Mary 26
Allen, Marcia 28, 65, 178, 183, 194
Aloneness 176
Alter Christus 328, 336
Ambiguity 240, 330
Anderledy, Anton 25
Andersen, Frank 299
Anita, Alice 279
Ann Teresa, Sister 215
Anne Marie, Mother 293
Annecy, France 54, 66, 240
Anonymity 11, 240
Aquinas, Thomas 99, 173, 220, 226
Arizona 53, 187, 283
Ashram Saint-Joseph 198
Associates 9, 11, 35-36, 77, 82, 127, 159, 164, 209, 211, 213, 253, 255, 257, 336-337, 342, 347
Augustine 4, 99, 172, 204, 310
Auvergne, region of 21, 102, 319
Baden 113, 190, 242, 296

Baptism 2, 53, 76, 145, 151, 175, 308, 312, 322,
Barth, Karl 314
Batlow 193
Battlers 250
Baxter Detention Centre 301, 302
Belo, Bishop 82
Berulle, Cardinal Pierre 13, 273, 274, 327
Bethany House, Erie 146, 147, 149
Betrayal 70, 207, 286-288
Bhubaneswar, India 282
Bigotry 72, 106, 108, 193, 202
Bird, Sister Jeanne, 113
Bishops 14, 18, 25, 26, 89, 104-108, 236, 258, 291-293, 315, 322-327, 342
Bisson, Diane 116, 149, 353
Body of Christ 6, 11, 31, 174, 175, 204, 209, 212, 299, 308, 310-313
Book of Instructions, A 29, 57, 140, 145, 233, 276, 318, 319
Bossuet, Jacques 180
Bourne, Sr Michael Joseph 19, 27, 55, 78, 81, 82, 107, 110, 111, 113, 114, 115, 240, 248, 252,282, 284, 285, 289, 292, 293, 331
Bravery 53, 266, 281
Brennan, Margaret 67, 68, 106, 192, 236, 278, 286, 287, 294, 298, 299, 323, 324, 333, 334
Bridge Over Troubled Waters 153
Brisbane 65, 143, 191, 235, 274, 275, 325
Broadmeadows 2812
Brown, Bishop of Orange 342
Brown, Raymond 88, 137
Brun, Anna 14, 352
Burdier, Margruerite 14, 16, 99, 352
Burford, Kathleen 249, 252, 329
Burra 113

Byrne, Patricia 16, 501, 53, 102, 105, 106, 107, 112, 119, 183, 184, 185, 212, 213, 214, 232, 271, 319, 347

Byrne, Sister Anne 74

Cambodia 205, 209

Canadaigua 236

Canonical Status of Apostolic Religious 48, 50, 71

Casanova, Mary-Ann 258

Catholic 20, 21, 24, 26, 53, 56-58, 62, 67, 90, 106-108, 113, 117, 120, 121, 136, 140, 144, 163, 166, 192-193, 199, 202, 229, 242, 282, 289, 305-312, 314, 317-319, 321, 322, 333, 335, 336, 340, 341

Caulfield, Alphonse 248

Chaleyer, Anna 14, 352

Chanel, Sister 154

Change 8, 17, 18, 29, 30, 44-47, 52, 59, 74, 84, 92, 118, 134, 140, 146-149, 152, 154, 165, 166, 168, 185, 206, 208, 240, 254, 277, 279, 286, 291, 293, 294, 342

Charism 6-29 (See Charism/Joseph)

Charles, Sister Marie 114

Chastel, Claudia 15

Chastity, vow of 16, 30, 147-151, 253

Chicago 280

China 296

Civil Rights Movement USA 153

Class distinction 9, 14, 16, 24, 49, 50, 92, 103, 109, 117, 118, 140, 141, 142, 187, 301

Clifton, Wales 331

Coburn, Carol 50, 53, 54, 56, 68, 72, 112, 115, 117, 122, 186, 187, 193, 231, 239, 280, 281, 291, 294, 295, 321, 333, 348, 349

Code of Canon Law 1917-18 15, 71, 195, 322, 333

Collaboration 39, 163, 168, 315-317, 338, 339

Collectivism 176, 177

Collegiality 314-316, 342

Colloquiums 34

Colorado 56, 193

Communication 2, 127, 147, 279, 289, 291, 292, 339, 343

Communio, Church as 75, 140, 309, 319, 334-346

Communion 35, 39, 63, 132, 137, 168, 169, 171-175, 184, 198, 204, 209, 212, 214, 221, 222, 259, 265, 266, 269, 295, 305, 308-318, 334-345

Communion of Saints 230, 312-314

Community 4-6, 16, 29, 32-38, 50, 52, 58, 62, 72, 75-83, 89, 105, 109, 113-122, 124-128, 133, 136, 142, 145, 147, 152, 156, 158, 163-166, 171, 174-214, 219, 233, 237-239, 241, 243, 244, 246, 248, 252, 265, 278, 279, 282, 288, 292, 294, 300, 305, 306, 311-312, 317-321, 325, 328, 331-333, 339, 344, 346, 347

Compassion 25, 34, 38, 39, 62, 122, 124, 132, 135, 138, 139, 143, 144, 146, 148-151, 159, 163, 169, 181, 184, 185, 188, 194, 196, 200, 202-204, 223, 264, 265, 270, 279, 298, 322, 329, 336, 344, 346-349

Competition 70, 72, 240, 241, 254, 340

Concordia 19, 112, 190, 243, 248

Conformity 71, 286, 333, 349Confraternities of mercy 10, 13, 145, 16, 33, 49, 76, 101, 336

Connectedness 139, 217, 219, 250, 257

Connelly, Susan 156

Consecration 27, 30, 32, 47, 122, 184, 230, 338,

Constitutions (Fed. Aust/NZ) 160, 194

Constitutions (Médaille) 50, 52, 100, 112, 116, 118, 119, 140, 183, 184, 185, 246, 317, 352

Constitutions (Srs St Joseph of Sac. Heart) 120, 185, 212, 293, 352

Conversion 31, 45, 46, 164, 305, 325, 342

Co-operation 175

Copenhagen 192, 295
Courage 36, 44, 51, 62, 122, 206, 219, 224, 240, 257, 264, 265, 271, 274, 302, 339
Cowan, Barbara 337
Cowan, Marian 133
Co-workers 33, 34, 77, 159, 161, 167, 209, 212, 331, 336
Crameri, Carmel 258
Creation 2, 41, 70, 88, 89, 120, 134, 144, 145, 171, 172, 214, 217-222, 229, 230, 250, 258, 259, 307, 308, 312, 341, 344
Creatures 2, 6, 172, 184, 191, 195, 218-221, 229, 233, 251, 258, 274, 302, 318, 342, 345
Cross, The 175, 236, 265, 266, 272, 273, 274, 277, 278-294, 298, 299, 305, 342
Crucifixion 226, 262, 265, 267
Cuff, Mother Antoinette 146, 248
Culliton, Michael 166, 167
Cunningham, Sister Xavier 112
Cyril of Jerusalem 306
Daughters of Charity 49, 340
De Chantal, St Jane Frances 48
De Chantal, Sister Mary 236
De Maupas, Henri 14, 17, 50, 102, 323
De Maurienne, Mother St John 55
De Montfort, Marie 48, 215
De Paul, St Vincent 49
De Sales, St Francis 48, 100, 112, 139, 178, 205
De Vaublanc, Benedicte 67, 112
Depression, The 71, 73, 113, 155, 156, 199, 243, 249
Devotion 13, 15, 25-27, 101, 178, 180, 185, 228, 269, 298
Dignity of persons 72, 80, 83, 106, 113, 114, 136, 137, 138, 140, 147, 148, 150, 154, 157, 161-163, 200, 209, 223, 231, 255, 265, 270, 300, 327, 335, 338, 344
Discernment 46, 126, 209, 338, 345

Divine Providence 22, 23, 55, 57, 65, 78, 146, 229-230, 246-249, 256-257, 270, 318
Dominican Sisters 192, 237
Domitilla, Mother 152
Double Union 15, 101-102, 125, 128, 143, 151, 334, 344
Dowry 13, 103, 117, 138
Dream 5, 6, 26, 29, 42, 44, 57, 147, 171, 283, 323
Duffy, Joan 83
Dunn, Sister Frances 154, 197
Earthiness 15, 123, 134, 160, 171, 173, 217-219, 220, 228, 229, 230, 247, 343
East Timor (Timor L'Este) 25, 82, 156, 255
Ecumenism 192, 308, 336
Education 9, 13, 17, 24, 39, 53, 56, 59, 73, 77, 80-82, 103, 109, 117, 136, 142, 142, 144, 157, 158-162, 165, 196, 238, 240, 241, 258, 337
Edwards, Denis 2, 42, 148, 172, 191, 195, 199, 219, 222, 223, 265, 269, 316, 350
Egalitarianism 59, 117, 128, 141, 142, 195, 235
Einstein, Albert 131
Encounter with the "Holy" 42, 76, 120, 182, 186, 198, 206, 225, 226, 228, 278, 299, 312
Engelbrecht, Kate 305, 308
Eucharist 17, 29, 39, 47, 85, 101, 140, 157, 168, 169, 182, 184, 204, 214, 221, 222, 231, 233, 259, 265, 266, 296, 299, 309-311, 314, 318, 334, 339, 344
Eucharistic Letter, The 26, 29, 101, 184, 231, 247, 352, 269, 270, 317, 318
Eudes, St John 27
Eureka (California) 202, 250, 283
Evian (France) 280
Exploitation 125, 218, 219, 230
Eyraud, Françoise 14
Facemaz, Mother Saint John 110
Faith 3, 22-23, 26, 29, 41, 57, 58, 59, 63, 66, 88, 89, 103, 118, 120, 124,

143, 151, 152, 157, 158, 174, 191, 198, 203, 204, 210, 212, 226, 235, 247, 263, 286, 299, 305- 307, 310-312, 317, 321, 325, 332, 339
Fatima College, India 188
Fear 1, 38, 41-43, 55, 59, 69, 72, 78, 79, 85, 94, 102, 108, 139, 150, 193, 208, 238, 254, 261, 263, 267, 271, 281, 283, 288, 289, 290, 292, 303, 343, 345, 347
Fesch, Cardinal 17, 52
Flavie, Mother Louise, 67
Fleming, Sister Zita 203
Flu Epidemic 202, 282
Foale, Marie 22, 24, 57, 61, 141, 142, 193, 248
Fontbonne, Mother St John 18, 51, 52, 271, 320
Foolishness 57, 63, 85
Fort Yuma 283
Francis of Assisi 2, 11, 218, 319
Fraser, Janet 257
Freedom 21, 89, 136, 230, 265, 271, 281, 295, 301, 302, 333, 342, 343
French Revolution 17, 26, 51, 52, 56, 58, 100, 104, 110, 113, 118, 141, 271, 320
French School of Spirituality 15, 25, 273
Friendship 35, 36, 37, 73, 167, 176, 190, 201, 203, 204, 262, 276, 286, 291, 298, 302, 338, 342
Frontier Women 53-56, 60
Fullerton, Lady Georgina 7, 8
Gap (France) 295
Gardiner, Paul 62, 64, 67, 111, 191, 193, 235, 237, 275, 277, 284, 286, 294 324, 325
Gardner, Virginia Ann 244, 245, 254, 280, 289, 290, 332, 340
Garnier, Sister St Julien 271
Geagley, Brad 27, 72, 73, 107, 113, 115, 154, 202, 204, 279, 288, 330, 332
General Strike 1926 289
Gentleness 27, 114, 199, 231, 246, 247

Geoghegan, Bishop 22, 56
Gilroy, Ann 59
Glaser, Jack 165, 349
Globalisation 38, 39, 45, 158-160, 169, 207, 209, 347
Gondal, Marie-Louise 13
Gosselin, Mother Alexine 288
Gosselin, Mother Bernard 26, 74, 115, 235, 279, 283
Goulburn 202
Gratitude 193, 229, 230, 243
Grenoble 238
Groupe Monde Ouvrier (Worker Sisters) 125, 126, 156, 205, 254
Guatemala 146
Gussin, Sister Gabriel Joseph 298
Hamilton (Canada) 34, 163, 236
Haunton 194
Healthcare 17, 34, 142, 156, 165, 166, 167
Healy, Joan 205, 350
Hennessy, Anne 10, 13, 42, 44, 47, 90, 91, 92, 93, 94, 95, 100, 101, 137, 179, 180, 181, 228, 266, 267, 268, 269
Herod Antipas 90, 95, 227, 267, 268
Holiness 4, 32, 75, 76, 87, 88, 99, 100, 117, 128, 186, 221, 228, 231
Holy Family 15, 28, 94, 178, 182, 185, 247, 344
Honour 9, 15, 26, 47, 92, 93, 95, 96, 178, 112, 182, 184, 211, 234, 238, 252, 266, 327, 343
Hope, virtue of 38, 39, 47, 49, 127, 144-147, 155, 157, 211, 224, 226
Hopkins, Gerard Manley 2, 96
Horan, Charles 275
Hospital Chaplaincy 290, 199
Hospitality 34, 95, 147, 173, 181-183, 189-190, 214, 258, 338, 344
Hospitals 50, 53, 57, 71-74, 82, 84, 110, 115, 154, 162, 163, 165, 192, 193, 197, 202, 206, 239, 240, 246, 250, 252, 288, 295, 321, 322, 326, 330, 348
Hostility 108, 282-283

Howley, Sister Calasanctius 69, 252
Huasa Huasi 286
Hughes, Gerard 46, 225
Human body 10, 217, 220, 221, 245, 255
Hume, Cardinal Basil 163
Humiliation 143, 222, 224, 236, 272, 275, 323
Humility 33, 65, 120, 218, 222-224, 226, 227, 228, 230-238, 239, 240, 242, 251, 254, 316, 344
Humour 54, 218, 225-226, 251-253
Humus 217, 218-219, 226
Ignatius of Antioch 224
Ignatius of Loyola 46, 100, 233
Image of God 2, 15, 220, 221, 225, 231, 244
Imitation of Christ, The 233
Incarnation 13, 43, 87-89, 126, 174, 176, 184, 207, 214, 221, 223, 227, 230, 349, 313, 338
Inclusivity 163, 186-189
Individualism 60, 175, 177, 208
Inglewood 201
Institutes 8, 74, 247
Interconnectedness 139, 217, 218, 219, 258, 344
Interdependence 75, 139, 167, 219, 223, 229, 343
Inter-religious relations 192-194
Irenaeus of Lyon 218, 220
Jansenism 120
Jaramillo, Elena 79
Jeremiah 5, 133
Jerome, St 4
Jesuit Fathers 13, 21, 23, 24, 25, 63, 104, 270, 275, 277, 325
Jewish assistance 62, 192, 193, 277
Jimnez, Margarita 250
Johnson, Elizabeth 90, 91, 92, 95, 96, 97, 99
Joseph 15, 42, 43, 47, 54, 55, 62, 65, 78, 85, 104, 151, 154, 193, 228, 229, 230, 232, 249, 250, 274, 286, 313

and community 178-183, 184, 185, 190, 230
and dreams 5-6
and faith 3-4, 69
and humility 226-228, 233, 253
and justice 137-140, 143, 145, 147, 157, 162, 169
and suffering 266-269, 288
ordinariness 89-99, 123, 124
as patriarch 43-44
charism of 9-12, 29, 33, 37, 39, 47, 55, 69, 72, 75, 77, 78, 83, 84, 101, 127, 159, 162, 165, 168, 204, 207, 209, 212- 214, 244, 253, 257, 259, 299, 301, 3023, 335-339, 343, 342-346
devotion to 13-14, 36, 185
Patron of the Church 313-317, 339
Josephite Community Aid (JCA) 36, 37, 38, 83, 128, 164, 206, 209, 256, 261, 262, 302, 346
Justice 7, 34, 124, 131, 132-169, 214, 222, 226, 263, 265, 270, 342, 343, 350
Kansas 56, 112, 146, 329
Kasper, Walter 70
Kelly, Tony 259
Kieran, Mother Mary John 106
Kindness 98, 136, 193, 199-201, 206, 329, 346
Kirby, Monsignor Tobias 25, 28, 68, 197, 273, 324
Ku Klux Klan 72, 283
Laity 30, 31, 32, 33, 76, 162, 309, 345
Lay Sisters of St Joseph 59
Le Puy 13, 14, 103, 111, 127, 231
Leary, Mother Stanislaus 68, 234, 278, 286, 299, 329
Leddy, Mary Jo 230, 295
Leto, Joe 256
Lincoln, Abraham 41, 87
Lirette, Mother Francis 72, 279, 330
Little Design 16, 49, 50, 101, 186
Little, Archbishop Frank 297

Local Church 106, 165, 310-312, 319-323, 330, 335, 343
Loneliness 47, 176, 267, 289
Lonergan, Bernard 123
Lonergan, Veronica 198, 284, 298, 340
Lung, Therese-Joseph 296
Lutheran community 62, 192
Mack, Anna Marie 48
Mackay, Hugh 226, 208, 227, 254
MacKillop, Donald 66, 29
MacKillop, Blessed Mary 7, 12, 22-23, 25-28, 34, 57-59, 61-64, 66, 68-69, 73, 77, 82, 85, 117, 140-141, 152, 185, 187, 191-193, 197, 200, 202, 232, 235, 238, 240, 249, 251, 252, 256, 277, 284-285, 290, 292, 293, 301, 318, 321, 324, 327, 328, 352
   and the Cross 151, 236, 272, 274, 281, 282, 286, 287, 294, 298
   and the ordinary 107-111, 115
   excommunication of 24, 60, 64, 192, 238, 274, 275, 276, 325
Manicka, Sister Mary 188
Markham, Donna 223, 226
Marsh, Sally 258
Mary MacKillop Institute of East Timorese Studies 82, 156
Mason, Ted 265
Materialism 343
Maura Ann, Sister 253
Maxims of Medaille 27, 28, 29, 65, 231, 238, 239, 257, 270
McBrien, Richard 306
McCord, H Richard 309
McCormack, Irene 296-298
McDonald, Lillian 299
McGlone, Mary 19, 81, 298
McMullin, Sister Josephine 65
McNerney, Eileen 77
McQuaid, Bishop of Rochester 286, 294, 323
Mealing, Donna 346
Médaille, Jean Pierre 14-17, 26-29, 37, 49-51, 65, 100, 101, 116, 118-120, 140, 142, 153, 178, 183, 184, 186, 199, 203, 204, 209, 230, 231, 238, 239, 246, 269, 270, 300, 317, 318, 334
Mediator 312
Melbourne 223, 158, 198, 208, 281
Micek, Louise Ann 146, 147
Mission 5-8, 11, 13, 14, 17, 18, 27, 31-34, 44, 47, 52, 55, 56, 63, 66-69, 75-81, 87, 93, 101, 104, 120, 125, 127, 142, 145, 146, 150, 158, 159, 161, 163, 171, 183, 187, 188, 203, 204, 206, 207, 210, 212, 213, 235, 238, 256, 273, 280, 281, 283, 284, 288, 307, 309, 311, 313, 316, 319, 320, 322, 329, 334-336, 340, 341, 347-349
Molinari, Paul 42, 44, 93
Monastic Orders 14, 16, 18, 71, 99, 100, 110, 233, 243
Monistrol, France 51
Monks and Nuns of Jerusalem 197
Montgomery 196
Moran, Cardinal Patrick 193, 293, 324
Morrow Park 188
Moslander, Bette 17, 158
Motor Missions 73, 79
Mount Hope, Canada 54
Movement of St Joseph 12, 35, 160, 342-346
Mundelein, Bishop (Chicago) 288
Murillo, Bartolome 178
Mutuality 196, 203-204, 210-212
Mysticism 6, 122, 152, 178, 344
Napoleon 18, 52, 328
Nazareth 65, 89-92, 94, 97, 171, 181, 185, 200, 267, 269
Nazareth House, Toronto 200
Necessity for the Institute, The 22, 58, 62, 68, 107, 318
Neale, Ann 166, 167
Nee, Meas 205, 209, 210, 212
Neighborhood Networks 82, 83, 114, 338
Nepper, Marius 26, 115, 129, 352

NETWORK, 166
Networking 159, 160, 161, 163, 168, 301, 321, 338
New Age movement 123
New York 112, 280
Newton, Kansas 329
Non-violence 154
Nouwen, Henri 174, 175, 177
O'Connell, Cardinal (Boston) 152
O'Connor, Nancy 84, 342
O'Leary, Sister Mary 253
Obedience 3, 9, 29, 68, 144, 151-158, 316, 326
Obedience, Vow of 3, 16, 151, 333
Olier, J J 6
Orange 165, 283, 342
Ordained Ministry 335, 341-342, 345
Ordinary 6, 8, 9, 10, 12, 43, 49, Ch3, 131, 167, 207, 225, 228, 243, 253, 269, 319, 338, 344, 346, 347, 349
Orthodox 307
Outback Sisters 60-63, 196, 282, 326
Pachmarhi, India 198
Pain 46-49, 60, 93, 150, 160, 176, 236, Ch7, 342
PALMS 337
Pandikattu, Kuruvilla 131
Papua New Guinea 25, 107, 332
Parish 22, 25, 35, 37, 81, 101, 105, 106, 115, 116, 119, 156, 188, 198, 199, 201, 212, 284, 285, 310-322, 326, 329, 332
Partnership 33, 34, 38, 75, 77, 82, 127-128, 132, 133, 142, 156, 163, 164, 206, 210, 229, 230, 255, 301, 327, 336, 337, 341, 345, 350
Patriarchy 43, 47, 91, 239
Patronage 9, 10, 48, 54, 92, 95, 316
Peace 134, 142, 144, 149, 150, 158, 159, 160, 165, 167, 168, 169, 297, 298, 303, 315
Pennsylvania 200

Penola 22, 23, 24, 111
Perrotta, Louis Bourassa 5, 43, 65, 91, 92, 93, 94, 138, 182, 183, 228, 313, 314
Persecution 43, 99, 284-285, 293, 300, 319
Philadelphia 67, 190, 243, 290
Pilcher, Carmel 157
Pilgrim People of God 307, 312, 335
Pope John XXIII 314, 315, 316
Pope John Paul II 3, 5, 39, 47, 77, 93, 139, 159, 168, 214, 309, 313, 314
Pope Leo XIII 137, 138, 140
Pope Paul VI 136, 165, 312
Pope Pius VII 52
Pope Pius IX 26, 313
Pope Pius XI 31, 138
Pope Pius XII 27, 31, 180, 208, 308, 334
Port Augusta 301
Port Lincoln 113, 243
Poverty 21, 56, 58, 98, 105, 109, 116, 128, 160, 163, 227, 241, 246, 247, 248, 265, 276
Poverty, vow of 16, 68, 110, 144, 145-147, 276, 277
Power 10, 14, 16, 29, 38, 41, 49, 78, 101, 104, 122, 133-137, 151, 158, 172, 180, 203, 208, 214, 219, 238, 242, 265, 298, 316, 322-334, 341-345
Power, misuse of 69, 144, 151, 154, 160, 218, 227, 267, 273, 291-294, 295, 317, 324, 325, 327, 328, 333, 342-345
Practicality 24, 65, 111-113, 114, 127, 128, 144, 147, 153, 156, 157, 163, 197, 199, 264, 283, 297, 319, 339, 342, 347, 349
Prejean, Helen 150, 213
Presence of God 6, 8-12, 83, 88, 96, 98, 101, 104, 118-122, 127, 157, 178, 195, 197, 198, 204, 212, 214, 218, 222, 226, 227, 258, 259, 299, 341, 344, 345
Press, Margaret 277, 278, 283
Programs of formation 16, 33, 36, 37, 77, 100, 158, 162, 205, 336

Propaganda, Rome 140, 293, 324
Prophetic, sign of justice 133, 144-158, 161, 297
Protestant Reformation 13, 20, 67, 192, 307, 319
Protestants 21, 56, 58, 67, 193, 238, 252, 284, 317, 318, 331
Prudence 63, 65, 189, 226
Queensland 62, 64, 68, 191, 196, 201, 258, 284, 291
Quinn, Bishop James 144, 324, 325
Quinn, Bishop Matthew 291, 292, 325
Radcliffe, Timothy 38, 107, 207, 208, 209, 210, 211, 212, 221, 226, 294
Ranson, David 32, 123, 124, 152, 153
Raper, Mark 159
Reconciliation 142, 143, 150, 161, 168, 191, 192, 194, 200, 204, 209, 210, 213, 215, 222, 306-308, 319, 344
Reconfiguring 19, 340, 341
Refounding 17, 104, 210
Re-framing program 166-167
Refugees 37, 79, 82, 147, 158, 164, 168, 188, 189, 247
Reign of God 63, 66, 84, 85, 89, 137, 139, 144, 145, 159, 162-164, 169, 181, 182, 198, 204, 214, 222, 253, 266, 270, 298, 347
Relationalism 31, 176, 201-203, 203, 211
Relaxation 127, 204, 225, 235
Reynolds, Bishop Christopher 59, 151, 328
Risk 43, 46, 48, 57, 60, 62-64, 66, 72, 80, 84, 257, 263, 281, 300, 333, 337, 347
Robespierre 52, 271
Rochejacquelein, Countess 18, 53
Rockhampton 327
Rogerson, Libby 158, 208
Rome 24, 25, 48, 68, 69, 71, 74, 95, 104, 267, 275, 276, 287, 292, 293, 310, 325, 327, 338
Rosati, Bishop 18

Rowe, N 85
Rublev, Andrei 173, 181
Russell, Bill 43, 227
Russell, Patrick 237, 286
Ryan, Joan 281
Ryan, Mother Leone 73
Sachs, John R. 211
Sacralism 76
Sacrament 6, 7, 28, 47, 63, 81, 108, 184, 202, 219, 222, 259, 271, 299, 309, 311, 320, 335, 341
Sacred Heart of Jesus 26, 27, 36, 73, 121, 154, 185, 232, 273, 274, 335
Sacred Heart, Mother 272
Sacrifice 47, 63, 98, 101, 157, 174, 177, 180, 218, 263, 266, 274, 279, 325, 327, 328
Saint-Didier 270
Salvation 10, 42, 43, 44, 65, 100, 117, 180, 220, 227, 270, 306, 313, 314, 325, 330
San Salvador 79
Santa Ana 206, 301
Schlick, Rose 258
Schneiders, Sandra 30, 31, 144, 145
Seasons for Growth, 301
Secularisation 38, 56, 151, 239, 240, 241, 268, 285
Self-denial 283
Self-gift 101, 125, 148, 179-180, 261, 266, 345
Self-sacrifice 175, 176, 180, 226, 239, 332
Self-surrender 177, 219, 242, 274, 276, 302
Sepphoris 90, 91, 94, 95, 267, 268
Service 6, 15, 30, 32, 36, 37, 49, 50, 53, 56, 71-74, 82, 83, 87, 102, 118, 120, 127, 140-142, 161, 162, 163, 178, 179, 180, 182, 183, 185, 186, 194, 196, 197, 199, 202, 203, 206, 209, 213, 214, 229, 231, 235, 238, 239, 246, 247, 268, 280, 299, 315-318, 322, 325, 329, 335, 341, 342, 344
Shaffer, Sister Gretchen 166

Shannon, Margaret 42, 226, 227
Sharing of the heart 120
Sheehan, Fintan 58
Sheil, Bishop Lawrence 59, 117, 240, 275, 276
Sicari, Antonio Maria 6, 8, 32, 139, 343-344
Silvestre, Louis Marie, 321
Simplicity 12, 21, 26, 35, 51, 185, 224, 230, 231, 238, 247, 277, 347
Sisters of Mercy 22, 191, 340
Sisters of Perpetual Adoration 277, 278
Sisters of St Joseph, Le Puy 12-17, 20, 24, 33, 48, 65, 79, 83, 100, 110, 111, 115, 117, 120, 127, 147, 231-232, 238, 319, 328, 334, 336, 340, 344, 352
Sisters of St Joseph 3, 9, 13, 18-21, 26, 29, 32-35, 38, 48, 49-51, 57, 63, 67, 69-71, 74-75, 77, 78, 99-102, 104, 105, 107, 109-111, 113-116, 118, 120- 122, 125-127, 137, 139, 140, 144, 145, 147-149, 156, 158, 160, 161, 183, 185-187, 190, 192, 194, 195, 197-200, 202, 203, 204, 209, 212, 213, 230, 233-235, 238-244, 246-251, 254, 256, 258, 269, 270, 272, 278, 285, 291-292, 295, 300, 317-319, 322-323, 326-327, 329-330, 334-345, 347-349
   in Africa 19, 20, 25, 80, 107, 113, 187, 285, 300
   in Algeria 321
   in Armenia 67
   in Brazil 21, 67, 80, 82, 196, 280, 281, 338
   in Central America 19, 79, 80, 107
   in England (Wales) 116, 194, 196, 235, 252, 284, 289, 331
   in Haunton 194
   in India 19, 20, 55, 66, 78, 80, 81, 107, 115, 122, 163, 187, 198, 199, 205, 248, 282, 285, 249, 300
   in Ireland 25, 80, 108
   in Italy 18, 19, 20, 67, 338
   in Maine 150
   in Mexico 80, 187
   in Mozambique 80
   in New Zealand 59, 69, 109, 113, 154, 252, 331, 336, 337
   in Northern Europe 19, 67, 147, 192
   in Peru 25, 36, 80, 127, 164, 187, 196, 206, 256, 296
   in Senegal 81
   in South America 20, 25
   in St Paul 71, 105, 241, 281
   in Tanzania 80
   in the Kimberley 81
Sisters of St Joseph
   of Argentina 19, 67
   of Annecy 19, 27, 80, 81, 100, 110, 284, 292, 300, 331
   of Baden 190, 242, 295, 296
   of Boston 83, 150, 152, 202, 207
   of Buffalo 194, 324
   of Carondelet 19, 53, 79, 80, 99, 105, 112, 114, 272, 283
   of Chambéry 19, 20, 67, 80, 81, 82, 127, 192, 196, 272, 280, 295, 321
   of Concordia 112, 190, 243, 248
   of Erie 149, 213, 253, 289, 323, 338, 339
   of Goulburn 114, 193, 202
   of Hamilton 34, 162, 163, 236, 255
   of La Grange 26, 288
   of Lochinvar 121, 247
   of London 255
   of Lyon 18, 34, 52, 67, 80, 82, 147, 151, 188, 247
   of Orange 26, 33, 72, 77, 78, 115, 146, 165, 196, 202, 235, 250, 279, 281, 283
   of Perthville 155, 255
   of Philadelphia 48, 67, 80, 106, 153, 190, 279
   of Rochester 27, 126, 210, 286
   of Springfield 148, 171, 148
   of Tasmania 39, 247
   of the Sacred Heart 12, 20, 23-

28, 36, 57, 61, 66, 73, 78, 80, 110, 115, 118, 121, 145, 185, 187, 217, 237, 297, 298, 324, 334, 344, 352
  of Tipton 72, 162
  of Toronto 148, 162, 200, 257
  of Wanganui 113, 336
  of Wheeling 158, 166
  of Wichita 329
Sisters of St Joseph, Federation of
  Australia/New Zealand 25, 160, 194
  Canada 19, 142, 159
  France 20, 34, 82, 124, 125, 142, 339
  Italy 20, 142
  USA 19, 143, 159
Smith, Martha 50, 53, 54, 56, 68, 72, 112, 115, 117, 122, 186, 187, 193, 231, 239, 280, 281, 291, 294, 295, 321, 333, 348, 349
Smyth, Elizabeth 116, 146, 149, 163, 188, 200, 247, 258, 353
Smyth, Sister Raymond 69, 117, 252
Social welfare 53, 56, 57, 142, 147, 192, 226, 238, 289, 340
Solomon Islands 281
Solomon, Emanuel 192, 193, 277
South Australia 21, 24, 57, 59, 61, 109, 111, 113, 149, 188, 217, 243, 272, 301
Spencer, Mother Agnes 324
Spirituality 13, 14, 21, 25, 26, 34, 64, 99, 100, 123-126, 128, 138, 160, 161, 192, 198, 207, 217, 249, 251, 257, 258, 269, 273, 299, 327, 337, 348, 350
Splett, Jorg 220, 221
Sponsored ministries 161-162, 258, 301, 340
St Catherine's College (St Paul) 241
St Joseph's Australian-Peruvian Mission Associates 164, 255
St Joseph's Healthcare 34, 84, 165-167
St Louis, USA 18, 67, 105, 111, 114, 187, 280, 291
St Mary's Orphan Asylum 286
Statuto, Rich 84
Steinhagen, Sister Rita 301
Stewardship 229
Suain, PNG 332
Suffering 28, 102, 106, 109, 139, 146, 150, 175, 213, 261, 263-299, 302, 319, 347
Sullivan, Francis 307, 309
Sullivan, Maria 206
Sullivan, Mary Cornelia 244
Superstition 313
Sury, France 320
Sydney 36, 63, 69, 73, 74, 82, 83, 156, 164, 248, 256, 277, 324
Symbol 2, 4, 5, 26, 30, 34, 60, 76, 98, 182, 197, 204, 219, 226, 230, 265, 280, 296, 311, 319, 320, 333, 335
Synagogue 96, 97, 137
Tambacounda (Senegal), 82
Teresa of Avila 13
The Beautiful Daughters 337-338
The Collaborators 210
The Two Trinities 15, 101, 178
Thomas, Evangeline 106, 146, 234, 248, 329, 329
Tillard, J M R 308, 310, 311
Timon, Bishop of Rochester 236, 323
Torah 97
Townley, Ruth 262, 302
Townsville 284
Trinity 15, 172, 173, 178, 182-186, 344
Truth 4, 87, 224, 225, 238-242, 265, 275, 287, 305, 328
Tumberumba 203
Turin 338
UN NGO, *The Congregations of St Joseph* 160-161
Uniformity 18, 52, 70, 121, 327, 333, 349
Union 15, 29, 30, 31, 39, 49, 75, 76,

84, 87-89, 96, 99-102, 104, 117, 119, 125, 140, 142-145, 168, 172, 174, 178, 182, 184, 185, 197, 210, 212, 270, 305-308, 309, 315, 317, 318, 330, 341, 348, 350

Unity 31, 39, 59, 117, 142-144, 150, 151, 157, 161, 168, 186, 188, 190-192, 204, 209, 219, 221, 265, 270, 298, 306, 307-311, 314-317, 320, 334, 336, 339-341, 343, 343, 347, 350

USA 19, 33, 48, 53, 72, 73, 79, 84, 113, 114, 153, 159, 166, 167, 171, 186, 187, 190, 193, 196, 234, 236, 272, 296

Vacher, Therese 49, 50, 58, 99, 101, 102, 104, 110, 112, 120, 122, 186, 232, 232, 237, 238, 270, 320, 322, 347, 348

Vatican II 8, 19, 29, 31, 32, 39, 74, 76, 87, 89, 121, 122, 125, 136, 185, 187, 1890, 208, 279, 307-311, 314, 327, 334, 335

Vaughan, Archbishop Roger 325

Vey, Anna 14, 352

Vienne 110, 237, 347, 348

Virginity 4, 30

Visions 26, 64, 275, 278

Vocation 4-7, 14, 32, 117, 183, 186, 187, 191, 207, 221

Volunteers 35, 36-38, 53, 55, 77, 79, 83, 149, 161, 164, 201, 227, 256, 280, 336, 346

Von Bunning, Mother Martha 236

Vulnerability 12, 46, 139, 148, 151, 171, 224, 254, 286, 299

Walsh, Mother Bernard 293

Walsh, Sheila, 126

Ward, Mary 49

Wars of Religion 13, 102, 319

Western Australia 11, 247, 252, 297

Wholeness 100, 161, 221, 230, 343, 344

Wicks, Linda 116, 146, 149, 163, 188, 200, 247, 258, 353

Will of God 3, 4, 15, 28-29, 46, 59, 60, 137, 140, 146, 151, 155, 161, 185, 246, 249, 267, 273, 286, 249, 298, 299, 306, 309, 313, 345

Willcock, C 85

Willis, Sister Thomasine 188

Wisdom 51, 85, 124, 132, 223, 224, 226, 227, 234, 240, 254, 263, 266, 343, 345

Woods, Julian Tenison 12, 20-22, 23, 24, 27, 37, 57, 58, 61, 64, 66, 108, 109, 111, 121, 140, 141, 143, 145, 185, 199, 232, 240, 247, 249, 250, 256, 258, 273, 274, 275, 276, 287, 303, 317, 318, 325

Woodward, Evelyn 203, 207, 213

World War I 70

World War II 75, 200, 201, 295

Worthing, Mark 219

Young Christian Workers 31

Zeal 15, 61, 63, 65, 101, 107, 116, 144, 277, 279, 332

Zinn, Carol 160, 343

Zullo, James 45, 46

—